Equity Valuation and Analysis with eVal

Equity Valuation and Analysis with eVal

Second Edition

Russell Lundholm
University of Michigan

Richard Sloan
University of Michigan

McGraw-Hill
Irwin

Boston   Burr Ridge, IL   Dubuque, IA   Madison, WI   New York
San Francisco   St. Louis   Bangkok   Bogotá   Caracas   Kuala Lumpur
Lisbon   London   Madrid   Mexico City   Milan   Montreal   New Delhi
Santiago   Seoul   Singapore   Sydney   Taipei   Toronto

McGraw-Hill
Irwin

EQUITY VALUATION AND ANALYSIS WITH eVAL

Published by McGraw-Hill, a business unit of The McGraw-Hill Companies, Inc., 1221 Avenue of the Americas, New York, NY, 10020. Copyright © 2007 by The McGraw-Hill Companies, Inc. All rights reserved. No part of this publication may be reproduced or distributed in any form or by any means, or stored in a database or retrieval system, without the prior written consent of The McGraw-Hill Companies, Inc., including, but not limited to, in any network or other electronic storage or transmission, or broadcast for distance learning.

Some ancillaries, including electronic and print components, may not be available to customers outside the United States.

This book is printed on acid-free paper.

1 2 3 4 5 6 7 8 9 0 DOC/DOC 0 9 8 7 6

ISBN-13: 978-0-07-310026-5
ISBN-10: 0-07-310026-9

Editorial director: *Stewart Mattson*
Editorial assistant: *Megan McFarlane*
Executive marketing manager: *Rhonda Seelinger*
Media producer: *Greg Bates*
Project manager: *Marlena Pechan*
Manager, New book production: *Heather D. Burbridge*
Coordinator freelance design: *Artemio Ortiz Jr.*
Media project manager: *Matthew Perry*
Cover design: *Chris Bowyer*
Typeface: *10/12 Times New Roman*
Compositor: *Interactive Composition Corporation*
Printer: *R. R. Donnelley*

Library of Congress Cataloging-in-Publication Data

Lundholm, Russell James.
    Equity valuation and analysis with eVal/Russell Lundholm, Richard Sloan.—2nd ed.
      p. cm.
    Includes index.

    ISBN-13: 978-0-07-310026-5 (alk. paper)
    ISBN-10: 0-07-310026-9 (alk. paper)
    1. Corporations—Valuation. 2. Business enterprises—Valuation. 3. Stock price forecasting.
4. Investment analysis. 5. eVal (Electronic resource) I. Sloan, Richard G. II. Title.
HG4028.V3L796 2007
332.63'221028553—dc22

                  2006014698

www.mhhe.com

About the Authors

Russell J. Lundholm

Russell J. Lundholm is the chairman of the Accounting Department at the University of Michigan's Ross School of Business. He holds a PhD in Business Administration and a Master of Science in Statistics from the University of Iowa. He has taught at the University of Michigan since 1993 and at Stanford University from 1987 to 1993.

Professor Lundholm's research interests lie at the intersection of accounting, finance, and economics, and his findings have been published in the *Journal of Accounting Research, Accounting Review, Journal of Finance, Review of Financial Studies, Journal of Political Economy,* and *Econometrica*. His research also has been the subject of articles in *BusinessWeek, Fortune, The New York Times,* and *The Wall Street Journal*. He teaches graduate-level financial statement analysis, with a particular emphasis on stock valuation, and graduate-level financial economics. He speaks regularly at hedge funds and mutual funds on various topics concerning stock valuation and market inefficiency, and he serves as a consultant to numerous professionals in the investment industry.

Richard G. Sloan

Richard G. Sloan is the Victor L. Bernard PricewaterhouseCoopers Collegiate Professor of Accounting, Professor of Finance, and Director of the Tozzi Electronic Finance Center at the University of Michigan's Ross School of Business. He received his PhD at the University of Rochester and previously served on the faculty of the Wharton School at the University of Pennsylvania.

Professor Sloan's research focuses on the role of accounting information in investment decisions. His research is widely published in journals including the *Accounting Review, Journal of Accounting and Economics, Journal of Accounting Research, Journal of Finance, Journal of Financial Economics,* and *Review of Accounting Studies*. His research is regularly featured by the business press and has received numerous awards, including the 2001 American Accounting Association Notable Contributions to the Accounting Literature Award and the 2003 Q-Group Roger F. Murray First Prize.

Professor Sloan currently teaches financial statement analysis, security valuation and investment management in BBA, MAcc, MBA, PhD, and executive courses at the University of Michigan's Ross School of Business. He is an editor of the *Review of Accounting Studies,* an associate editor of the *Journal of Accounting and Economics,* and a member of the editorial boards of the *Accounting Review, Accounting and Finance,* and *Journal of Financial Economics*. He also serves as a speaker and consultant for various organizations in the investment management industry.

Brief Contents

Contents

Preface

WHY THIS BOOK?

We wrote this book because we saw a void between the abstract theoretical treatment of equity valuation and the practical problem of valuing an actual company using real-world data. We give serious treatment to the underlying theory of financial analysis and valuation, but our main goal is to be able to arrive at a pragmatic answer to the all-important question, "what is this company really worth?" To answer this question, we adopt a very different approach from other textbooks. The key differences can be summarized as follows:

1. Our focus is on generating good financial statement forecasts.
2. We provide detailed practical guidance on how to obtain and analyze relevant real-world data.
3. We demystify the mechanics of equity valuation.

Our overriding theme is that good forecasts of the future financial statements are the key input to a good valuation. Most other aspects of the valuation process are mechanical and can be programmed into a computer. In fact, this text is supplied with eVal, an Excel-based computer program that takes care of these mechanical tasks. As with many other textbooks, we discuss topics like business strategy analysis, accounting analysis, financial ratio analysis, and so forth. However, we always do so with a clear view to how these analyses help us to generate better financial statement forecasts.

We also provide plenty of advice on where to go to obtain the most relevant raw data. eVal is supplied with historical financial statement data for over 8,000 companies and you can use eVal to access companies' SEC filings, investor relations' Web sites, analysts' forecasts, and news releases. Armed with such a rich source of data, we are able to provide you with plenty of practical examples and limitless opportunities for you to practice doing your own analyses.

A final goal of this book is to demystify the valuation process. In the past, we have seen students become lost in a sea of valuation formulas and inconsistent spreadsheet models. For example, students get confused as to whether they should use the DDM, DCF, or RIM valuation formula and whether they need to use the CAPM, APT, or MFM to compute their WACC. They become obsessed with learning acronyms and formulas but flounder when asked to provide a plausible valuation for an actual company. Using eVal, we demonstrate that these different formulas are easily reconciled and refocus students on developing the best set of financial forecasts to plug into these formulas. This reinforces our main point that the key to good valuations is good forecasts.

THE eVal SOFTWARE

We wrote the software because we realized that students were spending way too much time building and debugging their valuation spreadsheets and, consequently, way too little time thinking about the forecasts that they put into their spreadsheets. The tail was definitely wagging the dog. They also couldn't talk to one another because each student tackled the spreadsheet problem differently—it could take hours just to figure out why Jill's value estimate differed from Jack's value estimate. By building one "mother-of-all spreadsheet valuation models" and making it completely transparent and completely general, we turned our students' attention back to the real problem at hand, which is forecasting the future financial statements. Thus, eVal was born. As we used the early version of the program with students, we discovered that we could use eVal to organize the entire historical analysis, forecasting, and valuation process. All the pieces of the puzzle could finally be kept in one place. Later we realized that, if we loaded the program with tons of company data and provided Web links to even more data, eVal could become the final one-stop shop for valuation analysis. We also found that once we had familiarized students with eVal, we could effectively teach complex valuation cases that would previously have been overwhelming.

The eVal software helps in doing valuation and it helps in *learning* valuation. There are many software products and Web services today that take a few forecast inputs from you and then spit out a valuation, as if by magic, but how they arrived at the result is hidden in a black box. In contrast, this book and the eVal software that accompanies it are designed to be completely transparent at every stage of the valuation process. The software displays the valuation implications of your forecasts in both discounted cash flow models and residual income models, and it shows exactly how the flows of value from these models are linked to your financial statement forecasts.

HOW DOES ALL THIS HELP YOUR STUDENTS?

Besides the practical value of focusing our book in this way, we think that students find financial analysis and forecasting much more compelling when the theory of valuation is closely linked to real-world applications. The abstract theory of financial statements, ratios, and valuation formulas can be covered in one or two very boring lectures. What makes this topic exciting is seeing how an organized approach to studying a real company leaves you so much better informed about the firm's future. Is Dell really the highly efficient manufacturer of computers that everyone claims? The answer is yes, as you can see in their turnover statistics. Netflix is scorching a new trail in the DVD rental market and sporting growth rates and valuation multiples that leave competitors like Blockbuster in the dust. Is it really the superstar stock that Wall Street analysts and bankers claim it to be? A careful analysis suggests that its strategy is unsustainable and the quality of its earnings is suspect, suggesting it is not such a superstar after all. Royal Caribbean Cruises wants to build six more cruise ships in the next three years, but can they generate enough cash from the existing ships to pay for the new ones? A careful study of their cash flows shows that they will almost certainly be borrowing lots of money to buy these boats. Financial statements, accounting rules, financial ratios, and valuation models are all pretty dull beasts on their own, but if we can use them to answer questions such as these, we can really bring them to life. By blending the theory of equity analysis with practical application, we feel that students learn both more effectively.

Throughout the text, we use the retail department store chain Kohl's as an illustrative example. It is also the default company in eVal, so you can readily see how the theory translates into real forecasts and valuation implications. And because eVal comes preloaded with data for over 8,000 public companies, you can analyze your own favorite company with just a few mouse clicks.

CASES AND WEB SITE

The back of the book contains a series of cases for classroom illustrations and student assignments. Most of the cases require students to analyze real-world companies. These cases are an integral part of the learning experience. We find that students only really begin to understand the material when they try to apply it to real-world cases. The final section of each chapter identifies which cases and questions are relevant to the material covered in that chapter. Many of these cases are revisited in consecutive chapters. One chapter will address business strategy analysis, the next will address accounting analysis, and so on. We recommend that you pick a subset of the cases and follow them throughout the book. It is hard to do a meaningful job of evaluating a firm's financial ratios if you haven't first analyzed its strategy and accounting policies. This is why we put the cases at the end of the book instead of trying to allocate entire cases to specific chapters. Several of the cases are tailored directly to the eVal software, and financial data for these cases are included in the eVal software.

A challenge in writing cases on real-world companies is the determination of the information to include along with each case. Traditionally, case writers have preselected the most relevant information for inclusion in the case. This approach has two disadvantages. First, the case writer is robbing the student of the opportunity to learn one of the most important skills in equity analysis: identifying the relevant information. Second, to the extent that the case writer omits relevant information, the richness of the case is compromised. We adopt a new approach to this problem by posting a broader set of information on a dedicated Web site. Each case contains links out to its own set of information, and the student must take responsibility for identifying the relevant information. For example, we may provide a 100-page Form 10-K along with the case, and the student must be able to navigate the 10-K and extract the relevant information. We think that the ability to extract relevant information is one of the most important skills of a real-world equity analyst, and our cases provide students with the opportunity to develop this skill.

In addition to providing case material online, eVal also has a dedicated Web site containing answers to frequently asked questions and notifications of new developments. The URL for the Web site is http://www.mhhe.com/eval2007. We also have a series of PowerPoint slides and associated instructional materials for the text and cases. If you are an instructor, contact your McGraw-Hill representative to obtain these materials.

CHANGES FOR THE SECOND EDITION

The first edition of eVal was generally well-received by students and instructors alike, so we haven't attempted any major changes in the second edition. Users of the first edition should therefore be able to transition to the second edition very smoothly. The biggest change in the second edition is the inclusion of a set of cases at the end of the book. Some of these cases were previously posted on the eVal Web site. With this second edition, we have expanded the set of cases to provide more complete coverage and included them at the end of the book. With this change, the second edition of eVal is a one-stop shop for your equity analysis and valuation coursework. It now includes a textbook, software, cases, data, and a variety of online resources.

While the number and titles of the chapters in the text remain the same, we have updated various chapters to incorporate recent developments and iron out a few wrinkles from the first edition. Chapter 2 (Information Collection) now incorporates recent changes in disclosure requirements, particularly those related to the passage of the Sarbanes Oxley Act. Our data provider also changed hands once again, so while the structure of the data is the same, the new owner is Hemscott and the new title is Hemscott Data. We also have updated all of the links to the latest and greatest sources of information on the Internet. Chapter 4 (Accounting Analysis) now includes a comprehensive set of examples illustrating the impact of aggressive and conservative accounting on the financial statements (students just didn't dig the terse algebraic treatment in the first version). Chapter 5 (Financial Ratio Analysis) includes a more insightful discussion of the cross-sectional ratio analysis for Kohl's versus Target. Note that we decided to retain Kohl's fiscal 2001 financial statements as the basis for the running example for the book. We think that it provides a good example from a pedagogical perspective, and having several years of subsequent data now enables us to evaluate the accuracy of our forecasts in Chapter 8 (Forecasting Details). Chapter 6 (Cash Flow Analysis) includes an extended discussion of the use of cash flow analysis to evaluate the quality of earnings. Chapter 9 (The Cost of Capital) incorporates a discussion of the computation of the implied cost of capital. This computation is now available in the updated version of the eVal software. It allows a user to solve for the cost of capital that equates a given set of financial statement forecasts to a given market price.

ACKNOWLEDGMENTS

Before getting down to business, we would like to thank everyone who has helped us in the preparation of both the first edition and this revised second edition. Patricia Dechow and Kai Petainen have been involved throughout and have provided valuable and timely feedback. We also would like to thank the following list of people for excellent suggestions on how to improve the text: Noel Addy, Mississippi State University; Ervin Black, Brigham Young University; Mike Calegari, Santa Clara University; Ted Christensen, Brigham Young University; Bryan Church, Georgia Institute of Technology; Paul Hribar, Cornell University; Bruce Johnson, University of Iowa; Joshua Livnat, New York University; Sarah McVay, New York University; Steve Monahan, University of Chicago; Michael Sandretto, University of Illinois; Akhtar Siddique, Georgetown University; Richard Simonds, Michigan State University; Sarah Tasker, University of California at Berkeley; and Peter Wysocki, Massachusetts Institute of Technology. We also thank our entire publication team on the second edition, with a special thanks to the following individuals. Steve Delancey and Stewart Mattson, our editors at McGraw-Hill, provided inspiration and guidance throughout the publication process. Robin Reed, our developmental editor at Carlisle Publishing Services, worked tirelessly to help keep the publication process on track. Megan McFarlane and Marlena Pechan at McGraw-Hill kept us both organized. Finally, we'd like to thank our significant others, friends, students, colleagues, families, pets, and everyone else who had to put up with us while we worked on this project.

PART ONE

Text

Introduction

1.1 GETTING STARTED

On a typical business day, well over 4 billion shares are traded on major U.S. stock markets. The combined market value of these trades exceeds $75 billion. Most of the shares traded represent equity interests in the business activities of corporations. The prices at which these trades take place determine both the fortunes of the traders and the allocation of much of the economy's scarce capital resources. Our objective in this book is to make you an expert in determining the fair value of these equity interests. If we are successful, you not only will be in a position to make a decent living, but also will be making the whole economy more efficient.

This book and the associated eVal software provide you with a systematic framework for valuing equity securities. There are many books written on the topic. Our approach is unique in that we seek to provide the best possible marriage between theory and practice. We provide a framework that is both theoretically rigorous and readily amenable to practical implementation. The eVal software is a flexible tool for the analysis and valuation of equity securities. It will provide you with hands-on experience in building financial models and estimating the value of equity securities. The use of spreadsheet-based financial modeling software is ubiquitous in practice. However, such software can be a dangerous weapon in the hands of the inexperienced user. Our aim is to provide you with a firm grounding in valuation theory and a good understanding of the techniques that have evolved to facilitate practical application of the theory. The end result is that you should be able to confidently produce sound valuations for just about any equity security.

Valuing equity securities necessarily involves uncertainty. We give plenty of guidance on what constitutes a reasonable forecast in an uncertain world. We also point out many sources of data that are available to aid you in constructing your forecasts. We are living in the middle of an information explosion. The Internet puts an ever-increasing array of financial data at our fingertips. In the spirit of practical advice, we will suggest places to find the best, juiciest tidbits of information and how to incorporate them into your analysis. All this work will reduce the uncertainty in your forecasts, but plenty will still remain. No one knows exactly how the future will unfold; uncertainty is the nature of the beast.

This introductory chapter outlines our equity analysis and valuation framework. We begin with an overview of the nature of business activities. Next, we provide a brief discussion of equity valuation theory. We then explain the critical importance of the financial statements in the practical application of equity valuation theory. Finally, we outline the steps in our systematic approach to valuation and show you how eVal guides you through these steps. Throughout the book, we use Kohl's as a working example. In case you haven't heard of this firm, Kohl's is a rapidly growing department store chain featuring clothing items and housewares. This chapter provides a road map for the entire equity valuation process, and we will refer back to this road map frequently as we walk you through each of the intermediate steps.

1.2   OVERVIEW OF BUSINESS ACTIVITIES

Equity securities represent ownership claims in the business activities of profit-seeking entities. The valuation of an equity security must therefore begin with a thorough analysis of the entity's underlying business activities. Business activities can be divided into three broad categories to facilitate analysis: *operating activities, investing activities,* and *financing activities*. Each category is described below.

Operating Activities

Businesses typically generate profit for their owners by providing customers with goods and services in return for cash or other consideration. As long as the consideration received exceeds the costs incurred in providing the goods and services, profit is generated. *Operating activities* are activities that are directly related to the provision of goods and services to customers. For example, in a restaurant business, the purchase, preparation, and serving of food to customers are all examples of operating activities. Washing the dishes and cleaning the restrooms are also operating activities, since these are part of the package of services that a restaurant provides to its customers. The operating activities are clearly the bread and butter of any business and the primary means through which the owners of the business hope to profit from their investment.

Investing Activities

Nearly all businesses must make investments in productive capacity before they can begin to provide goods and services to their customers. For example, a restaurant business requires a restaurant building, furniture, and cooking equipment. Purchases and sales of resources that provide productive capacity are referred to as *investing activities*. We define investing activities with respect to the nature of the goods and services that the firm is in the business of providing. If the firm is in the business of selling cooking equipment, then the purchase of an oven is an operating activity. However, if the firm is in the business of selling restaurant meals, then the purchase of an oven is an investing activity, because it provides the productive capacity required to produce and sell meals.

Why bother to distinguish between operating activities and investing activities? Investing activities involve resource commitments that are expected to provide benefits over long periods of time. Investments take place in anticipation of future operating activities and the profits from operating activities ultimately must provide a competitive return for the investment to have been worthwhile. Because the resources acquired in investing activities provide benefits for long periods of time, it can take a long time to find out how profitable these investments have been. In addition, the investing activities that a company makes today may be used to support operating activities of a very different scale and scope in the future. It is therefore useful to separate our analysis of the performance of a business's current operating activities from its investments in productive capacity to support future operating activities. In the long run, however, operating and investing activities are closely linked. Operating activities are made possible by a specific set of past investing activities, and the profits from operating activities should be evaluated in relation to the cost of the investing activities that made them possible.

Financing Activities

In order to acquire the resources necessary to engage in operating and investing activities, businesses require financing. The owners of the business provide the initial source of financing in the hope that the business will provide them with a competitive return on their capital. In a corporation, these owners are the holders of the common equity securities. If a business is financed solely by its equity holders, and immediately distributes the cash flows generated by its operating and investing activities back to its equity holders, its *financing activities* consist of these simple cash flow transactions. In practice, however, there are many other sources of financing. For example, a business can issue debt, preferred stock, and warrants, to name just a few alternatives. In addition, a business need not immediately distribute all the cash generated by its operating and investing activities. Instead, the business may choose to invest this cash in financial assets, such as treasury bonds or financial securities issued by other businesses. Financing activities incorporate all such transactions.

Financing activities are distinct from operating and investing activities. A firm can finance a given set of operating and investing activities many different ways without affecting the nature of the operating and investing activities. But this does not mean that the firm cannot add value through financing activities. Financing activities create the opportunity for the owners of the business to leverage the return from their operating and investing activities, to minimize taxes and transactions costs, and to exploit inefficiencies in capital markets. Investment bankers specialize in determining the amount and type of capital that takes best advantage of these financing opportunities, and the large fees charged by investment bankers speak to the potential value that can be created.

1.3 OVERVIEW OF EQUITY VALUATION THEORY

The basic theory of equity valuation is straightforward and well established. Equity securities are financial instruments, and, as such, their value is equal to net present value of the future cash distributions that they are expected to generate.

These cash distributions traditionally have taken the form of cash dividend payments, and so the value of equity often is expressed as the net present value of the expected future dividend payments, as shown in the following equation:

$$\text{Value}_0 = \sum_{t=1}^{\infty} \frac{\text{Cash Dividend}_t}{(1 + r)^t}$$

where

Value$_0$ = value of equity at time 0

Cash Dividend$_t$ = expected amount of cash dividends to be paid in period t

r = discount rate (cost of capital)

This valuation model is widely known as the dividend-discounting model. However, dividends are not the only way that cash can be distributed to equity holders. Stock repurchases have become increasingly popular. While dividends represent routine cash payments made on a pro rata basis to all equity holders, stock repurchase involves the business buying back its own stock from specific equity holders. Nevertheless, both transactions involve distributing cash from the business to its equity holders. Another consideration in the valuation of equity securities is that companies often seek new cash infusions through the issuance of additional equity securities. These equity issuances can be thought of as negative cash distributions that should be netted against the positive cash distributions associated with dividends and stock repurchases in order to determine the net cash distributions to equity. So the dividend-discounting model is more precisely expressed as

$$\text{Value}_0 = \sum_{t=1}^{\infty} \frac{\text{Cash Dividend}_t + \text{Stock Repurchases}_t - \text{Equity Issuances}_t}{(1 + r)^t}$$

where

Cash Dividend$_t$ = expected amount of cash dividends to be paid in period t

Stock Repurchases$_t$ = expected amount of cash to be paid out via stock repurchases in period t

Equity Issuances$_t$ = expected amount of cash to be raised via equity issuances in period t

Throughout the remainder of the text, we will avoid this mouthful and simply refer to the numerator as "distributions to equity holders."

What determines the amount and timing of distributions to equity holders? Since equity holders are the owners of the business, they have the residual claim on the net cash flows available from a business's operating, investing, and nonequity financing activities. In practice, distributions to equity holders are made at the discretion of management, based on a variety of factors. The major factors are

- How much cash did the business's operating activities generate?
- How much cash was used for investing activities in order to maintain or expand the scale and scope of the business's operating activities?

- How much cash is required to make scheduled payments to providers of non-equity capital, such as interest and principal payments on loans?
- How much cash should be raised (used) issuing (retiring) nonequity capital, such as debt and preferred stock?
- How much cash should be retained in the business in the form of financial assets to provide for future cash flow needs?

In the long run, the free cash flows generated by a business's operating and investing activities are the key driver of its distributions to equity holders. However, the other factors listed above can make the amount and timing of a business's free cash flows very different from the amount and timing of its cash distributions to equity holders.

In summary, while the basic theory of equity valuation is quite straightforward, the devil is in forecasting the future cash distributions to equity holders. There are many different equity valuation formulas floating around academia and practice. These formulas implicitly use different variables to forecast future distributions to equity holders. For example, practitioners are fond of substituting variables like earnings, "EBITDA," and "NOPAT" for cash distributions. These substitutions can be justifiable if done in a way that maintains consistency with the underlying dividend discounting model. However, practitioners all too often throw caution to the wind and come up with formulas that require heroic assumptions to reconcile with sound valuation theory.

1.4 THE ROLE OF FINANCIAL STATEMENTS

The financial statements are the primary device for bridging the gap between theory and practice in equity valuation. Traditional valuation texts often criticize financial statements and their underlying accounting principles on the basis that they do an imperfect job at measuring value. However, these criticisms represent a basic misunderstanding of the role of financial statements in equity valuation. Financial statements are not designed to directly estimate equity value, and accounting book values rarely match market values. Instead, the role of the financial statements is to provide a detailed description of the financial implications of a firm's historical business activities. In other words, the financial statements summarize the historical operating, investing, and financing activities of a firm, and show how these activities affect the past, present, and expected future cash flows. The purpose of the historical financial statements is not to directly forecast the cash flow implications of future operating, investing, and financing activities.

Given that the historical financial statements do not directly forecast how future business activities will affect future cash flows, you may be questioning their role in equity valuation. Their role is twofold:

- They provide the language for translating forecasts of future business activities into forecasts of cash flows.

- By describing the cash flow implications of past business activities, they provide a good starting point for determining the cash flow implications of future business activities.

The first role of the financial statements in valuation is to provide a language for describing how a firm's future business activities will affect its future cash flows. We cannot forecast cash flows in a vacuum. The role of the financial statements is to identify and categorize the activities of a firm that have cash flow implications. A set of financial statements tells us how the various operating, investing, and financing activities of a firm combine to produce cash flows. In order to forecast a firm's future cash flows, we first need a set of financial statements that capture the various intended operating, investing, and financing activities of the firm. We can then begin the process of forecasting the cash flow implications of each of these activities. For instance, by forecasting sales and the change in accounts receivable, we can compute the cash collections from customers. By constructing a complete set of forecasted financial statements, we can systematically derive the cash distributions to equity holders.

The second role of the financial statements is to provide historical data on the cash flow implications of a firm's past business activities that may prove useful in forecasting its future cash flows. Many firms engage in similar business activities for long periods of time. Over time, these business activities are subject to change. Nevertheless, these changes are rarely so drastic as to make the results of past business activities completely irrelevant to the prediction of future results. Thus, the most common forecasting procedure is to start with the past financial statements and then modify those statements based on changes that are anticipated to occur in the future. The effectiveness of this procedure varies widely. For firms in mature industries with established products and stable customer bases, past results can be a very good predictor of future results and the past financial statements will be very relevant in estimating firm value. In contrast, for start-up firms in emerging industries with evolving products and growing customer bases, past results can be a poor predictor of future results. Past results also will be a poor predictor of future results for firms making significant acquisitions or significant changes to their business strategies. But we have to start somewhere, and the past is usually the best place to start when thinking about the future.

1.5 THREE STEPS TO EQUITY ANALYSIS

The discussion thus far indicates that the equity valuation process can be broken down into three distinct steps, which are illustrated in Figure 1.1. *Understanding the past* is the first step. This analysis must go beyond simply looking at the firm's past financial results. You need to understand the firm's results in the context of the industry and economy in which the firm operates, and you need to look for clues about planned changes in the future business activities. Second, we need to use our analysis of the past in *forecasting the future*. This step is structured around forecasting the future financial statements, from which we will derive our estimates of

FIGURE 1.1 **Framework for Equity Valuation**

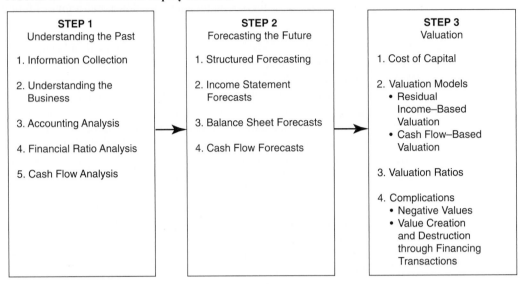

cash distributions to equity holders. The third step comprises *valuation*. In this step, we convert our estimates of future cash distributions into a single estimate of intrinsic value. The eVal software provided with this book will guide you through each of these steps. In this section, we give an overview of the three steps and introduce you to eVal.

Understanding the Past

The first step in the equity valuation process is to examine all relevant information about the business. This step begins with the systematic collection of pertinent information, which we refer to in Figure 1.1 as *information collection*. If the equity security is publicly traded on a major exchange in the United States, then the usual starting point for information collection is the firm's financial filings with the Securities and Exchange Commission (SEC). However, there are a myriad of other information sources that should be investigated, ranging from company press releases to industry and macroeconomic data. Today, much of this information is available via the click of a mouse. We provide a more detailed discussion of the most important information sources in Chapter 2.

Once the pertinent information has been gathered, we begin the process of analyzing this information. The first task is *understanding the business*. This process is primarily qualitative in nature and is aimed at developing a detailed understanding of the business activities in which the firm is engaged. What does the business make, how is it made, and who buys it? Who are the main competitors, what are the industry characteristics, and how does this industry fit into the general economy? We also want to identify the elements of a firm's business strategy that are expected to make it more successful than its competitors. Just as investors strive to find securities that will provide abnormally high investment returns, company managers strive to find real investment opportunities that will provide abnormally high profits. Competition among managers limits the availability of such investment opportunities. Your business analysis should leave you with a clear understanding of the firm's business plan, and some opinions about whether this plan represents a viable strategy for generating abnormally high profits. We cover the basics of business analysis in Chapter 3.

Armed with a thorough understanding of the business, we can start to scrutinize the historical financial statements. *Accounting analysis* is the first task. The objective here is to develop a thorough understanding of how the economic consequences of the firm's business activities are reflected in the financial statements. The financial statements report on the periodic financial position and operating performance of a business. Over long periods of time (i.e., many years), the cash flows from a firm's operating and investing activities become known with perfect certainty, and so the economic consequences are easy to measure. But over short periods of time (i.e., a quarter or a year), the short-run cash flows can have little relation to the long-run economic consequences. This problem arises because a firm's operating and investing cycles often span many years. Firms can hold or produce inventory for long periods, they can advance credit to customers for long periods, they invest in assets that will generate benefits over long periods, and they reward employees with retirement benefits that will be paid over long periods. As a result, the net cash flows to a firm over short periods of time provide a very noisy signal of the long-run cash flow consequences of the firm's activities.

This is where financial accounting comes to our aid. The primary objective of accrual accounting is to provide a better indication of the long-run cash consequences of a firm's business activities. For instance, investing in a productive asset is not merely a cash outflow; the accrual accounting system tracks the store of future benefits that this investment represents by recording an asset on the balance sheet. But, while the accrual accounting process undoubtedly creates useful information, it is also fraught with distortions. The distortions are sometimes the benign errors that come from estimating uncertain events, and they are sometimes intentionally created by management manipulation of the reported results. Accounting analysis is concerned with understanding a firm's accrual accounting policies and their implications for the interpretation of the financial statements. A solid accounting analysis will help you understand the key strengths and weaknesses of a firm's financial statements, identify where management may have attempted to mislead you, and help you draw informed conclusions about the economic consequences of the firm's past business activities. Accounting analysis is the subject of Chapter 4.

Once you have a solid understanding of the firm's financial statements, you are set to use the financial statements to evaluate the financial performance of the firm. Chapter 5 develops a systematic *financial ratio analysis* framework to facilitate this task. This analysis shows us how the components of a firm's financial statements interact to produce overall financial performance. What margin does the firm earn on its sales? How much investment is required to generate the sales? How aggressively does the firm use nonequity sources of financing? This analysis enables us to quickly identify the key drivers of financial performance and spot any irregularities. When combined with accounting analysis, financial ratio analysis provides the basis for evaluating the economic consequences of a firm's past business activities and the success of its business strategy.

Ratio analysis focuses almost exclusively on a firm's accrual accounting statements—the income statement and the balance sheet. However, in order to remain solvent, fund new business opportunities, and ultimately make cash flow distributions, a firm also must carefully manage its cash. A firm's cash flows are detailed in its statement of cash flows, and the analysis of this information is the topic of Chapter 6. *Cash flow analysis* is concerned with understanding the articulation of the cash flows between a firm's operating, investing, and financing activities. A sound business strategy should anticipate the cash needs associated with operating and investing activities and provide for their timely and efficient financing. Also, firm value is ultimately dependent on the distribution of cash flows to equity holders. Unfortunately, some firms choose to invest surplus cash flows in wasteful ways rather than making timely distributions to equity holders. These and other related issues are explained in Chapter 6.

Forecasting the Future

Once you understand the past, you are ready to forecast the future. The tasks involved in this step are summarized in the second box of Figure 1.1. Our goal in this step is to forecast the future financial statements. Recall from our earlier discussion that the financial statements represent the language for converting forecasts of future business activities into forecasts of future cash flows. In Chapter 7 we introduce *structured forecasting*—the systematic way that we go about developing forecasts. Rather than attempting to forecast each line item of the financial statements in isolation, we frame the forecasting problem using the same types of ratios that you studied in Chapter 5. You express your forecasts about the firm's operating, investing, and financing activities by developing forecasts of these ratios, and then derive the implied values for the underlying financial statement line items.

Chapter 7 also discusses earnings-per-share (EPS) forecasts. EPS forecasts are the most popular way of summarizing expectations of financial performance for equity securities. On the surface, the computation of EPS might sound pretty simple—take the forecasted earnings and divide it by the number of shares. But what number of shares should you use? Our forecast of the future number of shares depends on both our forecast of the amount of new equity that is expected to be issued/repurchased between now and the forecast date and the stock prices at which the issuances/repurchases are expected to occur. While our pro forma financial statements will provide us with dollar forecasts of issuances and repurchases, they do not provide us with forecasts of future issuance and repurchase prices. Thus, per-share analysis turns out to be quite a complex topic involving some thorny issues.

The eVal software requires a number of specific forecasting assumptions. In Chapter 8 we give you advice concerning *detailed forecast construction*. The process begins with the very first line on the income statement, the "Sales" forecast. Most firms have business models that center around providing goods and services to customers in return for sales revenue. The sales forecast is the single most important forecast; it represents the key driver of most other business activities. For example, most of the remaining lines in the income statement capture the costs that are incurred in the firm's operating activities, and many of these costs depend on the level of business activity, as described by the sales forecast. But the costs also depend on the efficiency with which the business is run and the prices at which the inputs for the business (such as materials and labor) are purchased, so forecasting these costs is not as simple as taking a fixed percentage of sales.

Income statement forecasts concern operating activities. Balance sheet forecasts concern the impact of the operating, investing, and financing activities on the resources and obligations of a firm. The forecasting of the balance sheet can be divided into two distinct tasks. First, we must forecast the resources and obligations necessary to sustain the operating activities that we forecast on our income statement. Operating activities typically require investments in working capital (e.g., inventory) and long-term capital (e.g., property, plant, and equipment) and can also result in obligations (e.g., accounts payable and pension benefits for employees). The forecasted amount of operating resources and obligations depends on both the forecasted level of operating activity and the efficiency with which the firm is forecasted to conduct its operations. The second distinct task is to forecast the resources and obligations associated with the firm's financing activities. Most firms hold some financial resources (e.g., cash and marketable securities) and use some nonequity financing (e.g., debt and preferred stock). The forecasting of the individual financial resources and obligations on the balance sheet provides a systematic process for determining the amount and mix of financing that is used to support the firm's operating and investing activities.

The next task is to create cash flow forecasts. As we discussed earlier, the financial statements provide the language we use to describe the economic consequences of business activities. Ultimately, these economic consequences are represented by cash flows and the statement of cash flows reports these cash consequences. Contained within the cash flow forecasts are implied forecasts of the net cash distributions to equity holders, a key input for equity valuation, so this is an important step. Fortunately, cash flow forecasting is quite straightforward. As you may recall from your accounting classes, we can derive a statement of cash flows from an income statement, along with the associated beginning and ending balance sheets. So, we simply use our income statements and balance sheet forecasts to construct our cash flow forecasts. In fact, the *eVal* software can handle this step for us.

The forecasted financial statements are often referred to as "pro forma" financial statements ("pro forma" is Latin for "a matter of form"). The last step is to apply the same ratio analysis and cash flow analysis that we discussed in Chapter 5 to the pro forma financial statements. This final step provides a reality check on the plausibility of our forecasts. For example, we may find that our forecasting assumptions imply a level of profitability for a firm that far exceeds the historical industry average. Such performance may be justified through some unique feature of the firm's business strategy. However, if we do not see anything particularly unique, we should probably revise the forecasting assumptions to bring profitability back to more reasonable levels. Similarly, our pro forma cash flow analysis may reveal that our forecasting assumptions imply that a firm must raise substantial additional capital. If the firm has no plans to raise new capital, or would have difficulty accessing capital markets on favorable terms, we should revise our forecasting assumptions accordingly.

Valuation

With your forecasts of the future under your belt, you are ready for step number three, valuation. The tasks involved in the valuation step are summarized in the third box of Figure 1.1. First you need to decide on the necessary valuation parameters. The most important of these is the "discount rate," or *cost of capital,* which enters the denominator of our equity valuation model. Unfortunately, there is much disagreement concerning the selection of an appropriate discount rate. In Chapter 9, we will discuss some of the most popular techniques for computing the discount rate and provide some general advice on how to handle this issue.

The remaining tasks consist of the equity valuation computations themselves. The good news here is that eVal does all of the work for you. eVal provides computations using both a "residual income valuation model" (RIM) and a "discounted free cash flow" (DCF) model. Why do we need two valuations? Well, we don't, and it turns out that both of these valuations will give you exactly the same answer. These are simply two different algebraic formulations of our basic valuation theory. Regardless of the formula used, it is your forecasts of the future financial statements, along with your valuation parameters, that ultimately determine the value of the equity. The only issue here is whether you would like to look at computations based on earnings or cash flows. By providing you with both sets of computations, you will be able to effectively communicate your equity valuation work to fans of either model.

A second issue in constructing the valuation models is whether we choose to discount the cash distributions directly to equity holders using the cost of equity capital, or whether we discount cash flows to all providers of capital (i.e., common equity plus preferred stock and debt) using a weighted average cost of capital, and then subtract the value of the nonequity capital to derive equity value. Again, *eVal* does the valuation both ways, both ways give the same answer, and the choice between the two approaches is largely a matter of taste. Chapter 10 provides a detailed explanation of the valuation gymnastics involved in these alternative *valuation models.*

Financial analysts often communicate their beliefs about the value of a firm in terms of *valuation ratios.* Some of these are quite straightforward, such as the price-to-earnings ratio, defined as the market price divided by EPS. Others are much more complex, like the PEG ratio (don't ask). In Chapter 11 we discuss some of these ratios, what they represent, and how they can be used to screen for underpriced or overpriced stocks. These ratios are commonly used shortcuts, but they are just that; they are no substitute for a full-blown valuation analysis.

The final step in the equity valuation process is to consider some *complications*. If you are lucky, none of these complications will apply to your valuation. Unfortunately, one or more of these monsters often rear their ugly heads. We mention them here briefly only to alert you to their existence; Chapter 12 provides more detailed coverage.

The first complication concerns negative equity values. Stock prices cannot be negative in practice, but models can be constructed in eVal that generate negative equity values. If you find yourself with a negative equity valuation, then you should read Chapter 12. A second and related complication concerns the abandonment option. If you come up with a positive equity valuation, but your sensitivity analysis reveals that negative valuations are also reasonably likely, then you need to consider the abandonment option.

A third complication arises when we introduce the possibility that a firm may create or destroy value through transactions in its own mispriced securities. For example, if a firm's stock is overpriced relative to its intrinsic value, it can create value for its existing equity holders by issuing additional shares of the overpriced stock. Thus, not only do we have to correctly determine the intrinsic value of a firm's operating and investing activities, but we also have to forecast how much additional value will be created or destroyed through the firm's financing activities. A final and related complication concerns contingent equity claims. Contingent equity claims provide their holders with the option, but not the obligation, to purchase shares of common stock for a prespecified exercise price. Firms issue contingent claims on their equity for a variety of reasons. For example, firms can raise capital by issuing warrants, firms can reduce the interest rate paid on debt by issuing convertible debt, and firms can compensate employees using employee stock options. Because the holders of contingent claims only have to exercise their claims when it is profitable to do so, the claims themselves will have value as long as there is some probability of a profitable future exercise. These claims can therefore result in equity securities being issued for consideration less than fair value.

1.6   THE ROLE OF eVal

We are now at an ideal point to introduce eVal, our Excel-based financial modeling software (see Appendix A for instructions on how to install eVal on your computer). Remember that you MUST enable macros for eVal to work. We promise that we haven't programmed anything evil, so click "Enable Macros" when prompted. Each time you start a new model in eVal, you will be greeted by the eVal introductory screen, shown in Figure 1.2. This screen contains some boilerplate legal notices, and, after acknowledging them, you simply hit the OK button to start using eVal. Clicking the OK button takes you to the User's Guide worksheet, shown in Figure 1.3.

FIGURE 1.2
eVal Start-Up Screen

FIGURE 1.3
eVal User's Guide

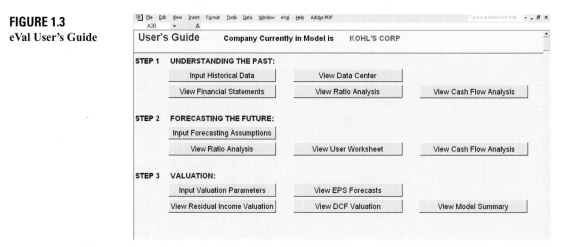

The User's Guide worksheet is eVal's control center, and you will use this worksheet to guide you through the construction of your financial models. Note that this worksheet is organized around the same three steps that we outlined in the equity valuation framework. The worksheet consists of a series of ordered buttons. Clicking a button takes you to another worksheet, where you will either input required valuation data or view financial data prepared by eVal. Each sheet that you are taken to will have a Go To User's Guide button in the top left corner. When you have finished with a sheet, click this button to take you back to the User's Guide

FIGURE 1.4   **The Role of eVal in the Application of Our Equity Valuation Framework**

STEP 1 Understanding the Past	STEP 2 Forecasting the Future	STEP 3 Valuation
What You Do: Obtain and analyze financial and nonfinancial information on the business **What eVal Does:** Imports historical financial data using **eVal's** standardized format Provides links to company data Performs systematic ratio analysis on historical data Performs systematic cash flow analysis on historical data	**What You Do:** Select forecast horizon Modify **eVal's** default forecasting assumptions based on the insights from your analysis in STEP 1 **What eVal Does:** Creates forecasting template and prompts you for key forecasting assumptions Provides historic values and suggests default values for forecasting assumptions Prepares pro forma financial statements from forecasting assumptions Performs ratio and cash flow analysis on pro forma financials	**What You Do:** Provide cost of equity capital and other valuation parameters **What eVal Does:** Performs residual income valuation to both common equity holders and all capital providers Performs discounted cash flow valuation to both common equity holders and all capital providers Maintains internal consistency between the two valuation models Provides EPS forecast schedule Provides model summary and sensitivity analysis

worksheet. While we have organized the buttons so as to systematically walk you through the entire equity valuation process, you are free to skip between buttons and worksheets as you wish while you build your model.

Figure 1.4 summarizes the role played by eVal in each of the three steps of our valuation framework. The first box in Figure 1.4 summarizes how eVal assists you in step one, *understanding the past*. eVal begins by importing the firm's historical financial data into a standardized spreadsheet format and provides you with a variety of links to company data. Next, eVal performs systematic financial ratio analysis and cash flow analysis on the firm's historical financial statements. These repetitive and tedious data input and data manipulation tasks are done for you automatically. However, there is no escaping the inevitable fact that you must perform the vast majority of the work in this first step yourself. A thorough understanding of all the relevant information concerning a business can only be achieved through your own detailed information collection and analysis.

The second box in Figure 1.4 summarizes how eVal helps you in step two, *forecasting the future*. eVal will initially prompt you for a forecast horizon. It will then generate a forecasting template and prompt you for the individual forecasting assumptions required to build the forecasted financial statements. The structure in eVal is designed to simplify an otherwise daunting task, yet remain sufficiently flexible to hit any desired set of financial results. eVal also provides default forecasting assumptions that are reasonable for the average firm in the average industry in the average year. However, you should avoid relying too heavily on these defaults. We are not licensed soothsayers; our defaults are simply based on the naïve extrapolation of past data. You should use your detailed information analysis from step one to provide more accurate forecasting assumptions. Once you have updated the assumptions, eVal will prepare the pro forma financial statements implied by these assumptions and will perform a detailed financial ratio analysis and cash flow analysis on the pro forma financial statements.

The third box in Figure 1.4 summarizes how eVal helps you in step three, *valuation*. You have already done most of the hard work in steps one and two, leaving eVal to do most of the work in step three. eVal begins by presenting detailed valuation calculations using both the residual income (RIM) and discounted free cash flow (DCF) valuation models. You can use the formulas in the valuation spreadsheets to trace all of the amounts entering the valuation calculations back to the pro forma financial statements prepared in step two. eVal also will ensure that the valuations obtained using the RIM and DCF models are identical. While this feature is simply a reflection of the consistent application of valuation theory, it is important from a practical perspective. One of our strongest motivations for creating eVal was the hundreds of hours that we spent trying to reconcile the inconsistent valuation models of students. eVal also provides a detailed analysis of the earnings-per-share (EPS) implications of your pro forma financial forecasts, which helps you to benchmark your forecasts with those of Wall Street analysts. EPS is the most closely tracked summary measure of firm performance and EPS surprises are a big catalyst for stock price changes. If your EPS forecasts are more accurate than the consensus forecasts of Wall Street analysts, the differences between your forecasts and the consensus should provide the basis for a lucrative investment strategy. Finally, eVal provides a summary of your valuation model and a sensitivity analysis tool that allows you to quickly determine the sensitivity of your valuation estimate to changes in the key assumptions. These features are designed to summarize the key ingredients of your valuation model for others.

1.7 CLOSING COMMENTS

In this chapter, we provided you with an overview of the theory of equity valuation and introduced a framework for its practical application. We also highlighted the role played by the eVal financial software in helping you to apply this framework more efficiently and communicate the key ingredients of your analysis more effectively. If you have a reasonable background in accounting and finance, this overview is probably enough to get you up and running with eVal. However, the "garbage-in, garbage out" maxim rules the day. Even software like eVal cannot protect you from your own bad forecasting assumptions. In the chapters that follow, our main purpose is to provide you with a framework for deriving the best possible forecasting assumptions from the available information. Let's face it: valuation software like eVal costs just a few dollars. It stands to reason that such a tool by itself cannot give you the edge in the competitive world of Wall Street. So for those of you who want to make it big in the investment world, there are still 11 more chapters and a lifetime of diligent work ahead of you.

Information Collection

2.1   INTRODUCTION

The heart of a good valuation is a good forecast, and a forecast is only as good as the information that is used to support it. So the more relevant information you collect, the more accurate your forecast will be. You may be thinking that information collection is time consuming and costly, and that our "more is better" advice ignores this aspect of the trade-off. But our advice comes from years of experience watching students and practitioners underinvest in information collection. The chapters that follow talk in more detail about how to interpret the specific information you collect. This chapter focuses on describing the most important sources of information and how eVal can help you obtain and process this information. By focusing your information collection effort where it yields the highest returns, and using tools such as eVal to leverage your data collection and processing abilities, you will maximize the payoff to information collection.

We begin by identifying the key sources of company-specific data. For public companies whose securities trade in the United States, filings with the Securities and Exchange Commission (SEC) are the most important source of company-specific information. We identify the most important filings and describe their contents. We then discuss other data sources, such as company Web sites, company press releases, news stories, and analysts' reports. Next, we identify and briefly discuss the key sources of industry and macroeconomic data. Finally, we explain the various options for importing historical financial statement data into eVal.

Throughout this chapter, we will give you links to sources of information on the Internet. We simply name the site in the text and, at the end of the chapter, give you the URL that gets you to the site. The most important company-specific links can be found on the Data Center sheet in eVal. Other more general links can be found under the eVal menu.

2.2   COMPANY DATA

You should spend most of your time collecting company-specific data. Two-thirds of the variation in a typical stock's price is company-specific and unrelated to market or industrywide movements. We recommend that you spend at least two-thirds of your time on the analysis of company-specific data. The major sources of company-specific data are explained in Figure 2.1.

SEC Filings

Public companies issuing securities in the United States are required to file a number of detailed financial reports with the Security and Exchange Commission (SEC), which in turn makes these reports available to the public. These SEC filings represent the most important source of company-specific information and provide the natural starting point for the collection of company data. A summary of the most important SEC filings is provided in Figure 2.1. A more detailed description of SEC forms is available on the SEC's Web site.

FIGURE 2.1   **Guide to Common SEC Filings**

Filing	Description
Form 10-K	This is the annual report filed by most companies. It provides a comprehensive overview of the company's business (see Figure 2.2 for details). Depending on company size, it must be filed within 60 days of the close of the fiscal year.
Form 10-Q	This is the quarterly financial report filed by most companies. It includes unaudited financial statements and provides a continuing view of the company's financial position during the year. Depending on company size, it must be filed within 35 days of the close of the quarter.
Form 8-K	This is the "current report" that is used to report the occurrence of any material events or corporate changes that are of importance to investors and have not been previously reported.
Proxy Statement (Form DEF 14A)	The proxy statement provides official notification to designated classes of shareholders of matters to be brought to a vote at a shareholders' meeting.
Form 13F	This is the quarterly report filed by institutional investors managing over $100 million. It lists the name and amount of each security held at the end of each quarter.
Schedule 13D	This filing is required by 5 percent (or more) equity owners within 10 days of the acquisition event.
Schedule 13E	These are filings required by persons engaging in "going private" transactions in the company's stock or by companies engaging in tender offers for their own securities.
Schedule 13G	This is similar to Schedule 13D but is only available in special cases where control of the issuer is not compromised.
Schedule 14D	These are filings required pursuant to a tender offer.
Form 3, Form 4, and Form 5	These are statements of ownership filings required by directors, officers, and 10 percent owners. Form 3 is the initial ownership filing, Form 4 is for changes in ownership, and Form 5 is a special annual filing.
Registration Statements (Forms S-1 and S-3)	These are filings that are used to register securities before they are offered to investors. The most common registration filings are Forms S-1 and S-3.
Prospectus (Rule 424)	This document is made available to investors in a security offering. It comes in varieties 424A, 424B1, 424B2, 424B3, 424B4, 424B5, 424B6, and 424B7.

Listed first in Figure 2.1 is the annual Form 10-K, the most useful SEC filing. All domestic publicly traded companies are required to file this form within 60 days of their fiscal year end. If you were going to read only one document about the company before starting your valuation, this would be the one. This can be quite a lengthy document, but it follows a standardized format and familiarizing yourself with this format will improve your ability to efficiently process the contents.

The basic format of a Form 10-K is summarized in Figure 2.2. The first item, the description of the business, provides a detailed discussion of the company's past and expected future business activities. Companies are required to provide a

FIGURE 2.2 **Items of Disclosure Contained in Form 10-K**

Item	Description
Cover Page	Lists company name, fiscal year end, state of incorporation, each class of publicly traded securities, and other information.
Item 1—Business	Identifies principal products and services of the company, principal markets and methods of distribution, and other key attributes and risks of the business.
Item 2—Properties	Location and character of key properties.
Item 3—Legal Proceedings	Brief description of material pending legal proceedings.
Item 4—Submission of Matters to Vote	Information relating to the convening of a meeting of shareholders, whether annual or special, and the matters voted upon.
Item 5—Market for Common Stock	Principal market in which common stock is traded; high and low quarterly stock prices for the last two years; number of stockholders; dividends paid during the last two years; future dividend plans.
Item 6—Selected Financial Data	Five-year summary of selected financial data, including net sales and operating revenue, income from continuing operations, total assets, and long-term obligations.
Item 7—Management's Discussion and Analysis	Discussion of results of operations, liquidity, capital resources, off-balance-sheet arrangements, and contractual obligations. Discussion should include trends, significant events and uncertainties, causes of material changes, effects of inflation and changing prices, and critical accounting policies.
Item 7A—Disclosures about Market Risk	Provides qualitative and quantitative disclosures about market risk (e.g., interest rate, exchange rate, and commodity price risk). Requirements apply to financial instruments and commodity instruments.
Item 8—Financial Statements and Supplementary Data	Two-year audited balance sheets, three-year audited statements of income, three-year audited statements of cash flows, along with supporting notes and schedules.
Item 9—Changes in and Disagreements with Accountants	Description of any changes in and disagreements with independent auditors on any matter of accounting principles or practices, financial statement disclosure, or auditing scope of procedure.
Item 9A—Controls and Procedures	Opinion of top management and auditors regarding the effectiveness of the company's internal controls and procedures over financial reporting.

long list of information on things such as the principal products sold, sources and availability of raw materials, key patents, trademarks and licenses, seasonalities, key customers, competitive conditions, government regulations, and risk factors associated with the business. The SEC designed this item to be a thorough and objective overview of a company's business activities, and is a great starting point for getting to know a company.

The next three items in the Form 10-K provide information about other aspects of the company that the SEC decided were worth singling out. Item 2 requires a description of the property of the company, Item 3 requires a description of any material pending legal proceedings against the company, and Item 4 requires a description of any matters submitted during the fourth quarter to a vote of security holders. You should scan this information for anything important, but there isn't usually too much here. Item 5 requires summary information concerning recent stock price and dividend activity and Item 6 provides summary financial data for the last five years. You can obtain the information in Items 5 and 6 in more detail from other sources, but since it provides a convenient summary, you may want to scan through it.

Item 7 contains management's discussion and analysis of the firm's financial condition, results of operations, off-balance-sheet arrangements, contractual obligations, and critical accounting policies. Referred to as the "MD&A," this is a "must read." The discussion and analysis of financial condition requires management to identify any factors that might cause the company's liquidity to change. It also requires a description of the company's material capital expenditure commitments, the purpose of such commitments, and the anticipated sources of funding for the commitments. Finally, the company is required to discuss any pending changes in the company's capital structure. The discussion and analysis of results of operations requires management to walk the reader through the line items in the company's income statement, identifying any unusual or nonrecurring items and explaining any significant changes during the last two years. The discussions concerning off-balance-sheet arrangements, contractual obligations, and critical accounting policies are recent additions in response to the accounting scandals at Enron and WorldCom. These discussions can be useful for identifying potential problem areas in the company's financial reports. But if a company is really "cooking the books," it is unlikely to tell you exactly how it is doing it right here. Lastly, because much of the material in the MD&A is forward-looking, it normally finishes with a long list of all the risk factors that add uncertainty to these forecasts. As you can see, the management discussion and analysis requires management to divulge a wealth of information that is useful in forecasting. Moreover, the company's auditor is required to perform a reality check on the information in the MD&A. So read the MD&A carefully and completely.

Following the MD&A is Item 7A, requiring disclosures about the company's exposure to certain market risks, such as interest rate risk and currency risk. This item is important for financial services companies and other companies holding large amounts of financial instruments or engaging in significant hedging activities. Next is the all-important Item 8. Item 8 contains the company's financial statements and supplementary data. This item includes annual balance sheets for the last two years and annual income statements and statements of cash flows for the past three years. This section also must include a detailed description of significant accounting policies, detailed supporting notes and schedules, and an auditor's opinion. The analysis of these financial statements is one of our most important tasks, and is the subject of Chapters 4, 5, and 6.

Item 9 contains information about changes in and disagreements with the independent auditors on accounting practices and financial disclosures. It basically requires disclosure if the company's auditor either resigned or had a major accounting disagreement with management in the past two years. Most of the time you will find nothing in this section, but you should always check it out just to be sure. It takes a whopper of a disagreement for the company and auditors to get to the point of hanging out their dirty laundry in Item 9. A recent addition to Form 10-K is Item 9A. This item was added by the Sarbanes-Oxley Act and basically requires the senior management and auditors to attest to the effectiveness of the company's controls over its financial reporting system.

To summarize, Form 10-K is the most important SEC filing and your starting point for analyzing a company. The most important parts of Form 10-K are the description of business in Item 1, the MD&A in Item 7, and the financial statements in Item 8. The main drawback of Form 10-K is that it is only made available once a year. Our main interest in the other SEC filings in Figure 2.1 is to access more timely information.

The second filing listed in Figure 2.1 is the Form 10-Q filing. This is the quarterly version of Form 10-K; it must be filed within 35 days of the end of the quarter, for each of the first three quarters of the fiscal year (the annual 10-K filing handles the fourth quarter). These filings are not as detailed as the 10-K and do not give you the description of the business and much of the other information that comes with the 10-K. But, obviously, they are more current. They typically contain a summary version of the MD&A and abbreviated, unaudited financial statements. You should plan on reviewing all Form 10-Qs filed since the most recently available Form 10-K. You also should make sure that you are familiar with the information in the most recent 10-K before attempting to read the intervening 10-Qs, since the 10-K provides the necessary context to understand the information in the 10-Q.

The third filing listed in Figure 2.1 is the Form 8-K filing. This filing is used to report significant current events on a timely basis. Examples of events that warrant a Form 8-K filing include a change in control of a company, the acquisition or disposition of a significant portion of the company's business operations, bankruptcy, change in auditors, and the resignation of key directors or officers. The Form 8-K filing must generally be made within four days of the event being reported.

There are lots of other forms that a firm must file with the SEC; the most common ones fill out the rest of Figure 2.1. Most of these other filings aren't as relevant for our purposes as the 10-K, 10-Q, and 8-K, but here are a few of the more interesting ones. Whenever shareholders are required to vote on something (which is usually at least once a year at the annual meeting), the firm must file a proxy statement. This statement gives spicy details about management compensation. So if you think management is skimming too much off the top, this is the place to see just how much they are taking. There are a few different filings related to proxy statements, but the most common one is filed under the designation DEF 14A. Insider trades (i.e., trades by management in the company's stock) are reported on Forms 3, 4, and 5. Note that these forms are filed directly by the managers themselves, rather than under the name of the company. Finally, if a company issues new securities, it will typically file a Form S-3 to register the securities and a Form 424B3 for the final prospectus.

All of these filings can be accessed directly from the EDGAR database on the SEC's Web site. However, this site is not the world's best example of a user-friendly Web interface. To assist you in tracking down SEC filings, eVal includes direct links to each company's Form 10-K and Form 10-Q filings, as well as the complete list of all SEC filings. To use this feature, click the Data Center button on the User's Guide sheet in eVal. This will take you to the Data Center sheet shown in Figure 2.3.

This sheet contains a listing of all companies with financial statement data available from Hemscott and covers over 8,000 U.S. companies. To find a specific company in the list, use the Search button at the top of the screen. The company, sector, and industry tickers on the left-hand side of the screen allow you to import financial statement data into eVal; we discuss these data import functions later in the chapter. The company links on the right-hand side of the screen allow you to link directly to a variety of company-specific information sources on the Web. You must be connected to the Internet to use these links. The first three links are the

FIGURE 2.3 **eVal Data Center Sheet**

	A	B	C	D	E	F	G	H	I	J	K
1	**Data Center**				**Annual Financial Data is originally from April 2006**						
2	Go To User's Guide	KSS	Go	Search	Click Here for an annual update						
3	To import historical data double-click any cell or enter ticker above:										
4			Industry Code LookUp								
5	Company Name	Ticker	Industry	Sector	**Links to SEC filings, Company Websites, News and Analyst Forecasts**						
6	1-800 CONTACTS INC	CTAC	MG520	MG5	Form 10-Ks	Form 10-Qs	All Filings	Home Page	Investor Relations	News	Forecasts
7	1-800-FLOWERS.COM CL A	FLWS	MG852	MG8	Form 10-Ks	Form 10-Qs	All Filings	Home Page	Investor Relations	News	Forecasts
8	1ST CENTENNIAL BANCORP	FCEN	MG411	MG4	Form 10-Ks	Form 10-Qs	All Filings	Home Page	Investor Relations	News	Forecasts
9	1ST COLONIAL BANCORP	FCOB	MG411	MG4	Form 10-Ks	Form 10-Qs	All Filings	NA	NA	News	Forecasts
10	1ST NET TECHNOLOGIES INC	FNTT	MG826	MG8	Form 10-Ks	Form 10-Qs	All Filings	NA	NA	News	Forecasts
11	1ST SOURCE CORP	SRCE	MG414	MG4	Form 10-Ks	Form 10-Qs	All Filings	Home Page	Investor Relations	News	Forecasts
12	1ST STATE BANCORP INC	FSBC	MG419	MG4	Form 10-Ks	Form 10-Qs	All Filings	NA	NA	News	Forecasts
13	21ST CENTURY HOLDING CO	TCHC	MG432	MG4	Form 10-Ks	Form 10-Qs	All Filings	Home Page	Investor Relations	News	Forecasts
14	21ST CENTURY INSURANCE	TW	MG430	MG4	Form 10-Ks	Form 10-Qs	All Filings	Home Page	Investor Relations	News	Forecasts
15	21ST CENTURY TECHNOLOGIE	TFCT	MG423	MG4	Form 10-Ks	Form 10-Qs	All Filings	NA	NA	News	Forecasts
16	24/7 REAL MEDIA INC	TFSM	MG852	MG8	Form 10-Ks	Form 10-Qs	All Filings	Home Page	Investor Relations	News	Forecasts
17	24HOLDINGS INC	TFHD	MG826	MG8	Form 10-Ks	Form 10-Qs	All Filings	NA	NA	News	Forecasts
18	3CI COMPLETE COMPLIANCE	TCCC	MG637	MG6	Form 10-Ks	Form 10-Qs	All Filings	Home Page	Investor Relations	News	Forecasts
19	3COM CORP	COMS	MG814	MG8	Form 10-Ks	Form 10-Qs	All Filings	Home Page	Investor Relations	News	Forecasts
20	3D SYSTEMS CORP	TDSC	MG820	MG8	Form 10-Ks	Form 10-Qs	All Filings	Home Page	Investor Relations	News	Forecasts
21	3M COMPANY	MMM	MG210	MG2	Form 10-Ks	Form 10-Qs	All Filings	Home Page	Investor Relations	News	Forecasts
22	3SI HOLDINGS	TSIH	MG850	MG8	Form 10-Ks	Form 10-Qs	All Filings	Home Page	Investor Relations	News	Forecasts
23	4KIDS ENTERTAINMENT INC	KDE	MG763	MG7	Form 10-Ks	Form 10-Qs	All Filings	Home Page	Investor Relations	News	Forecasts
24	4NET SOFTWARE INC	FNSI	MG210	MG2	Form 10-Ks	Form 10-Qs	All Filings	NA	NA	News	Forecasts
25	5G WIRELESS CMMCTNS INC	FGWC	MG840	MG8	Form 10-Ks	Form 10-Qs	All Filings	NA	NA	News	Forecasts
26	724 SOLUTIONS INC	SVNX	MG852	MG8	Form 10-Ks	Form 10-Qs	All Filings	Home Page	Investor Relations	News	Forecasts
27	7-ELEVEN INC	SE	MG734	MG7	Form 10-Ks	Form 10-Qs	All Filings	Home Page	Investor Relations	News	Forecasts
28	8X8 INC	EGHT	MG841	MG8	Form 10-Ks	Form 10-Qs	All Filings	Home Page	Investor Relations	News	Forecasts
29	99 CENT STUFF INC	NNCT	MG852	MG8	Form 10-Ks	Form 10-Qs	All Filings	NA	NA	News	Forecasts
30	99 CENTS ONLY STORES	NDN	MG732	MG7	Form 10-Ks	Form 10-Qs	All Filings	Home Page	Investor Relations	News	Forecasts
31	A CONSULTING TEAM INC	TACX	MG824	MG8	Form 10-Ks	Form 10-Qs	All Filings	Home Page	Investor Relations	News	Forecasts
32	A O SMITH CORPORATION	AOS	MG314	MG3	Form 10-Ks	Form 10-Qs	All Filings	Home Page	Investor Relations	News	Forecasts
33	A. SCHULMAN INC	SHLM	MG322	MG3	Form 10-Ks	Form 10-Qs	All Filings	Home Page	Investor Relations	News	Forecasts
34	A.C. MOORE ARTS & CRAFTS	ACMR	MG745	MG7	Form 10-Ks	Form 10-Qs	All Filings	Home Page	Investor Relations	News	Forecasts

User's Guide | **Data Center** | Financial Statements | Ratio Analysis | Cash Flow Analysis | Forecasting

Ready

10-K link, the 10-Q link, and the link to all SEC filings. Clicking on these links will take you directly to the corresponding company filings on the SEC's EDGAR database. Another useful Web site for accessing SEC filings is the Pricewater-houseCoopers EDGARSCAN Web site. This site provides a nicer user interface than EDGAR and also performs some useful processing and formatting of the data. Finally, MSN Money provides standardized financial statement data that you can cut-and-paste into eVal.

Even after visiting the above sites, it can sometimes be a challenge to find the exact filing that you are looking for. Companies frequently file one form and then later file an amendment to the form (appending a "/A" to the form name). They also incorporate information in a required filing by referencing another filing. But be persistent, especially when seeking the 10-K and 10-Q. They must be out there somewhere.

Company Web Site

You can learn much about a company's business by surfing its Web site. Most companies have a dedicated investor relations section of their Web site providing financial information about the company. In fact, the development of the Internet and the passage of Regulation FD (Fair Disclosure) by the SEC have proved to be a boon to small investors. Regulation FD was introduced by the SEC in 2000 and basically prohibits companies from selectively disclosing nonpublic information to a few individuals, such as portfolio managers or Wall Street analysts. In order to comply, most companies put out on their Web site any information they have disclosed to other investors. The Data Center sheet in eVal provides links to each company's main homepage and investor relations homepage.

One "must read" in the company Web site is the press release section. Company press releases often provide more timely information than SEC filings. However, you also should remember that the information in these press releases is not subject to the same standards as the company's SEC filings. Good examples are press releases related to quarterly earnings announcements. These press releases are made days or even weeks ahead of the corresponding Form 10-Q filing. However, companies often make up their own pro-forma measures of earnings in their press releases and typically emphasize good information and downplay bad information. So always read these press releases with a grain of salt. Another document that you will often find on the Web site is the annual report to shareholders. Be careful not to confuse the firm's annual report with its official Form 10-K filing. There are fewer required disclosures in the annual report than in the 10-K and, for many companies, the annual report is little more than a marketing document. You will see lots of fancy graphs and photographs of happy employees and customers all designed to convince you that the company is financially healthy, very profitable, an exemplary corporate citizen, and especially kind to animals and small children.

If you check out the company's Web site shortly after an earnings announcement, you will frequently find an audio file that replays the conference call that management had with analysts to discuss the quarter's results. This can be a rich source of information, but can be short-lived; most companies remove them from the Web site after a week or two. After listening to a few of these, you will notice that they are very short sighted and long winded. Most analysts are only interested in forecasting the next quarter's results, and most CEOs are counseled to refrain from expressing opinions about the future.

Financial Press

The company isn't the only one talking. A very active financial press scurries about trying to uncover interesting, and sometimes scandalous, facts about the company. The company will not rush to write a press release about their own questionable accounting practices, but the financial press will not hesitate to do so. And the company will not generally compare itself to other firms in the same industry, but a good news article frequently does this. The only word of warning we offer is that writers for the financial press are paid to write exciting stories that people will be drawn to read; being accurate is desirable but not paramount. Frequently the financial press is the first to call attention to a firm's questionable accounting practices, but, in our experience, only about half the time does the accounting really turn out to be bad.

Most of the major financial portals on the Web have links to recent news stories, along with the firm's press releases. The Data Center sheet in eVal provides you with a link to each company's news page on the Yahoo! Finance portal. This link follows immediately after the investor relations link. Other free sites that we recommend include Reuters and MSN Money. If you want to join the professionals, then a real-time subscription to the Dow Jones News Service will give you access to the most timely and comprehensive newswire service.

Lots of regional newspapers also write about companies in their own backyard, and the major news services may not pick up these stories. One way to be sure you haven't missed something big—and we hesitate to recommend this—is to check out the investment message boards for the company. Yahoo, Motley Fool, and several other sites sponsor boards where investors exchange views about particular stocks along with insults about one another's intelligence. The analysis offered by the average user of these boards is suspect, but you can benefit from the board's collective eyes and ears. If a great story about the company appeared in a local newspaper, or some other source you have overlooked, the odds are high that somebody on the message board has posted something about it. Look for message titles with headlines like "Did anyone else see the article on Hurricane Corporation in the Miami Herald?"

Analyst Research Reports

One final source for company-specific information is the research distributed by analysts working for the independent research firms and the research departments of brokerage houses. Analysts working for brokerage houses are referred to as sell-side analysts to distinguish them from the buy-side analysts working for institutional investors. Buy-side research is used internally by the institutional investor and is not typically made available to other investors. Sell-side research is primarily produced for brokerage clients, but a number of services now collect and redistribute these research reports. The largest service is Investext, a division of Thomson Research. This is a subscription-based service that is offered through many business school libraries.

Sell-side research reports generally provide very precise and confident forecasts based on a rudimentary analysis of a company. Our experience suggests that students and other neophyte investors are often taken in by the apparent confidence with which these reports are written and their association with prestigious investment houses. Historically, however, the recommendations and price targets contained in these reports have been unreliable. Moreover, sell-side analysts rarely charge a direct fee for the research they issue to clients. Instead, they generate revenue from two indirect sources. First, they help their brokerage business to generate brokerage commissions by attracting clients and encouraging them to trade. Second, the analysts often work for brokerage houses that are affiliated with investment banks. By issuing positive research on current and potential investment banking clients, sell-side analysts help to generate investment-banking business. As you can imagine, the fact that sell-side analysts generate revenue through these indirect sources poses a great conflict of interest. One strategy we recommend is to zero in on the research report of the analyst issuing the least favorable recommendation on a stock. This way, you are more likely to find solid analysis rather than superficial hype.

Given the limitations of sell-side research discussed above, we encourage you to read this research with a healthy dose of skepticism. However, sell-side research does have its redeeming features. First, sell-side analysts tend to be industry specialists. A sell-side research report may give you some deep industry insights that you missed in your own industry analysis. Second, sell-side analysts are usually up to date on recent company news and guidance. They can be a good place to check that you have all the latest and greatest company-specific information. Third, sell-side research almost always contains earnings forecasts for the next year or so. One of the strongest catalysts for a stock price change is an earnings surprise, whereby a company announces earnings that differ from the consensus forecast of sell-side analysts. A number of services collect sell-side analysts' forecasts and construct consensus earnings estimates from these forecasts. The leading services are First Call and Zacks. The Data Center sheet in eVal provides you with a link to each company's First Call consensus earnings estimates through the Yahoo! Finance portal. The MSN Money portal provides the Zacks consensus estimates, so it is worth checking both sites.

2.3 MACROECONOMIC AND INDUSTRY DATA

Careful analysis of company-level data is where you are most likely to generate the best insights. However, a good understanding of industry and economywide factors is also useful in the interpretation of past company data and the forecasting of future company data. We have had many experiences where students have become excited about stocks that look "cheap" relative to past fundamentals, only to learn that the students have overlooked some key macroeconomic shifts. Examples include "cheap" oil services stocks in periods immediately following dramatic declines in the price of crude oil and "cheap" banking and home construction stocks in periods immediately following dramatic rises in interest rates. You don't have to be an expert macroeconomist to do sound equity analysis and valuation. But you do need to have a good idea of the macroeconomic factors that impact the industry and company you are analyzing. And you should track the consensus view of where these macroeconomic factors are heading. Macroeconomic and industry analysis is covered in Chapter 3. In this section, we tell you how to collect the necessary data for your analysis.

The Global and Domestic Economy

A taxonomy for conducting macroeconomic and industry analysis is provided in Figure 2.4. At the broadest level, we have the global economy. As the economies of the many countries in the world become increasingly integrated, the healths of domestic economies are increasingly linked to the health of the global economy. Global economic trends are measured by summing the trends in domestic economies. Countries with the largest domestic economies, such as the United States, Japan, and the United Kingdom, tend to dominate global economic trends. However, economic crises in smaller countries, such as those in the Middle East and Latin America, can have a material impact on the global economy. There are a number of Web sites tracking the global economy. We recommend the DismalScientist, offered through Moody's Economy.com Web site.

FIGURE 2.4
Taxonomy for Conducting Macroeconomic and Industry Analysis

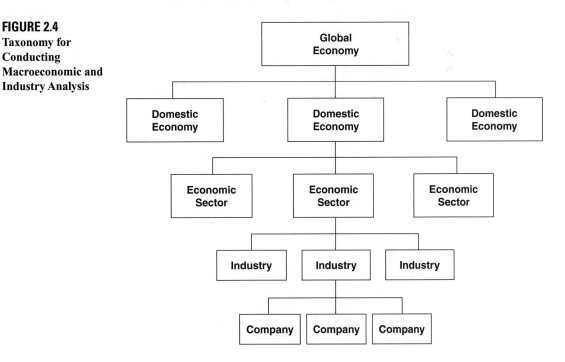

Armed with data on the global economy, you should next collect data on the domestic economy. The operations of most businesses are concentrated in a particular country and the health of this country's domestic economy is a key driver of profitability. Our discussion focuses on the U.S. economy. There is a wealth of free data available on the domestic U.S. economy, most of it made available courtesy of the U.S. government. Five good portals are

- Dr. Ed Yardeni's Economic Network
- FreeLunch.com
- Economagic
- FedStats
- The White House Economic Statistics Briefing Room

The underlying sources for most of this information are government bureaus, where you can find even more juicy details. The U.S. Census Bureau provides information on the population and how it is changing. It also conducts an economic census, which contains a wealth of data on consumer spending habits by industry, and collects "e-stats," which are e-commerce statistics such as Web-generated sales by industry. The Bureau of Economic Analysis provides three main types of data. First, they report GDP data and their components, by industry and by state. Second, they also report input-output statistics, which document the flow of goods between industries. Finally, their fixed-asset surveys report on new investment, net holdings, and average age of major classes of assets. For example, it gives the amount the electrical machinery industry spent on metal-working machinery (lots) versus farm tractors (very little). The Bureau of Labor Statistics reports many labor-related statistics, and also conducts an annual consumer expenditure survey. This is a great source of information about the buying habits of American consumers, including data on their expenditures, income, and consumer unit (families and single consumers) characteristics. The Federal Reserve is a good source of information for industrial capacity statistics and periodic releases on consumer, real estate, and business credit. If you take an evening and peruse the above sites, you will no doubt be left with the following two thoughts: (1) there is an unbelievable amount of economic information available on the Web and (2) our government spends way too much time collecting all of it.

As we discuss in the next chapter, the success of many companies is tied to the success of the U.S. economy. While the previous links describe the past very well, what you are really interested in is how the future economy will evolve. Two good sources for forecasts of future gross domestic product in the United States are the Conference Board and the Congressional Budget Office.

Finally, you should keep track of major economic announcements by following an economic calendar of events. The Yahoo! Finance Economic Calendar provides a good free economic calendar that includes detailed descriptions and additional links for many economic statistics. We'll give you a framework for interpreting all of this domestic economic data in Chapter 3.

Sectors and Industries

Economic sectors and industries are the next two levels in our taxonomy. Before we can discuss sources of data for analysis at these levels, we need to define what we mean by "sector" and "industry." An economic sector consists of a group of industries that engage in related activities. For example, "consumer goods" defines an economic sector consisting of firms that manufacture goods for consumers. Examples of industries included in this sector are automotive and tobacco. The production technologies are very different across these two industries, but it is their common customer base that places them in the same economic sector.

Within each sector are many industries. Industries are defined by the nature of the good or service that is provided by the business. Firms in the same industry provide similar goods and services and will typically use similar inputs and production technologies. Because of these similarities, similar analysis techniques can be applied to firms in the same industry. Also, because firms in the same industry typically compete for market share, analysis of the competitive structure of input and output markets is usually conducted at the industry level. While the macroeconomic and sector-level analysis provides necessary background, the industry level is where we really get to understand the operating characteristics and competitive environment facing a company.

There are several competing classification systems for allocating firms to sectors and industries. To make matters more confusing, the U.S. government has its own system, the North American Industrial Classification System (NAICS). Since the data in eVal are supplied by Hemscott, we use their classification system. While the similarities between this system and other competing systems outnumber the differences, it is important to use a single classification system consistently; otherwise, you can end up double-counting some companies and missing others altogether. Figure 2.5 provides an overview of the Hemscott sector and industry classification system.

There are 12 sectors and over 100 industries in the Hemscott classification system. Hemscott has a mnemonic code for each sector and industry; some are shown in Figure 2.5 and a complete list is given in Appendix B. In addition, listed next to the name and ticker symbol for each company on the Data Center worksheet in eVal is the mnemonic code for the company's sector and industry. Clicking the Industry button on this worksheet allows you to sort firms by industry in order to easily identify the individual firms in each industry. You also can import financial data into eVal that is averaged across all available firms in that sector or industry by double-clicking on a sector or industry code. This is a great way to assess what the typical firm in the industry or sector looks like—how big it is, how profitable it is, and how rapidly it is growing. We describe how you can use these sector and industry averages as part of your financial analysis in Chapter 5.

Beyond the Hemscott data, the very best starting point to begin analyzing a new industry is the pertinent Standard & Poor's Industry Survey. Unfortunately, these surveys are only available on a subscription basis. However, most business school libraries have them available on the Internet through a subscription to the

FIGURE 2.5
**The Hemscott Sector
and Industry
Classification System**
The sector weights are
based on market
capitalizations for the
firms in the S&P 1500
Supercomposite Index
as of January 25, 2006.

Sector (industry codes)	Sector Weight	Major Industries (industry codes)
Basic Materials (110–136)	10.8%	Chemicals (110–113) Energy (120–125) Metals & Mining (130–136)
Conglomerates (210)	4.5%	Conglomerates (210)
Consumer Goods (310–351)	8.5%	Consumer Durables (310–318) Consumer Non-Durables (320–327) Automotive (330–333) Food and Beverage (340–348) Tobacco (350–351)
Financial (410–449)	20.6%	Banking (410–419) Financial Services (420–427) Insurance (430–434) Real Estate (440–449)
Healthcare (510–528)	12.4%	Drugs (510–516) Health Services (520–528)
Industrial Goods (610–637)	2.6%	Aerospace/Defense (610–611) Manufacturing (620–628) Materials and Construction (630–637)
Services (710–716)	20.3%	Leisure (710–716) Media (720–729) Retail (730–739) Specialty Retail (740–745) Wholesale (750–759) Diversified Services (760–769) Transportation (770–776)
Technology (810–852)	16.5%	Computer Hardware (810–815) Computer Software (820–827) Electronics (830–837) Telecommunications (840–846) Internet (850–852)
Utilities (910–914)	3.8%	Utilities (910–914)

Standard and Poor's NetAdvantage service. There is also a wealth of industry-specific information available on the Web. A good portal for accessing this information is Polson Enterprises Industry Portals.

In closing this section, we offer a final word of advice. The list of information given above may seem quite daunting. You may be asking, *"Do I really need to gather and read all of this every time I want to value a company?"* The answer is probably *Yes* if this is the first time you have ever studied the company and you know nothing about it, the economy, or the industry in which it resides. But a more typical situation is that you already have a good knowledge of general macroeconomic trends and may have good industry knowledge from following other companies operating in the same industry. With experience, you also should become quicker at identifying what is relevant and what is irrelevant, and you can zoom right in on the facts that will yield you a better forecast.

2.4   INPUTTING HISTORICAL DATA INTO eVal

When you are ready to start building a valuation model, the first step is to obtain the company's historical financial statement data. These data will provide the foundation on which you will build your forecasts of the future financial statements. eVal provides a number of options that simplify the process of importing historical financial statement data into eVal's standardized spreadsheet format. The very first button in eVal's main User's Guide sheet is the Input Historical Data button. Clicking this button will provide you with four data input options, as shown in Figure 2.6. Most of the time, you will want to choose the first option, Go to Data Center, but there are times when you may want to use one of the other three choices, as we discuss below.

eVal uses up to five years' worth of historical data but will operate effectively with as few as two years. The basic data input requirements for eVal are the historical income statement, the historical balance sheet, historical dividends, and the number of shares outstanding at the most recent fiscal year end. All of these data items can be readily obtained from a company's annual financial statements. Unfortunately, companies do not create their financial reports using a standardized template; rather, each company chooses its own line items. This disparity in company financial reports has given rise to services such as Hemscott that standardize the financial data, making it usable in computerized applications. This

FIGURE 2.6
eVal Data Input Options

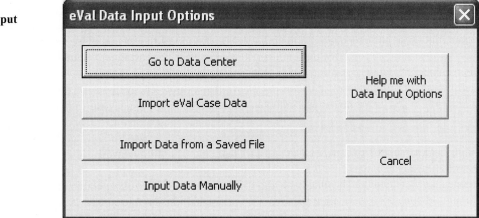

standardization process ensures that every line item appearing on a firm's income statement and balance sheet is included as part of a line item in eVal's standardized financial statements. The process by which all the various line items that can be reported in a firm's actual financial statements are mapped to a standardized line item in eVal is described in more detail in Appendix C.

This standardization process has important advantages and disadvantages. The most important advantage is that it provides a common and familiar framework for analyzing and valuing companies. The most important disadvantage is that detailed information about many line items is discarded in the standardization process. For this reason, you *must* have a copy of the company's financial statements on hand so that you can figure out how the line items on those financial statements have been translated to the standardized financial statements in eVal (as noted above, links to the actual financial statements in the 10-K filings are available on the Data Center sheet).

2.5 USING eVal's DATA CENTER

Included with the eVal software is standardized financial statement data supplied by Hemscott for over 8,000 publicly traded U.S. companies. To import the data for a specific company into eVal, hit the Go to Data Center button in the Data Input Options dialog box or simply click the View Data Center button on the User's Guide sheet. This will take you to the Data Center sheet, where you will find a list of all companies with data available in eVal. If you know the ticker of the company whose data you are after, enter it in the input box at the top of the screen and click the adjacent Go button. The company's recent financial statement data will load into eVal, and you will be returned to the User's Guide worksheet.

If you do not know the company's ticker, you can sort the list by company name, ticker, industry, or sector and then scroll through it to find the company you are looking for, or you can use the search function. To search the list, click the Search button at the top of the screen, enter the company name (or some fragment thereof) in the input box of the resulting dialog box, and click the Find Next button. To import the data, either double-click on the company name or type the ticker into the input box at the top of the sheet and hit Go. The list also includes sector and industry financial statement averages, named using the industry and sector mnemonics listed in Appendix B. These averages can be imported just like a regular company by either double-clicking on the mnemonics or typing the mnemonic in the input box at the top of the page and clicking the Go button.

2.6 IMPORTING eVal CASE DATA

The eVal book and software are supplied with a number of instructional cases. You will find these cases at the back of this book. Some of these cases require you to analyze company data in eVal. Many of these cases relate to particularly interesting points in companies' histories. As such, we are interested in having you analyze the historical data that were available at the time of the case. To save you time inputting these historical data into eVal, we have coded and stored them along with the eVal software. Note that the cases provide you with the historical financial statements from which we obtained these data. Also, as with the data described in the last section, all of the case data are in eVal's standardized format, so you should be sure to reconcile these data back to the original financial statements.

To load eVal case data, click the Import eVal Case Data button in the Data Input Options dialog box. This will take you to a case data options box, where you select the option button for the appropriate case and click the Load Data for Selected Case button.

2.7   IMPORTING DATA FROM A SAVED FILE

In addition to providing immediate access to Hemscott data, eVal is able to use standardized financial data from other data providers, including Thomson Research and Wharton Research and Data Services (WRDS). If you choose to use one of these other data import options, inputting the historical data is a two-step process. First, you access the data from the third-party source and save it in the particular format that we describe in Appendix D. This step does not involve eVal directly, although we provide you with some basic guidance in the appendix. Second, you import the data into eVal by clicking the Import Data from a Saved File button in the Data Input Options dialog box and selecting the database option that matches your data source. You will then be prompted to locate and load your saved file.

2.8   INPUTTING DATA MANUALLY

Manual input is somewhat tedious, but it is sometimes the only option. If you are studying a private company, or a division of a company, then you won't find pre-coded financial data. This option, however, does have two redeeming features. First, since it requires that you manually map data from the published financial statements to eVal's standardized format, you will develop a detailed knowledge of the underlying line items listed in the published statements. This will help you conduct a more informed analysis. Second, standardized financial data are gradually becoming available for free on the Internet, and they are usually the most current data available. You can simply cut and paste these data into eVal using the manual input option. One free and respectable source of historical financial statement data is MSN Money, which provides data sourced from Hemscott. Since eVal also sources its data from Hemscott, this is a great source if you simply want to update the data supplied with eVal.

Clicking the Input Data Manually option in eVal will take you to the Financial Statements worksheet with an empty set of financial statements. You are required to enter your company's historical financial information in all of the yellow cells. All other cells in the worksheet are write-protected to prevent you from accidentally changing them. You can enter a maximum of five years of income statement and balance sheet data, but you don't have to complete the whole spreadsheet to use eVal. The minimum amount of data that we recommend is the company name, the number of shares outstanding, the most recent fiscal year end, and the financial statement data for each of the two most recent fiscal years.

You should enter all dollar and share amounts in thousands. You also should make sure to put the most recent year's financial statement data in the rightmost column and then gradually work back to the left for earlier years. Finally, you need to make sure that you follow eVal's conventions for positive and negative numbers. All amounts that increase net income, assets, liabilities, or equities are entered as positive amounts, while all amounts that decrease net income, assets, liabilities, or equities are entered as negative amounts. For example, costs and expenses such as Cost of Goods Sold are entered as negative numbers, even though they are usually shown as positive numbers in firms' actual financial statements. You can check your signing decisions by making sure that the subtotals of various line items computed in eVal are the same as the corresponding subtotals in your firm's actual financial statements.

You will have to exercise some judgment in mapping line items from the as-reported financial statements to the standardized line items in eVal. Many line items will have different names from the names that we have used in eVal. For example, some firms refer to Cost of Goods Sold as "Cost of Sales." Also, many companies report detailed line items that you will have to aggregate into a single line item in eVal. For example, some firms report marketing expenses and administrative expenses as separate line items, while eVal aggregates these expenses into the single line item SG&A Expenses. We provide detailed guidelines concerning the definitions for each of eVal's standardized line items in Appendix C. However, it is not critical that you follow these guidelines to the letter. The most important thing is that you find a home for every single line item appearing on the as-reported financial statements. And, as you are doing this, you should remember the nature of the as-reported line items underlying each eVal line item so that you can meaningfully interpret ratios computed using these line items.

eVal also has built-in alerts to warn you if your data input decisions seem unreasonable. For example, the message "Error! -Exp?" indicates that you have entered an expense as a positive number, when expenses should be entered as negative numbers. In some cases, you may actually mean to do this; for instance, if interest revenue and interest expense are netted together and the revenue exceeds the expense, then the amount of net interest expense should be entered as a positive amount. But, generally, the expense lines will be negative. The message "Error! A=L+E?" means that your balance sheet does not balance. This error is less forgivable—the entire financial analysis in eVal is suspect if this error is present. In sum, eVal will pick up some, but not all, data input errors, so you should exercise care and make sure that all the financial statement totals in eVal are the same as the corresponding totals in the as-reported financial statements.

2.9 CASES, LINKS, AND REFERENCES

Cases

There is no list of assigned cases for this chapter. However, many of the cases assigned to later chapters require you to apply the information retrieval techniques described in this chapter. A simple exercise that we encourage you try right now is to load a company of your choice into eVal, access the company's recent Form 10-Ks using the link in the Data Center, and then try to reconcile the company's as-reported financial statements to the standardized financial statements in eVal's Financial Statements sheet. This is not always as easy as it first sounds, and going through this process now will alert you to some of the complications. If you want a challenge, try doing this for General Electric Co. (Ticker = GE)—this one's a real stinker!

Links to Company-Specific Information

- SEC Web site: http://www.sec.gov

  The Security and Exchange Commission's official site.

- Description of SEC forms: http://www.sec.gov/info/edgar/forms/edgform.pdf

  Companies file many forms with the SEC. Here is the guide to help you find the interesting ones.

- EDGAR database: http://www.sec.gov/edgar/searchedgar/webusers.htm

  This is where the SEC stores the official financial statement filings for all the companies that are registered in the United States.

- EDGARSCAN Web site: http://edgarscan.pwcglobal.com/

  A free service provided by PriceWaterhouseCoopers that provides SEC filings in a more user-friendly format than the SEC's Web site.

- MSN Money: http://moneycentral.msn.com/investor/invsub/results/statemnt.asp

  This is a link within the MSN Money site. It provides standardized financial statements using Hemscott data (the same data used in eVal).

- Yahoo! Finance: http://finance.yahoo.com

  This is our favorite general-purpose financial portal. Also a good source for Thomson Financial (First Call) consensus analyst estimates.

- Reuters Investing: http://today.reuters.com/investing/

  Another great general-purpose financial portal.

- MSN Money: http://moneycentral.msn.com

  Yet another great general-purpose financial portal. A good source for Zack's consensus analyst estimates.

- Dow Jones Newswire Service: http://www.djnewswires.com/

  This is where Wall Street gets up-to-the-second company-specific news (a subscription-based service).

- Thomson Research: http://research.thomsonib.com/

  This service provides access to a broad set of published analyst reports (a subscription-based service).

Link to Global Macroeconomic Information

- Dismal Scientist: http://www.economy.com/dismal/

  The name says it all. This is a great free source for global economic news and data. It is now owned by Moody's.

Links to U.S. Domestic Macroeconomic Information

- Dr. Ed Yardeni's Economics Network: http://www.yardeni.com/

  A great portal to many economic statistics.
- FreeLunch: http://www.economy.com/freelunch

  Another great portal to many economic statistics.
- Economagic: http://www.economagic.com/

  Yet another great portal to many economic statistics.
- FedStats: http://www.fedstats.gov/

  A comprehensive collection of government statistics, but not always described very well. You really need to use its search engine to find anything. But, if diligent, you can find the amount spent on fish consumption for each state in the United States in 1992. Cool?
- White House Econ/Stat Briefing Room: http://www.whitehouse.gov/fsbr/esbr.html

  This site has great graphs but is not as comprehensive as some other portals.
- U.S. Census Bureau: http://www.census.gov

  Contains juicy details about the changing demographics of the U.S. population.
- Bureau of Economic Analysis: http://www.bea.gov

  Lots of statistics on the components of the gross domestic product.
- Bureau of Labor Statistics: http://www.bls.gov

  A good source for labor statistics. It also reports results of consumer expenditure surveys that document the changing spending habits of American households.
- Federal Reserve: http://www.federalreserve.gov

  Good source on monetary policy and consumer credit.

Links to Gross Domestic Product Estimates and Announcements

- Conference Board: http://www.conference-board.org/economics/index.cfm

  Offers free estimates of future gross domestic product. A subscription gets you many more juicy forecasts.

- Congressional Budget Office: http://www.cbo.gov/

  This is the government's official estimate of future gross domestic product. It also goes farther into the future than the Conference Board.
- Yahoo! Economic Calendar: http://biz.yahoo.com/calendar/

  A good summary of what macroeconomic statistic gets announced when.

Links to Industry Information

- S&P Industry Surveys: http://sandp.ecnext.com/coms2/page_industry

  A subscription service with great (but expensive!) industry surveys.
- Standard and Poor's NetAdvantage: http://www.netadvantage.standardandpoors. com/

  A common package of services that contains the S&P industry surveys.
- Polson Enterprises Industry Portals: http://www.virtualpet.com/industry/ mfg/mfg.htm

  A free portal organized by industry with links to many industry-specific data sources.

CHAPTER THREE

Understanding the Business

3.1 INTRODUCTION

After collecting the wealth of data described in Chapter 2, your next task is to weave it together in a meaningful way. Your goal is to develop a thorough knowledge of the macroeconomic environment, the industry structure, and the operations and strategies of the particular business you are studying. We encourage you to adopt a top-down approach. First, you should consider the general macroeconomic conditions. This will help you understand how the current economic climate affects the performance of each of the industries in which the business operates. Next, you should consider each of the industries in which the business operates. Most professional analysts concentrate on just one or two industries, and they know these industries like the back of their hand. So, if you are going to produce work of similar quality, you also will need to develop a thorough knowledge of the industry. The final stage is a detailed analysis of the operations and strategies of the business. What is the source of competitive advantage in each of the industries in which the company operates, and what are the synergies between the different segments? We briefly review each of these steps below and refer you to the appropriate texts for a more detailed treatment.

Before devoting the next month to pouring over macroeconomic data and reading strategy textbooks, we also encourage you to use a healthy dose of economic intuition and common sense in your analysis. Macroeconomic and industry factors are only useful if you can draw a link between them and the particular firm you are studying. And the strategy literature has seen many fads over time—remember the "new economy"? Don't just join the herd and assume that any firm that pours resources into implementing the latest fad will have stellar growth and staggering profitability for the foreseeable future. Your goal at this stage is to develop a working understanding of the business you are studying and how it fits into the larger economy.

3.2 MACROECONOMIC FACTORS

A top-down approach to understanding a business must start with the global economy. Most domestic businesses have direct exposure to the global economy through their product markets, input markets, or foreign operations. Even businesses without direct exposure to global markets are sensitive to the global economy because the U.S. economy is becoming increasingly sensitive to global economic conditions. You need to understand the state of the global economy and the consensus among experts about where it is headed. You also should be aware of the state of the individual domestic economies that your business is exposed to and their individual sensitivities to the global economy. In particular, you should be aware of the expected economic growth rates, political risks, and currency risks in each of the domestic economies in which the firm operates. These factors can vary widely across countries. For example, expected growth is relatively low in large, mature markets such as the United State and Europe. Expected growth rates are much higher in emerging markets, such as Asia and South America, but these economies also tend to have the greatest political risks and currency risks.

Armed with a basic understanding of the global economic environment, you should next focus on the domestic economy. For most U.S. firms, operations and customers are concentrated in the United States and, consequently, the U.S. economy is where you should begin your analysis. The overall state of the domestic economy and its future prospects can be summarized by a few key economic statistics. We review these below.

Gross Domestic Product

Gross domestic product (GDP) is the most widely used measure of macroeconomic performance. It measures the market value of final goods and services produced domestically. Figures for GDP are released quarterly by the Commerce Department. These figures are typically expressed in real (i.e., inflation-adjusted) terms as an annualized quarter-to-quarter percentage change, which is referred to as the real GDP growth rate. The overall rate at which the economy is growing is an important determinant of the rate at which many businesses can grow, which explains why the GDP growth rate is such a closely watched statistic. Over the last 40 years, the real GDP growth rate has averaged about 3 to 4 percent, reaching highs of over 10 percent and lows of less than –5 percent. The most commonly used definition of an economic recession is two consecutive quarters of negative real GDP growth. Economists carefully monitor many leading indicators of GDP growth in an attempt to predict its future movements. Common leading indicators include unemployment insurance claims, consumer spending, consumer confidence, business orders, business productivity, and housing and construction activity.

Interest Rates

Interest rates reflect the cost of borrowing money and affect business performance in two important ways. First, interest rates determine the price that a firm must pay for its own capital. Other things equal, lower interest rates mean less interest expense and higher profits. Low interest rates also reduce the cost of capital, increasing the number of viable investment opportunities. For consumers, low interest rates also reduce the cost of current consumption relative to future consumption. For example, you have a greater incentive to buy a new car today if the cost of borrowing declines. A decline in interest rates tends to spur consumer spending, thereby increasing sales growth for many businesses. It is important to note that it is *changes* in interest rates that cause changes in consumer spending. If interest rates are low today, but have been low for many years, then consumers are not going to suddenly rush out today to increase their current consumption. However, if interest rates have been running at high levels in recent years and suddenly drop to more moderate levels, we will see an increase in consumption as the relative cost of current versus future consumption has just dropped. Interest rates reflect not only the cost of current versus future consumption, but also expected inflation and credit risk. We can abstract from the credit risk portion of interest by examining the interest rate on low-credit-risk borrowings such as the federal funds rate or the yields on the bills, notes, and bonds issued by the U.S. Treasury. Over the past 40 years, nominal (i.e., not inflation-adjusted) interest rates on low-risk borrowings have ranged from less than 2 percent to over 15 percent, with an average of about 7 percent.

Inflation

Inflation is defined as a general rise in price levels. Inflation creates the gap between real and nominal economic effects. In times of high inflation, businesses will generally find that they are better off in nominal terms because they are selling their goods for higher prices. But if those incoming dollars buy fewer goods and services, the businesses may actually be worse off in real terms. Armed with the inflation rate, it is possible to adjust nominal dollars into real dollars and get a clearer picture of economic performance. Inflation has other more pernicious effects. In times of high and uncertain inflation, the risk from investing in financial assets increases and the credibility of the domestic currency is undermined in global currency markets. Faced with such risk, investors will take their capital to countries without such uncertainty or invest directly in commodities such as gold that provide a hedge against inflation. The inflation rate is most commonly measured using the rate of change in the Consumer Price Index (CPI), published monthly by the Bureau of Labor Statistics. The CPI measures the price of a fixed basket of goods bought by a typical U.S. consumer. Over the past 40 years, the annual rate of inflation, as measured by the CPI, has ranged from less than 0 percent to over 12 percent, and has averaged around 4 percent.

Foreign Exchange Rates

Foreign exchange rates describe how many units of one currency can be bought with a unit of another currency. Many of the inputs bought and outputs sold by domestic businesses are in transactions with foreign entities. As the relative value of the U.S. dollar rises, the cost of foreign inputs decreases and the revenue from foreign sales also decreases. Thus, the impact of foreign exchange rate fluctuations on a business depends not only on whether exchange rates go up or down, but also on whether the firm is a net importer or exporter in a particular currency. Foreign exchange rates are driven by a complex variety of factors, including the relative productivity of capital and labor, relative inflation rates, and relative real interest rates.

Oil Prices and Other Key Commodity Prices

Commodity prices affect the costs of all businesses. The most important commodity price at the macro level is the price of oil. Oil is critical to the successful functioning of an industrialized economy. Oil prices tend to be volatile, due to the concentration of a large proportion of the world's oil reserves in a small number of countries. Increases in oil prices lead to increases in transportation and energy costs that affect nearly all businesses. Increases in oil prices also reduce the amount of income that consumers have to spend on other products. Other important commodity prices include natural gas and various metals. Obviously, different industries have different key commodity inputs: the price of steel is important for the auto industry and the price of palladium is important for the semiconductor industry. Make sure you identify the commodities that are important to the industry that you are studying.

Aside from the economic indicators above, other important factors to consider in your macroeconomic analysis are corporate hedging activities and the business cycle.

Hedging

A firm can effectively hedge its exposure to interest rates, foreign exchange rates, and most commodity prices. Consequently, two firms in the exact same business may have completely different exposures to these factors. For instance, one gold-mining firm may sell its entire production forward, so that its economic profits are unaffected by changes in gold prices,[1] while another firm may not, so that its profits are tied closely to the price of gold. Similarly, financial institutions can alter their interest rate exposure by entering into various interest rate derivative contracts. Firms also can create natural hedges by the way they structure their business. For instance, a firm that expects a large increase in receivables denominated in a foreign currency can arrange its operations in such a way that it also has a large increase in payables denominated in the same currency. The currency gains or losses on receivables will offset the gains or losses on the payables. The point is that, even if a firm's underlying business is exposed to changes in interest rates, foreign exchange rates, or commodity prices, you won't know its net exposure until you understand its hedging activities. Recall from Chapter 2 that Item 7A of

---

[1] We emphasize economic profits here. Thanks to some crazy accounting rules, a firm that has a good economic hedge may have extremely volatile accounting earnings. This unfortunate situation arises because firms are usually required to carry their financial instruments (such as their hedging contracts) at fair value but are not allowed to carry the hedged real assets at fair value.

Form 10-K requires disclosure of exposures to macroeconomic risks. This is the best place to learn about a company's net exposure to interest rate, currency, and commodity risk.

The Business Cycle

The *business cycle* is an important concept for understanding the current state and future prospects of the domestic economy. Historically, domestic economies have exhibited systematic periods of expansion (characterized by high GDP growth, low unemployment, and high consumer confidence) and contraction (characterized by low GDP growth, high unemployment, and low consumer confidence). While there is no guarantee that these cycles will continue, many macroeconomists believe that they are a permanent feature of the economy. Hence, you should have a good sense of the current state of the business cycle and when and how it is most likely to change. The profitability of some sectors is much more sensitive to movements in the business cycle than others, as we will discuss below.

A Realistic Goal for Macroeconomic Analysis

If you set out to become an expert in all the factors that influence the global and domestic economies, you may never get to the point of analyzing your particular firm. Your goal should be to understand the general consensus about major macroeconomic factors. You don't need to develop your own independent forecasts of future GDP or interest rate movements, but you should understand what the experts are saying about these factors and how they might influence your firm's performance in the future.

3.3 INDUSTRY FACTORS

Before considering the details of one particular firm, it is important to think about the industry that the firm resides in. Professional analysts tend to specialize in particular economic sectors and industries to achieve efficiencies in business analysis. Industry analysis has three primary objectives:

- To understand the sensitivity of the industry to key macroeconomic factors.
- To understand how the industry operates and the key performance metrics for evaluating these operations.
- To understand the competitive structure of the industry.

We discuss each of these objectives in more detail below.

Sensitivity to Macroeconomic Factors

Recall from Chapter 2 that economic sectors represent groups of industries that have similar exposures to key macroeconomic factors. Figure 3.1 provides an overview of the sensitivities of each economic sector to three key macroeconomic factors: the GDP growth rate, interest rates, and oil prices.

FIGURE 3.1
Sensitivity of Sector
Profitability to Key
Macroeconomic
Factors

Sector	Macroeconomic Factor		
	GDP	Interest Rate	Oil Price
Basic materials	++	− −	− −
Energy	++	−	++
Conglomerates	+	−	−
Consumer goods	++	− −	−
Financial	+	− −	−
Health care	+	−	−
Industrial goods	++	− −	− −
Services	+	−	−
Technology	++	− −	−
Utilities	+	−	− −

Key: ++ = strong positive relation; + = positive relation; − = negative relation; − − = strong negative relation.

The GDP growth rate is a key driver of profitability for all sectors of the economy. However, some sectors are much more sensitive to this than others. For example, the basic materials, consumer goods, industrial goods, and technology sectors all have high sensitivity to the GDP growth rate. Many of the industries in these sectors have high operating leverage (i.e., relatively high fixed costs), so small movements in economic activity have big impacts on profitability.

Increases in interest rates tend to have a negative effect on the profitability of all sectors, but some sectors are affected more than others. The industrial goods and technology sectors are particularly sensitive to the reductions in corporate capital expenditures that accompany increased interest rates. The financial sector also suffers directly from the reduced borrowing activity associated with higher interest rates.

Increases in oil prices also tend to have a negative effect on the profitability of all sectors. The one obvious exception is the energy sector, which consists largely of companies involved in the exploration, production, transportation, refining, and marketing of oil.

Industry Operation and Key Industry Ratios and Statistics

Firms in the same industry generally produce similar goods and services using similar production technologies. You should begin your industry analysis by figuring out how the industry operates. This involves finding the answers to questions such as: What is the nature of the production process that takes place in the industry? What are the key inputs in the production process? What is the nature of the marketing and distribution process? Is service after the sale a significant factor?

Once you understand how the industry operates, you should identify the key ratios and statistics that capture the financial health of the industry and firms within the industry. The particular metrics vary widely based on the nature of the industry's operations. In the oil production industry, for example, key statistics include oil prices, the current demand for oil, crude oil and petroleum inventories, oil refinery capacity utilization rates, and oil services equipment utilization rates. In contrast, in the semiconductor industry, key ratios and statistics include the semiconductor industry monthly global sales report, the semiconductor equipment book-to-bill ratio, wafer fabrication plant utilization rates, the purchasing managers' index, and business capital spending.

Competition Structure of Industry

Your study of the industry should include an assessment of the intensity of competition. As a benchmark, recall the old microeconomic concept of perfect competition. In a perfectly competitive market, there are many firms using the same production technology and facing the same input and output prices. In equilibrium, just enough firms enter the market to ensure that the equilibrium price provides a "normal" return on the invested capital to all firms in the market. In such a market, valuation is easy. In expectation, each firm simply generates a normal return on its invested capital. Thus, if we know the magnitude of the invested capital and the normal rate of return, we simply multiply the two together to forecast the expected profit. Indeed, this is exactly the logic that is applied to securities markets by efficient market theorists: in an efficient market, each investor is simply expected to earn a normal return on his or her investment. However, it is generally accepted that there are inefficiencies in the market for real assets. Firms in certain industries have been known to generate abnormally high returns for extended periods of time. For example, Coke and Pepsi have both sustained high profitability over prolonged periods, and they do so selling sugared water (with a touch of addictive caffeine)! When studying the industry, you should look for characteristics that might allow firms to generate abnormal profits over a prolonged period of time.

Famed strategist Michael Porter highlights five forces that determine the degree of competition in an industry. The first three forces relate to sources of direct competition. They are the rivalry among existing firms, the threat of new entrants, and the availability of substitute products. Let's apply these three forces to the restaurant industry, focusing particularly on chains of fast-food restaurants. Clearly there is intense rivalry among existing firms—next to every McDonald's is a Burger King, with Wendy's, Taco Bell, and Subway just around the corner. Similarly, new entrants face relatively low barriers to entry—patents are not available for food items, capital expenditures are relatively minor, and franchisees can help fund investment. The competitive pressure from substitute products depends entirely on how narrowly you define the industry. Customers of fast-food restaurants could switch to full-service restaurants at low cost. However, if the industry is defined as simply "restaurants," then the substitute product is cooking food in the home. The switching costs here are probably higher, insofar as this requires a significant lifestyle change on the part of customers. Putting the three forces together, one would have to conclude that the fast-food restaurant industry is highly competitive, possibly even approaching the textbook definition of perfect competition.

The final two forces in Porter's framework relate to a company's relative bargaining position with its suppliers and customers. In particular, both suppliers and customers can alter input and output prices in order to extract a firm's profits if they have a bargaining advantage. Consider the desperate situation of a small firm in the automotive parts industry, one that manufactures plastic parts. A few large corporations control the market for the raw plastic pellets that are used as inputs, leaving little room to negotiate a better price on the input side. And on the output side, the situation is even worse. The automotive firms have many alternative sources for plastic parts. They enjoy so much power over their suppliers that they occasionally give themselves price concessions on existing contracts. Without even consulting the supplier, they simply pay less than the full amount on their accounts payable, expecting that the supplier will either acquiesce or lose all business in the future.

As you analyze the industry, remember that less competition means that abnormal levels of industry profitability are easier to sustain. Of course, we also should remember that various regulatory bodies are charged with preventing business practices that restrain competition. In the United States, the Federal Trade Commission's Bureau of Competition and the U.S. Department of Justice's Antitrust Division are the pertinent regulatory bodies.

3.4   THE FIRM'S STRATEGY

Firm profitability is not solely a function of industry profitability. For example, McDonald's has been able to generate consistently high profits while operating in the highly competitive restaurant industry for many years. What explains this anomaly? Strategists would say that McDonald's has developed a strategy for creating and sustaining competitive advantage. Strategy textbooks attempt to identify and categorize such winning strategies. Three common categories are cost leadership, product differentiation, and focus. A cost leadership strategy aims for low production costs and thin margins, with profits coming from a high volume as customers are attracted by the low price. Wal-Mart successfully implemented such a strategy in the variety retail industry. Product differentiation is achieved by producing a product with unique attributes that are valued by buyers who will pay a premium price, resulting in higher profits. Revlon pioneered this strategy in the cosmetics industry. Finally, the idea behind focus is to develop a niche strategy that supplies one segment of the market with exactly what they want, be it low cost or a differentiated product. Apple successfully implemented such a strategy in the PC industry.

In evaluating a company's strategy, the most important point to keep in mind is that it is extremely difficult to sustain a competitive advantage. Each of the generic strategies described above will be difficult to sustain in the long run. A cost leadership strategy is vulnerable to imitation and to shifts in technology that lead to new, lower-cost production methods. A differentiation strategy also is subject to imitation. Moreover, differentiation strategies are often short-lived fads. For example, the specialty retail and apparel industries are characterized by many differentiated brands that go in and out of style over time—Levi's are out and Antik Denim is in, at least as of this writing. Finally, a focus strategy also is subject to imitation and the risk that changes in market conditions make the targeted segment nonviable.

The best source for information concerning a firm's strategy for achieving competitive advantage is the first section of a firm's Form 10-K filing with the Securities and Exchange Commission. This section must provide a description of the registrant's business. The applicable securities laws require the description of business to include

> Competitive conditions in the business involved including, where material, the identity of the particular markets in which the registrant competes, an estimate of the number of competitors and the registrant's competitive position, if known or reasonably available to the registrant. Separate consideration shall be given to the principal products or services or classes of products or services of the segment, if any. Generally, the names of competitors need not be disclosed. The registrant may include such names, unless in the particular case the effect of including the names would be misleading. Where, however, the registrant knows or has reason to know that one or a small number of competitors is dominant in the industry it shall be identified. The principal methods of competition (e.g., price, service, warranty or product performance) shall be identified, and positive and negative factors pertaining to the competitive position of the registrant, to the extent that they exist, shall be explained if known or reasonably available to the registrant.[2]

Thus, management is required to give its best shot at describing both the degree of industry competition and the firm's own perceived source of competitive advantage. However, you should always take management's ravings about their own wonderful sources of competitive advantage with a grain of salt. Simply admitting that the firm doesn't really have any competitive advantage would probably not sit well with investors, so management will typically spin some sort of yarn. Your job is to check that the alleged source of competitive advantage is real and delivers superior financial performance.

Synergy Analysis

Not all firms operate a single business in a single industry. Corporate synergy analysis focuses on how firms can generate abnormal profits by bringing two or more businesses under the same corporate umbrella. Theories abound in this area. Synergies are created by leveraging proprietary assets, eliminating transaction costs, eliminating redundant overhead, increasing market power, or any number of other activities. The important point to remember here is that the free market is a very good disciplining mechanism, but it is eliminated when activities are brought inside a single firm. For instance, it could be that synergy is created when a

---

[2] Extracted from SEC Regulation S-K, Item 101(c)(1)(x).

sawmill company acquires a timber company, or it could be that the timber segment no longer harvests trees efficiently, because it no longer has to sell logs on the open market—the sawmill segment simply takes their timber as an input. Without the discipline of competing in an open market, the timber segment may respond to inefficient transfer prices or simply get lazy. Empire-building managers are often quick to identify the benefits of mergers but fail to appreciate the costs that can result from coordination and control issues that surface once market discipline is removed.

3.5 CONCLUSION

When you purchased eVal, you were probably hoping that it would take all the hard work out of equity analysis and valuation. If so, then you should now realize that you were sorely wrong. There is no substitute for a thorough understanding of the business underlying the equity security. Anyone who tries to convince you that you can accurately value a business by extrapolating past trends or applying fixed multiples to key historical financial statement variables is wrong. But the good news is that there are many investors out there who use such simple rules to value equity securities. If enough of these investors trade using these simple rules, then they will have an impact on price. Armed with a thorough understanding of the underlying business, you will be in a position to determine when these simple rules give the wrong answer and take these rookie investors to the cleaners.

But there is still plenty of work to do before you are ready to value a firm's equity. We still need to talk about how to use the financial statements to evaluate the effectiveness of the firm's strategy and how to develop good forecasts of the future financial statements. These forecasts are the ultimate drivers of your valuation. We turn to these tasks in the remaining chapters.

3.6 CASES, LINKS, AND REFERENCES

Cases

- Turnaround at Bally Total Fitness? (Question 1)
- Boston Chicken, Inc. (Questions 1 through 3)
- Netflix, Inc. (Questions 1 and 2)
- Overstock.com (Questions 1 and 2)
- Pre-Paid Legal Services (Question 1)
- Can Salton Swing? (Question 1)

References

Further Readings in Macroeconomics

- *Macroeconomics,* by Andrew Abel and Ben Bernanke (2005), is a good standard text on macroeconomics. The main focus is the domestic macroeconomy, but it also includes coverage of the global macroeconomy.

Further Readings in Strategy

- *Competitive Strategy,* by Michael Porter (1998), is a landmark book in the strategy literature. It lays out Porter's five forces for industry analysis and his three generic strategies for achieving competitive advantage.
- *Economics of Strategy,* by David Besanko, David Shanhove, Mark Shanley, and Scott Shaefer (2003), brings a structured microeconomics-based approach to the analysis of corporate strategy.
- *Gaining and Sustaining Competitive Advantage,* by Jay Barney (2001), is an easy read and covers the basics.
- *Strategic Management,* by Garth Saloner, Andrea Shepard, and Joel Podolny (2000), weaves economics and organizational theory together in the search for a sustainable competitive advantage.

Accounting Analysis

4.1 INTRODUCTION

Traditional valuation texts are usually very good at telling you how to value a business assuming that you already know the future cash flows. But, in practice, forecasting these cash flows is the most important and difficult task in conducting a valuation. Moreover, past cash flows are rarely a good indicator of either past performance or future cash flows. For example, successful growth firms often generate negative cash flows as they invest to expand their future business activities. The problem with cash flows is that they measure the distribution of value rather than the creation of value. For this reason, financial statements, prepared in accordance with generally accepted accounting principles (GAAP), have evolved to provide more useful information about value creation in a business. These statements provide a "language" for evaluating a firm's past performance and forecasting its future performance. It is the language that is spoken by the financial community, and it is the language that we will use throughout the valuation exercise.

At this point, you may ask yourself, "If accountants already measure value creation, what is left for the rest of us to do?" It turns out that financial statements are not designed to value a company. Instead, the financial statements are intended to provide information that is useful in helping others to conduct their own valuation. Since we are the "others" who actually get to do the valuation, we must understand three aspects of accounting information:

1. What information do financial statements provide?
2. How does this information help in valuation?
3. What are the key limitations of this information?

The purpose of this chapter is to address these questions.

We begin by reviewing the conceptual underpinnings of accounting. Our objective is not to teach you basic accounting. In fact, we assume that you already have a working knowledge of basic accounting principles. Instead, our objective is to discuss the nature of the information provided in the financial statements and how this information relates to firm value. We also discuss the limitations of financial statement information, including managerial manipulation of accounting information.

4.2 THE UNDERPINNINGS OF ACCOUNTING

Although we assume you already know basic accounting principles, we fear that you may have lost the forest among the trees. So let's review the basics. The building blocks of accounting are assets and liabilities. Assets represent future benefits and liabilities represent future obligations. Accountants periodically identify and assign dollar values to a firm's assets and liabilities. The difference between the value of the assets and the value of the liabilities represents the accountants' value of the equity in the firm that belongs to the owners. The owners' equity is also referred to as the *net assets* or *book value* of the firm. This relation, rearranged and given as an equation, is

$$\text{Assets} = \text{Liabilities} + \text{Equity}$$

Because this accounting equation must always hold, the balance sheet must always balance (hence its clever name!). At the end of each accounting period, accountants prepare a *balance sheet* or *statement of financial position* listing and valuing the firm's assets and liabilities. The balance sheet and its relation to the other financial statements are illustrated in Figure 4.1.

If accountants recognize all assets and liabilities and record each item on the balance sheet at its fair market value, taking into account interactions between items, then the value of equity on the balance sheet would equal the fair market value of the firm. But accountants are adamant about the fact that they are not

FIGURE 4.1
Overview of Basic Building Blocks of Accounting

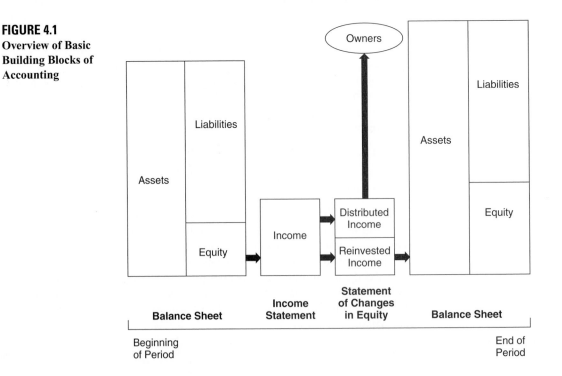

measuring the fair market value of every asset and liability, so the resulting value of equity is not a measure of the equity's fair market value. Instead, accountants ignore many future benefits and obligations altogether and value others at amounts having little connection with their fair market value. Why do accountants employ rules that result in incorrect valuations? It turns out that once we move away from simple examples such as bank accounts or lemonade stands, it would be impossible to reliably measure the fair market value of many assets and liabilities. The accountant may know the value of some equipment immediately after the company purchases it, but what about halfway through its useful life? And how should our humble accountant deal with the fact that the equipment will produce goods whose value is partially determined by the success of the firm's advertising campaign? In deciding what information to provide, accountants trade off relevance with reliability. We may all want to know the present value of the cash flows associated with a firm's business activities. This would be very relevant information. But any attempt to measure this value would be highly subjective, and therefore quite unreliable. The historical acquisition costs of operating assets, on the other hand, can be measured reliably. Accountants view their role as providing the capital markets with reliable information, while leaving the more subjective forecasting of the unreliable but highly relevant stuff to us.

Given the limitations inherent in accounting, the primary role of accounting analysis is to determine which benefits and obligations have been ignored in the financial statements and which have been recognized but incorrectly valued. We start with the accounting rules governing the recognition and measurement of assets and liabilities.

Assets

Accountants define assets as probable future economic benefits obtained or controlled by a firm as a result of past transactions or events. This rather dry definition imposes two important hurdles for a future economic benefit to be recognized as an asset. First, the future benefit must be *probable*. Accountants have developed a long list in GAAP to help determine whether a benefit is sufficiently probable to make it into the financial statements. Important examples of future benefits that are *not* deemed to be probable include those associated with most research and development and marketing activities. Second, the future benefits must have resulted from past transactions or events. The most important manifestation of this hurdle is that future benefits associated with selling goods and services cannot be recognized until the sale has actually been consummated (the realization principle). So future benefits associated with anticipated future sales revenues are not recognized. It is virtually certain that General Electric will generate more than zero dollars' worth of sales during the next few years, but the accounting system does not recognize the value of these future transactions. And many start-up pharmaceutical companies have zero current sales (because they have not yet marketed their first drug) but are valued by the stock market as being worth millions of dollars. The market is valuing cash flows from anticipated future sales. Accountants ignore such future benefits.

So what future benefits are the accountants willing to recognize? There are three broad types of assets. First, there are cash and cash equivalents, which are valued quite simply at their face value. Second, there are amounts of cash owed to the firm as a result of past transactions or events (e.g., trade receivables and loans). These monetary receivables are generally valued using the net present value of the expected future payments. Third, there are future benefits acquired by the firm as part of a past transaction or event (e.g., marketable securities, inventory, property, acquired intangibles). If the acquired future benefits are financial assets, such as marketable securities, they are generally valued using their observed market value. If the acquired future benefits are nonfinancial assets, such as a truck or a building, they are generally valued at historical cost, adjusted downward to the extent that the anticipated future benefits have either been used up or impaired.

Overall, accountants do a good job at recognizing and valuing future benefits associated with financial resources but do a poor job at recognizing and valuing future benefits associated with operating resources. Accountants only recognize a subset of the future benefits associated with operating resources and they usually value these benefits based on what they cost rather than on the value of the cash flow streams they are expected to generate.

Liabilities

Liabilities are defined as the reverse of assets. Liabilities are probable future sacrifices of economic benefits arising from present obligations as a result of past transactions or events. The recognition hurdles imposed on liabilities correspond closely to those imposed on assets. The future sacrifices must be *probable*. Important examples of future sacrifices that are *not* deemed probable include the expected costs associated with unsettled litigation and third-party loan guarantees. The future sacrifices also must arise from present obligations as a result of past transactions or events. For example, we may have contracted with employees to purchase their services in the future. But we are not obliged to recognize a liability for the promised future payments until such time as we receive the promised services. Most liabilities are monetary in nature and are valued based on the present value of the promised payments. Obligations to provide future goods and services to customers represent an important exception and are valued based on the price paid by the customer to receive the future goods/services. While this sounds like a simple valuation rule, things can get tricky. For example, assume that a software company sells a software program bundled with a contract to service the software. The accountant must decide how to divide the selling price between the software program and the future service obligation. The latter is recognized as a liability on the balance sheet until the service envisioned by the contract has been provided.

Changes in Equity

Recall that equity is equal to the difference between assets and liabilities, so we don't need a separate set of recognition and measurement rules to determine the book value of equity. But it is useful to distinguish between two broad reasons why a firm's equity changes over time. One reason is that the owners of the firm can contribute new assets to the firm (e.g., equity issuances) or withdraw existing assets from the firm (e.g., dividends). Such transactions are recorded in the *statement of changes in equity*. The other reason is that the firm's business operations inevitably lead to changes in assets and liabilities. This is the miracle of value creation (or, in the case of negative net changes, the misfortune of value destruction). Through this second source of change, assets and liabilities not only provide the building blocks for the balance sheet, but also for the *income statement*. While the balance sheet lists the assets and liabilities of a firm at a point in time, the income statement measures changes in these assets and liabilities over a period of time. But it is important to remember that the income statement only reports changes in assets and liabilities resulting from the firm's business operations, not from financing transactions with the owners. Recalling that equity equals assets less liabilities, periodic income is the "plug" in the following equation:

$$\text{Ending Equity} = \text{Beginning Equity} + \text{Income}$$
$$- \text{Net Distributions to Equity Holders}$$

and rearranging gives

$$\text{Income} = \text{Change in Equity} + \text{Net Distributions to Equity}$$

This relation is known as the *clean surplus relation*—change in equity on the balance sheet plus distributions to equity holders represent income that is generated by the firm for its equity holders. The change in equity component of income is often referred to as *reinvested income* or *retained earnings,* while the distributions to equity holders component of income is often referred to as *distributed income.* Intuitively, the income statement measures the net benefits generated by the firm's business operations over a period of time. And it does this using the same restrictive definitions of future benefits (i.e., assets) and future obligations (i.e., liabilities) as the balance sheet. Figure 4.1 illustrates the relation between the balance sheet, the income statement, and the statement of changes in equity.

Armed with the balance sheet from the beginning of the period, the balance sheet from the end of the period, and the amount of net distributions to/from owners during the period, it is a simple matter to compute income. So what is the incremental role of the income statement? The real information in the income statement isn't just the bottom line; rather, it is the classification of the various changes in assets and liabilities into different components of income. The income statement provides insights into how the firm's business operations generate changes in assets and liabilities over the course of the period. The key components of the income statement are illustrated in Figure 4.2. Each of these components has a different definition that facilitates the interpretation of past performance and forecasting of future performance. We describe each component in more detail below.

Revenues

Revenues are defined as increases in assets or reductions in liabilities that arise from the provision of the goods and services in the course of a firm's operating

FIGURE 4.2

Classification of Components of Income

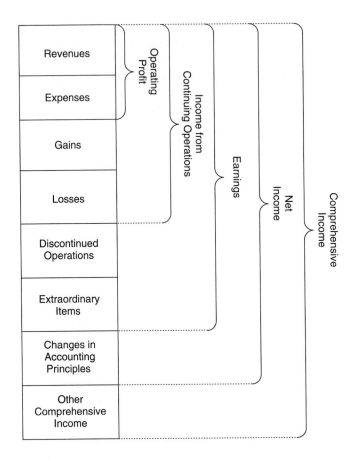

activities. For the most part, revenues are simply the proceeds received by the firm in return for providing goods and services. Note that the goods and services sold must be part of the firm's intended operating activities. If a firm that is in the business of operating restaurants sells an entire restaurant, the proceeds from the sale will not be recorded as part of revenue, because the firm's intended operating activity is operating rather than selling the restaurant. Instead, it will be reported as part of either the gain or loss on the sale of the restaurant (more on this below).

A central question in accounting for revenues is establishing exactly when the revenues are earned. In what period do the associated assets increase in value? The general revenue recognition rule is called the *realization principle* and states that revenue is recognized when an exchange transaction has taken place, the earnings process is substantially complete, and collection of the proceeds is reasonably assured. While this sounds very reasonable, it clearly leaves room for interpretation. Consider a company that purchases land, does some minor improvements, subdivides it, and then sells plots to customers who pay 10 percent of the selling price and sign a 10-year mortgage for the balance. Is the selling price recognized as revenue when the firm purchases the land, when it finishes the minor improvements, when a customer pays the initial 10 percent, or when the customer pays off the mortgage? In most situations, the accounting rule is easy: revenue is recognized when a sale is made and the customer takes possession of the goods. But even this seemingly simple rule has received its share of abuse, as we discuss later.

Sales transactions are the key driver of most other activities in a firm. Once a sale transaction occurs and revenues are recognized, the accounting rules attempt to measure the assets that are consumed in generating these revenues. Revenue recognition is the kick-off event for the measurement of income and, because of this, plays a central role in ratio analysis and forecasting.

Expenses

Expenses are defined as the mirror image of revenues: they are decreases in assets or increases in liabilities that arise from the provision of goods and services in the course of a firm's operating activities. As with revenues, the costs must be associated with the firm's intended operating activities. For example, the carrying value of a restaurant that is sold by a restaurant operating company would not be an expense (see discussion on gains and losses below).

Wherever possible, expense recognition rules attempt to match the consumption of specific assets to the production of specific revenues, but these rules frequently have to resort to ad hoc allocations of costs. For example, we might all agree that the cost of the raw materials used to produce finished goods should be matched against the revenue generated by the sale of the goods. But exactly how much property, plant, and equipment was consumed to convert the raw materials into finished goods? How much of the corporate Lear jet was consumed in the production of the goods? What about the cost of deferred compensation to the sales force? What about interest on the money that was borrowed to purchase the equipment that was used to convert the raw materials into finished goods?

Operating Profit

The difference between a firm's revenues and expenses represents the profit associated with the firm's ongoing operating activities. This amount is often referred to as the *operating income* or *operating profit* of the firm and is the primary driver of firm value. If a firm can't generate a respectable operating profit, then it probably won't be around for very long.

An important role for the income statement is in distinguishing operating profit from the myriad of other, largely nonrecurring transactions and events that cause assets and liabilities to change. Revenues and expenses are intended to capture the financial consequences of a firm's ongoing operating activities. The remaining bits and pieces of income are discussed below. But just because an item is classified as revenue or expense does not rule out the possibility that it may be nonrecurring. Even the ongoing operations of a company are subject to nonrecurring demand and supply shocks. And it is not uncommon for companies to generate recurring sources of nonoperating income from investments they have made in other companies. Recall from Chapter 2 that the management discussion and analysis provided in Forms 10-K and 10-Q is required to identify any potentially nonre-curring components of revenue and expense. As you study the firm's income statements, think carefully about the extent to which each item is likely to be recurring.

Gains

Gains are increases in the net assets of a firm that occur in the normal course of business and contribute to the earnings of a firm but are incidental or peripheral to the firm's operating activities. Returning to our previous example of the restaurant operating firm that sells an entire restaurant, if the proceeds from the sale exceed the carrying value of the restaurant sold, then we would report a gain. Since we are not in the business of selling restaurants, the proceeds and costs associated with the sale are not classified as revenues and expenses. Instead, they are netted and recorded as a gain in the income statement. By separating gains from revenues and expenses, we can discriminate between profitability that is directly associated with the firm's ongoing business operations and profitability that is due to incidental transactions and events. This distinction is very useful from a forecasting perspective, because these incidental transactions and events are much more likely to be one-off occurrences. Common examples of gains include proceeds from the sale of assets, awards from winning a lawsuit, and certain increases in the value of marketable securities.

Losses

Losses are decreases in the net assets of a firm that occur in the normal course of business and reduce the earnings of a firm but are incidental or peripheral to the firm's operating activities. If our restaurant operating firm sells an entire restaurant and the proceeds from the sale are less the carrying value of the restaurant sold, then we would report a loss. As with gains, losses are likely to be one-off occurrences, so it is useful to distinguish them from revenues and expenses. Transactions and events resulting in losses include asset disposals, legal settlements, asset impairments, and restructuring charges.

As shown in Figure 4.2, revenues, expenses, gains, and losses combine to produce a firm's *income from continuing operations*.

Other Items

There are a few other oddities on the income statement that are zero for most firms most of the time. Most of these items are nonrecurring. If a firm sells a major division or segment of its business, any operating income, gains, or losses related to that segment must be reported separately on the income statement as Discontinued Operations. There is also a separate line item reserved for extraordinary gains and losses. To be extraordinary, gains and losses must be both unusual in nature and infrequent in occurrence. However, GAAP define these terms so narrowly that even business losses associated with the September 11 terrorist attacks were not deemed to be extraordinary. So what can be put here? Gains and losses associated with the early extinguishment of debt are allowed, as are certain losses associated with natural catastrophes and confiscation of assets by foreign governments. As shown in Figure 4.2, revenues, expenses, gains, losses, discontinued operations, and extraordinary items combine to produce a firm's earnings. Earnings measure the performance of the firm for the period, and include all components of periodic performance, regardless of whether they are expected to recur.

If the accounting rule makers change the rules, the cumulative effect on retained earnings from the change in accounting principle must be reported separately following extraordinary items in the income statement. The reason that this component of income is not included in earnings is that it is unrelated to current period performance. Instead, it is a *catch-up* adjustment that measures the cumulative effect of the change in earlier periods. As shown in Figure 4.2, revenues, expenses, gains, losses, discontinued operations, extraordinary items, and changes in accounting principles combine to produce a firm's net income. Net income is the traditional *bottom line*. However, if the company has preferred stock, then any dividends declared on the preferred stock are deducted from net income to arrive at net income available to common stock. This is the real bottom line to common equity holders.

The final component of the income statement is other comprehensive income. This component consists of a variety of other changes in equity that accountants could not bring themselves to include in earnings. Remember that accounting is a political process, and corporations lobbied to keep the items in this section out of earnings. But because they involve changes in assets and liabilities that cause equity to change, they had to be put somewhere—hence this category. Examples include unrealized gains and losses on marketable securities, foreign currency translation adjustments, and minimum pension liability adjustments. These last adjustments make sure that we preserve the clean surplus relation, written precisely as

Comprehensive Income Available to Common Equity
= Change in Common Equity + Net Distributions to Common Equity Holders

On the bottom of the Financial Statements sheet in eVal, you will notice a line item titled Clean Surplus Plug (Ignore). We use this item to clean up the company's prior financial statements by putting all the other comprehensive income items here. But because these items are not expected to recur, we force it to be zero in the forecast financial statements. That's why we ask you to "ignore" the clean surplus plug. In addition, we use the shorthand "Net Income" for "Comprehensive Income Available to Common Equity"; typically, they are the same (or at least very similar) amounts.

4.3 ACCOUNTING INFORMATION AND VALUATION

By now, we should have driven home the point that the financial statements are not intended to yield a final measure of firm value. Instead, they provide information that assists in the determination of value. In this section, we explain why and how accounting information is useful. We'll be kind to accounting in this section, concentrating on the positive ways in which it provides information that facilitates valuation decisions. But accounting information also has many shortcomings, and we will discuss them in the next section.

In most businesses, the accounting system can be thought of as classifying the business into a series of current and expected future *sales transactions*. The balance sheet measures the cumulative amount that has been invested in the past to generate future sales transactions. The income statement measures the expected cash flow consequences of sales transactions consummated during the current period. The sales transaction is the critical event that leads to the recognition and measurement of value in the financial statements. A sale triggers the recognition of revenues, representing the net assets created by the sales transaction, and expenses, representing the net assets used to generate the sales transaction. The difference between these revenues and expenses is recorded as operating profit in the income statement.

It is important to note that the operating income resulting from sales transactions during a period rarely coincides with the actual net cash receipts generated by these transactions during the period. The accounting rules that measure changes in assets and liabilities are collectively known as *accrual accounting,* and the differences between accounting income and cash receipts are referred to as the *accruals*. Differences between net income and the net cash receipts arise from changes in noncash assets and liabilities on the balance sheet (i.e., a completely cash-based accounting system would have no noncash assets or liabilities). But, over the long run, net income and cash flows will be similar. Accrual accounting just changes the timing of the recognition of cash receipts and payments.

Accountants go to great lengths to make sure that the net assets resulting from a particular sales transaction include all the past and expected future cash consequences of that sales transaction. Some examples should make this clear:

- The expected future cash collections associated with credit sales are usually recognized in revenues in the period that the sales transaction occurs.
- The cash outflows associated with inventory purchases are usually not recognized as expenses until the inventory is sold.
- The cash outflows associated with the purchase of a machine are usually recognized as expenses gradually over the periods in which the machine is expected to generate sales.
- The expected future cash outflows associated with postretirement benefits earned by workers producing sales in the current period are recognized as expenses in the current period.

Although the financial statements do not attempt to measure the expected future cash consequences of future sales transactions, they nevertheless provide a rich source of information to help in forecasting the future cash flows associated with these transactions. Most firms operate in the same lines of business for many accounting periods and their competitive environments change slowly over time.

Hence, by measuring the cumulative cash consequences of current sales transactions, the financial statements provide useful information for forecasting the cash consequences of anticipated future sales transactions. For example:

1. Historical balance sheets provide a detailed breakdown of the investment that was required to generate historical sales.
2. Historical income statements provide a detailed breakdown of the cash consequences of the firm's historical sales.
3. The most recent balance sheet accumulates past investment that is expected to generate future sales.

Accounting Information and Value

To develop the link between accounting information and firm value, recall the basic valuation model we introduced in Chapter 1 (and will discuss in more detail in Chapter 10). Equity value V_0 is equal to the net present value of the future net cash distributions made by the firm to its stockholders:

$$\text{Value}_0 = \sum_{t=1}^{\infty} \frac{\text{Distributions to Equity}_t}{(1+r)^t}$$

where r is the cost of equity capital. Distributions to equity can be derived from the financial statements using the clean surplus relation. Recall from the clean surplus equation in the previous section that net income measures all changes in equity over a period except for net distributions to owners. This gives us

$$\text{Distributions to Equity} = \text{Net Income} - \text{Change in Equity}$$

One important implication of this relation is that we cannot value a firm by simply discounting its income. We first need to adjust for changes in equity. The intuition for this adjustment is simple. Net income is the result of accrual accounting and so may consist of cash receipts and disbursements relating to past or future periods. But whenever we record net income without an associated distribution to equity, we also must have either added assets to or removed liabilities from the balance sheet. By subtracting changes in equity from net income, we work back to cash distributions to equity. The increase in equity is also what we refer to in Figure 4.1 as *reinvested income*. Thus, if we can forecast the income statement and the beginning and ending balance sheets, we can easily solve for the implied forecast of distributions to equity.

By directing us to forecast income statements and balance sheets, accrual accounting organizes the forecasting process into three distinct tasks. First, we forecast future sales revenues. The sales transaction is the trigger for recognizing benefits associated with a firm's ongoing business operations, and so the sales forecast is the starting point for forecasting income statements and balance sheets. Second, we forecast the other income statement components, many of which are driven by the forecasted sales revenues. Third, we forecast the balance sheet components, many of which are driven by the forecasted sales revenues. Each of these tasks is discussed in much greater detail in Chapters 7 and 8. For now, we simply want to emphasize that the past financial statements provide the starting point for forecasting the future financial statements, and the future financial statements are used to value the firm.

4.4 LIMITATIONS OF ACCOUNTING INFORMATION

Unfortunately, our love fest with accounting lasts only a short while. It's time to look at accounting's dark side. In order to think about the limitations of accounting, it is useful to introduce a "perfect accounting" benchmark. This benchmark should reflect what accounting would be like if we could overcome all its limitations. Let's start by considering a bank savings account. In a bank savings account, an initial amount is invested in order to generate a future stream of interest. Over a period of time, interest is earned on the account and contributions or withdrawals can be made from the account. The ending balance in a savings account is equal to the beginning balance plus interest earned less any withdrawals:

$$\text{Ending Balance} = \text{Beginning Balance} + \text{Interest} - \text{Withdrawals}$$

Rearranging gives

$$\text{Interest} = \text{Withdrawals} + \text{Increase in Balance}$$

This equation is just the clean surplus relation applied to a savings account.

The key measure of investment performance for a savings account is the interest rate earned on the balance, computed as

$$\text{Interest Rate} = \text{Interest/Beginning Balance}$$
$$= (\text{Withdrawals} + \text{Increase in Balance})/\text{Beginning Balance}$$

The equality between the two prior expressions is important. The first expression tells us that we can compute the interest rate by directly putting the amount of interest in the numerator. The second expression says that we also can compute the interest rate without direct reference to the amount of interest. This is because any interest that is not withdrawn from the account must have been reinvested. So we can always impute the amount of interest by adding withdrawals to the increase in the savings account balance.

The accounting for a savings account is pretty simple. The reason accounting works so well in this case is because we know exactly how much interest has accrued over any time period. Equivalently, at any point in time, we know exactly what the account is worth. Now extend the same logic to an equity investment. Simply replace the savings account balance with the book value of equity and the savings account withdrawals with the distributions to equity. The clean surplus relation given earlier is now written as

$$\text{Net Income} = \text{Distributions to Equity} + \text{Increase in Equity}$$

Following the same procedure as we did for the savings account to compute the rate of return on the equity investment gives

Return on Equity = Net Income/Beginning Equity

= (Distributions to Equity + Increase in Equity)/Beginning Equity

The return on equity (ROE) perfectly measures the economic rate of return on the equity investment only if the accounting rules can perfectly measure the income earned over a period or, equivalently, if the accounting rules can perfectly measure the amount of the equity investment at a point in time. But, while such measurements are easy with a savings account, they are almost impossible for an equity investment.

To illustrate how ROE is affected by imperfections in accounting measurements, we will introduce some new notation. Suppose that, due to divine intervention, we could create the perfect accounting system. Let Economic Income denote the amount of income and Investment denote the book value of equity under this perfect accounting system. (We really only need one of these measures; with one, we can compute the other.) The clean surplus relation for this perfect accounting system would be

Economic Income = Distributions to Equity + Increase in Investment

The underlying economic rate of return is given by

Economic Rate of Return = Economic Income/Beginning Investment

= (Distributions to Equity + Increase in Investment)/Beginning Investment

Now define ε as the *measurement error* in equity. It is the difference between the book value of equity, as computed by the imperfect accounting system, and the true value of the Investment, computed with our hypothetical perfect accounting system:

$$\varepsilon = \text{Equity} - \text{Investment}$$

Solving for the relation between accounting net income and economic income gives

Net Income = Distributions to Equity + Increase in Equity

= Distributions to Equity + Increase in Investment + Increase in ε

= Economic Income + Increase in ε

So ROE can be expressed as

ROE = (Economic Income + Increase in ε)/(Beginning Investment + Beginning ε)

Measurement error in equity has a two-pronged effect in distorting ROE relative to the economic rate of return. First, changes in the measurement error between two dates are reflected in the numerator. This is because accounting net income picks up the effects of any changes in the book value of equity between two

FIGURE 4.3 The Effects of Accounting Measurement Error (ε) on Beginning Equity, Net Income, and ROE, Along with Associated Accounting Scenarios

	Change in ε < 0 (Net Income Understated)	Change in ε = 0 (Net Income Correct)	Change in ε > 0 (Net Income Overstated)
Beginning ε < 0 (equity understated)	Effect ambiguous Permanently conservative accounting with increasing investment	ROE > ERR Permanently conservative accounting with constant investment	ROE > ERR Reversal of temporarily conservative accounting Permanently conservative accounting with declining investment
Beginning ε = 0 (equity correct)	ROE < ERR Origination of temporarily conservative accounting	ROE = ERR Perfect accounting	ROE > ERR Origination of temporarily aggressive accounting
Beginning ε > 0 (equity overstated)	ROE < ERR Reversal of temporarily aggressive accounting Permanently aggressive accounting with declining investment	ROE < ERR Permanently aggressive accounting with constant investment	Effect ambiguous Permanently aggressive accounting with increasing investment

Note: ROE is the accounting return on equity (defined as net income divided by beginning equity), ERR is the true economic rate of return, and ε is the measurement error in accounting, defined as the book value of equity minus the true amount of investment.

periods. Second, the level of error at the beginning of the period is reflected in the denominator. The overall distortion in ROE relative to the economic rate of return (ERR) depends on the relative size of the numerator and denominator effects. Possible alternatives are listed in Figure 4.3.

A negative beginning ε causes a positive bias in ROE, because the denominator in the ROE calculation is overstated (and vice versa for a positive beginning ε). A negative change in ε causes a negative bias in ROE, because the numerator in the ROE calculation is understated (and vice versa for a positive change in ε). If the sign of the beginning ε and the change in ε are the same, the two biases work in the opposite direction, and the overall bias in ROE is ambiguous (see the top-left and bottom-right cells of Figure 4.3). In this case, we need to quantify the errors in order to determine the exact nature of the bias.

At this point, you may be thinking that the above analysis is just an abstract exercise in basic algebra (if not, we suggest you apply to an accounting Ph.D. program). So let's move from algebra to a simple example with real numbers in which perfect accounting is well defined. We will then extend the example to illustrate how we could arrive at each of the scenarios identified in Figure 4.3.

Our simple example considers a firm that engages in business for five periods. In each period, the firm makes an initial investment of $100. This investment generates sales in the next period, and nothing thereafter. The proceeds from these sales are assumed to be collected in cash, and the firm also is assumed to incur additional cash operating costs in generating these sales. Cash sales are assumed

FIGURE 4.4
**Cash Flow Analysis
for Simple Example**

	Period				
	1	**2**	**3**	**4**	**5**
Investment	100	100	100	100	0
Cash flows:					
Cash from sales	0	165	165	165	165
− Cash operating expenses	0	−55	−55	−55	−55
− Investment	−100	−100	−100	−100	0
= Net cash distributions	−100	10	10	10	110

to be 165 percent of the prior period's investment and cash operating costs are assumed to be 55 percent of the prior period's investment. These are the only consequences of the investment. Thus, the firm invests $100 in each period in order to generate a net cash inflow of $110 (= $165 − $55) in the next period. The economic income on this investment is therefore $110 − $100 = $10 and the economic rate of return is $10/$100 = 10%. We will assume that the firm invests $100 in each of the first four periods, and then ceases to make any further investments in period five and beyond. We also will assume that any surplus cash is immediately distributed to the owners of the firm.

Figure 4.4 presents a basic cash flow analysis for our simple example. Net cash distributions are −$100 in period one. This is the period in which the initial $100 investment is made, but since sales are not generated until the next period, cash sales and cash operating costs are both $0. Thus, in period one, the owners of the firm must invest $100 in the firm. In periods two through four, net cash distributions to the owners are $10 per period. This represents the excess of the $110 operating cash flows from the period's sales, less the $100 investing outflow to support the next period's sales. Finally, net cash distributions are $110 in period five. Since no new investment is made in period five, all operating cash flows are distributed to the owners. Note that net cash distributions provide an accurate measure of economic income in periods two through four, but are a poor measure of economic income in periods one and five. This is because there is a one-period lag between investing cash flows and operating cash flows. The main objective of accrual accounting is to match investment costs to the benefits that they generate, thus providing a superior measure of periodic performance. We next turn to Figure 4.5 to see how this is accomplished.

Panel A of Figure 4.5 presents the "perfect" accrual accounting scheme that exactly matches the cost of investment to the benefits generated. This accounting scheme perfectly captures the underlying economics of the business. Recall that a $100 investment in a given period generates $110 of cash flows in the subsequent period and is then "used up." The perfect accounting therefore adds an asset of $100 in the period the $100 investment is made, and then removes that asset in the following period. In accounting parlance, we *capitalize* the $100 investment in the period it is made and then expense (i.e., amortize) the asset as it is used up.

Each panel of Figure 4.5 employs a different set of accounting assumptions. The only potential future benefits or obligations in this example are the future

FIGURE 4.5
Accounting
Measurement Error
Scenarios

Panel A. Perfect Accounting (all investment is capitalized in all years)

	Period				
	1	2	3	4	5
Accounting Assumptions:					
Capitalized investment costs	100	100	100	100	0
+ Capitalized operating costs	0	0	0	0	0
Balance Sheet:					
Assets = Equity	100	100	100	100	0
Accruals (change in assets)	100	0	0	0	−100
Measurement Error (ε):					
Beginning ε	0	0	0	0	0
Change in ε	0	0	0	0	0
Income Statement:					
Sales	0	165	165	165	165
− Operating expense	0	−55	−55	−55	−55
− Amortization expense	0	−100	−100	−100	−100
− Investment expense	0	0	0	0	0
= Operating income	0	10	10	10	10
Return on equity		10.0%	10.0%	10.0%	10.0%

Panel B. Temporarily Aggressive Accounting (perfect accounting, except that 120% of investment costs are capitalized in period 3)

	Period				
	1	2	3	4	5
Accounting Assumptions:					
Capitalized investment costs	100	100	100	100	0
+ Capitalized operating costs	0	0	20	0	0
Balance Sheet:					
Assets = Equity	100	100	120	100	0
Accruals (change in assets)	100	0	20	−20	−100
Measurement Error (ε):					
Ending ε	0	0	20	0	0
Change in ε	0	0	20	−20	0
Income Statement:					
Sales	0	165	165	165	165
− Operating expense	0	−55	−35	−55	−55
− Amortization expense	0	−100	−100	−120	−100
− Investment expense	0	0	0	0	0
= Operating income	0	10	30	−10	10
Return on equity		10.0%	30.0%	−8.3%	10.0%

FIGURE 4.5
Accounting
Measurement Error
Scenarios
(*Continued*)

Panel C. Temporarily Conservative Accounting (perfect accounting, except that 80% of investment costs are capitalized in period 3)

	Period				
	1	2	3	4	5
Accounting Assumptions:					
Capitalized investment costs	100	100	80	100	0
+ Capitalized operating costs	0	0	0	0	0
Balance Sheet:					
Assets = Equity	100	100	80	100	0
Accruals (change in assets)	100	0	−20	20	−100
Measurement Error (ε):					
Ending ε	0	0	−20	0	0
Change in ε	0	0	−20	20	0
Income Statement:					
Sales	0	165	165	165	165
− Operating expense	0	−55	−55	−55	−55
− Amortization expense	0	−100	−100	−80	−100
− Investment expense	0	0	−20	0	0
= Operating income	0	10	−10	30	10
Return on equity		10.0%	−10.0%	37.5%	10.0%

Panel D. Permanently Aggressive Accounting (perfect accounting, except that 120% of investment costs are capitalized in all periods)

	Period				
	1	2	3	4	5
Accounting Assumptions:					
Capitalized investment costs	100	100	100	100	0
+ Capitalized operating costs	20	20	20	20	0
Balance Sheet:					
Assets = Equity	120	120	120	120	0
Accruals (change in assets)	120	0	0	0	−120
Measurement Error (ε):					
Ending ε	20	20	20	20	0
Change in ε	20	0	0	0	−20
Income Statement:					
Sales	0	165	165	165	165
− Operating expense	20	−35	−35	−35	−55
− Amortization expense	0	−120	−120	−120	−120
− Investment expense	0	0	0	0	0
= Operating income	20	10	10	10	−10
Return on equity		8.3%	8.3%	8.3%	−8.3%

(*Continued on next page*)

FIGURE 4.5
Accounting
Measurement Error
Scenarios
(*Continued*)

Panel E. Permanently Conservative Accounting (perfect accounting, except that 80% of investment costs are capitalized in all periods)					
	Period				
	1	2	3	4	5
Accounting Assumptions:					
Capitalized investment costs	80	80	80	80	0
+ Capitalized operating costs	0	0	0	0	0
Balance Sheet:					
Assets = Equity	80	80	80	80	0
Accruals (change in assets)	80	0	0	0	−80
Measurement Error (ε):					
Ending ε	−20	−20	−20	−20	0
Change in ε	−20	0	0	0	20
Income Statement:					
Sales	0	165	165	165	165
− Operating expense	0	−55	−55	−55	−55
− Amortization expense	0	−80	−80	−80	−80
− Investment expense	−20	−20	−20	−20	0
= Operating income	−20	10	10	10	30
Return on equity		12.5%	12.5%	12.5%	37.5%

benefits generated by the investment expenditure. It provides a future benefit, because it generates positive cash flows in the next period. Therefore, the only accounting issue that we need to consider is the amount of the investment to list on the balance sheet as an asset. In panel A, we employ perfect accounting and so the first row lists capitalized investment costs equal to $100 in each period that a $100 investment is made. The next row lists our accounting for capitalized operating costs. Note that since we assume that operating costs only generate a benefit in the period that they are incurred, none of these costs should be capitalized under a perfect accounting system (we will use this row later, when we consider imperfect accounting systems). The next row lists the total assets of the firm, which are simply equal to the sum of the capitalized costs. This is the asset side of the balance sheet for the firm in our simple example. Since the firm has no future obligations, there are no liabilities, and so the liability and equity side of the balance sheet simply consists of an equity account with a balance equal in value to total assets (recall that we plug to equity to make the balance sheet balance).

The next three rows list various diagnostics for our accounting scheme. The first of these rows lists the amount of accounting *accruals*. Recall that accruals are simply equal to the net change in noncash assets on the balance sheet. In our example, they are simply equal to the change in total assets (since we have no cash or liabilities on the balance sheet). Accruals are $100 in period one, zero in periods two through four, and –$100 in period five. The positive accruals in period one arise because this is the first period we make an investment. The negative accruals in period five arise because this is the period in which we cease making investments. In the intervening periods, the originating accrual of $100 relating to the current period investment is exactly offset by the reversal accrual of –$100 relating to the prior period investment. The next two rows record the measurement error (ε) and the change in the measurement error respectively. We will use these two rows to see how our examples correspond to the scenarios identified in Figure 4.3. Panel A employs perfect accounting, so the amounts in both of these rows are zero in all periods. This corresponds to the center cell in Figure 4.3.

The next set of rows in panel A of Figure 4.5 presents the income statement corresponding to our perfect accounting system. The amounts in the income statement are all zero for period one, since we capitalize all of the period one investment and we don't have any other cash receipts or disbursements in period one (recall that these benefits come one period after the investment is made). In periods two through five, we generate cash receipts from sales of $165 and incur cash expenses of $55 (from our prior period investment). We also amortize 100 percent of the investment that was capitalized in the prior period, resulting in an additional expense of $100. Thus, we have operating income of $10 in each period. This is exactly equal to the economic income generated by our investment. The final row of panel A lists the return on equity, computed as current period operating income divided by prior period equity. The return on equity is 10 percent for periods two through five, which is exactly equal to the economic rate of return on investment. Thus, with perfect accounting, operating income equals economic income and return on equity equals economic rate of return.

Unfortunately, perfect accounting is the exception rather than the rule, so it's now time to consider imperfect accounting. We begin in panel B of Figure 4.5 by engaging in temporarily aggressive accounting. We will do perfect accounting in periods one and two. Then, in period three, we will do some aggressive accounting. We will then revert back to perfect accounting in periods four and five. The term *aggressive accounting* is applied to the situation where the net assets of the firm are overstated, by either overstating assets or understating liabilities. Opportunistic managers often use temporarily aggressive accounting when they would otherwise fall short of important earnings targets, such as meeting bonus plan thresholds or meeting analysts' forecasts. To engage in aggressive accounting in our simple example, we will capitalize some of the operating costs incurred in period three. Recall that these costs all relate to the revenues generated in period three, and so a perfect accounting system should expense them all in period three. For the purposes of this example, we will capitalize an amount of these costs equal to 20 percent of the current period investment. Thus, we will be overstating our assets by 20 percent. The accounting assumptions shown at the top of panel B implement temporarily aggressive accounting by capitalizing $20 of operating costs in period three. This causes the period three balance sheet to be overstated by $20, showing total assets and equity of $120. The period three ε is therefore 20, and the change in ε for period three is 20 (since ε is zero in period two). This puts us in the center-right cell of Figure 4.3. Moving down to the income statement, operating expenses are understated by $20, causing operating income to be overstated by $20. This overstatement in operating income causes return on equity to be 30 percent, overstating the economic rate of return of only 10 percent. Note that even though we return to perfect accounting in period four, operating income and return on equity understate their "perfect" levels in period four. This is because we have to amortize an extra $20 worth of capitalized operating costs in period four. The period three ε is 20 and the period four ε is 0, so the change in ε is -20. This puts us in the bottom-left cell of Figure 4.3. Since the numerator of return on equity is understated and the denominator is overstated, ROE must be understated. Note that the reversal of the aggressive accounting occurs in period four because we assume that the firm reverts to perfect accounting in this period. Thus, temporarily aggressive accounting has two consequences. First, it causes operating income and ROE to be overstated in the period in which the aggressive accounting originates. Second, it causes operating income and ROE to be understated in the period in which it reverses.

In practice, temporarily aggressive accounting must eventually reverse, though it may take more than one period for the reversal to occur. In panel B, we could have assumed that the firm capitalized another $20 of operating costs in period four, which would have delayed the reversal of the aggressive accounting to period five. Temporarily aggressive accounting is the most common type of accounting manipulation that occurs in practice. In fact, our example resembles the well-known accounting debacle at WorldCom. Managers at WorldCom capitalized almost $10 billion of operating costs in PP&E during 1999 and 2000, only to have it all reverse in 2001, precipitating WorldCom's bankruptcy.

Panel C of Figure 4.5 illustrates temporarily conservative accounting, which is just the flipside of temporarily aggressive accounting. The term *conservative accounting* is applied to the situation where the net assets of the firm are understated, by either understating assets or overstating liabilities. Opportunistic managers can use temporarily conservative accounting to temporarily avoid regulatory scrutiny for excess profits or to create "cookie jar" reserves that can be used to boost future profitability. To engage in conservative accounting in our simple example, we immediately expense some of the current period investment. For the purposes of this example, we will expense an amount equal to 20 percent of the current period investment in period three. Thus, we will be understating our period three assets by 20 percent. The accounting assumptions shown at the top of panel C reflect this temporarily conservative accounting, with only $80 of the period three investment being capitalized. The period three balance sheet is understated by $20, showing total assets and equity of only $80. The period three ε is -20, and the change in ε for period three is -20. This puts us in the center-left cell of Figure 4.3. Moving down to the income statement, we have an additional investment expense of $20, causing operating income to be understated by $20. The understatement of operating income causes return on equity to be -10 percent, understating the economic rate of return of 10 percent. We return to perfect accounting in period four, but operating income and return on equity overstate their "perfect" levels in period four. This is because amortization expense is only $80 in period four. The period three ε is -20 and the period four ε is 0, so the change in ε is 20. This puts us in the top-right cell of Figure 4.3. Since the numerator of return on equity is overstated and the denominator is understated, ROE must be overstated. Thus, temporarily conservative accounting causes operating income and ROE to be understated in the period in which it originates and overstated in the period in which it reverses.

So far, we have considered temporarily aggressive and temporarily conservative accounting. Can accounting be permanently aggressive or permanently conservative? It is unlikely that management could commit serious violations of GAAP that would never be detected by auditors. It is, however, possible that a company could engage in permanently aggressive or conservative accounting in a manner that is allowed or even required by GAAP. A good example is the GAAP requirement that research and development expenditures be immediately expensed. This accounting principle results in permanently conservative accounting. Examples of permanently aggressive accounting are less common, because GAAP are guided by the *conservatism convention,* which encourages the understatement, but discourages the overstatement, of assets. Nevertheless, managers have been creative over the years in exploiting loopholes in GAAP to structure transactions that receive permanently aggressive accounting. Employee retirement benefits are a good case in point. For many years, firms were not required to recognize a liability for nonpension retirement benefits. The result was an explosion in the use of such benefits to compensate employees. Accounting regulators in the United States finally addressed this GAAP loophole with the release of Statement of Financial Accounting Standard (SFAS) No. 106, which requires these liabilities to be estimated and recognized on the balance sheet. New types of permanently aggressive accounting are likely to be invented by tomorrow's generation of creative managers (no doubt with the eager assistance of their investment bankers and auditors). We will therefore examine the effects of both permanently aggressive and permanently conservative accounting.

Panel D of Figure 4.5 illustrates permanently aggressive accounting. This is achieved by capitalizing operating costs equal to 20 percent of investment in all periods. Consequently, assets and equity are equal to $120 for all but period five (when investment ceases and both are equal to zero). Accruals are $120 in period one (when investment commences), $-$120 in period five (when investment ceases), and zero in the intervening periods. Measurement error is 20 in periods one through four and 0 in period five, so the change in measurement error is 20 in period one, -20 in period five, and 0 in the intervening periods. Moving to the income statement, operating expenses are understated by $20 in the first four periods and amortization expense is overstated by $20 in the final four periods. The net result is that operating income is overstated by $20 in period one and understated by $20 in period five. In periods two through four, the understatement of operating expenses is exactly offset by the overstatement of amortization expense. Note that in every period, the change in measurement error equals exactly the amount by which accruals and operating income misstate their "true" levels from panel A. The final row of panel D lists the return on equity, which is 8.3 percent in periods two through four and −8.3 percent in period five. For periods two through four, the level of the measurement error is 20 and the change in measurement error is 0, so operating income is correctly stated and equity is overstated, resulting in the understatement of ROE. This corresponds to the bottom-center cell of Figure 4.3. For period five, the level of the measurement error from the prior period is still 20, but the change in the measurement error is −20, putting us in the bottom-left cell of Figure 4.3 and causing an even more severe understatement of ROE.

Finally, panel E of Figure 4.5 illustrates permanently conservative accounting. This is achieved by capitalizing only 80 percent of investment in all periods. Consequently, assets and equity are equal to $80 for all periods except period five (when investment ceases and both are equal to zero). Accruals are $80 in period one (when investment commences), −$80 in period five (when investment ceases), and zero in the intervening periods. Measurement error is −20 in periods one through 4 and 0 in period 5, so the change in measurement error is −20 in period one, 20 in period five, and 0 in all of the intervening periods. Moving to the income statement, investment expense is overstated by $20 in the first four periods and amortization expense is understated by $20 in the final four periods. The net result is that operating income is understated by $20 in period one and overstated by $20 in period five. In periods two through four, the overstatement of investment expense is exactly offset by the understatement of amortization expense. The final row of panel E lists the return on equity, which is 12.5 percent in periods two through four and 37.5 percent in period five. For periods two through four, the level of the measurement error is −20 and the change in measurement error is 0, so operating income is correctly stated and equity is understated, resulting in the overstatement of ROE. This corresponds to the top-center cell of Figure 4.3. For period five, the level of the measurement error from the prior period is still −20, but the change in the measurement error is 20, putting us in the top-right cell of Figure 4.3 and causing an even more severe overstatement of ROE.

We'll finish this section by summarizing what we've learned about permanently aggressive and permanently conservative accounting. Aggressive accounting always overstates equity ($\varepsilon > 0$), while conservative accounting always understates equity ($\varepsilon < 0$). The effects on operating income are more complex and depend on the rate of growth in investment. Constant investment combines with aggressive and conservative accounting to correctly state operating income (as shown in periods two through four of our example). Declining investment combines with aggressive (conservative) accounting to understate (overstate) operating income (as shown in period five of our example). Increasing investment combines with aggressive (conservative) accounting to overstate (understate) operating income (as shown in period one of our example). Thus, opportunistic managers in growing companies can boost income through the use of permanently aggressive accounting. But doing so also increases equity, resulting in an ambiguous effect on ROE. Figure 4.3 summarizes these effects.

4.5 COMMON SOURCES OF ACCOUNTING MEASUREMENT ERROR

So far, we've talked a lot about accounting theory, enjoyed some fancy algebra, and cooked up some contrived examples. Now it is time to get practical and talk about what actually causes the book value of equity to measure the true value of the investment with error. Recall from the accounting equation that equity is the difference between assets and liabilities. So measurement error in equity must arise from measurement error in the underlying assets and liabilities. We can divide the sources of measurement error into three broad categories:

1. Measurement error caused by GAAP.
2. Measurement error caused by lack of perfect foresight in the use of accounting estimates.
3. Measurement error caused by management's intentional manipulation of accounting estimates.

We discuss each of these sources of error in more detail below.

Measurement Error Caused by GAAP

The major source of measurement error introduced by GAAP is in the recognition and valuation of nonfinancial assets. Measurement error arises because investments made in nonfinancial assets are typically expected to generate uncertain benefits over multiple future periods. Because the timing and amount of these benefits are not known early in the life of the asset, measurement error is unavoidable. But worse still, the accounting rules for many types of investments often result in systematic and predictable measurement errors. Recall that GAAP accounting rules trade off relevance and reliability, with reliability often winning the day. Consequently, GAAP often require simple and objective procedures because they can be reliably computed and easily verified. Examples include the immediate expensing of certain investment expenditures and the use of mechanical depreciation and amortization schedules for others. We discuss the biases created by these simple procedures next.

Immediate Expensing of Internally Generated Intangibles

This is an example of an asset that GAAP ignores. Under GAAP, expenditures made on internally developed intangible assets are required to be expensed immediately. In other words, it is assumed that these expenditures produce no benefits beyond the accounting period in which they are incurred. Examples include most research and development expenditures, expenditures to develop patents, most advertising expenditures, and most administrative expenditures. Many of these expenditures clearly generate benefits that extend well beyond the period in which they are incurred, but, rather than attempt to estimate the unused amount of these investments, GAAP use the safe and reliable value of zero. So a firm gets to capitalize the cost of constructing a new building, but not the cost of developing a valuable patent. Immediate expensing of internally developed intangibles is a classic example of permanently conservative accounting. This accounting results in systematically negative measurement error in equity (because assets are understated) in all periods during which there has been a past expenditure that is expected to generate future benefits.

As with other cases of permanently conservative accounting, the impact of this accounting distortion on net income relative to economic income depends on the growth rate in investment. If the firm is increasing its investments in internally developed intangibles, then immediately expensing the investment lowers net income relative to economic income. If investment is constant, there is no effect on net income. Finally, if investment is decreasing, net income is overstated relative to economic income.

The overall effect on ROE is also ambiguous. The systematic understatement of equity inflates ROE due to the denominator effect (i.e., it puts us in the first row of Figure 4.3). If we are in a period when investment on internally generated intangibles is increasing, income is understated and the numerator and denominator errors move ROE in different directions, so the overall nature of the bias is ambiguous (i.e., we are in the top-left cell of Figure 4.3). But if we are in a period when investment is decreasing, income is overstated and ROE is biased upward (i.e., we are in the top-right cell of Figure 4.3). Finally, if we have to guess quickly, the rule of thumb is that the denominator effect dominates, so in a steady state, ROE will be overstated (i.e., we are in the top-middle cell of Figure 4.3).

Depreciation and Amortization of Capitalized Nonfinancial Assets

Unlike internally developed intangible assets, GAAP generally allow for the capitalization of expenditures on tangible assets (e.g., property, plant, and equipment) and purchased intangibles (e.g., patents). The accounting for such expenditures at their inception is straightforward. Since these expenditures are investments that are expected to generate future benefits, the full amount of the expenditures is initially *capitalized* on the balance sheet as an asset. The difficult part is deciding how to subsequently reduce the value of the asset over the future periods in which it generates benefits. This process is known as *depreciation* for tangible assets and *amortization* for purchased intangible assets. Ideally, the depreciation/amortization method should reflect the flow of expected future benefits generated by the initial investment expenditure. However, implementing such a method would entail subjective forecasts of the future benefits. So GAAP generally sacrifice relevance for reliability, requiring firms to follow a predetermined depreciation schedule, with the most common method being straight-line, whereby the initial value of the asset is reduced in equal increments over the expected life of the asset.

The general effect of these measurement errors is to understate asset values by depreciating them too quickly. This leads to permanently conservative accounting, resulting in the same biases as for the immediate expensing of expenditures on internally developed intangibles. However, the degree of bias is not as great, because we simply depreciate the asset too quickly rather than expensing the entire asset immediately. One consequence of this is the so-called *old plant trap*. Firms with old plant that has been almost completely depreciated will have low book values that result in high accounting rates of return. But once this old plant is replaced, book values will increase, causing accounting rates of return to fall. The old plant trap is sprung when investors mistake the high accounting rates of return for firms with old plant for high economic rates of return.

Asset Impairments

As discussed above, GAAP generally require that nonfinancial assets be carried at their amortized historical cost. This means that the carrying value of the asset represents a fraction of the amount that was originally invested in order to generate future benefits rather than a forecast of the value of the expected future benefits. However, GAAP also contain an important exception to this rule. If it is determined that an asset has been impaired—that is, its carrying value is greater than the undiscounted sum of the cash flows it is expected to generate—GAAP require that the asset be restated to fair value. This rule is a manifestation of the aforementioned conservatism convention, and it introduces a nasty asymmetry into asset valuations. If an asset's value falls below its carrying value, it gets revalued downward based on the estimated future benefits, but if the asset's value exceeds the current carrying value, no upward revaluation is allowed. Hence, we cannot interpret aggregate asset value as either an estimate of past investment or an estimate of expected future benefits. Rather, it is something of a mongrel, representing a mixture of the lower of these two amounts.

From a practical perspective, we need to remember that firms with asset impairments have potentially flawed business models. Corporate managers often encourage investors to focus on net income before asset impairment charges, reasoning that these charges are nonrecurring and are not indicative of future performance. Moreover, asset impairments represent prime examples of temporarily conservative accounting. By writing down the value of an asset today, equity goes down and future expenses go down, so future income and ROE are overstated (see top-right cell of Figure 4.3). You also should remember that an asset impairment is basically an admission by management that they have invested in an unprofitable business. If an asset impairment is recorded every time management makes a bad investment, it stands to reason that income and ROE before impairments will always look good, since they exclude the effects of all the bad investments. However, we should not draw the conclusion that management is doing a good job. We need to look at the aggregate performance of both the good and bad investments to draw overall conclusions about firm performance.

Omission of Contingent Liabilities

We have already discussed the fact that the accounting rules do not allow for the recognition of investments in internally generated intangibles as assets. The reason for this is that the future benefits are deemed to be so uncertain that they cannot be reliably measured. For the same reason, contingent liabilities also are not recognized on the balance sheet. A contingent liability is an expected future obligation that is not sufficiently probable or not reasonably estimable. Two common examples of contingent liabilities are ongoing litigation against a firm and potential environmental cleanup costs. Because liabilities are not recognized, net assets and equity are overstated. This results in permanently aggressive accounting, placing us in the bottom row of Figure 4.3. In the period that a contingent liability arises, measurement error increases, so net income is overstated and the impact on ROE is ambiguous (i.e., we are in the bottom-right cell of Figure 4.3). In subsequent periods, as long as the contingent liability remains contingent, equity will be overstated and there is no effect on net income, so ROE will be understated (we are in the bottom-center cell of Figure 4.3). Manufacturers of tobacco products represent good examples of companies with unrecognized liabilities. These companies have reported high past accounting profits, but these profits most likely overstate the companies' true economic profitability, because they ignore the cost of future litigation stemming from tobacco-related illnesses.

Measurement Error Caused by Lack of Perfect Foresight

The measurement of many assets and liabilities requires the estimation of future amounts. GAAP require that future amounts be measured with some minimum level of reliability before qualifying for recognition in the financial statements. However, this certainly doesn't mean that, just because accountants found the nerve to recognize them, the assets and liabilities in the financial statements have little estimation error. In fact, quite the opposite is often true. For example, the employee postretirement benefit liability requires a forecast of health care costs decades into the future. Even if management has made a good-faith estimate, we should recognize that the amount recorded on the balance sheet might differ greatly from the actual future obligations it represents.

If management has done a thorough job at estimating inherently subjective future amounts, then there is probably little that you can do to improve upon their estimates. However, it is very important that you understand the amount of potential estimation error involved in the various assets and liabilities presented on a company's balance sheets. Understanding estimation error is important for at least two reasons. First, the precision of forecasts based on financial statement data is directly related to the precision of the financial statement data themselves. Second, the inherent risk of a business is a direct function of the risk of its underlying assets and liabilities.

Unfortunately, there are only a few broad-brush rules we can give you for establishing the amount of potential measurement error associated with particular classes of assets and liabilities. For example, we can safely tell you that cash and short-term investments have little measurement error. For accounts receivable, however, the amount of potential measurement error can be very small or incredibly large. A bank that lends only to highly creditworthy customers will generally be able to measure its receivables with much less potential error than a firm that makes subprime loans. A detailed understanding of the nature of the assets and liabilities being measured and the techniques used to measure them is required to make a good assessment of the amount of potential measurement error. This can only be accomplished through a careful analysis of Form 10-K, with particular emphasis on the notes to the financial statements.

Measurement Error Caused by Managerial Manipulation

The final source of error in the financial statements is introduced through intentional managerial manipulation (shock and horror!). Given the many estimates that GAAP entail, it is an inevitable fact that some managers will use this discretion to achieve their own short-term objectives. The most common type of managerial manipulation is temporarily aggressive accounting. This allows management to temporarily boost earnings and ROE. Possible motivations include hitting key bonus thresholds, meeting analysts' earnings forecasts, and creating the illusion of a profitable business for the purpose of raising new capital. Temporarily aggressive accounting can be accomplished by overstating assets or understating liabilities. This results in either the overstatement of revenue (e.g., overstating receivables, understating deferred revenues) or understatement of expenses (e.g., overstating inventory or understating pension liabilities). But temporarily aggressive accounting must ultimately reverse, so this type of *earnings management* is really about shifting income from one period to another. It simply isn't possible to inflate income forever.

The key to detecting temporarily aggressive accounting is to pin down the assets and liabilities over which management exercises the most discretion. This typically rules out things like cash, short-term investments, debt, and most payables. GAAP for these items are fairly rigid and there isn't much room for managerial manipulation.[1] As we advised in the previous section, you should devote extra attention to assets and liabilities that require the most estimation. This is where managers are most likely to perpetrate their dastardly deeds. Recall that Item 7 of Form 10-K requires management to describe their firm's critical accounting policies. This represents a good starting point for the identification of likely areas for earnings management. But you should not stop here, since management may have been sneaky enough not to tell you where the earnings management is taking place.

Another important technique in the detection of earnings management is to look for signs of temporarily aggressive accounting. Referring back to panel B of Figure 4.5, we see that accruals are inflated during periods of temporarily aggressive accounting. Unfortunately, high accruals do not always signal temporarily aggressive accounting. Accruals are also high in period one of panel B. This is because "true" investment is increasing in period one. High accruals can represent either the origination of temporarily aggressive accounting or growth in "true"

---

[1] The accounting scandal at Parmalat reminds us that even cash and short-term investments can occasionally be subject to considerable managerial manipulation. But keep in mind that Parmalat's financials were audited by Italians.

investment. Without a more detailed analysis, it is difficult to discriminate be-tween these two determinants of accruals. We'll provide you with guidance on how to conduct a more detailed analysis in Chapters 5 and 6.

We will categorize common earnings management techniques based on how they impact on the income statement. Below, we briefly discuss each category, identifying the assets and liabilities that are most likely to be involved.

Revenue Manipulation

Revenue manipulation is the most common type of earnings management. The sales transaction is a key trigger for the recognition of future benefits under GAAP, so there is no better place to start looking for earnings management. The asset most commonly involved in revenue manipulation is accounts receivable. A cash payment from a customer is a pretty good indication that the customer is committed to the transaction (although the revenue may still not have been earned—more on this below). However, when the customer has not yet paid, the balance lives in the accounts receivable, and there is greater uncertainty about whether the payment will be made. The customer may not be committed to the transaction, may not know about the transaction, or may not have the ability to make the contracted payment.

A common form or revenue manipulation is *trade loading* or *channel stuffing*, whereby product is shipped to a customer before the customer really needs it. This type of activity is most prevalent at the end of a reporting period. Management is effectively stealing from next period's sales in order to inflate this period's sales. Another form of revenue manipulation overstates the value of the net receivables by understating the allowance for uncollectible accounts. It is easy to increase the volume of sales transactions by granting more generous credit terms or by selling on credit to customers with lower credit quality. However, the cost of increasing sales in this way is the increased amount of expected uncollectible accounts. If accounts receivable is not adjusted downwards to reflect the increased expected un-collectibles, then accounts receivable, revenue, and earnings will all be overstated.

A variety of ratio analysis techniques can be used to identify firms that are po-tentially overstating revenue and accounts receivable, and we discuss them in Chapters 5 and 6. However, it is important to analyze these ratios in the context of the firm's business strategy and accounting policies. There have been examples of firms that have made strategic choices to loosen their credit terms that have paid off nicely. While unusually high receivables are an important red flag, they are not a definitive indicator of revenue manipulation.

Accounts receivable is not the only account that can be used for revenue ma-nipulation. Suppose a customer pays in advance for a product or service, such as a subscription or a product that includes a servicing agreement. In such cases, GAAP require that revenue recognition should be delayed until the good or service is delivered to the customer. This creates a liability representing the future obligation of the firm to provide the promised goods/services. Common titles for such a liability are Unearned Revenue and Advances from Customers. Unfortu-nately, the total sales price is allocated to different periods based on subjective proration schedules. Unlike receivables, the collection of cash is already assured. It is simply the timing of the revenue recognition that is at issue. Nevertheless, understatement of the liability to provide future goods/services can be a powerful tool for revenue manipulation. For example, a firm can boost current period revenues by promising to provide enhanced future service or additional future products at discounted prices. If the cost of these future obligations is not recorded as a liability, then current period equity and earnings will be overstated.

Expense Manipulation

Whenever an asset is used up or a liability is created in the process of providing goods and services to customers, GAAP require an expense to be recognized. The theory is straightforward. However, like revenue recognition, there are many gray areas that open the door for earnings management.

Perhaps the biggest gray area is the capitalize versus expense decision. Whenever an asset is used up in a firm's operating activities, an expense must be recognized *unless* a new asset is created. In other words, there must be a future benefit that satisfies the criteria for recognition as an asset. Therefore, earnings can be manipulated by capitalizing costs that should really be expensed. This is exactly what we did in our aggressive accounting examples in panels B and D of Figure 4.5. It is also the means by which WorldCom perpetrated its well-known earnings management scheme. WorldCom capitalized approximately $10 billion of its line operating costs as part of Property and Equipment. Another common real-world example is the aggressive capitalization of costs incurred to develop and produce software. GAAP require that only costs incurred beyond the point of technological feasibility can be capitalized. But the determination of technological feasibility is subjective and lends itself to manipulation. In order to lower expenses, management can simply claim technological feasibility has been achieved. The auditor, not being an expert in software development, is in a poor position to question such a judgment. In an interesting twist on earnings management, Microsoft has been accused of understating income by expensing all software development costs, regardless of technological feasibility. Following the permanently conservative accounting example from panel E of Figure 4.5, we should expect that when Microsoft slows its investment in new software, its earnings will predictably increase. A good check for expense manipulation of this kind is to compare the total proportion of costs that are capitalized by a firm with its industry counterparts. If a firm is capitalizing a very different proportion of its costs from other firms in the industry, it is more likely to be manipulating earnings. But it is always possible that the firm really is different from its industry counterparts and its capitalization policies are appropriate.

Inventory accounting also lends itself to expense manipulation. In times of changing prices, the cost flow assumption used to account for inventory (FIFO, LIFO, etc.) can be very important in determining the cost of inventory that has been used up and therefore recognized as cost of goods sold. Management can time inventory purchases and change cost flow assumptions in order to manipulate earnings. They also can manipulate the allocation of joint costs. In a slaughterhouse that produces pork products, how should we allocate the cost of the pig between bacon and sausage? If we sell bacon more quickly than we sell sausage, we can temporarily boost earnings by assigning more costs to sausage, hence leaving these costs in inventory longer.

Yet another technique for manipulating earnings using inventory accounting is to purchase a diverse range of inventory and offer it for sale at a high markup. The firm makes big profits on the product that sells and leaves the product that doesn't sell in inventory. The problem here, of course, is inventory obsolescence. This type of earnings management is particularly prevalent in the specialty retail industry, where seasonal fashions are difficult to predict. By failing to write down the obsolete inventory on a timely basis, management can understate expenses.

Another avenue for expense manipulation involves noncurrent assets that are used up gradually over many periods, such as property, plant, and equipment. GAAP call for these assets to be depreciated, amortized, or impaired over time using a variety of rules. However, all of these rules provide management with considerable latitude in determining the periodic expenses recorded. An interesting example here is Blockbuster, a video rental chain. In the early years of video, Blockbuster depreciated its rental videos over a longer time period than its competitors. At the time, there was considerable uncertainty concerning the useful lives of rental videos, particularly because the demographics of video renters were changing rapidly as video players became more affordable. As a result, Blockbuster looked more profitable than its competitors, and so attracted more capital and cemented its position as the leading player in the industry.

Expense manipulation is not restricted to assets. Understating liabilities is another technique for understating expenses. Consider the accounting for warranty liabilities. When a firm sells a product with a warranty, the expected future costs of the warranty should be recognized as an obligation of the company at the same time that the sales transaction is recognized. This will result in an increase in liabilities and a decrease in equity and earnings. By understating or ignoring the warranty liability, management can overstate earnings. One spectacular example of expense manipulation in this vein involved Regina Company. Regina manufactured vacuum cleaners that were reputably so durable that they would last a lifetime. In fact, Regina offered a lifetime warranty on its products, but the high quality of its products meant that few warranty costs were ever incurred. Then, a new CEO boosted Regina's earnings and stock price by using cheaper components in the vacuum cleaners. The lower costs meant higher profits in the short run. But, as you would expect, costs associated with the lifetime warranty started to skyrocket, and Regina subsequently went broke. The higher expected warranty costs should have been recorded as a liability, and an associated expense recognized in the income statement. If this had been done, Regina would never have shown higher profits in the first place.

A final important area for expense manipulation is employee pensions and other retirement benefits. GAAP require these amounts be estimated, recognized as a liability, and charged off as an expense in the period that employees earn the right to these future benefits. There is huge subjectivity involved in estimating these amounts. What will be the ultimate amount of the benefits? What rate of return will be earned on benefit plan assets? What discount rate should be used to calculate the present value of the benefits? Small changes in these assumptions can have huge impacts on the financial statements, so management has considerable leeway to manipulate earnings. Again, you should conduct an industry comparison of the accounting assumptions to determine whether a particular firm appears to be managing earnings.

In summary, most earnings management involves accruals that create associated assets or liabilities on the balance sheet. Consequently, the key to detecting earnings management is a careful examination of the balance sheet. So far, we have focused exclusively on traditional revenue and expense manipulation. However, there are other more subtle forms of financial statement manipulation. We provide a brief discussion of four of the most common forms below.

Related-Party Transactions

A key prerequisite for the recognition of many assets and liabilities on the balance sheet is a transaction with another party. The maintained assumption under GAAP is that these transactions represent arm's-length business dealings. For example, if inventory is purchased, the underlying assumption is that the purchase price represents the fair market value at the date of purchase. Also, if a sale is made, the assumption is that the sale will not be reversed at a later date.

Given GAAP's heavy reliance on transactions with other parties, one possible technique for manipulating the financial statements is to engage in "sham" transactions with related parties. For example, a firm with an earnings shortfall could sell product to a customer with a verbal agreement that the sale will be reversed or the customer reimbursed in some other manner (e.g., a stock option grant). Such practices are technical violations of GAAP, but they can be difficult to prove. Further, related-party transactions are not confined to earnings management. A director may make a "long-term loan" to a company just before the end of a reporting period in order to create the impression of improved short-term liquidity on the balance sheet, and then reverse the loan shortly thereafter.

Fortunately, U.S. reporting requirements require that all material related-party transactions must be disclosed in the financial statements of the reporting entity. The nature of the relationship and the amount and nature of the transactions must be reported in the notes to the financial statements. Unfortunately, if management really wants to deceive you with related-party transactions, it is unlikely that they will say so in plain English in the financial statement footnotes.

Off-Balance-Sheet Entities

Off-balance-sheet entities have many similarities with related-party transactions. With off-balance-sheet entities, management creates a separate legal entity that is not required to be consolidated in the firm's financial statements. Management nevertheless exercises influence over this new entity and uses the entity to manipulate the firm's financial statements. Management usually exercises influence over the off-balance-sheet entity by appointing related parties to the management of the entity or by being a key financier, supplier, customer, or guarantor of the entity. Once established, there are several ways in which the off-balance-sheet entity can then be used to manipulate the financial statements of the firm. For example, the off-balance-sheet entity may purchase goods and services from the firm at inflated prices, directly boosting equity and earnings. In many past cases, these purchases have been funded by loans from the firm itself and simply represent sham transactions designed with the sole intent of boosting earnings. Alternatively, a firm could boost revenue by using an off-balance-sheet entity to provide customers with loans for making purchases from the firm. If the firm itself guarantees these loans, then the risk associated with the loans is ultimately borne by the firm but is hidden from investors because the loans themselves are in the off-balance-sheet entity. Off-balance-sheet entities also can be used to hide financial leverage and other sources of risk from investors.

The analysis of off-balance-sheet entities can be extremely difficult. Firms that create such structures in order to manage the financial statements will go to great lengths to make it as difficult as possible for investors to figure out what is going on. Moreover, because we typically don't have financial information for these off-balance-sheet entities, we really don't have much to work with. The well-known rise and sudden fall of Enron was primarily attributable to the aggressive use of off-balance-sheet entities to boost earnings and hide risks from investors. The best advice we can give you here is that if you see any sign that off-balance-sheet entities are being used, you should make sure that you understand how they are being used. If you don't feel that you have enough information to make a meaningful assessment, you should assume the worst.

How do you know if any off-balance-sheet entities are out there? There are three potential disclosures in the notes to the financial statements that you should look for. First, there is the related-party note. This note must report any unconsolidated transactions with entities in which the firm has ownership, control, or significant influence. Second, there is the note relating to equity investments and other unconsolidated investments. You should ascertain whether any of these investments give the firm influence over the operating policies of the investee. Finally, there is the contingent liabilities note. If the firm has guaranteed the debt of any unconsolidated entities, then these guarantees should be identified in the contingent liabilities note.

Off-Balance-Sheet Financing

Off-balance-sheet financing is used to finance the acquisition of resources without showing the associated assets and liabilities on the balance sheet. By doing so, the firm usually hopes to create the impression that it has less financial risk than it really does. The most common technique for implementing off-balance-sheet financing is the operating lease. A firm enters into a contract in which it acquires the right to use an asset in return for periodic payments to the owner of the asset. If the contract covers a substantial portion of the useful life of the asset, then the economic substance of the transaction is identical to one in which the firm borrows money and then buys the asset. But because the legal form of the transaction is a lease contract, no assets and liabilities are recognized.

GAAP have developed a complex set of rules to determine whether leases can be kept off the books as operating leases or must be put on the books as capital leases (the future benefits and obligations associated with capital leases must be estimated and placed on the balance sheet). While we won't drag you through all the rules, suffice it to say that creative accountants have found ways to help management get whatever accounting treatment they want, regardless of the economic substance of the lease transaction. As a result, most leases remain off balance sheet.

Fortunately, figuring out the impact of operating leases is straightforward. Firms are required to disclose future minimum lease payments on most operating leases in the notes to the financial statements. By taking the present value of these payments, you can immediately get a good idea of how much off-balance-sheet financing is attributable to operating leases.

Operating leases are not the only way off-balance-sheet financing can be achieved. Any contract in which a firm acquires the right to use a resource and incurs future obligations in return represents off-balance-sheet financing. Other common forms of off-balance-sheet financing include take-or-pay contracts, sale of receivables with recourse, unconsolidated finance subsidiaries, joint ventures, and equity investments. You should be able to discover the existence of these and other off-balance-sheet financing techniques by studying the notes to the financial statements, particularly the investments and contingent liabilities notes.

Nonrecurring Charges and Pro Forma Earnings

A final form of financial statement manipulation that has become popular of late is the strategic use of nonrecurring charges, such as asset impairments, losses on the sale of long-lived assets, and restructuring charges. Because these charges are nonrecurring, it has become usual for management, analysts, and investors to focus on the recurring component of earnings that excludes such charges. This non-GAAP definition of earnings is often referred to as *pro forma* earnings in analyst reports and firms' press releases.

In recent years, the magnitude and frequency of nonrecurring charges has exploded. Moreover, firms have started to exclude recurring charges from pro forma earnings with the lamest of excuses. The idea is to reclassify as many recurring expenses as possible into a nonrecurring charge and, hence, report higher recurring or pro forma earnings. For example, if a firm writes down its fixed assets today in a nonrecurring impairment charge, recurring earnings will be higher moving forward, because the carrying value of these assets is lower and hence future depreciation expense will be lower. As a result, many firms are consistently reporting large nonrecurring charges year after year. Management wins twice with this manipulation. First, they convince you to ignore the nonrecurring charge in the period they take it, arguing that it is old news that is irrelevant to the future. Second, expenses in the future are lower because of the writedown of assets in the current period. Ignoring expenses that management labels as nonrecurring is like evaluating a fund manager after she throws out the bottom 10 percent performers in her portfolio. You should determine what is really included in these charges and make a careful assessment of their implications for the soundness of the firm's financial health. A bad management team will blunder from one bad business decision to the next. Are the losses associated with each of these bad decisions nonrecurring simply because they relate to different business decisions? The answer is no.

4.6   CONCLUSION

You should take away three lessons from this chapter. First, the GAAP-based financial statements provide the universal language for evaluating past performance and forecasting future performance. Second, the financial statements only provide timely information on a subset of value-relevant events. The financial statements are not the accountants' attempt to value the firm. Rather, the goal of the financial statements is to provide people like us with information that is useful in conducting our own valuations. Third, while the financial statements are restricted to reasonably reliable information, lots of subjectivity is still involved in the estimation of assets and liabilities. This opens the financial statements to potential errors and managerial manipulation. A careful examination of a firm's assets and liabilities is the best starting point for identifying potential errors and manipulation.

To build a good valuation model, you must become intimately familiar with a firm's financial statements and the accounting policies underlying those financial statements. Are the accounting policies consistent with the firm's business operations and strategies? What important events are captured in the financial statements on a timely basis and what events are missing? Which assets, liabilities, revenues, and expenses are measured with the least reliability? Is there any evidence suggesting management is manipulating the financial statements? You need to answer all of these questions before you attempt to forecast the firm's future financial statements and produce a valuation.

4.7   CASES, LINKS, AND REFERENCES

Cases

- Boston Chicken, Inc.
- EnCom Corporation (Stages 1 and 2)
- GAAP versus the Street
- Netflix, Inc. (Questions 1 through 5)
- Overstock.com (Questions 1 through 6)
- Pre-Paid Legal Services

CHAPTER FIVE

Financial Ratio Analysis

5.1 INTRODUCTION

Valuing an equity security requires you to interpret and forecast a huge quantity of financial data. Ratio analysis provides a framework for doing this in an organized and systematic manner. By converting the financial statement data into ratios, we standardize it in a way that identifies basic relationships. For instance, margin analysis reveals how much profit a firm makes from each dollar of revenue it generates and turnover analysis reveals the amount of assets needed to generate each dollar of revenue. It is extremely important that you learn to evaluate a firm's performance in terms of the financial ratios presented here. This is the language that analysts and management use to discuss a company's performance, and we will use this language to construct forecasts of the future. Ratio analysis is traditionally applied to historical data to evaluate past performance, but we also will use it to evaluate the plausibility of our forecasted future financial statements.

5.2 TIME-SERIES AND CROSS-SECTIONS

Ratio analysis involves comparing individual ratios with their levels in prior years and their levels in other firms. Comparing a firm's ratios to their levels in prior years is called *time-series analysis*. Time-series analysis identifies changes in financial performance and helps to detect the underlying cause. It also helps you see whether the firm's most recent performance is unusual, in which case it is unlikely to recur in the future, or whether it is just one in a series of normal outcomes. If you have a flair for quantitative analysis, you might be tempted to estimate a complicated time-series model of a firm's past ratios in order to predict their future values, but we don't recommend such an approach. As a general rule, financial ratios don't follow mechanical time-series models. Instead, it is more important that you evaluate changes in ratios in the context of changes in the underlying business operations and strategies of the firm. eVal provides you with five years of historical data, which is about as far back as you should usually need to go in your time-series analysis.

Comparing a firm's ratios with the corresponding ratios in competitor firms is called *cross-sectional analysis*. This type of ratio analysis also is called *comparative analysis* (often shortened to *comps*). If management has done a consistently good job, then this will not be readily apparent in a time-series analysis. But it will be revealed by a cross-sectional ratio analysis with competitors. Does the company command a higher margin on its products? Is it the most efficient producer in its industry? Is it gaining market share from competitors? These are the types of questions that you can only answer by comparing a firm's financial ratios with competitor firms or the industry average. It isn't always easy, but you should try to triangulate a firm's ratios with its business strategy. If the firm is attempting to differentiate its product, it should enjoy higher margins than its competitors. If a firm is attempting to be a cost leader, it should have higher asset turnover than its competitors. We'll discuss how different strategies influence particular ratios later in the chapter.

You can conduct cross-sectional analysis in eVal by loading a competitor firm into eVal and then comparing ratios across the two firms. To see a list of competitors in the same industry, you first sort the companies on the Data Center sheet by industry (click the Industry button at the top of the industry column). Next, locate your firm on the data sheet by using the Search button on the top of the sheet. This will take you to your firm's row, which will now be surrounded by its industry brethren. You can load an industry competitor by clicking on its name or ticker. Alternatively, you can load the industry or sector averages. You do this by simply clicking on the industry or sector code that is listed next to the company name and ticker on the Data Center sheet. The advantage of using the industry average is that it abstracts from any unusual events that might distort the financials for an individual competitor. The disadvantage is that you may be able to find a competitor that is very similar to your firm, while the industry average may contain less-similar firms.

If you don't have any idea of a firm's closest competitors, and the list of firms in the same industry on the Data Center sheet is too long to be useful, then you can get some help from the Yahoo! Finance Web site. The easiest way to do this is to click the News link for your firm in eVal's Data Center sheet. This will take you to the Yahoo! Finance news page for your company. Over on the left-hand side of this Web page, you will see a Competitors link. Click on this link to see the company's major competitors (as selected by Hoover's, Inc). Note that some of these competitors may be private companies, in which case it will be difficult to obtain financial data for a cross-sectional analysis. But if they are public companies, you should be able to find them on eVal's Data Center worksheet and load them up.

Ratios Tend to Mean-Revert

From a valuation perspective, the main reason we want to study the historical performance of a firm's financial ratios is to guide us in forecasting the future values of these ratios. To this end, you should remember a common theme in the evolution of financial ratios over time: they tend to mean-revert. This means that, if they are unusually high, they tend to come down and, if they are unusually low, they tend to come up. For example, firms that experience an extremely high or extremely low return on equity (net income over common equity) in a given year probably had something unusual happen—a windfall gain on the sale of an asset, a write-off of inventory, a surprisingly successful advertising campaign, or an embarrassing product recall, to list just a few possibilities. In these cases, it is unlikely that the extremely high or extremely low return will persist into the future, because the unusual event that happened once is unlikely to happen again.

We don't want to oversell the power of mean reversion. It is an observable tendency for many different ratios in a large sample of firms, but there are many exceptions. And, as we discuss below, how quickly and how completely a ratio mean-reverts varies greatly by both ratio and firm.

5.3   SOME CAVEATS

Despite their usefulness, ratios are also frequently misunderstood and abused. So, before launching into a discussion of specific ratios, we offer some important caveats regarding ratio analysis.

There Is No "Correct" Way to Compute Many Ratios

Many people assign the same name to ratios that are computed quite differently. Consider the return on assets (ROA) ratio. The numerator (income) is sometimes measured on a before-tax basis and sometimes measured on an after-tax basis. It is sometimes measured on a before-interest basis and sometimes on an after-interest basis. It may or may not include any nonrecurring and/or nonoperating items for the period. The denominator (assets) usually represents total assets, but it is sometimes measured as net operating assets (in which case the ratio is sometimes referred to as the return on net operating assets). The key point here is that there are no standards such as GAAP governing the computation of ratios. Basically, anything goes, and both management and sell-side analysts can be creative in coming up with ratios that put firms in the best possible light. Thus, when interpreting a ratio, you should make sure you understand how it was computed.

Ratios Do Not Provide Answers; They Just Tell You Where to Look for Answers

It is common to hear of rules of thumb that attach certain interpretations to ratios falling in certain ranges. For example, a firm with an interest coverage ratio less than two is often alleged to be financially distressed, or a firm with an ROA less than the yield on U.S. Treasuries is labeled a "dog." Unfortunately, financial analysis is not that simple. There are many reasons why ratios can have unusual values: from accounting distortions to subtle differences in a firm's business environment. Ratio analysis guides you in your search for answers, but ratios themselves rarely provide the answers.

Managers Know That Investors Use Ratios

Managers are well aware that investors rely on ratios to summarize their firm's financial performance. Hence, they can and do use their discretion over accounting, operating, investing, and financing decisions to make their key ratios look more appealing. A common example is the use of operating leases and other off-balance-sheet financing techniques to reduce leverage ratios. It is therefore important to anticipate and undo the effects of any managerial "window dressing" of a firm's financial ratios.

5.4 A FRAMEWORK FOR RATIO ANALYSIS

With these caveats in mind, we will now describe how to conduct a comprehensive ratio analysis of a firm's financial performance. We encourage you to follow along by working through Kohl's ratio analysis, which is the default company in eVal. If you haven't heard of Kohl's before, it is a department store chain located primarily in the Midwest and Midatlantic. It targets middle-income families with a niche strategy combining product differentiation with reasonable prices. Our analysis is based on financial statement data through fiscal 2001, which ended on February 2, 2002, for Kohl's. We end our analysis of past data in fiscal 2001 so that we have some future data to look back at when we cover forecasting in Chapter 8.

Target Stores (ticker symbol TGT) is one of Kohl's chief competitors, so our ratio analysis will compare Kohl's with Target and with the Retail Department Stores industry as a whole (Industry Code 731). Since we are analyzing Kohl's at the end of fiscal 2001, we also want data on Target and the Retail Department Stores industry for the same period. To load these data from within eVal, go to the eVal menu and select the Kohl's 2001 Data and Resources menu item. From here, you can load fiscal 2001 data for Kohl's, Target, and the Retail Department Stores industry. You also will find a link to Kohl's fiscal 2001 Form 10-K. We will refer to this document frequently as we interpret Kohl's ratios. Note that if you go to the Data Center sheet and load data for Kohl's, Target, or the Retail Department Store industry, the most recently available data will load. These are not the data we are discussing here, since our analysis uses historical data ending in fiscal 2001.

The results of eVal's ratio analysis are displayed on the Ratio Analysis sheet, the top of which is reproduced in Figure 5.1. To access this sheet, simply click on the View Ratio Analysis button from eVal's User's Guide sheet. You will find it helpful to display Excel's formula bar so that you can see how the ratios in each cell have been computed. The formula bar can be displayed by selecting the Formula Bar menu item from the View menu in eVal. You also may want to load Target into eVal and then print out its Ratio Analysis sheet to compare with Kohl's.

Ratio analysis begins with the two pillars of firm value: *growth* and *profitability*. Profitability measures the return that a firm is generating on its invested capital. Growth measures changes in the magnitude of invested capital base on which the firm is able to generate profitability. To create maximum value, a firm must

FIGURE 5.1
Ratio Analysis Sheet for Kohl's in Fiscal 2001

	A	B	C	D	E	F
1	**Ratio Analysis**	Growth and Profitability		Margin, Turnover and		
2	Go To User's Guide	Dupont Models		Analysis of Credit Risk		
3						
4	**Company Name**	KOHL S CORP				
5						
6		Actual	Actual	Actual	Actual	Actual	For
7	**Fiscal Year End Date**	1/31/1998	1/30/1999	1/29/2000	2/3/2001	2/2/2002	2/2
8						
9	**Annual Growth Rates**					
10	Sales		20.3%	23.8%	35.0%	21.7%
11	Assets		19.5%	51.4%	31.5%	27.9%
12	Common Equity		21.8%	45.0%	30.7%	26.7%
13	Earnings		36.1%	34.3%	44.2%	33.2%
14	Free Cash Flow to Investors			#N/A	#N/A	#N/A	#
15	Sustainable Growth Rate			18.1%	19.1%	19.9%
16						
17						
18	**Profitability**					
19	Return on Equity		0.182	0.181	0.191	0.199
20	Return on Equity (b4 non-recurring)		0.181	0.180	0.190	0.197
21	Return on Net Operating Assets		0.150	0.147	0.152	0.153

simultaneously achieve high growth and high profitability. Our ratio analysis starts with summary measures of each. We then examine their underlying drivers to identify the cause of any unusual performance.

5.5 GROWTH

The analysis of growth is relatively straightforward. Growth rates are commonly reported for a variety of performance metrics, including sales, earnings, and cash flows. But *growth in sales* is the key long-term driver of growth in all other metrics. Growth rates in assets, common equity, and earnings are closely related to the growth rates in sales. In fact, when sales growth and profitability reach steady state, the growth rates in all key performance metrics quickly converge to the steady-state sales growth rate. However, during years when sales growth and profitability are fluctuating, the growth rates in the other performance metrics will generally differ from the growth rate in sales. The intuition behind these differences is usually straightforward. For example, asset growth will differ from sales growth when there is a change in the level of assets that is required to generate a given level of sales.

The final growth ratio that we report is the *sustainable growth rate*. This ratio is computed as

Sustainable Growth Rate = Return on Equity * (1 − Dividend Payout Ratio)

Given its current level of profitability and dividend policy, the sustainable growth rate is the maximum rate that a firm can grow without resorting to additional external financing. If a firm's forecasted sales growth rate exceeds its sustainable growth rate, be sure you understand how the additional growth will be financed. One possibility is through increased future profitability. However, if the increased profitability is not achieved, then the growth plans may be curtailed. Alternatively, the additional growth may be financed externally through the issuance of debt and/or equity. This also introduces uncertainty, because capital markets must be receptive to the firm's growth plans if they are going to provide financing. A final option is for the firm to cut its dividend payout ratio. However, given that the dividend payout ratio is usually zero for growth firms, this final option often is not available.

Analyzing Kohl's Growth

Turning to eVal, you will note that Kohl's growth in assets and common equity is more volatile than its growth in sales between 1999 and 2002. As discussed above, this is because Kohl's sales growth and profitability have yet to reach steady state. Note also that earnings growth exceeds sales growth in every period. This occurs because Kohl's margins have improved in every period, as we will see more directly when we examine profitability ratios. If a growth rate is shown as #NA, as is the case for Free Cash Flow to Investors, this means that the value of the underlying series is negative at the beginning of the period, so a growth rate is not defined.

Kohl's sales have grown consistently between 20 and 35 percent between fiscal 1998 and fiscal 2001. By comparison, Target's sales have grown at only about 10 percent and sales for the Retail Department Sales industry have been flat. These growth statistics reflect the fact that big-box strip mall stores such as Kohl's and Target have been stealing market share from traditional department stores such as JC Penney and Sears. Kohl's sales have grown considerably faster than Target's because of Kohl's more aggressive growth strategy. Page 8 of Kohl's fiscal 2001 Form 10-K indicates that Kohl's store count has increased from 182 at the end of 1997 to 382 at the end of 2001. Target is a much more mature company with over 1,000 stores already in operation. While Target is opening stores at about the same rate as Kohl's, the new store openings represent a smaller percentage of the total store count.

5.6 PROFITABILITY

While the analysis of growth is relatively straightforward, the analysis of profitability has an endless number of nuances. The starting point for the analysis of profitability, and the ultimate ending point, is the *return on equity,* computed as

$$\text{Return on Equity (ROE)} = \frac{\text{Net Income}}{\text{Average Common Equity}}$$

ROE is the accounting measure of the rate of return that the firm has provided to its common stockholders. It represents the amount of profit generated per dollar of book value of common equity. It is analogous to the interest rate that is generated by a fixed income investment. However, accounting rates of return are complicated by two factors. First, the income-generating process for a firm is much more complicated and uncertain than for a fixed-income security. Second, as discussed in Chapter 4, GAAP accounting does not recognize many economic assets and liabilities. Consequently, common equity and net income are both distorted, causing ROE to provide a distorted measure of true economic performance.

Because ROE is the ultimate accounting measure of a firm's performance, it will be the focus of our financial analysis of the past and our forecasts of the future. We therefore devote most of the remainder of this chapter to the analysis of ROE.

Benchmarking the Return on Equity

ROE is one of the few ratios where it makes sense to make comparisons with a well-defined benchmark. If you were considering investing in a fixed-income investment, you would compare its interest rate to the interest rates offered by like investments. Similarly, to evaluate firm profitability, you can compare the firm's ROE with its competitors' ROEs. Other things equal, the higher a firm's ROE, the greater the return generated per dollar of equity invested in the firm. Moreover, to value a firm, you must estimate the firm's cost of equity capital. Loosely speaking, the cost of equity capital represents the expected return that an equity investment must generate to make it competitive with similar investment opportunities. Just as you would rather invest in a bank CD with an above-average interest rate, you would rather invest in a firm with an above-average ROE. Thus, the cost of equity capital is a natural benchmark by which to judge a firm's ROE. Indeed, this is the logic behind some much-hyped performance measurement systems, such as Stern Stewart's EVA system.[1] Historically, the cost of equity capital has been estimated at about 10 percent for the average firm in the U.S. economy, so this is a crude benchmark you can use to assess a firm's ROE. Unfortunately, there are two key drawbacks with such comparisons. First, it is difficult to estimate a particular firm's cost of equity capital with any certainty. Second, as we have mentioned before, the vagaries of GAAP accounting rarely result in measures of net income and common equity that correspond with their economic counterparts. So, to make these constructs more meaningful, we need to do more work.

ROE is computed by dividing net income for the period by the *average* book value of common equity that was used to generate the net income. Ideally, we would like to use a time-weighted average of the equity that was invested during the year. But we generally only get to see balance sheets for the last day of each fiscal period, so we follow the common convention of dividing net income for the

---

[1] Visit http://www.sternstewart.com/evaabout/whatis.php to learn more about the EVA performance measurement system and see a nice picture of Bennett Stewart. A good understanding of the material in this book should help you develop your own performance measurement system at a much lower cost, and you'll be in a better position to understand the system's strengths and weaknesses.

period by the simple average of the beginning and ending balances of common equity. This can lead to a distorted ratio when there have been large changes in common equity near the beginning or the end of the year. For example, if a firm dou-
bled its common equity on the second day of the fiscal year, the average common
equity calculation would understate the true magnitude of the equity base that was
available for most of the year, leading to an overstatement of ROE. This limitation
arises anytime we compute a ratio that compares flow variables (amounts generated over the course of the year—such as those found on the income statement)
with stock variables (cumulative amounts present on the first or last day of the
year—such as those found on the balance sheet).

Mean Reversion in ROE

We stated earlier that many measures of financial performance tend to mean-
revert, and ROE is no exception. Figure 5.2 shows the mean reversion in return on
equity for the entire sample of publicly traded firms between 1951 and 2001. We
sort the firms into five groups in year 0 from lowest to highest ROE and then we
plot the median ROE for each of these groups over the next 10 years. As the plot
shows, the highest groups move down over time and the lowest groups move up
over time, consistent with the notion of mean reversion.

There are a few other observations to take away from Figure 5.2. First, the drastic improvement in the lowest ROE group in year 1 is a bit misleading (note that the
actual values in years 0 and 1 are technically off the chart at −0.50 and −0.44,
respectively). If the firm goes bankrupt, it drops out of the sample, leaving only
those firms that improved their performance enough to stay alive and, hence, remain on the graph. Even with this selection bias, it takes this bottom group six
years to get back to zero ROE. So they mean-revert, but very slowly. Second, while
the top two ROE groups decline and the bottom two groups improve, at no time do
the lines completely converge. Even after 10 years, the highest group has an ROE
of almost 13 percent and the lowest group has an ROE of just over 4 percent. While

FIGURE 5.2

**Mean Reversion in
Return on Equity**

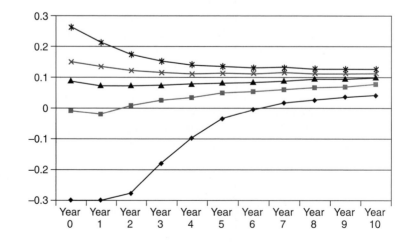

mean reversion has definitely brought the two groups closer together, it has not completely eliminated the disparity in ROE.

Why does ROE tend to mean-revert? The short answer is competition. If a firm enjoys a high return on equity, this catches the attention of other firms. Existing rivals undercut the firm's prices and new firms enter the market. As the firm responds to these competitive threats with a price cut of its own, its profitability suffers, driving down the ROE. Why is the mean reversion in ROE less than complete? For reasons we discussed in Chapter 3, many firms enjoy imperfect competition and are therefore partially shielded from competitive forces. In addition, accounting distortions can generate long-term disparity in ROE across firms. Firms in the pharmaceutical industry report among the economy's highest ROEs, but this is partly due to the fact that their most prominent economic asset—their recent past R&D expenditures—is expensed immediately. Because an asset is not recorded, assets and common equity are understated, causing ROE to be overstated.

It is reasonable to expect that some of the amounts on the income statement are more persistent than others. For this reason, we also compute *return on equity before nonrecurring items*. The idea is to exclude from the numerator items that are likely to completely disappear in subsequent years, thus providing a better indication of a firm's long-run sustainable ROE. We expect that ROE before nonrecurring items will mean-revert more slowly than regular ROE. Nonrecurring items are most commonly found in the extraordinary items and discontinued operations, other income and nonoperating income line items on the income statement. Thus, eVal excludes these line items from the definition of net income used to compute ROE before nonrecurring items. Nonoperating income is a pretax item on the income statement, so it must be tax-adjusted before adding it back to net income. eVal does this by using the effective tax rate for the year. The resulting measure is as follows:

$$\text{Return on Equity (b4 nonrecurring)} = \frac{\text{Net Income} - \text{After-Tax Nonrecurring Items}}{\text{Average Common Equity}}$$

where

After-Tax Nonrecurring Items = Extraordinary Items & Discontinued Operations + Other Income (Loss) + (1 − Tax) * (Nonoperating Income (Loss))

Tax = Effective Tax Rate = Income Taxes/EBIT

You should remember that while eVal mechanically spits out ROE before nonrecurring items, it is only a general guide and you should engage in more detailed analysis in order to classify items as recurring or nonrecurring. For example, the Other Income line item sometimes includes earnings from equity affiliates, which may well be recurring. In the case of Kohl's, examining the actual financial statements in their Form 10-K reveals that the Other Income line item is interest income, which will recur as long as Kohl's keeps the associated investments, so you probably shouldn't treat this income as nonrecurring. Also, nonrecurring items may be buried in other line items on the income statement, such as the effects of

FIGURE 5.3
Basic Dupont Model

ROE = Net Profit Margin $\times$ Asset Turnover $\times$ Total Leverage

$$= \frac{\text{Net Income}}{\text{Sales}} \times \frac{\text{Sales}}{\text{Average Total Assets}} \times \frac{\text{Average Total Assets}}{\text{Average Common Equity}}$$

an inventory write-down, which will usually be hidden in cost of goods sold (but can be recovered from the financial statement footnotes).

Decomposing ROE—The Basic Dupont Model

It is very useful to decompose ROE into a few fundamental drivers of profitability. The basic Dupont model, pioneered by management at a predecessor of the DuPont Chemical Company, factors ROE into three components, as shown in Figure 5.3.

The basic Dupont model does a good job at highlighting the three key drivers of the accounting rate of return on equity. First, the net profit margin measures the amount of net income generated per dollar of sales. Second, the asset turnover ratio measures the amount of sales generated per dollar of assets. Third, the total leverage ratio measures the amount of assets that can be supported by a dollar of common equity. By combining the three, we arrive back at the amount of net income generated per dollar of common equity, which is just our accounting rate of return on equity.

The Dupont breakdown is useful for a variety of reasons. First, if a firm can't earn a respectable net profit margin, or at least a positive one, then it doesn't matter how efficiently it operates its assets or how much leverage it applies. The first order of business at any hotdog stand is to sell the hotdogs for more than the cost of the meat and buns. The net profit margin extends this intuition all the way to the bottom line of the income statement—how much of each sales dollar remains after all expenses are deducted. Second, assuming the firm is making a net profit, the trick is to do so with the minimum investment in assets. If selling hotdogs requires an elaborate kiosk, or a fleet of home-delivery trucks, then the profit made might not be sufficient to justify the investment. Fortunately for the hotdog business, most stands run a large volume past a relatively inexpensive investment in assets; hence, the asset turnover is high.

The first two components of the basic Dupont model capture the operations of the business. How does the firm use its assets to make sales, and how profitably can it convert the sales into net income? These two components tend to trade off against one another; if you multiply them together, you get Net Income/Average Total Assets, labeled the *return on assets* (but beware of this term; it gets computed many subtly different ways). We can characterize different firms and industries by the different trade-offs that are required between margin and turnover. Capital-intensive industries, such as construction and heavy equipment manufacturing, have low turnovers and therefore must charge higher margins to get a competitive return on assets. On the other end of the spectrum, discount retailers and fast-food chains generally have high turnover and therefore competition drives their margins relatively low. Within industries, we also can characterize firms

FIGURE 5.4

Trade-Off between Margin and Turnover for May Department Stores and Wal-Mart

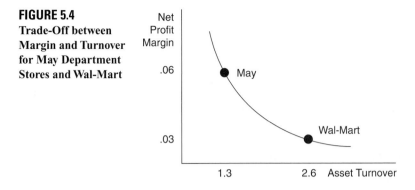

based on the different margin and turnover trade-offs that they make. Firms that choose a cost leadership strategy, producing at the lowest possible cost and selling in large quantities, tend to have low margins and high turnover. On the other hand, firms that choose a product differentiation strategy, producing a premium product and selling in smaller quantities, tend to have higher margins and lower turnover.

As an example, consider the net profit margin and asset turnover of Wal-Mart and May Department Stores, as shown in Figure 5.4. For the year ending in January 2002, both Wal-Mart and May had a return on assets of about 8 percent, but the route by which they got there was very different. In retailing, Wal-Mart would be classified as a cost leader, with low margins and high turnover, while May Department Stores would be classified as a product differentiator, with relatively higher margins and lower turnover. While both firms would like to have a high margin *and* a high turnover, in practice this is very hard to do. If Wal-Mart were to raise its prices in order to improve its margin, its sales volume would probably suffer, driving down its asset turnover. And if May were to carry lower quantities of less expensive inventory in an effort to improve its asset turnover, its customers would probably be unwilling to pay its higher margins. The very nature of each firm's strategy dictates where they will be on the margin versus turnover trade-off.

The trade-off between margins and turnover plays out in a number of different business decisions. Putting inventory on sale lowers the profit margin but improves the asset turnover (assuming, of course, that the sale causes a buying frenzy among customers). Outsourcing production improves turnover but lowers margin. Aging wine longer improves the quality and allows the winemaker to charge a greater margin, but necessarily lowers the asset turnover.

The first two terms in the basic Dupont model determine the firm's return on total assets. The return on equity can be made larger than the return on assets by leveraging the assets. This effect is captured by the third factor in the basic Dupont model, total leverage. Imagine a firm whose assets are financed by a small amount of equity and a large amount of liabilities. The small equity base claims the entire return on assets and will therefore enjoy a very high return on equity.

Management has lots of control over the firm's leverage, so why don't all firms increase their ROE simply by borrowing more money? Ignoring for a moment the added risk that additional leverage brings, the more basic answer is that the additional debt comes with additional interest expense, and interest expense lowers net income and therefore lowers the net profit margin. Thus, as total leverage increases, the net profit margin decreases. Which effect dominates depends on whether the interest rate on the borrowed money is less than the pre-interest return that the firm earns with the borrowed money. This last effect is a weakness of the basic Dupont model; it doesn't cleanly separate operating decisions from financing decisions. For this, we must turn to the advanced Dupont model.

Decomposing ROE—The Advanced Dupont Model

The advanced Dupont model isolates operating performance much more cleanly by introducing a new measure of profitability: the *return on net operating assets* (*RNOA*). This core measure of operating performance is then adjusted for the effect of leverage. While this decomposition more cleanly separates operating and financing effects, it is also more complicated. Before we can present detailed definitions and computations, we need to associate each line item on the income statement and balance sheet with either operating or financing activities.

The income statement items are divided into net operating income (NOI) and net financing expense (NFE). Both amounts are net of tax, so that Net Income = NOI − NFE. The tax rate used is not arbitrary; it is the effective tax rate for the period, defined as Income Taxes/EBT (where EBT denotes earnings before taxes). The balance sheet assets and liabilities are divided into net operating assets (NOA) and net financial obligations (NFO), so that Common Equity = NOA − NFO. Obviously, there are many different ways we can sort line items into either operations or financing, and there will be some ambiguous items, but the general goal is to isolate the effects of operating activities from financing activities. The most important thing is to be consistent across classifications on the income statement and balance sheet. It would be wrong, for instance, to classify the interest on capital leases as part of net financing expense but then classify the capital lease obligation as part of net operating assets. Similarly, it would be wrong to classify the minority interest in earnings as part of net operating income but then classify the minority interest on the balance sheet as part of net financial obligations. Figure 5.5 illustrates how eVal has made these classifications.

Having allocated the line items in the income statement and balance sheet into operating and financing components, we can now conduct our ratio analysis on each activity separately, and then examine how they come together to determine ROE. The two key ratios are shown at the bottom of Figure 5.5. They are

$$\text{Return on Net Operating Assets (RNOA)}$$
$$= \frac{\text{Net Operating Income (NOI)}}{\text{Average Net Operating Assets (NOA)}}$$

and

$$\text{Net Borrowing Costs (NBC)} = \frac{\text{Net Financing Expense (NFE)}}{\text{Average Net Financial Obligations (NFO)}}$$

FIGURE 5.5
Decomposing the Financial Statements into Operating and Financing Components

Income Statement

	Sales (Net)
−	Cost of Goods Sold
=	Gross Profit
−	R&D Expense
−	SG&A Expense
=	EBITDA
−	Depreciation & Amortization
=	EBIT
−	Interest Expense
+	Nonoperating Income (Loss)
=	EBT
−	Income Taxes
−	Minority Interest in Earnings
+	Other Income (Loss)
=	Net Income before Ext. Items
−	Ext. Items & Disc. Ops
−	Preferred Dividends
=	Net Income (available to common)

Balance Sheet

	Operating Cash and Market. Sec
+	Receivables
+	Inventories
+	Other Current Assets
=	Total Current Assets
+	PP&E (Net)
+	Investments
+	Intangibles
+	Other Assets
=	Total Assets
	Current Debt
+	Accounts Payable
+	Income Taxes Payable
+	Other Current Liabilities
=	Total Current Liabilities
+	Long-Term Debt
+	Other Liabilities
+	Deferred Taxes
+	Minority Interest
=	Total Liabilities
+	Preferred Stock
+	Paid in Common Capital (Net)
+	Retained Earnings
=	Total Common Equity

Net Operating Income (NOI) =

	(EBIT + Nonoperating Income) ∗ (1 − tax)
−	Minority Interest in Earnings
+	Other Income (Loss)
−	Ext. Items and Disc. Ops.

Net Financing Expense (NFE) =

	Interest Expense ∗ (1 − tax)
+	Preferred Dividends

where the effective tax rate (tax) = Income Taxes/EBT

Net Income = NOI − NFE

Net Operating Assets (NOA) =

	Total Assets
−	Accounts Payable
−	Income Taxes Payable
−	Other Current Liabilities
−	Other Liabilities
−	Deferred Taxes
−	Minority Interest

Net Financial Obligations (NFO) =

	Current Debt
+	Long-Term Debt
+	Preferred Stock

Common Equity = NOA − NFO

Return on Net Operating Assets (RNOA) = $\dfrac{\text{NOI}}{\text{NOA}}$

Net Borrowing Cost (NBC) = $\dfrac{\text{NFE}}{\text{NFO}}$

where

Net Financing Expense (NFE) = Interest Expense ∗ (1 − tax) + Preferred Dividends

Net Operating Income (NOI) = Net Income + Net Financing Expense

Net Financial Obligations (NFO) = Current Debt + Long-Term Debt + Preferred Stock

Net Operating Assets (NOA) = Common Equity + Net Financial Obligations

Effective Tax Rate (tax) = Income Taxes/Earnings before Taxes

Each ratio associates the income statement flows with the balance sheet items that caused them. Consider the RNOA. In the numerator, NOI represents the after-tax income earned by the operating assets; equivalently, it is net income with the after-tax financing charges added back. In the denominator, NOA represents the operating assets used to generate the NOI. Equivalently, it is common equity with the net financial obligations added back, which represent the sources of capital that are used to finance the net operating assets. The result is a measure of the firm's operating performance that abstracts from the manner in which these operations are financed. RNOA is not affected by the firm's level of debt, the interest rate it borrows at, or the tax shield that the interest creates. All these effects are isolated in the net borrowing cost (NBC), which associates the after-tax income statement flows that go to debt and preferred stock providers with the amount of capital they provided.

The absolute interpretation of the RNOA as a performance measure is similar to the interpretation of ROE. The key difference is that the long-term *hurdle rate* for RNOA is the after-tax weighted average cost of capital—a blend of the cost of equity capital and debt capital that we will discuss later in Chapter 9.

A final word of warning regarding RNOA. In practice, there are many different definitions and terminologies used for RNOA. For example, it is not uncommon to use total assets in the denominator, in which case the measure is usually referred to simply as return on assets (ROA). Another common variant measures the numerator before taxes, in which case the measure is usually referred to as the pre-tax RNOA. Finally, the term *return on invested capital* (ROIC) is also frequently used in place of the term *RNOA*. Recall that net operating assets are equal to invested capital (which is equal to the sum of debt, preferred stock, and common stock). So the terms *net operating assets* and *invested capital* are used interchangeably. The bottom line is that when you see a return on "something," you should make sure that you understand how it is computed before attempting to interpret it.

Putting all the pieces together, the advanced Dupont model decomposes ROE as[2]

$$\text{ROE} = \text{RNOA} + \text{Leverage} \times \text{Spread}$$

where

$$\text{Leverage} = \frac{\text{Average NFO}}{\text{Average Common Equity}}$$

$$\text{Spread} = \text{RNOA} - \text{NBC}$$

and the other terms are as defined earlier.

Note that Leverage in this decomposition differs from the Total Leverage definition in the basic Dupont model. This measure of leverage only includes financial obligations in the numerator, whereas the basic Dupont model used total assets. The advanced Dupont model describes ROE as RNOA plus an adjustment for the amount of leverage the firm employs times the *spread* between RNOA and NBC.

---

[2] If you remember your high school algebra, you should be able to prove that the above relation holds. We omit the proof for brevity (trust us!).

To interpret this relation, first recall that RNOA measures a firm's operating performance. ROE, on the other hand, measures the return to the common equity holders after satisfying the claims of all the other capital providers that are funding the firm's operations. The common equity holders are the residual claimants on any operating earnings that remain after satisfying these other capital providers. Thus, if a firm's RNOA exceeds its net borrowing costs (NBC), then the ROE will exceed the RNOA, because the common equity holders get more than a proportionate share in the net operating income. The extent to which ROE exceeds RNOA depends on the *spread* between RNOA and the NBC, and the amount of leverage the firm applies.

As a simple illustration, consider a bank that borrows funds at one rate and lends at another (hopefully higher) rate. The bank's RNOA is given by its lending rate (i.e., the rate it earns on its operating assets, which consist of its loan portfolio). The ROE generated for the bank's owners depends on its borrowing rate relative to its lending rate (i.e., its spread) and the proportion of its lending that is funded by the bank's own debt. For example, if a bank lends at 10 percent and funds its lending with nine dollars of debt for each dollar of equity, and it borrows the debt at 8 percent, then the bank's ROE is given by

$$ROE = 10\% + \frac{9}{1}(10\% - 8\%) = 28\%$$

In this case, the leverage is 9 and the spread is 2 percent, adding 18 percent to the RNOA of 10 percent to yield an ROE of 28 percent. Note that leverage does not always increase ROE relative to RNOA. If a firm has a negative spread, then additional leverage reduces ROE relative to RNOA. For example, assume that the bank in our example can only lend at 6 percent. In this case, we have

$$ROE = 6\% + \frac{9}{1}(6\% - 8\%) = -12\%$$

Thus, higher leverage increases ROE when RNOA is greater than the cost of nonequity financing and reduces ROE when RNOA is less than the cost of nonequity financing. In other words, additional leverage makes the good times really good and the bad times really bad. This is just another way of saying that additional leverage increases the risk of the returns to common equity holders.

The next stage of the advanced Dupont model is to decompose RNOA into net operating margin and the net operating asset turnover, much like we did in the basic Dupont model:

$$RNOA = \text{Net Operating Margin} * \text{Net Operating Asset Turnover}$$

where

$$\text{Net Operating Margin} = \frac{\text{Net Operating Income}}{\text{Sales}}$$

$$\text{Net Operating Asset Turnover} = \frac{\text{Sales}}{\text{Average Net Operating Assets}}$$

Thus, RNOA is increasing in both the margin that a firm generates on its sales and the amount of sales that can be generated per unit of assets, just as in the basic Dupont model. The difference between the two models is that the margin and turnover measures are based on "cleaner" measures of operating activities in the advanced model, and this has some important consequences. First, the net operating margin isn't polluted by interest expense or preferred dividends, as it was in the basic Dupont model. Second, the treatment of operating liabilities is very different between the two models. In the basic Dupont model, operating liabilities are included in the denominator of the asset turnover ratio. In the advanced Dupont model, they are netted against total assets to compute net operating assets, and hence excluded from the denominator of the net operating asset turnover ratio. The basic Dupont model treats operating liabilities as a type of financial leverage. The advanced Dupont model treats them as a reduction in the amount of operating assets. The latter treatment makes more sense, as we don't usually think of accounts payable and related operating liabilities as arising from financing activities.

Figure 5.6 summarizes the advanced Dupont model in all its glory. As you can probably tell, we like this model a lot.

eVal classifies all cash and marketable securities as part of net operating assets. Yet in many cases, these are really financial assets that are not directly tied to the operations. The firm needs to maintain some balance of cash to fund its ongoing operating activities, but this is rarely more than a few percent of sales. To pick an extreme example, if you load Google into eVal (ticker = GOOG), you will see that, in recent years, its operating cash and marketable securities line item exceeds 100 percent of sales. Google doesn't need to maintain this much cash for normal operations; rather, it is accumulating financial assets (probably as part of Larry and Sergey's evil plan to take over the world). How should we deal with these financial assets in our advanced Dupont model? Ideally, we would net them against the net financial obligations and we would net the investment income they produce against net financing expense. They aren't really part of operations, so we should shuffle them into financing. eVal doesn't do this for a few reasons. First, we would be hard-pressed to specify for all firms at all times what the right amount of operating cash

FIGURE 5.6
Advanced Dupont Model

$$\text{ROE} = \text{RNOA} + \text{Leverage} \times (\text{RNOA} - \text{NBC})$$

$$= \frac{\text{NOI}}{\text{NOA}} + \frac{\text{NFO}}{\text{Common Equity}} \times \left(\frac{\text{NOI}}{\text{NOA}} - \frac{\text{NFE}}{\text{NFO}} \right)$$

and

$$\text{RNOA} = \text{Net Operating Margin} \times \text{Net Operating Asset Turnover}$$

$$= \frac{\text{NOI}}{\text{Sales}} \times \frac{\text{Sales}}{\text{NOA}}$$

where ROE is return on common equity, RNOA is return on net operating assets, NBC is net borrowing cost, NOI is net operating income, NOA is net operating assets, NFO is net financial obligations, and NFE is net financing expense, as defined in Figure 5.5.

is, making it almost impossible to isolate the true financial assets. Second, without examining the "as reported" financial statements and footnotes, it is impossible to know where the investment income has been included on the income statement, and, hence, it is impossible to know where the data standardization process has allocated this income in our data. It could be netted against Interest Expense and therefore included in that line item, it could be included in Nonoperating Income (Loss), or it could be netted against SG&A Expense. As we discussed in Chapter 2, you need to look at the "as reported" financial statements and make sure that eVal's standardized income statement and balance sheet are in good order. Part of that exercise is making sure that the line item Interest Expense is only the interest outflow on the current and long-term debt; any interest income should be included in Nonoperating Income (Loss). An early indicator that your financial statements might have a problem in this regard is an extremely low (or even negative) net borrowing cost. For example, if you load May Department Stores (ticker = MAY) into eVal, you will see that their net borrowing cost is less than 1 percent in recent years. It isn't the case that May can really borrow at such a low rate; rather, they have netted some interest income against their interest expense.

Decomposing Kohl's ROE

Let's take a look at what the Dupont models tell us about Kohl's ROE. You can locate this analysis in eVal by going to the Ratio Analysis sheet and clicking the Dupont Models button. We reproduce this analysis in Figure 5.7.

Kohl's ROE has hovered between 18 and 20 percent in recent years, while its RNOA has hovered around 15 percent. The basic Dupont model indicates that

FIGURE 5.7
Dupont Models for Kohl's in Fiscal 2001

	A	B	C	D	E	F	
1	**Ratio Analysis**	Growth and Profitability		Margin, Turnover and			
2	Go To User's Guide	Dupont Models		Analysis of Credit Risk			
3							
4	**Company Name**	KOHL S CORP					
5							
6		Actual	Actual	Actual	Actual	Actual	For
7	**Fiscal Year End Date**	1/31/1998	1/30/1999	1/29/2000	2/3/2001	2/2/2002	2/2
23	**Basic Dupont Model**						
24	Net Profit Margin	0.046	0.052	0.057	0.060	0.066	
25	x Total Asset Turnover		2.071	1.873	1.813	1.705	
26	x Total Leverage		1.679	1.709	1.745	1.759	
27	= Return on Equity		0.182	0.181	0.191	0.199	
28							
29	**Advanced Dupont Model**						
30	Net Operating Margin	0.051	0.056	0.061	0.065	0.071	
31	x Net Operating Asset Turnover		2.685	2.429	2.320	2.161	
32	= Return on Net Operating Assets		0.150	0.147	0.152	0.153	
33	Net Borrowing Cost (NBC)		0.044	0.040	0.043	0.037	
34	Spread (RNOA - NBC)		0.106	0.107	0.109	0.117	
35	Financial Leverage (LEV)		0.295	0.317	0.364	0.388	
36	ROE = RNOA + LEV*Spread		0.182	0.181	0.191	0.199	

Kohl's net profit margin has gradually improved from 4.6 to 6.6 percent, while asset turnover has gradually declined from 2.071 to 1.705. Finally, leverage has increased from 1.679 to 1.759. On balance, the increased margins and leverage have outweighed the declining asset turnover, resulting in small improvements in ROE. The advanced Dupont model tells a similar story. Gradual improvements in margins and leverage have offset corresponding declines in turnover. Note that the spread between Kohl's RNOA and NBC is consistently over 10 percent, indicating that leverage will have a big impact in increasing ROE relative to RNOA. Unfortunately, Kohl's financial leverage is less than 40 percent, so the 10 percent spread translates into only a 4 percent increase in ROE relative to RNOA. One wonders why Kohl's doesn't use more leverage, given its healthy spread. A probable explanation is that Kohl's has a lot of off-balance-sheet leverage in the form of operating leases for its stores. Thus, the reported leverage ratio of 40 percent probably understates Kohl's economic leverage. While there is relatively little time-series action in Kohl's Dupont decompositions, there is definite evidence of an increase in margins and a reduction in turnover in fiscal 1999 relative to fiscal 1998. What explains this trend? Inspection of Kohl's Form 10-Ks indicates that Kohl's shifted from a strategy of opening new stores itself to a strategy of both opening new stores and acquiring and rebranding existing stores. The acquisition of existing stores involved payments for goodwill and favorable lease rights that boosted Kohl's assets and reduced its turnover. At the same time, these existing stores yielded higher margins, so the net effect on ROE and RNOA was a slight improvement. It appears that the strategic shift is successful, at least for now.

While there is relatively little time-series action in Kohl's ratios, a cross-sectional analysis with Target reveals some major differences. Both firms generate ROEs of around 20 percent, but the way that they get there is very different. First of all, Target's RNOA of 11.1 percent in fiscal 2001 is considerably lower than Kohl's RNOA of 15.3 percent. While Target enjoys a slightly faster net operating asset turnover than Kohl's, its net operating margin is much lower, coming in at 4.2 percent in fiscal 2001, as compared to 7.1 percent for Kohl's. Both firms have similar net borrowing costs of about 4 percent, so, before even looking, we can conclude that Target must get back to the same ROE by using much more financial leverage than Kohl's. Indeed, Target's average financial leverage has been about 100 percent in the past few years, while Kohl's has been less than 40 percent. Thus, Target is making up for its lower operating margins through more aggressive use of leverage. But why are Target's margins so much lower? We investigate this issue next.

5.7   PROFIT MARGINS

The net operating margin used in the advanced Dupont model represents after-tax operating income divided by sales. In order to understand the drivers of net operating margin, we must look at each of the components of after-tax operating income as a proportion of sales. Note that the Forecasting Assumptions sheet in eVal expresses many of the income statement line items as a proportion of sales. Rather than repeating this analysis, our ratio analysis focuses on just a few key margins. If the bottom line net operating margin is unusual, then work your way down this list of intermediate margins to identify the underlying line items that are driving this behavior.

The starting point is the *gross margin,* which measures the difference between sales and cost of goods sold as a proportion of sales:

$$\text{Gross Margin} = \frac{\text{Sales} - \text{Cost of Goods Sold}}{\text{Sales}}$$

This is the first level of profitability—the markup on the product. For each dollar of sales, how much more can the firm charge over the cost of making or buying the product. It is generally all downhill from here, so if a firm can't generate a decent gross margin, there is not much point in looking any further. This is also the ratio to watch if you are worried about increased competition. If the firm is lowering its prices to retain market share, you will see it here.

The next key margin we report is the *EBITDA margin,* which gives earnings before interest, taxes, depreciation, and amortization as a proportion of sales. Another way to define the numerator is sales less cost of goods sold, R&D expense, and SG&A expense, as shown below:

EBITDA Margin

$$= \frac{\text{Sales} - \text{Cost of Goods Sold} - \text{R\&D Expense} - \text{SG\&A Expense}}{\text{Sales}}$$

The firm may enjoy a large markup on its product, but it could be that the key costs aren't the actual manufacturing and production of the goods. For instance, if you load Pfizer into eVal (ticker = PFE), you will note that their gross margin is approximately 85 to 90 percent for the past few years. But the real cost to a pharmaceutical company is R&D and SG&A; the actual manufacturing of the drug is a relatively minor component. Consequently, Pfizer's EBITDA margin is about 35 percent. If you discover that the EBITDA margin is unusual, then you should go back to the detailed income statement to identify the specific line items that are responsible. Note that this ratio excludes depreciation and amortization, so it can be quite high for capital-intensive firms. It is often touted by analysts on the basis that depreciation and amortization represent noncash charges. But don't be fooled into relying too heavily on this ratio (as many Telecom investors were in the late 1990s). While depreciation and amortization are accounting adjustments, they nevertheless represent the allocation of past capital expenditures. A capital-intensive firm may look great on an EBITDA basis, but it will have to reinvest in its capital base in order to stay in business.

The *EBIT margin* is the EBITDA margin with the "DA" taken out. As such, it provides a useful summary measure of operating performance. The numerator is sales less all expenses except interest and taxes; hence the name "earnings before interest and taxes":

$$\text{EBIT Margin} = \frac{\text{Earnings before Interest and Taxes}}{\text{Sales}}$$

The after-tax operating margin can fluctuate due to changes in leverage or tax rates. The EBIT margin abstracts from these effects, providing a clean measure of underlying operating performance.

As we move down the page from gross margin to EBIT margin, the relation between sales and profits gets weaker. As sales increase, cost of goods sold will necessarily have to increase—the firm needs to pay for the goods that it is selling—so the gross margin is relatively stable over time. But an increase in sales does not necessarily mean that R&D expense will increase, as this is a much more discretionary expenditure. Similarly, administrative expenses bear no direct relation to sales. In the long run, a firm needs these expenses to generate its sales, but in a given year there is no reason why they should vary in proportion to sales.

The final margin that we report is the *net operating margin before nonrecurring items*. This margin starts with net operating income but then adds back any nonrecurring expenses, adjusted for their tax consequences (specifically, it adds back tax-adjusted nonoperating income, other income, and extraordinary items and discontinued operations). Unusual behavior in this margin that does not show up in the EBIT margin is attributable to taxes or costs of nonequity capital (specifically, tax-adjusted interest expense and preferred dividends).

$$\text{Net Operating Margin before Nonrecurring Items}$$

$$= \frac{\text{Net Operating Income} + \text{After-Tax Nonrecurring Items}}{\text{Sales}}$$

Finally, any unusual behavior in the bottom-line net operating margin that does not show up in the above margin is due to nonrecurring items. As mentioned above, eVal makes a leap of faith in classifying tax-adjusted nonoperating income, other income, and extraordinary items and discontinued operations as nonrecurring. You should identify the nature of these items from the Form 10-Ks and make sure you are confident that they are indeed unusual and unlikely to recur.

Economies of Scale and Operating Risk

Many young and growing firms have negative net operating margins. They all claim that this is a temporary situation and that once they grow past some critical size, they will be hugely profitable. Of course, many of them never achieve this dream and fail, but the ones that succeed do so because they experience some economies of scale. A typical situation might be a firm with a positive gross margin but a negative EBITDA margin, due mainly to its SG&A expense. If the SG&A expense is composed of mostly fixed costs, then as sales grow, the SG&A expense does not increase proportionately, and eventually the EBITDA margin becomes positive. Moreover, expenditures on R&D and marketing have to be expensed immediately but usually benefit future sales. Be on the lookout for such effects as you study a company's margins. If sales are growing and the margins are steadily improving, this is a sign that the firm is exploiting economies of scale. Alternatively, if a firm claims that it will not be profitable until it grows to some larger size, but its past sales growth has not generated any significant improvement in its margins, then you should be suspicious. The company's claims of great margins in the future may be nothing more than wishful thinking.

While a cost structure with a large fixed-cost component helps achieve economies of scale, it also imposes *operating risk* (also referred to as *operating leverage*) on the company. If the sales volume is highly variable, then, in periods of low volume, the firm will be stuck with its fixed costs and insufficient revenue to cover them; in periods of high volume, it will easily cover its fixed costs and enjoy huge margins. In other words, the good times are really good and the bad times are really bad. As an example, compare a firm's decision to buy equipment or enter short-term rental contracts for said equipment. Short-term rentals can be varied with sales, resulting in lower operating risk. Managers often attempt to lower their operating risk by outsourcing many aspects of production. Frequently, however, they find that there is little profit left over when they do this. No risk often means no reward. For example, most oil exploration companies rent exploration equipment from dedicated oil services companies. This lowers their operating risk. But when the price of oil is high, the oil services firms jack up their rental rates, cutting into the potential profits of the oil exploration companies.

Analyzing Kohl's Margins

Let's take a look at the breakdown of Kohl's margins. Margin analysis directly follows the Dupont models on eVal's Ratio Analysis worksheet. Kohl's margin analysis for fiscal 2001 is reproduced in Figure 5.8. We see that the gross margin has increased slightly over the last few years, adding up to about 1 percent between fiscal 1997 and fiscal 2001. But this is only part of the story, because the EBITDA

FIGURE 5.8
Margin and Turnover Analysis for Kohl's in Fiscal 2001

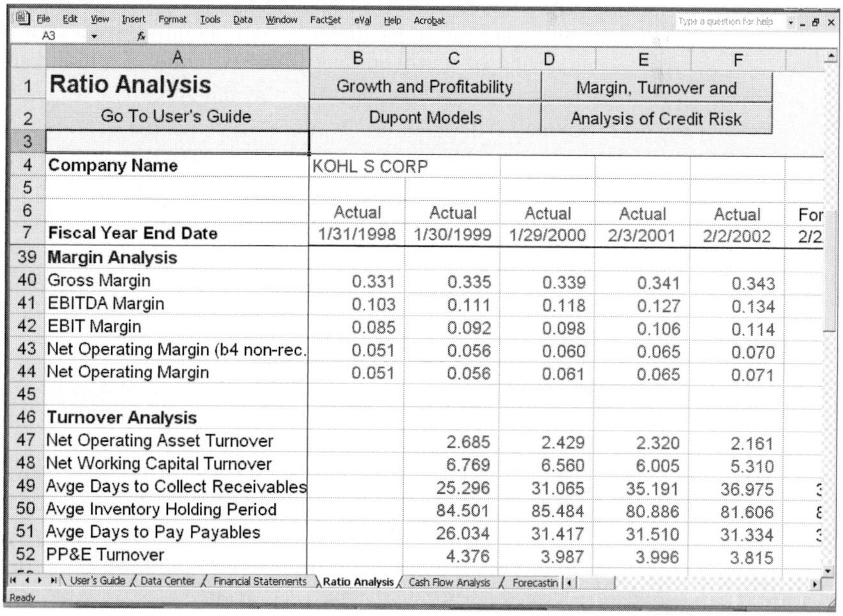

	A	B	C	D	E	F	
1	**Ratio Analysis**	Growth and Profitability		Margin, Turnover and			
2	Go To User's Guide	Dupont Models		Analysis of Credit Risk			
3							
4	**Company Name**	KOHL S CORP					
5							
6		Actual	Actual	Actual	Actual	Actual	For
7	**Fiscal Year End Date**	1/31/1998	1/30/1999	1/29/2000	2/3/2001	2/2/2002	2/2
39	**Margin Analysis**						
40	Gross Margin	0.331	0.335	0.339	0.341	0.343	
41	EBITDA Margin	0.103	0.111	0.118	0.127	0.134	
42	EBIT Margin	0.085	0.092	0.098	0.106	0.114	
43	Net Operating Margin (b4 non-rec.	0.051	0.056	0.060	0.065	0.070	
44	Net Operating Margin	0.051	0.056	0.061	0.065	0.071	
45							
46	**Turnover Analysis**						
47	Net Operating Asset Turnover		2.685	2.429	2.320	2.161	
48	Net Working Capital Turnover		6.769	6.560	6.005	5.310	
49	Avge Days to Collect Receivables		25.296	31.065	35.191	36.975	
50	Avge Inventory Holding Period		84.501	85.484	80.886	81.606	
51	Avge Days to Pay Payables		26.034	31.417	31.510	31.334	
52	PP&E Turnover		4.376	3.987	3.996	3.815	

margin increased by about 3 percent over the same period. By toggling to the Forecasting Assumptions worksheet, we see that the other main force behind this improvement is a decline in the ratio of SG&A to sales. Kohl's has been growing rapidly in the past few years and it would appear that they are enjoying some economies of scale. The MD&A on page 10 of Kohl's fiscal 2001 Form 10-K confirms that Kohl's is experiencing economies of scale in advertising and corporate overhead as well as reducing store operating costs. Another minor contribution to the net operating margin comes from a declining effective tax rate (also seen on the Forecasting Assumptions sheet). If you get Kohl's 10-K for fiscal 2001 and find the tax footnote way in the back of the report, you will see that this is due to a decline in the state income tax rate in the states where Kohl's operates.

Comparing Kohl's with Target, we see that Kohl's higher net margins come primarily from its higher gross margin. Kohl's gross margin is consistently 3 to 4 percent higher than Target's gross margin, and this difference flows down to the bottom line. This difference suggests that Kohl's is successfully differentiating its products and/or services from Target's. But this leaves a puzzle. A differentiation strategy usually involves higher margins but lower turnover. How is Kohl's able to generate higher margins than Target while maintaining asset turnover ratios that are similar to Target's? We address this issue next.

5.8   TURNOVER RATIOS

We now turn our attention to ratios measuring the amount of assets that the firm requires to generate its sales, known as turnover ratios. These ratios also are referred to as efficiency ratios, because they tell us how efficiently management is employing the firm's assets. A net operating asset turnover ratio of two indicates that $.50 of net operating assets is required to generate $1.00 of sales. We use turnover analysis to examine how the underlying operating asset and liability line items on the balance sheet contribute to the overall net operating asset turnover ratio. The basic approach is to compute a turnover ratio for specific groups of operating assets and operating liabilities. A commonly cited turnover ratio is the *net working capital turnover ratio*, computed as

$$\text{Net Working Capital Turnover} = \frac{\text{Sales}}{\text{Average Net Working Capital}}$$

where

Net Working Capital = Current Operating Assets −
Current Operating Liabilities

This ratio measures how efficiently a firm is managing its working capital accounts. Ideally, a firm would like to generate sales with a minimum investment in working capital. Obviously, this presents the firm with trade-offs. It is difficult to minimize the investment in inventory while still presenting the customers with a wide variety of choices and fast delivery. And all firms would like to collect on their sales immediately and pay their accounts payable very slowly, but such actions usually have consequences that hurt the firm in other ways.

It is common to compute individual turnover ratios for the three most important components of working capital—receivables, inventories, and payables—and there are a number of common modifications that are made to these ratios. First, they are often stated in the form of the average number of days that a dollar sits in the account. The relation between a turnover ratio and the average days outstanding metric is simply

$$\text{Average Days Outstanding} = \frac{365}{\text{Turnover Ratio}}$$

For example, if we turn over our receivables 12 times per year, then the average receivable must have a life of approximately 365/12 = 30 days. Using this approach, the average days to collect receivables is given by

$$\text{Average Days to Collect Receivables} = 365 * \frac{\text{Average Receivables}}{\text{Sales}}$$

Similarly, the average inventory holding period is given by

$$\text{Average Inventory Holding Period} = 365 * \frac{\text{Average Inventory}}{\text{Cost of Goods Sold}}$$

Note that we made an additional modification in computing the average inventory holding period; we replaced sales with cost of goods sold. This is because inventories are carried at cost, and so we want a flow variable that measures the cost of inventories consumed during the period. Lastly, the average days to pay payables is computed as

$$\text{Average Days to Pay Payables} = 365 * \frac{\text{Average Payables}}{\text{Purchases}}$$

where

$$\text{Purchases} = \text{Cost of Goods Sold} + \text{Ending Inventory} - \text{Beginning Inventory}$$

Note here that the denominator is measured using purchases. This represents the amount of payables that were added during the period, and so is directly comparable with the average balance in the payables account in the numerator.

The final turnover ratio that we report is property, plant, and equipment (PP&E) turnover, computed as

$$\text{PP\&E Turnover} = \frac{\text{Sales}}{\text{Average Net Property, Plant, and Equipment}}$$

PP&E isn't literally consumed in the sale the same way that inventory is. Nonetheless, it is an asset that is necessary in the production of sales, albeit indirectly at times. In the short run, Kohl's corporate headquarters could probably blow up and sales in the department stores wouldn't be affected, but, in the long run, headquarters are probably necessary. We want to know if the firm is using its PP&E

efficiently. Does it have idle capacity? Does it invest too heavily in nonproducing assets, such as lavish headquarters and Lear jets? Comparing the PP&E ratio of the firm with a few of its close competitors can frequently shed light on these questions.

Note that there are additional accounts, such as intangibles, that also may drive unusual turnover. You should identify and understand these accounts. For example, if a firm has engaged in an acquisition involving significant goodwill, this will typically drive the net operating asset turnover down relative to the company's competitors. However, this is not necessarily a bad sign, and competitors may have similar amounts of internally generated goodwill that is not recognized on their balance sheets.

Analyzing Kohl's Turnover

Kohl's turnover analysis for fiscal 2001 is shown in Figure 5.8, immediately following margin analysis. As noted previously, Kohl's net operating asset turnover has been declining steadily through 2001, almost perfectly offsetting the steady improvement in net operating margin. A more detailed analysis of Kohl's turnover ratios shows that their average days to collect receivables have been steadily increasing, from 25 days in fiscal 1997 to 37 days in fiscal 2001. This trend warrants further investigation. Page 12 of Kohl's 2001 Form 10-K indicates that Kohl's has been increasing its proprietary credit card operations and retaining more of the receivables generated by this program. Thus, this increase looks like it is part of a strategic shift to bring the credit operation in-house. But we should make sure that the credit operations are contributing to Kohl's margins and that Kohl's uncollectibles are in line with their allowances. On the positive side, Kohl's has reduced its inventory holding period and increased its days to pay payables, indicating more efficient management of working capital.

Finally, Kohl's PP&E turnover has been falling. It could be that same-store sales have been dropping. But page 8 of the 2001 Form 10-K indicates that sales per square foot have steadily increased, from $265 per square foot in fiscal 1998 to $283 per square foot in fiscal 2001, and page 9 indicates that same-store sales growth has been increasing. So what gives? The decline is probably explained by Kohl's strategic shift toward purchasing existing stores as an alternative to opening new stores. Some of the costs associated with establishing a new store must be expensed as incurred (such as administrative costs incurred at the corporate office), but when Kohl's buys an existing store, these costs will be included in the purchase price and, hence, capitalized on the balance sheet.

Before leaving Kohl's time-series turnover analysis, we should ask ourselves whether we have considered all the balance sheet items that could have contributed to Kohl's significant reduction in NOA turnover. We've looked at working capital items and PP&E, but Kohl's standardized balance sheet also shows a significant increase in Other Assets. The as-reported financial statements in Kohl's Form 10-K indicate that these other assets are Favorable Lease Rights. These assets were acquired as part of Kohl's strategic shift to purchasing existing stores. Kohl's basically purchased stores with existing lease agreements that locked in lease rates below current competitive levels. The costs associated with purchasing these lease rights are capitalized on the balance sheet and amortized over the lease term. These lease rights no doubt contributed to Kohl's slowing NOA turnover. But as long as the lower lease rates translate into higher margins for Kohl's, the net effect should be a wash on ROE.

Next, we compare Kohl's turnover ratios with the corresponding ratios for Target. This is where we get to revisit the puzzle that arose in our margin analysis. Recall that Kohl's has the margins of a product differentiator but the turnover of a cost leader. Starting with working capital, we see that Kohl's turnover ratios are substantially worse than Target's. Kohl's collects its receivables more slowly, holds its inventory longer, and pays its payables more quickly. These differences are all consistent with Target's successful implementation of a cost leadership strategy. But then things get confusing. Kohl's PP&E turnover is substantially better than Target's. Target's cost leadership strategy should give it higher PP&E turns. Fortunately, there is a simple explanation for this difference. Kohl's leases 56 percent of its stores under operating leases while Target leases only 12 percent of its stores. Recall that stores held under operating leases are not recorded on the balance sheet, leading to an understatement of PP&E and long-term debt for Kohl's relative to Target. Based on the information on page F13 of Kohl's 2001 Form 10-K, we can infer that the capitalized value of Kohl's operating lease commitments is probably in excess of $1.5 billion. Inclusion of this capitalized amount in PP&E would increase PP&E by almost 100 percent and cut Kohl's PP&E turnover ratio almost in half. This would render Kohl's PP&E turns and NOA turns significantly below Target's. Thus, we have the solution to the puzzle we were left with at the end of our margin analysis. Kohl's has the higher margins of a product differentiator, and once we consider Kohl's leased stores, it also has the lower turns of a product differentiator.

5.9   LEVERAGE

In both the basic and advanced Dupont decompositions, financial leverage makes the good times better and the bad times worse. As we analyze the firm's past, we can see how much leverage the firm employed and whether it amplified superior or inferior operating performance. But leverage has a forward-looking feature that the previous ratios lacked. Leverage increases the riskiness of the expected future cash flows. Levered firms commit themselves to making fixed payments to creditors, and the common equity holders must ultimately surrender control of the firm to the creditors if these payments cannot be met. The more financial leverage a firm has, the greater the chance that unexpected poor performance will be amplified to the point that the firm cannot pay its creditors. The likelihood of defaulting on amounts owed to creditors is known as *credit risk*. Many of the ratios we discuss in this section form the basis for the debt covenants between the firm and its creditors. In addition, a firm may have great long-term potential, but if it runs into short-term liquidity problems, it may not live to see the long term. For this reason, the analysis of credit risk also includes a detailed examination of the firm's ability to meet its obligations in the next year or two. Our Dupont decompositions examined how financial leverage contributes to the level and variability of ROE; now we want to assess the amount of credit risk that the leverage imposes on the equity holders.

In this section, we first discuss some summary measures of a firm's capital structure and short-term liquidity. We then discuss how these and other variables can be combined to make an explicit prediction of the likelihood of default.

Long-Term Capital Structure

A firm's capital structure—its mix of debt and equity—is the primary long-term driver of credit risk. The most common way to represent a firm's capital structure is the ratio of total debt to total common equity:

$$\text{Debt to Equity Ratio} = \frac{\text{Current Debt} + \text{Long-Term Debt}}{\text{Total Common Equity}}$$

This ratio is similar to the definition of financial leverage used in the advanced Dupont model. It differs in that we exclude preferred stock from the numerator, because preferred stockholders typically have fewer rights than debt holders in the case of a skipped payment. In the context of credit analysis, this ratio provides an overall indication of the extent of a firm's long-term credit commitments. Other things equal, higher debt to equity implies a higher probability of financial distress. The weakness of this ratio is that it fails to take into account the firm's ability to pay off its creditors. For example, firms with very stable and predictable cash flows, such as utilities and commercial banks, frequently run very high debt-to-equity ratios. This is because they know there is very little risk that they won't be able to meet their debt payments, and so a high debt-to-equity ratio is not necessarily an indication of financial distress for these firms.

Our next ratio is funds from operations to total debt, computed as

$$\text{Funds from Operations to Total Debt}$$

$$= \frac{\text{Funds from Operations}}{\text{average(Current Debt} + \text{Long-Term Debt)}}$$

Funds from operations represent the amount of working capital created or destroyed by the firm's operations (funds from operations are computed on the Cash Flow Analysis worksheet in eVal). This measure directly compares the amount of debt with the flow of funds that will be used to service the debt. Thus, this measure overcomes the shortcoming described above for the debt-to-equity ratio. One benchmark for this ratio is the interest rate that the company pays on its debt. Unless funds from operations can comfortably cover interest payments, the probability of default is high. A potential shortcoming of this ratio is that working capital can be tied up in illiquid current asset accounts, such as prepayments and inventories. In reality, it will be difficult to pay creditors with these assets. Thus, a common variant of this ratio is the cash from operations to debt ratio. This ratio backs the noncash working capital accounts out of the numerator to get cash from operations (CFO, also computed on the Cash Flow Analysis worksheet in eVal):

$$\text{CFO to Total Debt} = \frac{\text{Cash from Operations}}{\text{average(Current Debt + Long-Term Debt)}}$$

This ratio is a useful check, but you should not interpret it too literally. Growth firms frequently run negative cash from operations as they invest in working capital to generate sales growth. This growth is not necessarily a bad thing, but we need to make sure that the firm has the necessary plans in place to finance this growth.

Short-Term Liquidity

The above ratios focus on the firm's capital structure to assess the credit risk created by the firm's long-run financial obligations. Our final set of ratios focus on short-term liquidity. These ratios provide an indication of the firm's ability to meet its short-term cash commitments as they come due. The first ratio is the current ratio, measured as the ratio of current assets to current liabilities:

$$\text{Current Ratio} = \frac{\text{Total Current Assets}}{\text{Total Current Liabilities}}$$

Current assets represent the assets that the firm expects to convert to cash over the next 12 months. Current liabilities represent the obligations that the firm must pay with cash over the next 12 months. A current ratio greater than one indicates that the company has enough current assets to meet its current liabilities. An obvious shortcoming of this measure is that, in the event of financial distress, some of the current assets may not be readily converted into cash at their book values. If no one is buying the company's inventory, then it might not be worth its book value, and you can imagine the difficulty in converting prepaid rent back into cash. An alternative measure of the ability to meet current liabilities is the quick ratio:

$$\text{Quick Ratio} = \frac{\text{Cash and Marketable Securities + Receivables}}{\text{Total Current Liabilities}}$$

This ratio restricts the numerator to cash, marketable securities, and receivables, which are all likely to be converted into cash on short notice at close to their book values.

The next two ratios are called *interest coverage ratios*. These ratios provide an indication of the ability of a firm to cover its interest charges based on its ongoing operating profits. The first ratio uses EBIT (earnings before interest and taxes) in the numerator and interest expense in the denominator, while the second ratio replaces the numerator with EBITDA (earnings before interest, taxes, depreciation, and amortization):

$$\text{EBIT Interest Coverage} = \frac{\text{EBIT}}{\text{Interest Expense}}$$

$$\text{EBITDA Interest Coverage} = \frac{\text{EBITDA}}{\text{Interest Expense}}$$

The key difference between the ratios is the exclusion of depreciation and amortization expense from the numerator of the second ratio. The rationale for excluding depreciation and amortization is that it represents a noncash charge, and therefore does not reduce the amount of cash available to meet interest payments. On the other hand, a firm ultimately must replace its depreciable assets in order to stay in business, and so it also can be argued that inclusion of these charges provides a more meaningful indicator of long-term solvency.

Analyzing Kohl's Leverage

In the advanced Dupont decomposition for Kohl's, we noted that its average debt to equity of about 40 percent is much lower than Target Stores', which is about 100 percent. eVal reports a more detailed leverage analysis immediately following the turnover analysis on the Financial Ratio's worksheet. Applying this analysis to Kohl's versus Target indicates that Target has higher leverage and lower liquidity across all the measures of leverage discussed above. But remember that Kohl's financial statements omit over $1.5 billion of off-balance-sheet leverage associated with its operating leases. Inclusion of this debt on Kohl's balance sheet would cause debt to increase by over 100 percent and make Kohl's leverage ratios much more similar to Target's. This reminds us of an important limitation of leverage analysis that we mentioned at the start of this chapter. Managers can take advantage of accounting and disclosure requirements to manipulate common ratios. The use of operating leases to improve leverage and turnover ratios is a classic example.

Let's finish this section by summarizing what we learned about Kohl's relative to Target. Kohl's has higher margins, lower leverage, and similar turnover to Target. But once we adjust for the impact of Kohl's more aggressive use of operating leases, Kohl's has higher margins, similar leverage, and lower turnover than Target. Both companies are generating a healthy rate of return and these differences reflect Kohl's successful implementation of a product differentiation strategy versus Target's successful implementation of a cost leadership strategy.

5.10 MODELING CREDIT RISK

The analysis of leverage in the previous section gives us some interesting ratios, but it doesn't directly quantify the probability of default. Predicting the likelihood that a company will default on its debt is one of the most common uses of financial statement analysis. Every junior loan officer at every local bank requires financial statements from a commercial loan applicant and, if the loan is granted, then requires that financial statements be submitted on a regular basis in order to monitor the financial health of the company. The loan contract contains covenants that limit subsequent borrowing or equity distributions by the company and establishes periodic tests of financial health. If the company fails a health test, then the loan is declared to be in technical default and it becomes immediately due and payable in full. The idea is that, if the company starts to look sufficiently sick, the bank can rush back in and grab assets before they are all gone.

Being in technical default on a loan doesn't necessarily mean the firm will fail, or seek bankruptcy protection, but these events are highly correlated. In any case, defaulting on a loan has enormous consequences: legal fees skyrocket, suppliers stop granting credit, and customers can stop buying goods and services. Regardless of whether the firm can work out the default with its lenders or is forced into liquidation, default is a situation all parties wish to avoid.

Clearly, lenders and company management want to avoid default, but who beyond this cares about estimating the likelihood of default? Investors in corporate bonds also care about the probability of default. Bond rating agencies specialize in issuing credit ratings for corporate debt to help bond investors assess credit risk. More surprisingly, in certain contexts, the default probability can be an important input in pricing a firm's equity. If the firm defaults, the value of the equity is approximately zero, so the expected value of the equity is really the probability that it won't default times the value of the equity given that it continues as a going concern. For most firms, the probability of default is so low that we ignore default when valuing the equity. But for a firm with a high probability of default, default should not be ignored. You can think of an equity investment in a troubled firm as purchasing an option—the default probability is the likelihood that the option ends up out of the money, in which case the equity holders can abandon their claim of the firm. We often refer to this option as the abandonment option, and we discuss it in more detail in Chapter 12.

Estimating the Likelihood of Default

Broadly speaking, you should approach default forecasting in the same way as any other financial statement analysis topic: use the past financial statements to get a clear understanding of the company's past financial performance and current financial position, and then forecast how you believe the firm will evolve in the future. But there are a few twists. First, for the purposes of assessing the risk of default, we don't really care how successful a firm is beyond the point where we are confident that it will avoid default. The difference between good financial performance and great financial performance matters when forecasting the cash distributions to equity holders but makes little difference to the cash distributions that flow to creditors. All the creditors get is the agreed-upon interest and principal payments. Second, we have a very specific notion of what unsuccessful is: failure to make contractual interest and principal payments or a violation of debt covenants.

The long-term capital structure and short-term liquidity ratios discussed earlier give you a qualitative feel for the firm's credit risk. In this section, we attempt to attach specific probabilities of default to different levels of these and other ratios. Specifically, at the bottom of eVal's Ratio Analysis worksheet, there are six ratios that have been shown to be predictive of future default. Under each ratio, we report the historical frequency that firms with a ratio near this value defaulted on their debt during the subsequent five years. As a benchmark, over the past two decades, the probability that an industrial firm will default during a five-year period has been about 5 percent.

Before proceeding with our model of default probability, we want to issue a word of warning. The actual covenants found in a typical loan contract are extremely detailed. They spell out exactly how each ratio will be measured, what line items will be included and excluded over what time periods, and what the consequences are for violating different hurdle rates for each ratio. By comparison, the ratios below are simple and standardized. For example, as illustrated by our Kohl's example, these ratios ignore operating lease obligations that would typically be included in an actual covenant. You should consider the ratios below as a general guide for the types of ratios found in actual debt covenants, knowing that in practice the ratios are highly customized.

Figure 5.9 graphs each of the six ratios we use to build our model of default probability. The distribution of each ratio is computed for the entire sample of public firms between 1980 and 1999, excluding banks, insurance companies, and real estate companies (because their financial characteristics are so different from the majority of firms). For each ratio, we sort these data into 10 equal-sized groups, called *deciles*, and then plot the frequency that firms in each decile defaulted over the next five years.[3] Each graph also shows the cutoffs for each decile just above the axis; for instance, the value shown above deciles 5 and 6 is the median value of the ratio for the entire sample.

Profitability

For the purposes of predicting default, we measure profitability as the return on total assets before extraordinary items: (Net Income – Extraordinary Items)/Total Assets. Regardless of the firm's other financial characteristics, if it is sufficiently profitable, then it will generate enough cash each year to pay its creditors. But how much more likely is it for a firm to default on its debt when its profitability for the year is in the top 10 percent of all firms than if this ratio is in the bottom 10 percent? To get a feel for this, consider the top-left graph in Figure 5.9. As expected, the graph slopes down: firms with higher levels of profitability are less likely to default on their debt. To quantify this, the graph shows that the median firm has a return on total assets of 2 percent, and an implied default probability of about 4 percent. However, the bottom decile of firms have return on total assets of less than –45 percent and the odds that they will default in the next five years jumps to over 8 percent, while the top decile of firms have a return on total assets of 12 percent or more and a default probability of only 2 percent. In other words, it is over four times more likely that a firm in the bottom decile will default than a firm in the top decile.

---

[3] The default probabilities associated with different levels of each ratio are taken from Falkenstein, Boral, and Carty (May 2000).

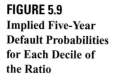

FIGURE 5.9
Implied Five-Year Default Probabilities for Each Decile of the Ratio

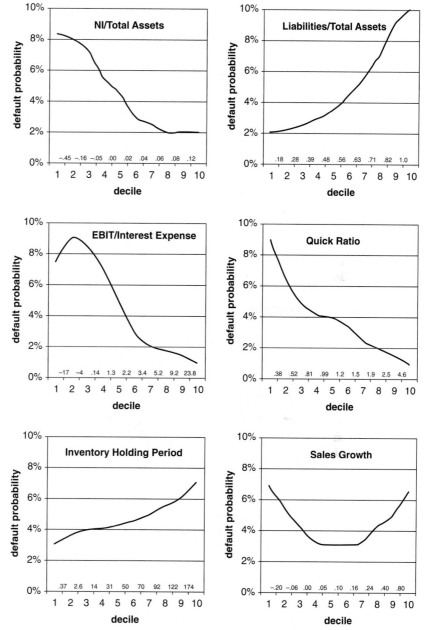

Leverage

The greater a firm's financial leverage, the less the cushion that is available if profits fail to generate the necessary cash flow to pay creditors. Because some firms have negative equity (and this would mess up our graph), Figure 5.9 plots

Total Liabilities/Total Assets rather than Debt/Equity, which is the more traditional measure of leverage. As a firm's leverage increases, the default rate increases steadily, starting at 2 percent for the firms in the lowest decile and increasing to 10 percent for firms in the highest decile.

Interest Coverage

Interest coverage is typically computed in a very precise and complicated way in most debt covenants. But for our purpose, we simply graph EBIT/Interest Expense. Between the second and sixth deciles, the slope of the interest coverage graph is very steep, showing that this ratio does a good job of discriminating winners from losers inside this region. The graph flattens out on the high end because it doesn't really make much difference if you are covering your interest eight times or 10 times. On the low end, the graph actually slopes up, which seems counterintuitive. But for firms with negative EBIT, an increase in interest expense lowers the EBIT/Interest ratio, which probably explains the unusual shape of the curve in the low region. As a crude benchmark, the median EBIT/Interest ratio is 2.2.

Liquidity

If you have enough cash, or assets that will soon become cash, you can surely pay your bills, hence the importance of liquidity ratios in credit analysis. As we discussed earlier, it is difficult to pay debt holders with inventory and certain other current assets, so the quick ratio (cash, marketable securities, and receivables divided by current liabilities) is the ratio we use to predict default. As Figure 5.9 shows, the quick ratio is predictive across the entire distribution, but the slope is steepest for the worst firms, those in the first two deciles. The default probability is 9 percent for firms with a quick ratio less than .38 but drops to 5 percent in the third decile, where firms have quick ratios between .52 and .81.

Inventory

The inventory holding period is less predictive than the previous measures, as seen by its modest slope in Figure 5.9. We include it nonetheless because it captures information that is very different from the previous default predictors. Previously, we described the inventory holding period as a measure of how efficiently the company manages its inventory. All else equal, a shorter holding period is better. In the context of default prediction, if the holding period is very long, then, besides suggesting inefficient inventory management, it may indicate an even more serious problem. It could be that the firm is having trouble selling its inventory and, consequently, may suffer financial distress in the future. Firms in the lowest decile of this ratio are probably service firms that have little or no inventory, so the ratio doesn't really apply to them; as a benchmark, the median inventory holding period is about 50 days.

Sales Growth

Unlike the previous graphs, sales growth has a U-shaped relation with default probability, as seen in the bottom-right graph in Figure 5.9. While this makes it more difficult to interpret, we include it because it captures information that is very different from the more traditional ratios. In the lowest deciles, sales are declining (i.e., negative sales growth), which is clearly a bad sign. But more curiously, the odds of default are high for firms with the highest sales growth. The intuition is that the set of firms with rapidly growing sales includes a greater proportion of firms with unprofitable sales (think of Overstock.com's). Further, such rapid sales growth is more likely to be financed by additional borrowing, further increasing the risk of default. As a benchmark, the median annual sales growth for the sample is 10 percent, and this corresponds to the lowest default risk. Sales declines of more than 20 percent or sales growth of more than 80 percent imply twice as high a probability of default.

Final Thoughts on Credit Risk

As a summary statistic, the Ratio Analysis worksheet reports the simple average of the default probabilities from the six individual ratios. As seen at the bottom of this sheet, Kohl's faces very little risk of default. They are profitable and have a relatively low amount of financial leverage, their quick ratio is well above 1.0, and they cover their interest expense more than 14 times. It isn't surprising, therefore, that the model estimates only a 3 percent chance that they will default in the next five years, well below the 5 percent overall average probability of default. Target Store's average default probability is slightly higher, at 3.6 percent, but it too is relatively small when compared to the population of default risk.

We stress once again that the ratios given here capture the spirit, but not the actual details, of the financial health tests specified in an actual debt contract. Further, if your forecasts imply that a poorly performing firm will turn around and be wildly profitable in the future, then the implied default probabilities based on its historical performance don't really mean much.

5.11   CONCLUSION

Ratio analysis is an indispensable part of equity valuation and analysis. Ratios are the tools that you will use to evaluate financial performance. If you make a career in financial analysis, then you'll soon be reeling off with reckless abandon the financial jargon we've introduced in this chapter. But you should always remember the important caveats of ratio analysis. First, you should make sure you know how a ratio is computed before you start interpreting it. Second, ratios don't provide answers; they only guide you in your search for answers. Unusual ratios tell you which part of a firm's Form 10-K you need to delve into to get your answers. Finally, management knows that you'll be computing all these ratios, and they'll go to great lengths to make sure these ratios look nice. Be particularly skeptical of ratios that management flaunts in their press releases and be vigilant in your search for evidence of creative accounting.

5.12 CASES, LINKS, AND REFERENCES

Cases

- Interpreting Margin and Turnover Ratios
- Netflix, Inc. (Questions 6 through 9)
- Overstock.com (Questions 7 through 9)
- Forecasting for the Love Boat: Royal Caribbean Cruises in 1998 (Part A)
- Can Salton Swing? (Questions 2 through 5)
- A Tale of Two Movie Theaters

Reference

- Falkenstein, E., A. Boral, and L. Carty. (2000). "RiskCalc for Private Companies: Moody's Default Model." Moody's Investor Service Global Credit Research. Available online at http://papers.ssrn.com/sol3/papers.cfm?abstract_id=236011.

CHAPTER SIX

Cash Flow Analysis

6.1 INTRODUCTION

One of the novel features of accrual accounting is that firms can report oodles of accounting earnings in periods when they generate very little cash. As a simple example, a firm selling its goods on credit records sales revenue but doesn't actually receive any cash unless and until the customer pays. More complicated transactions can create even larger gaps between accounting earnings and cash flows. This is why companies like Enron and WorldCom were able to report healthy earnings one quarter, then go broke in the next. Their earnings turned out to be based on unrealistic accounting assumptions rather than cash flows. The fact that earnings and cash flows are different isn't, by itself, a sure sign of trouble. As we discussed in Chapter 4, the accrual accounting process was designed to generate more timely measures of wealth creation than cash-basis accounting. Nonetheless, generating cash, not earnings, is the ultimate long-term goal of the corporation. Cash is what the firm needs to buy assets and pay creditors, and it is what investors ultimately want to receive as a return on their investment.

This chapter describes how eVal creates pro forma statements of cash flows based on eVal's standardized income statements and balance sheets. We then describe how to use the information in the resulting cash flow statements to evaluate the cash consequences of the company's operating, investing, and financing activities. Are they generating positive cash from their operations? Are they reinvesting operating cash flow? If not, what are they doing with it? We'll also help you to evaluate whether the cash flow implications of your forecasted financial statements make sense. There is no point in assuming that a firm will raise gobs of new cash through an equity issuance at an extremely high price if the company's stock is currently out of favor with Wall Street.

Next, we'll show you how eVal uses its standardized financial statements to compute the inputs into discounted cash flow valuation models. We defer the technical development of the models to Chapter 10; here we simply describe how to compute the main inputs and discuss how they can be interpreted as measures of wealth distribution.

Finally, we'll finish with an extended discussion of how we can study differences between earnings and cash flows to evaluate the quality of earnings. You may recall from Chapter 4 that accounting distortions cause earnings to temporarily deviate from cash flows but that these distortions usually reverse.

Examining differences between earnings and cash flows can help us to identify such distortions and forecast their reversals. But how do we distinguish legitimate accruals from illegitimate distortions? While the only sure method is to corner the company's chief accounting officer in a dark alley, we offer some less reliable but more pragmatic alternatives.

6.2 THE STATEMENT OF CASH FLOWS

We begin with a brief review of how to construct a statement of cash flows. If this task is completely new to you, then we recommend you consult an intermediate accounting textbook.

eVal's pro forma statement of cash flows sets out to reconcile the beginning and ending balances in the Operating Cash and Marketable Securities line item given on the eVal Financial Statements sheet (this is our definition of *cash* and is one commonly used by companies[1]). You can intuitively think of the statement of cash flows as a summary of all the transactions that ran through the company's checking account during the year. The statement of cash flows summarizes these transactions by dividing them into operating, investing, and financing activities. To illustrate the logic behind the construction of this statement, we start with the basic accounting equation: Assets = Liabilities + Equity. We next divide assets into cash and noncash assets, take the change in each item over the year (denoted by Δ), and rearrange to get

$$\Delta\text{Cash} = -\Delta(\text{Noncash Assets}) + \Delta\text{Liabilities} + \Delta\text{Equity}$$

The statement of cash flows explains the change in Cash on the left-hand side of the equation by decomposing the changes in Noncash Assets, Liabilities, and Equity on the right-hand side of the equation. The statement then organizes the reasons for changes in these accounts into three familiar categories: operating, investing, and financing. We have listed common transactions summarized in each of these categories in Figure 6.1. Operating cash flows increase with (i) decreases in receivables (which is reflected as a decrease in Noncash Assets in the above equation); (ii) increases in accounts payable (which is reflected as an increase in Liabilities in the above equation); and (iii) net income (which is reflected as an increase in the retained earnings component of Equity in the above equation). For example, consider

---

[1] We note that *Statement of Financial Accounting Standards 95,* "Statement of Cash Flows," requires a more restrictive definition of cash than the one used in eVal. The standard requires that only marketable securities representing short-term, highly liquid investments be classified as *cash equivalents.* We use a more general definition of cash equivalents that includes all marketable securities held as current assets. We do this both because these assets are typically readily convertible into cash and because some standardized financial statement databases do not distinguish between cash equivalents and other short-term marketable securities. As a practical matter, most companies with large "cash" balances put a sizeable portion in short-term marketable securities in order to generate more competitive returns than offered by bank accounts. For example, Microsoft has accumulated balances of cash and short-term investments of over $35 billion, and parks about $30 billion of this amount in marketable securities, including sizeable investments in corporate bonds and municipal securities.

FIGURE 6.1
Common
Transactions
Summarized in the
Statement of Cash
Flows

ΔCash	=	−ΔNoncash Assets	+ ΔLiabilities	+ ΔEquity
Operating Cash Flows	=	+↓Receivables	+↑Payables	+Net Income
Investing Cash Flows	=	−↑PP&E		
Financing Cash Flows	=		+↑Debt	−Dividends

the collection of cash on a credit sale that was made in a prior period. This transaction triggers a decrease in accounts receivable that is accompanied by an operating cash inflow. Investing cash flows and financing cash flows work similarly. Selling (purchasing) PP&E or issuing (retiring) debt increases (decreases) cash.

To see some of these computations in action, let's look at Kohl's pro forma statement of cash flows, shown on the Cash Flow Analysis sheet in eVal and reproduced in Figure 6.2. Note that the Operating section starts with Net Income at the top and ends with Cash from Operations at the bottom. In between these two amounts are all the adjustments necessary to convert from the accrual measure of performance, Net Income, to a cash flow measure of performance, Cash from Operations. The first adjustment, adding back Depreciation & Amortization,

FIGURE 6.2
Pro Forma Statement
of Cash Flows for
Kohl's

	A	B	C	D	E	F	G
1	**Cash Flow Analysis**	**($000)**					
2	Go To User's Guide	View Statement of Cash Flows					
3		View FCF Computations					
4	**Company Name**	Kohl's Corporation					
5							
6		Actual	Actual	Actual	Actual	Forecast	Forecas
7	**Fiscal Year End Date**	1/30/1999	1/29/2000	2/3/2001	2/2/2002	2/2/2003	2/2/200⁴
8	**Pro Forma Statement of Cash Flows**						
9							
10	Operating:						
11	Net Income	192,288	258,142	372,148	495,876	590,761	70
12	+Depreciation & Amortization	70,049	80,523	126,966	157,165	193,540	23
13	+Increase in Deferred Taxes	8,683	12,695	17,774	29,872	23,082	25
14	+Increase in Other Liabilities	5,108	4,886	8,609	6,680	9,813	1C
15	+Increase in Minority Interest	0	0	0	0	0	
16	+Preferred Dividends	0	0	0	0	0	
17	=Funds From Operations	276,106	364,246	525,517	689,493	817,195	96
18	-Increase in Receivables	(31,087)	(234,306)	(176,246)	(154,690)	(168,916)	(187
19	-Increase in Inventory	(101,572)	(177,077)	(208,851)	(195,017)	(242,137)	(26
20	-Increase in Other Current Assets	(9,904)	(21,573)	(21,779)	(28,562)	(18,932)	(2
21	+Increase in Accounts Payable	62,247	123,506	63,507	78,931	96,763	107
22	+Increase in Taxes Payable	10,090	15,383	48,972	12,158	25,275	28
23	+Increase in Other Curr. Liabilities	22,015	36,621	35,042	70,735	52,456	5
24	=Cash From Operations	227,895	106,900	266,162	473,048	561,705	68
25							
26	Investing:						
27	-Capital Expenditures	(253,411)	(508,468)	(500,480)	(630,209)	(637,983)	(725
28	-Increase in Investments	0	0	0	0	0	
29	-Purchases of Intangibles	5,200	5,200	5,200	5,200	(1,887)	(2
30	-Increase in Other Assets	(10,216)	(136,737)	(16,824)	(64,441)	(51,872)	(5
31	=Cash From Investing	(258,427)	(640,005)	(512,104)	(689,450)	(691,742)	(784
32							
33	Financing:						
34	+Increase in Debt	234	279,137	233,067	287,189	224,664	249
35	-Dividends Paid on Preferred	0	0	0	0	0	
36	+Increase in Pref. Stock	0	0	0	0	0	
37	-Dividends Paid on Common	0	0	0	0	0	
38	+/-Net Issuance of Common Stock	15,731	264,582	144,988	93,091	(26,714)	(7:
39	+/-Clean Surplus Plug (Ignore)	0	0	0	0	0	
40	=Cash From Financing	15,965	543,719	378,055	380,280	197,951	176
41							
42	Net Change in Cash	(14,567)	10,514	132,113	163,878	67,914	75
43	+ Beginning Cash Balance	44,161	29,594	40,108	172,221	336,099	40⁴
44	= Ending Cash Balance	29,594	40,108	172,221	336,099	404,013	479

seems obvious because these are noncash expenses. But note that our cash flow equation is still doing the work. Depreciation & Amortization reduce Net Income and noncash assets by the same amount. By subtracting the change in noncash assets, our equation is adding back the amount by which depreciation and amortization reduced both noncash assets and Net Income. Cash is only consumed when noncash assets are initially purchased with cash, and these cash outflows are shown in the Investing section.[2] After Depreciation & Amortization, there are adjustments for a few other noncurrent operating accounts, leading to the subtotal Funds from Operations. This subtotal is the amount of working capital generated from operations; it makes no distinction between cash and other noncash sources of working capital. The final adjustments are for changes in all the noncash working capital accounts, leading to cash from operations of just over $473 million for Kohl's in fiscal 2001.

The Operating section of the cash flow statement is the trickiest one; the line items in the Cash from Investing and Cash from Financing sections are pretty straightforward. Note that eVal displays a cash outflow as a negative number. For example, in the most recent year, Kohl's invested $689 million, mostly in capital expenditures on PP&E. They paid for these investments partly with the $473 million of internally generated Cash from Operations and partly by raising $380 million in debt and equity financing, as shown in the Cash from Financing section. The net effect of Kohl's operating, investing, and financing activities is a Net Change in Cash of approximately $164 million in fiscal 2001.

The pro forma statements of cash flows shown in eVal are unlikely to exactly match the statements in the company's actual published financial statements. One reason is that our definition of cash may not match the company's definition (as is the case with Kohl's, which excludes certain marketable securities from its definition). A second reason is that we construct the cash flow statements based only on the information from the standardized income statements and balance sheets, so our classification of items into operating, investing, and financing activities may differ from the company's. The company's published statement of cash flows is usually the most accurate source of information about past cash activity. We construct pro forma statements for both the past and the forecasted future so that you can see a time series of cash flow data computed on a consistent basis.

6.3   EVALUATING A FIRM'S PAST CASH FLOWS

The statement of cash flows is the starting point for evaluating the firm's past cash flows. Recall from Chapter 2 that the MD&A section of Form 10-K includes a required discussion of the firm's liquidity and capital resources. It is useful to

---

[2] You should be aware of a classification issue related to Depreciation & Amortization in eVal. If the company lumps these expenses in with another line item, such as Selling, General, and Administrative or Cost of Goods Sold, then most standardized data providers will likely code Depreciation and Amortization as zero. The effect of this misclassification on the statement of cash flows is to understate cash from operations and overstate cash from investing.

review this discussion and have it close at hand while conducting your cash flow analysis. You should then work your way through each of the three sections of the statement of cash flows.

Evaluating Cash from Operations

The first section reports cash from operating activities. The first port of call is to see whether cash from operations is positive or negative. Positive cash from operations is generally good news. The company's operations are generating cash flow that can be either reinvested in the business or paid out to debt and equity holders. We'll find out exactly what the firm is doing with its cash flow in the next two sections. Negative cash from operations is a more mixed signal. One reason for negative cash from operations is that the company's operations are performing poorly. To see whether this is the case, check the company's net income. If net income is also negative, then poor operating performance is a likely explanation. In this case, you need to establish whether the company is likely to be able to turn its operating performance around, and whether it has sufficient financial resources to complete the turnaround. A second reason for negative cash from operations is that the company is investing in working capital. Investments in working capital, such as receivables and inventory, reduce cash from operations but do not reduce net income. That is why they are subtracted from net income to arrive at cash from operations. Investments in working capital can be both good and bad. If a company is experiencing healthy growth in its operating activities, then we expect working capital to grow at a corresponding rate. This is the good side of growth in working capital. On the other hand, if working capital is growing more rapidly than the company's operating activities, then this is usually a bad signal. For example, if a company's products are not selling, inventory will increase, and will probably have to be written down. This is the bad side of growth in working capital. But growth in working capital without accompanying growth in operations is not always a bad signal. For example, assume that a company implements a successful new credit program for its customers. Receivables will increase even if sales are flat, as customers take advantage of the new credit program. But if the interest rate charged on the credit plan is sufficient to provide the company with a healthy return on its incremental investment in receivables, the plan is justified.

There are a couple of other things to check before moving on from the operating section. First, if there is a big gap between net income and cash from operations, you should make sure that you understand what is driving this gap. Recall from Chapter 4 that the difference between net income and cash flows represents accounting accruals, and this is where accounting distortions are most likely to lurk. We'll talk more about how to identify accounting distortions in Section 6.6. For now, you should just realize that a big gap raises a red flag about earnings quality. What is a big gap? As a rule of thumb, if the difference between net income and cash from operations is greater than 5 percent of total assets, then you should follow the advice in Section 6.6.

The second thing to check is that cash from operations is not distorted by unusual one-time items. For example, a big one-off tax payment can temporarily depress operating cash flows. Or a cash receipt from the settlement of a major legal dispute can temporarily inflate cash flows. It is useful to separate these one-time items from recurring cash flows to evaluate the cash-generating ability of the firm's operations.

Evaluating Cash from Investing

The second section of the statement of cash flows reports cash from investing activities. While cash from operating activities is usually positive, cash from investing activities is usually negative. This is because most firms require ongoing capital expenditures to maintain their operating activities. For example, a trucking company must buy new trucks to replace spent ones that are taken out of service. A useful way to check whether a company is increasing or decreasing its investment base is to compare its capital expenditures in the investing section to the depreciation add-back in the operating section. If capital expenditures are greater than depreciation, then the company is growing its capital base. Growth in a company's capital base can be evaluated in much the same way as growth in working capital. If the growth in the capital base is accompanied by profitable growth in the firm's operations, all is usually well. But growth in the capital base that is not accompanied by profitable growth in the firm's operations should raise a red flag. Either the company is using its capital less efficiently or accounting distortions are inflating capital and earnings. We'll provide you with more advice for identifying such distortions in Section 6.6.

Apart from capital expenditures, you'll also find acquisitions and other investments in this section. For acquisitions, you should follow up and make sure that the acquisitions make good economic sense. Do the earnings of the acquired company justify the price that was paid for the acquisition? All too often, companies generate healthy cash flows from their existing operations, only to squander them by overpaying for acquisitions. Some managers would rather build an empire for themselves than return cash to debt and equity holders. For other investments, you should make sure you understand exactly what these investments are. They could be low-risk investments, such as treasury bonds. At the other extreme, they could represent investments in shady off-balance-sheet entities that could disappear overnight (as was the case with Enron).

As a final check on the investing section of the statement of cash flows, you should see whether the sum of operating and investing cash flows is positive or negative. Net operating and investing cash flows are frequently referred to as *free cash flow*. This is the cash flow that is free to be distributed to the debt and equity holders. If free cash flow is negative, then the company has to either dip into cash reserves or raise new capital to finance its operations. In this case, you should check that the company's operations have sufficient potential to warrant additional infusions of capital. If not, the company is unlikely to survive.

Evaluating Cash from Financing

The third and final section of the statement of cash flows reports cash from financing activities. This section tells us what the firm has been doing with its free cash flow. If free cash flow is positive, then the firm is probably distributing free cash flow to debt and/or equity holders. Such cash distributions are what give debt and equity securities value in the first place, so it is a good sign to see that a company is rewarding its investors by distributing free cash flow. If free cash flow is negative, then the firm is probably funding the shortfall by issuing new debt and equity securities. If the company is just issuing equity, this is a sign that there is considerable uncertainty about its ability to produce positive free cash flow in the near future.

Note that we qualified our statements about the relation between free cash flow and financing activities using the word *probably.* The reason for this qualification is that a firm can use its cash reserves to bridge differences between free cash flow and cash from financing activities. For example, firms with positive (negative) free cash flow can add to (subtract from) their cash reserves rather than engaging in financing activities. The last few lines of the statement of cash flows indicate whether this is the case. If a firm is funding negative free cash flows by using up its cash reserves, you should determine how long it can continue to do this before it runs out of cash. The ratio of negative free cash flows to cash reserves is termed the *burn rate;* the reciprocal of the burn rate provides an estimate of how long it will be before cash runs out. On the other hand, if a firm is squirreling away positive free cash flows as cash reserves, you should understand management's motives. Are they too selfish to pay this money back to investors? Are they empire builders who are planning value-destroying acquisitions? Firms that try to sell themselves as "growth" stocks are particularly reluctant to pay cash back to investors, because this basically amounts to an admission that they have no growth opportunities. Be wary of managers who hoard free cash flow.

Evaluating Kohl's Past Cash Flows

We'll now apply the above discussion to the evaluation of Kohl's cash flows. You should have a copy of the Liquidity and Capital Resources section of Kohl's MD&A from its fiscal 2001 Form 10-K close at hand. This document may be accessed from Kohl's 2001 Data and Resources menu item under the eVal menu in eVal, and the relevant section starts on page 11 of the document. Recall that eVal's pro forma statements of cash flows can be accessed by clicking the View Cash Flow Analysis button on eVal's User's Guide sheet. This cash flow analysis is reproduced in Figure 6.2. It is also important to remember that the cash flow amounts reported by eVal will differ somewhat from the corresponding numbers reported in the statement of cash flows reported in Kohl's Form 10-K. This is because eVal computes cash flows using Kohl's standardized financial statements. The main difference between the eVal cash flows and the Form 10-K cash flows is that eVal treats all short-term investments as cash equivalents, while the Form 10-K uses a narrower definition of cash equivalents.

Let's start with the operating section of eVal's cash flow analysis. Both cash from operations (at the bottom of this section) and net income (at the top of this section) are positive and have been growing over the last two years. Kohl's operating activities are generating a healthy stream of cash flows. Note that cash from operations is somewhat lower than net income in fiscal 2001 ($473,048 versus $495,676). Inspection of the other line items in the operating section indicates that Kohl's receivables and inventories are increasing, using up large amounts of cash in the process. These increases represent potential red flags. However, Kohl's discussion of liquidity and capital resources suggests that these increases are primarily due to the expansion of the company's proprietary credit card program and the opening of new stores. It appears that these increases represent an integral part of Kohl's healthy growth strategy.

Turning next to the investing section of the statement of cash flows, we see that Kohl's has been incurring significant capital expenditures in the past few years. Capital expenditures amounted to $630,209 in fiscal 2001. From the operating section, we see that depreciation and amortization is only $157,165. Kohl's is therefore aggressively growing its capital base. Page 9 of the Form 10-K indicates that Kohl's opened 62 new stores during fiscal 2001, increasing its total store count to 382. Moreover, the discussion of liquidity and capital resources on page 12 indicates that Kohl's plans capital expenditures of approximately $740,000 in fiscal 2002, to support the opening of another 70 stores. Is this explosive growth cause for concern? Recall from Chapter 5 that Kohl's is generating a healthy return on its existing operating assets. As long as Kohl's can continue to generate a similar return on its new investment, this growth should increase firm value. But we need to keep a watchful eye on future profitability. Firms often grow too big too quickly, resulting in diminishing marginal returns to new investment. The only other significant action in the investing section is an increase of $64,441 in "other assets" for fiscal 2001. A quick check of the as-reported balance sheet on page F-6 of Form 10-K reveals that this is due to the acquisition of favorable lease rights. Kohl's leases many of its retail locations, so the acquisition of these lease rights is an integral part of its growth strategy. Kohl's used a total of $689,450 cash in its investing activities during fiscal 2001. Given that it only generated $473,048 of cash from operations, free cash amounts to –$216,402. The remainder of the statement of cash flows will tell us how Kohl's financed this shortfall.

The financing section of Kohl's statement of cash flows indicates that Kohl's generated $380,280 cash from financing in fiscal 2001. Most of this financing came from increased debt, with the remainder coming from the issuance of equity. The discussion of liquidity and capital resources on page 12 of Kohl's Form 10-K identifies the source of this financing, indicating that Kohl's issued $300,000 worth of 6.3 percent unsecured notes in March 2001. The fact that Kohl's is issuing large amounts of debt indicates that its creditors expect it to generate a healthy stream of operating cash flows moving forward. Finally, we see that Kohl's cash from financing of $380,280 outstrips its negative free cash flow of –$216,402 by $163,878. Kohl's adds this amount to its cash reserves, increasing them from

$172,221 to $336,099. These reserves are no doubt earmarked to help fund Kohl's aggressive growth strategy for 2002.

6.4   EVALUATING A FIRM'S FUTURE CASH FLOWS

After you forecast the company's future income statements and balance sheets, you get the future statements of cash flow for free. eVal constructs these pro forma statements using the procedure described in Section 6.2. You should evaluate the forecasts of future cash flows in much the same way that you evaluated the past cash flows. In addition, you should make sure that the future cash flow forecasts make economic sense. For example, it is unrealistic to think that a firm could finance a long string of negative future operating cash flows by issuing debt. Creditors usually like to see a healthy stream of future cash to facilitate the timely repayment of debt.

As before, begin your evaluation with forecasted cash from operations. If it is significantly negative for the indefinite future, you should ask yourself whether the firm is really going to continue its operations. It doesn't make sense to continue losing money forever. Either the firm will ultimately generate positive operating cash flows or it will cease operations. You need to figure out which alternative is more likely and then go and adjust your forecast financial statements accordingly. Even if cash from operations is only forecast to be negative for a few years, you still need to ask yourself whether the company will be able to raise sufficient financing to keep afloat until positive operating cash flows arrive. While you might think that cash flows will be huge and positive in 10 years, other investors may disagree. Unless you are personally prepared to provide the firm's entire financing needs in the meantime, it may not survive long enough to reach that glorious day. Your evaluation of forecasted cash from investing should ask similar questions. If you have forecast that the firm is going to have significant capital expenditures, you should make sure that financing is likely to be available. If the firm's operations are forecast to be unprofitable, the firm may have a tough time convincing investors to provide financing to fund additional growth.

Finally, if there is any cash left after your forecasted cash from operations and cash from investing, what do your forecasts imply about where the money will go? Will the firm pay down debt or will it increase dividends? How do the implied financing cash flows compare with the firm's historical activity, and with any management communications about their plans for the future? It would be silly, for instance, to make forecasts that imply that the firm will pay large dividends in the near future when the firm has publicly stated that it has no intention of doing so. You should be particularly wary of firms with a record of wasting free cash flow on unsuccessful projects. Make sure that you don't inadvertently assume that such firms will stop this behavior and start graciously paying out all of their free cash flow as dividends.

6.5 CONSTRUCTING DCF VALUATION INPUTS

Chapter 10 covers valuation models, one of which is the discounted cash flow (DCF) model. Unfortunately, the cash flows reported in the statement of cash flows do not correspond exactly with the inputs to the DCF model. For this reason, eVal provides a separate set of *free cash flow* computations right after the statement of cash flows on the Cash Flow Analysis sheet. Recall from our discussion in Section 6.3 that the sum of cash from operations and cash from investing can be loosely referred to as *free cash flow*. The key difference between this measure of free cash flow and the measures of free cash flow used in DCF valuation models is that valuation models tailor their cash flow metrics to the claim(s) being valued. For example, if we are valuing equity, we only want to consider free cash flow that is distributed to equity holders. But the statement of cash flows measure of free cash flow includes all free cash flow, regardless of whether it is paid to equity holders, paid to debt holders, or held in cash reserves. The claims most commonly valued are common equity and the total for all investors (debt plus preferred stock plus equity). We present computations for the corresponding measures of free cash flow below.

Free Cash Flow to Common Equity

The *free cash flow to common equity* is simply the net cash distributions to common equity holders. If this amount is negative in a particular year, it means that common equity holders have contributed more cash to the firm than they have received. This is the input to the most basic valuation model—the DCF to common equity—alluded to in Chapters 1 and 4. We can compute this amount several different ways, and, if we do so properly, we will always get the same answer. Because different people prefer different computation methods, eVal computes the amount in all the common ways and demonstrates that they are, indeed, the same. Figure 6.3 shows eVal's free cash flow to common equity computations for Kohl's.

The first method of computation uses the clean surplus relation, as discussed in Chapter 4. Free cash flow to common equity is computed as net income less retained income. The computation is illustrated below using Kohl's fiscal 2001 results.

$$\text{Free Cash Flow to Common Equity} = \text{Net Income} \\ - \text{Increase in Common Equity}$$

$$-93{,}091 = 495{,}676 - 588{,}767$$

In this case, common equity holders invested an additional $93,091 in the company, so the net distribution to common equity is negative.[3]

---

[3] If you are industrious enough to try and trace these amounts to Kohl's Form 10-K for fiscal 2001, you will find that the statement of cash flows actually only lists $36,128 of proceeds from the issuance of common shares. Further investigation of the 10-K reveals that these proceeds come from the exercise of employee stock options, and the difference of $56,963 represents the tax benefit on the exercise of the options. This is a good example of the type of situation we alluded to earlier, where we have misplaced some cash flow in our pro forma statement of cash flow in eVal, because it is prepared mechanically from summary balance sheet and income statement data.

FIGURE 6.3

Free Cash Flow to Common Equity for Kohl's

	A	B	C	D	E	F
1	**Cash Flow Analysis**	**($000)**				
2	Go To User's Guide	View Statement of Cash Flows				
3		View FCF Computations				
4	Company Name	Kohl's Corporation				
5						
6		Actual	Actual	Actual	Actual	Forecast
7	Fiscal Year End Date	1/30/1999	1/29/2000	2/3/2001	2/2/2002	2/2/2003
47	Free Cash Flow to Common Equity					
48						
49	Net Income	192,266	258,142	372,148	495,676	590,761
50	- Increase in Common Equity	(207,997)	(522,724)	(517,136)	(588,767)	(564,047)
51	+/-Clean Surplus Plug (Ignore)	0	0	0	0	0
52	=Free Cash Flow to Common Equity	(15,731)	(264,582)	(144,988)	(93,091)	26,714
53						
54	Computation based on SCF:					
55	+Cash From Operations	227,895	106,800	266,162	473,048	561,705
56	-Increase in Operating Cash	14,567	(10,514)	(132,113)	(163,878)	(67,914)
57	+Cash From Investing	(258,427)	(640,005)	(512,104)	(689,450)	(691,742)
58	+Increase in Debt	234	279,137	233,067	287,189	224,664
59	-Dividends Paid on Preferred	0	0	0	0	0
60	+Increase in Preferred Stock	0	0	0	0	0
61	+/-Clean Surplus Plug (Ignore)	0	0	0	0	0
62	=Free Cash Flow to Common Equity	(15,731)	(264,582)	(144,988)	(93,091)	26,714
63						
64	Financing Flows:					
65	+Dividends Paid	0	0	0	0	0
66	-Net Issuance of Common Stock	(15,731)	(264,582)	(144,988)	(93,091)	26,714
67	= Free Cash Flow to Common Equity	(15,731)	(264,582)	(144,988)	(93,091)	26,714

Now we'll show you how we can arrive at the same answer using the amounts already computed in our statement of cash flows. One method is to back into free cash flow to common equity by taking free cash flow from the firm's operating and investing activities and then subtracting cash that is retained in the firm or paid out to debt holders. We start with the cash from operations and then subtract the increase in the cash balance. This adjusts for any cash flow that was retained in the firm. Next, add cash from investing and add (subtract) any cash that was received from (distributed to) debt or preferred stockholders. What's left must have been paid out to common equity holders. You will note that the answer on the Cash Flow Analysis sheet is exactly the –$93,091 we computed above.

The final computation is the most intuitive. Simply look in the Financing section of the statement of cash flows and pick out the two items that are cash transactions with the common equity holders—Dividends Paid and Net Issuance of Common Stock. Once again we see that common equity holders invested –$93,091 in Kohl's during the year.

You shouldn't be too distressed that Kohl's free cash flow to common equity is negative; this is often the case for healthy growing firms. Of course, you wouldn't want this number to stay negative forever. A quick rule for understanding whether a firm is growing healthily can be derived from the clean surplus relation discussed above. We can rewrite the clean surplus relation as

$$FCF = CSE_{beg}\left(\frac{Net\ Income}{CSE_{beg}} - \frac{CSE_{end} - CSE_{beg}}{CSE_{beg}}\right)$$

$$= CSE_{beg}(ROE - \%\ Growth\ in\ CSE)$$

where

FCF = Free cash flow to common equity

CSE = Common shareholders' equity at either the beginning (beg) or end of the period

ROE = Return on beginning common shareholders' equity

This rule tells us that FCF to common equity holders will be negative whenever the return on equity is less than the growth rate in common equity. But as long as the return on equity is sufficient to provide a competitive rate of return to equity holders, and is expected to stay that way, the firm's operations are healthy and growth should add value.[4]

We have already touched on the pluses and minuses of free cash flow to common equity as a measure of firm performance and equity value. It is a measure of wealth distribution, not a measure of wealth creation. As such, in any given period, it is probably a poor performance measure. In the long run, however, this is what the common equity holders actually get as a return on their investment. In this sense, it is final arbiter of equity value.

Free Cash Flow to Investors

Free cash flow to all investors is the net amount of cash distributed by the firm to all providers of capital: debt holders, preferred stockholders, and common equity holders. This is the primary input to the traditional DCF model. The traditional DCF model also incorporates another wrinkle. For reasons that aren't readily apparent, the cash savings from the tax deductibility of interest payments on debt are excluded from *free cash flow to investors*. The reason for their exclusion is not that these tax savings don't increase free cash flow—they do. Rather, it is because there is a tradition of valuing these cash inflows by reducing the discount rate that is applied to all other cash flows. The tradition involves the computation of another beast called the *weighted average cost of capital,* which we'll get to in Chapter 9. This all seems unnecessarily convoluted to us, but who are we to argue with tradition? eVal reports computations using this traditional method so that you can communicate with brainwashed b-school graduates who don't know any different. But we can assure you that you would get exactly the same valuation if you instead use the more direct approach of including these cash savings in free cash flow and leaving the discount rate alone.

As with the free cash flow to common equity, we can compute free cash flow to all investors a number of different ways and always get the same answer. Figure 6.4 shows eVal's computations of free cash flow to investors for Kohl's.

The first computation of free cash flow to investors makes use of the relation between net operating income and changes in net operating assets, and is analogous to the clean surplus relation that we used to determine the free cash flow to

---

[4] Remember that we have to adjust return on equity for accounting distortions before establishing whether it represents a healthy rate of return. Refer back to Chapter 4 for details.

FIGURE 6.4
**Free Cash Flow
to All Investors
Computation for
Kohl's**

	A	B	C	D	E	F	
	A3	▼	=				
1	**Cash Flow Analysis**	**($000)**					
2	Go To User's Guide	View Statement of Cash Flows					
3		View FCF Computations					
4	**Company Name**	Kohl's Corporation					
5							
6		Actual	Actual	Actual	Actual	Forecast	Fore
7	**Fiscal Year End Date**	1/30/1999	1/29/2000	2/3/2001	2/2/2002	2/2/2003	2/2/
70	**Free Cash Flow to All Investors**						
71							
72	Net Operating Income	206,028	276,207	402,467	531,216	635,635	
73	- Increase in Net Operating Assets	(208,231)	(801,861)	(750,203)	(875,956)	(788,712)	(8
74	+/-Clean Surplus Plug (Ignore)	0	0	0	0	0	
75	=Free Cash Flow to Investors	(2,203)	(525,654)	(347,716)	(344,740)	(153,016)	(1
76							
77	Computation based on SCF:						
78	Cash From Operations	227,895	106,800	266,162	473,048	561,705	6
79	-Increase in Operating Cash	14,567	(10,514)	(132,113)	(163,878)	(67,914)	
80	+Cash from Investing	(258,427)	(640,005)	(512,104)	(683,450)	(631,742)	(7
81	+Interest Expense	22,672	29,470	43,332	57,351	72,510	
82	-Tax Shield on Interest	(8,910)	(11,405)	(18,393)	(21,811)	(27,576)	
83	+/-Clean Surplus Plug (Ignore)	0	0	0	0	0	
84	=Free Cash Flow to Investors	(2,203)	(525,654)	(347,716)	(344,740)	(153,016)	(1
85							
86	Financing Flows:						
87	+Dividends on Common Stock	0	0	0	0	0	
88	+Interest Expense	22,672	29,470	43,332	57,351	72,510	
89	-Tax Shield on Interest	(8,910)	(11,405)	(18,393)	(21,811)	(27,576)	
90	+Dividends on Preferred Stock	0	0	0	0	0	
91	-Net Issuance of Common Stock	(15,731)	(264,582)	(144,388)	(93,091)	26,714	
92	-Net Issuance of Debt	(234)	(279,137)	(233,067)	(287,189)	(224,664)	(2
93	-Net Issuance of Preferred Stock	0	0	0	0	0	
94	=Free Cash Flow to Investors	(2,203)	(525,654)	(347,716)	(344,740)	(153,016)	(1
95							
96	Traditional Computation of FCF:						
97	EBIT	337,863	448,275	651,315	849,375	1,017,108	1,2
98	-Taxes on EBIT	(133,393)	(174,375)	(251,959)	(325,899)	(390,116)	(4
99	+Increase in Deferred Taxes	8,683	12,695	17,774	29,972	23,082	
100	= NOPLAT	213,153	286,595	417,130	553,548	650,074	1
101	+Depreciation & Amortization	70,043	88,323	126,386	157,165	193,540	2
102	+Minority Interest in Earnings	0	0	0	0	0	
103	+Non-Operating Income (Loss)	1,558	2,307	3,131	7,240	8,703	
104	+Other Income (Loss)	0	0	0	0	0	
105	+Ext. Items & Disc. Ops.	0	0	0	0	0	
106	=Gross Cash Flow	284,760	377,425	547,247	718,353	852,317	1,0
107	-Increase in Working Capital	(33,644)	(267,360)	(391,468)	(380,323)	(323,404)	(3
108	-Capital Expenditures	(253,411)	(508,468)	(500,480)	(630,205)	(637,383)	(7
109	-Increase in Investments	0	0	0	0	0	
110	-Purchases of Intangibles	5,200	5,200	5,200	5,200	(1,887)	
111	-Increase in Other Assets	(10,216)	(136,737)	(16,824)	(64,441)	(51,872)	
112	+Increase in Minority Interest	0	0	0	0	0	
113	+Increase in Other Liabilities	5,108	4,886	8,609	6,680	9,813	
114	+/-Clean Surplus Plug (Ignore)	0	0	0	0	0	
115	=Free Cash Flow to Investors	(2,203)	(525,654)	(347,716)	(344,740)	(153,016)	(1
116							

common equity above. We simply redefine net income as net operating income and book value of common equity as net operating assets. Recall from Chapter 5 how the advanced Dupont decomposition defines net operating income and net operating assets by isolating the income statement and balance sheet items that are associated with the firm's operating and investing activities. We can use the same approach to calculate the free cash flow generated by the firm's operating and investing activities. Define net operating income and net operating assets as follows (and as given in Chapter 5):

Net Operating Income (NOI)
= (EBIT + Nonoperating Income) * (1 − tax)
− Minority Interest in Earnings + Other Income (Loss)
− Extraordinary Items and Discontinued Operations

where the effective tax rate (tax) = Income Taxes/EBT, and

Net Operating Assets (NOA)
= Total Assets − Accounts Payable − Income Taxes Payable
− Other Current Liabilities − Other Liabilities − Deferred Taxes
− Minority Interest

Net operating income is defined before the tax savings accruing from the tax deductibility of interest on debt. We simply apply the firm's effective tax rate to earnings before interest and taxes, thus deducting how much tax the firm would have had to pay assuming no debt. As mentioned above, we'll incorporate any tax savings by reducing the discount rate in the valuation computation. Using Kohl's fiscal 2001 computations as an illustration, we can now write

Free Cash Flow to Investors = Net Operating Income
− Increase in Net Operating Assets
$$-344{,}740 = 531{,}216 - 875{,}956$$

Intuitively, this calculation starts with operating income that is available to all providers of capital and then deducts all amounts that are reinvested in the firm as opposed to being distributed to capital providers.

The next two methods of computing free cash flow to investors make use of measures already computed in the statement of cash flows. The first of these methods starts with cash from operating and investing activities, subtracts cash that is retained in the firm, adds back interest expense, and subtracts out the tax savings from interest. The reason that interest is added back is that interest is a cash flow to debt holders and not an operating expense. Accountants don't appreciate this distinction and so leave interest expense in the operating section rather than shifting it to the financing section of the statement of cash flows. The tax savings of interest are added back to conform to "the tradition." The next method takes the most direct route: it simply picks the appropriate cash flows out of the financing section of the statement of cash flows, again correcting for the misclassification of interest and the subtraction of tax savings on interest. Note that in all cases we get −$344,740 of free cash flow to investors for Kohl's fiscal year 2001.

There is one more common method of computing free cash flow to investors, which we label the "traditional" approach, because it is the recipe used in most finance textbooks. This approach starts with EBIT (i.e., earnings before interest and taxes) and then replicates many of the adjustments found in the operating and investing sections of the statement of cash flows. The traditional folk derived this method long before firms were required to report a statement of cash flows, and many of them still prefer to use this method rather than using the statement of cash flows as a shortcut. The general logic behind this approach is to start with EBIT, adjust for taxes, add back noncash charges (e.g., depreciation), subtract increases in working capital, and subtract investment expenditures. Note that we don't have to worry about adding back interest expense or subtracting tax savings on interest. This is because we started out with EBIT, which is before interest, and then applied the effective tax rate to EBIT, essentially ignoring the tax savings from interest. Adding back deferred taxes to the result of the above computation gives us *NOPLAT*, which stands for *net operating profit less adjusted taxes*. If you get out a large piece of paper and pour a tall cup of coffee, you can reconcile this last method with all the other more direct methods. The pieces are all the same; the jigsaw is just put together in a different order.

As with the free cash flow to common equity, we shouldn't be too concerned that Kohl's free cash flow to investors has been consistently negative. This is not uncommon for growing firms. It basically says that they are investing more than they are generating in operating cash flow. Following the logic from the previous subsection, a quick rule for understanding whether a firm is growing healthily is

$$FCF = NOA_{beg}\left(\frac{\text{Net Operating Income}}{NOA_{beg}} - \frac{NOA_{end} - NOA_{beg}}{NOA_{beg}} \right)$$

$$= NOA_{beg}(RNOA - \% \text{ Growth in NOA})$$

where

FCF = Free cash flow to all investors

NOA = Net operating assets at either the beginning (beg) or end of the period

RNOA = Net operating income divided by beginning net operating assets

This rule tells us that FCF to investors will be negative whenever the return on net operating assets (RNOA) is less than the growth rate in net operating assets (NOA). But as long as the RNOA is sufficient to provide a competitive rate of return to investors, and is expected to stay that way, the firm's operations are healthy and growth should add value.

6.6 CASH FLOWS AND EARNINGS QUALITY ANALYSIS

Recall from Chapter 4 that accounting distortions arise from imperfections in the accrual accounting process. Accrual accounting involves the estimation and recognition of future benefits and obligations in the current financial statements. But many accrual accounting estimates are subject to measurement error. This error can arise from limitations of GAAP, unintentional managerial forecasting errors, and intentional managerial manipulation. The examples we constructed in Section 4.4 of Chapter 4 indicate that accounting distortions often lead to systematic patterns in accruals and earnings. For example, temporarily aggressive accounting causes accruals and earnings to be temporarily high, while temporarily conservative accounting causes accruals and earnings to be temporarily low. Recall that accruals are simply the difference between earnings and cash flows. Accruals also manifest themselves as changes in assets and liabilities on the balance sheet. Now that we are armed with a good understanding of accruals, we are in a position to use this knowledge to help us identify accounting distortions. We refer to this process as earnings quality analysis, because we are primarily concerned with the impact of accounting distortions on earnings-based performance measures.

The main goal of earnings quality analysis is to distinguish between "good" accruals, which represent accurate estimates of expected future benefits and obligations, and "bad" accruals, which do not represent future benefits and obligations and are thus accounting distortions. There are two simple *red flags* that we can use to isolate suspect accruals. First, if a firm's accruals are unusually large, accounting distortions are more likely to be at work. Second, if the unusually large accruals relate to balance sheet accounts that typically consist of less reliable accrual estimates, accounting distortions are more likely at work.[5] For example, a big increase in the marketable securities account is unlikely to be due to an accounting distortion, because marketable securities can be measured with a high degree of reliability. On the other hand, a big increase in inventory is more likely to be due to an accounting distortion, because inventory is measured with a low degree of reliability. A big increase in inventory is a sign that obsolete inventory may be building up, meaning that inventory is overvalued and an inventory write-down is overdue. It is more difficult to establish the fair value of inventory than for marketable securities, so inventory accruals are inherently less reliable.

In order to help you use these red flags more effectively, we need to give you more guidance on what represents an unusually "large" accrual and which accrual categories are measured with low reliability. As a general rule, whenever any individual line item on the balance sheet changes by more than 5 percent of net operating assets, it represents a large accrual and warrants further investigation. In order to provide you with guidelines on the reliability of particular accruals, we first have to divide the balance sheet up into appropriate categories. We do this in Figure 6.5.

As a general rule, balance sheet items that are financial in nature are measured with a high degree of reliability, while balance sheet items that are operational in nature are measured with a lower degree of reliability. Figure 6.5 therefore begins by classifying all of the standardized balance sheet items in eVal as either operating or financial. This classification mirrors the classification we used in Figure 5.5 of Chapter 5, but with one important exception. Our objective in Chapter 5 was to distinguish between balance sheet items that are used in the firm's operations versus those that are not. Our objective here is to distinguish between balance sheet items that are financial in nature versus those that are not. In Chapter 5, we classified cash and marketable securities as part of operations, because firms typically need cash and marketable securities to facilitate their operations. But for the purpose of evaluating earnings quality, cash and marketable securities are financial assets that can be measured with a high degree of reliability. We therefore classify cash and marketable securities as financial assets. This results in the following modified definition of net operating assets:

Modified Net Operating Assets (NOA*)
= Total Assets − Cash and Marketable Securities − Total Liabilities
+ Current Debt + Long-Term Debt

---

[5] The technique of earnings quality analysis that we describe here is supported by extensive academic evidence. It doesn't just represent our own subjective opinions (though our opinions are almost as good as fact). We list the most relevant academic studies as references at the end of this chapter.

FIGURE 6.5   **Accrual Reliability Assessment by Accrual Category**

Accrual Category	Associated Balance Sheet Items in eVal	Reliability Assessment	Illustrative Examples
Change in noncash current operating assets	Receivables; Inventories; Other Current Assets	Low	Category is dominated by receivables and inventory. Receivables require the estimation of uncollectibles and are a common earnings management tool (e.g., channel stuffing). Inventory accruals entail subjective cost flow assumptions, allocations, and write-downs.
Change in current operating liabilities	Accounts Payable; Income Taxes Payable; Other Current Liabilities	Medium	Category is dominated by payables, which represent short-term financial obligations of the company that can be measured with a high degree of reliability. But it also can include more subjective accruals, such as deferred revenue and warranty liabilities.
Change in noncurrent operating assets	PP&E; Investments; Intangibles; Other Assets	Low	Category is dominated by PP&E and intangibles. Both PP&E and internally generated intangibles (e.g., capitalized software development costs) involve subjective capitalization decisions. Moreover, PP&E and intangibles involve subjective amortization and write-down decisions.
Change in noncurrent operating liabilities	Other Liabilities; Deferred Taxes; Minority Interest	Medium	Category includes long-term payables, deferred taxes, and postretirement benefit obligations. Best characterized as a mixture of accruals with varying degrees of reliability.
Change in financial assets and liabilities	Cash & Marketable Securities; Current Debt; Long-Term Debt	High	Category consists of financial assets and liabilities with reliably determined book values.

We reiterate that this definition of operating assets differs from the definition used in Chapter 5 only in that it excludes cash and marketable securities. We refer to this measure as NOA* to distinguish it from the NOA measure developed in Chapter 5.

We next classify the operating items based on whether they are assets versus liabilities. Operating assets are generally measured with less reliability than operating liabilities, because operating liabilities primarily relate to financial obligations that are measured with greater reliability (e.g., accounts payable). Thus, we classify operating assets as low reliability and operating liabilities as medium reliability. Finally, it is useful to distinguish between current and noncurrent items. Noncurrent items involve estimates into the more distant future, and hence tend to be less reliable. Figure 6.5 summarizes these reliability assessments and provides illustrative examples.

You should remember that Figure 6.5 summarizes general rules and not absolute truths. There have been some famous accounting scandals involving distortions in the measurement of supposedly high reliability accruals. For example, the well-known accounting scandal at Parmalat involved the overstatement of the cash balance (but it also involved Italian auditors). Nevertheless, the vast majority of accounting manipulations involve the overstatement of operating asset accounts. Therefore, the change in net operating assets provided a good summary measure of the amount of low reliability accruals that are included in earnings. This claim is supported by the results of a research study of accounting enforcement actions taken by the SEC. The study examines over 100 cases where the SEC alleged that firms had overstated their earnings in violation of GAAP. To examine whether these manipulations were perpetrated through the overstatement of operating assets, the researchers decomposed the return on net operating assets into a cash component and an operating accrual component:

$$\text{RNOA} = \underbrace{\frac{\text{FCF}}{\text{NOA}^*_\text{beg}}}_{\text{Cash Component}} + \underbrace{\frac{\text{NOA}^*_\text{end} - \text{NOA}^*_\text{beg}}{\text{NOA}^*_\text{beg}}}_{\text{Operating Accrual Component}}$$

where

FCF = Free cash flow to all investors

NOA* = Modified net operating assets at either the beginning (beg) or end of the period

RNOA = Net operating income divided by beginning net operating assets

They then tracked the behavior of each of the components around the year of the alleged earnings management. Figure 6.6 summarizes their results. As you can see, RNOA declines slightly in the year of the manipulation and then falls sharply thereafter. The operating accrual component increases in the year of the alleged manipulation and then decreases sharply thereafter. The cash component (not shown in Figure 6.6) must therefore decrease in the year of the alleged manipulation and level off thereafter. The clear message emerging from the figure is that accruals and RNOA are temporarily overstated in the year of the alleged manipulation and then reverse in the following years. This is exactly the scenario we labeled as *temporarily aggressive accounting* back in Chapter 4 (see Panel B of Figure 4.5 and associated discussion). The increase in accruals in the year of the alleged manipulation is a clear signal that accruals are temporarily inflated in that year.

FIGURE 6.6   **Event-Time Plots of RNOA and the Operating Accrual Component of RNOA (ACC) for Firms Subject to SEC Enforcement Actions**

Year 0 represents the year that a firm was subject to an SEC enforcement action for an alleged earnings overstatement. The solid (dashed) line reflects the mean (median) of the respective variable.

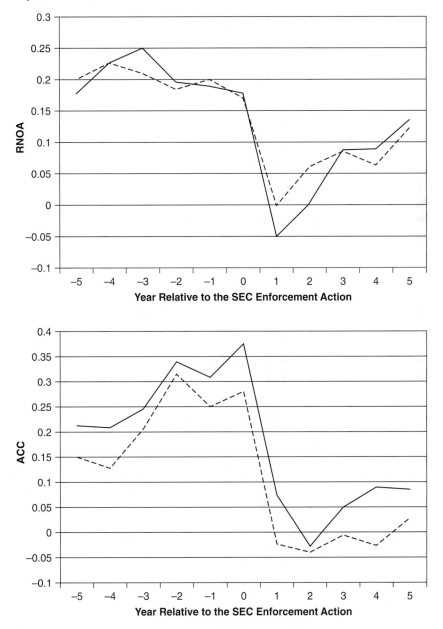

This should have tipped smart investors off to the precipitous earnings declines in the following year.[6]

To assist you in identifying accounting distortions and low-quality earnings, eVal computes various accrual metrics. You will find these metrics under the caption "Analysis of Earnings Quality" at the bottom of eVal's Cash Flow Analysis worksheet. The analysis begins by reporting the current and noncurrent portions of the operating accrual component of RNOA, defined as follows:

$$\underbrace{\frac{NOA^*_{end} - NOA^*_{beg}}{NOA^*_{beg}}}_{\text{Operating Accruals}} = \underbrace{\frac{COA_{end} - COA_{beg}}{NOA_{beg}}}_{\text{Current Operating Accruals}} + \underbrace{\frac{NCOA_{end} - NCOA_{beg}}{NOA_{beg}}}_{\text{Noncurrent Operating Accruals}}$$

where

COA = Current Net Operating Assets, defined as Current Assets − Cash and Marketable Securities − Current Liabilities + Short-Term Debt

NCOA = Noncurrent Net Operating Assets, defined as Total Assets − Current Assets − Total Liabilities + Current Liabilities + Long-Term Debt

If any of these components are unusually large, you should identify the balance sheet items that are responsible for the change and look for any evidence that the change is attributable to accounting distortions. What constitutes unusually large in this context? Using data from thousands of firms over the past 50 years, Figure 6.7 reports the cutoffs that would place a firm above the 50th, 75th, and 90th percentiles for each of these measures. At a minimum, you should conduct a detailed investigation of the underlying accruals for any component that comes in above the 90th percentile. To assist you in flagging these cases, eVal shades cells above the 90th percentile in light red.

Let's see how this quality of earnings analysis works out for Kohl's. Figure 6.8 reproduces eVal's analysis of earnings quality for Kohl's fiscal 2001 financial statements. On first blush, things don't seem so good. There is red shading in the noncurrent operating accrual cells for all years. Moreover, the current operating

FIGURE 6.7 **Percentile Cutoffs for the Historical Distributions of Accrual Components**

Accrual Component	50th Percentile	75th Percentile	90th Percentile
Operating Accruals/NOA*	0.08	0.20	0.38
Current Operating Accruals/NOA*	0.01	0.05	0.11
Noncurrent Operating Accruals/NOA*	0.02	0.06	0.14
% Sales Growth	0.09	0.21	0.39
− Increase in NOA Turnover	0.01	0.09	0.20

[6] An obvious question to ask at this point is whether stock prices act as if investors understand that high operating accruals signal low earnings quality. Academic research shows that firms with high accruals do tend to have future earnings declines but that investors don't appear to fully anticipate these earnings declines, resulting in predictably low future stock returns. For more details, see the References section at the end of this chapter.

FIGURE 6.8
Analysis of Earnings Quality for Kohl's

	A	B	C	D	E	
1	**Cash Flow Analysis**	**($000)**				
2	Go To User's Guide	View Statement of Cash Flows		View FCF to Investors Computations		
3		View FCF to Equity Computations		View Analysis of Earnings Quality		
4	**Company Name**	KOHL S CORP				
5						
6		Actual	Actual	Actual	Actual	Fore
7	**Fiscal Year End Date**	1/30/1999	1/29/2000	2/3/2001	2/2/2002	2/2/
117	**Analysis of Earnings Quality**					
118	(Red Shading = Quality Flag)					
119	Current Op. Accruals/NOA	0.039	0.178	0.116	0.076	
120	+ NonCurrent Op. Accruals/NOA	0.143	0.369	0.160	0.174	
121	= Operating Accruals/NOA	0.182	0.547	0.276	0.249	
122						
123	Sales Growth	0.203	0.238	0.350	0.217	
124	- increase in NOA Turnover	0.017	(0.250)	0.055	(0.026)	
125	- Interaction	0.004	(0.059)	0.019	(0.006)	
126	= Operating Accruals/NOA	0.182	0.547	0.276	0.249	
127	Fiscal Year	1998	1999	2000	2001	
128						
129						
130						
131						
132						
133						
134						

User's Guide / Data Center / Financial Statements / Ratio Analysis \ Cash Flow Analysis / Forecasting

Ready

accruals and total operating accruals also are shaded red in fiscal 1999. Inspection of Kohl's financial statements reveals that the biggest accruals have taken place in PP&E and inventory. These accruals should come as no surprise, since Kohl's has been opening new stores at a rapid pace. The store count has increased from 182 at the end of fiscal 1997 to 382 at the end of fiscal 2001. As long as the balance sheet amounts represent legitimate investment in profitable store growth, accounting distortions are probably not at work. Fiscal 1999, however, is a little more problematic. In that year, the financial statements indicate that Receivables increased from $270,705 to $505,010 and Other Assets increased from $38,708 to $175,445. Over this period, store growth increased by 22 percent, clearly a much lower growth rate than experienced in these accounts.

Here's where we need to dig deeper in Kohl's fiscal 1999 Form 10-K to understand what is going on. You can access Kohl's fiscal 1999 Form 10-K by going to the Data Center sheet, locating Kohl's, and clicking on the adjacent Form 10-K's link. The fiscal 1999 document is the one with the 2000-04-17 filing date. Inspection of the liquidity and capital resources section starting on page 10 of that document reveals the primary reasons for the high Receivables and Other Assets accruals.

With respect to Receivables, Kohl's typically sells its proprietary credit-card receivables for cash, but in 1999 it changed from selling receivables without recourse to selling receivables with recourse. This means that Kohl's is now on the hook for any unpaid receivables, and so GAAP require Kohl's to keep these receivables on the books. While we've got an explanation, we are not out of the woods yet. We should keep an eye on these receivables to make sure that the allowance for bad debts is reasonable; until we are confident that this is the case, we can't rule out accounting distortions.

With respect to the increase in Other Assets, Kohl's acquired 32 stores from Caldor Corporation in 1999 and booked $122 million in favorable lease rights associated with this acquisition. In other words, Caldor had long-term lease rights locked in at rates below current market levels. Kohl's had to pay a premium to purchase these lease rights and has booked the premium as an asset to be amortized over the lease period. Once again, while we have an explanation, we are not yet off the hook. We need to be sure that Kohl's did not pay too much for these lease rights. We'll have to keep an eye on profitability to make sure that the amortization of these lease rights is not a drag on future RNOA.

Our analysis of Kohl's earnings quality raises several red flags, but we have reasonable explanations for each of the red flags. This leads us to the broader question of what are the other common explanations for unusually large accruals. Other than accounting distortions, there are two common explanations. First, recall from the examples we considered in Chapter 4 that legitimate growth in investment will lead to increased net operating assets and hence high accruals. This is exactly what we saw at work in Kohl's inventory and PP&E accounts. How do we distinguish between legitimate growth in investment and illegitimate accounting distortions? Legitimate growth in investment should be accompanied by legitimate growth in sales. Thus, we should check that the sales growth rate is commensurate with the operating asset growth rate and that the sales themselves are not the product of revenue manipulation. For example, if there is a disproportionate increase in credit sales, we should make sure that the firm is not artificially inflating receivables in order to boost revenues.

The second legitimate explanation for increased accruals is a reduction in net operating asset turnover, whereby more assets are required to produce the same level of sales. A legitimate reduction in operating asset turnover occurs when more economic investment is required to produce the same level of sales. Examples include a shift to a more capital-intensive production process, offering longer credit terms to customers, and Kohl's decision to buy established store sites from Caldor instead of developing its own. Accounting distortions most often manifest themselves as reductions in operating asset turnover, so distinguishing between legitimate reductions in operating asset turnover and illegitimate accounting distortions can be tough. Nevertheless, we can offer a couple of good pointers. First, a legitimate reduction in operating asset turnover will usually be the result of an important strategic shift in the way that management conducts business. If you see no evidence of such a shift, then accounting distortions are likely at work. Second, as discussed in Chapter 5, a successful strategic shift to lower operating asset turnover should be accompanied by higher margins. It makes no sense to sacrifice turnover unless the reward is higher margins. Perhaps the most classic signal of an accounting distortion is declining inventory turnover in conjunction with flat or declining margins. This is a strong signal that inventory is overvalued and overdue for a write-down.

In order to help you distinguish between these two alternative explanations for high accruals, eVal decomposes operating accruals into a sales growth component and a turnover component, as shown below:

$$\underbrace{\frac{NOA^*_{end} - NOA^*_{beg}}{NOA^*_{beg}}}_{\text{Operating Accruals}} = \underbrace{\frac{Sales_t - Sales_{t-1}}{Sales_{t-1}}}_{\text{Sales Growth}} - \underbrace{\frac{\frac{Sales_t}{NOA^*_{end}} - \frac{Sales_{t-1}}{NOA^*_{beg}}}{\frac{Sales_t}{NOA^*_{end}}}}_{\text{NOA Turnover Growth}}$$

$$\underbrace{- \frac{Sales_t - Sales_{t-1}}{Sales_{t-1}} \times \frac{\frac{Sales_t}{NOA^*_{end}} - \frac{Sales_{t-1}}{NOA^*_{beg}}}{\frac{Sales_t}{NOA^*_{end}}}}_{\text{Interaction}}$$

where

Sales$_t$ = Sales for the current year

Sales$_{t-1}$ = Sales for the prior year

This algebraic decomposition is pretty nasty, but we can assure you that it holds. It demonstrates that operating accruals increase one-for-one with sales growth and decrease one-for-one with NOA turnover growth. We also have an ugly interaction term at the end, which we suggest you ignore. This decomposition serves two purposes. First, accounting distortions are more likely to reside in the NOA turnover growth component than the sales growth component, so a large NOA turnover growth component is an important red flag for accounting distortions. Second, as outlined above, the factors driving legitimate growth in accruals differ across the two components, so pinpointing the appropriate component will guide your search for explanations.

Figure 6.7 lists the cutoffs for each of these accrual components and Figure 6.8 shows this decomposition for Kohl's. Note that this decomposition involves subtracting the NOA Turnover Growth and Interaction components from the Sales Growth component, so positive (negative) values for the former components are listed as negative (positive) amounts in eVal. In other words, a positive amount for NOA Turnover Growth indicates that turnover has gone down, causing an increase in accruals. As before, eVal flags accrual components that are above the 90th percentile. This time, the only flags we see are for fiscal 1999 and relate to an unusually large increase in operating accruals resulting from an unusually large reduction in NOA turnover. These results reflect two aspects of our existing discussion of Kohl's accruals. First, the unusually high accruals in fiscal years 1998, 2000, and 2001 are primarily attributable to legitimate sales growth. There is no strong evidence of declining NOA turnover in these years. Second, the unusually high accruals in fiscal 1999 stem from the significant reduction in NOA turnover experienced in that year. The reduction in turnover, however, was attributable to the purchase of the 32 established Caldor Corporation stores and the decision to sell receivables with recourse. These changes represent real strategic shifts aimed at earning additional margin by sacrificing turnover. If we turn to the advanced Dupont model in eVal's Ratio Analysis sheet, we see that Kohl's NOA turnover fell

FIGURE 6.9

Analysis of Earnings Quality for WorldCom

	A	B	C	D	E	
1	**Cash Flow Analysis**	**($000)**				
2	Go To User's Guide	View Statement of Cash Flows		View FCF to Investors Computations		
3		View FCF to Equity Computations		View Analysis of Earnings Quality		
4	**Company Name**	WORLDCOM INC NEW				
5						
6		Actual	Actual	Actual	Actual	Fo
7	**Fiscal Year End Date**	12/31/1998	12/31/1999	12/31/2000	12/31/2001	12/3
117	**Analysis of Earnings Quality**					
118	**(Red Shading = Quality Flag)**					
119	Current Op. Accruals/NOA	(0.094)	(0.006)	0.018	0.003	
120	+ NonCurrent Op. Accruals/NOA	2.174	0.064	0.143	0.087	
121	= Operating Accruals/NOA	2.080	0.058	0.161	0.090	
122						
123	Sales Growth	1.262	1.038	0.089	(0.100)	
124	- increase in NOA Turnover	0.362	(0.481)	0.067	0.211	
125	- Interaction	0.456	(0.499)	0.006	(0.021)	
126	= Operating Accruals/NOA	2.080	0.058	0.161	0.090	
127	Fiscal Year	1998	1999	2000	2001	
128						
129						
130						
131						
132						
133						
134						

User's Guide / Data Center / Financial Statements / Ratio Analysis \ **Cash Flow Analysis** / Forecastin

Ready

from 2.685 in 1998 to 2.429 in 1999 to 2.320 in 2000. At the same time, margins climbed from 0.056 in 1998 to 0.061 in 1999 to 0.065 in 2000, resulting in flat to slightly higher RNOA. In sum, it appears that these are legitimate accruals resulting from real strategic changes in operations.

We've just gone through a lengthy analysis of earnings quality for Kohl's without identifying any major problems. For the purpose of comparison, let's take a look at another company where there are some problems. Figure 6.9 shows eVal's analysis of earnings quality for WorldCom through the end of fiscal 2001. You may recall that WorldCom seemed to be doing just fine until early in 2002, when the firm announced it had discovered some accounting irregularities. The firm filed for bankruptcy soon thereafter and ultimately wrote down assets by $70 billion (you'll excuse us for rounding to the nearest $10 billion). Most of the write-down amount related to asset impairments relating to the company's demise. The key accounting manipulations used by the company to prop up its sagging profitability in 2000 and 2001 involved the capitalization of operating costs in PP&E. The amounts incorrectly capitalized were approximately $2 billion in 2000 and $3 billion in 2001. You'll remember that this is exactly the kind of temporarily aggressive accounting that we modeled in Chapter 4. Wall Street analysts were caught off guard by these accounting distortions. Let's see if eVal's analysis of earnings quality could have alerted us to their presence.

Figure 6.9 shows multiple flags of accrual components in 1998. Operating accruals, noncurrent operating accruals, sales growth, and NOA turnover growth are all excessively high. The search for explanations for these accruals reveals that WorldCom engaged in a number of strategic acquisitions in that year. In particular, WorldCom acquired MCI late in 1998. The acquisitions boosted operating assets substantially. Sales also increased, but to a lesser extent, because World-Com acquired MCI late in 1998 and so only booked a few months of MCI sales in fiscal 1998. In 1999, sales growth is again high and NOA turnover drops. This is because 1999 includes a whole year's worth of sales from MCI. Thus, the red flags in 1998 and 1999 are primarily explained by the MCI acquisition.

eVal also flags WorldCom's noncurrent operating accruals in 2000. It is difficult to come up with legitimate explanations for these accruals. Noncurrent operating accruals are 14.3 percent, while sales growth is only 8.9 percent and current operating accruals are only 1.8 percent. Further inspection of WorldCom's financial statements reveals that the high accruals are entirely attributable to an increase in PP&E of approximately 30 percent. So why did PP&E increase by 30 percent when sales only increased by 8.9 percent? The only explanation offered in the MD&A accompanying WorldCom's fiscal 2000 Form 10-K is that "primary capital expenditures include purchases of transmission, communications and other equipment." This explanation is incomplete, as it does not mention any strategic shifts that would explain why PP&E is increasing so much faster than sales. Accounting distortions are therefore a likely explanation.

Finally, eVal flags WorldCom's NOA turnover growth in 2001. The amount shown is 0.211, indicating that NOA turnover declined by 21.1 percent in 2001. Inspection of the other accrual components for 2001 reveals that sales fell by 10 percent, while noncurrent accruals were 8.7 percent. Inspection of WorldCom's financial statements indicates that the high accruals are primarily attributable to a 4 percent increase in PP&E and a 9 percent increase in intangibles. The 9 percent increase in intangibles is explained by WorldCom's acquisition of Intermedia Communications in July 2001. But why did PP&E increase by 4 percent when sales declined by 10 percent? Again, the only explanation offered in the MD&A accompanying WorldCom's fiscal 2001 Form 10-K is that "primary capital expenditures include purchases of transmission, communications and other equipment." With hindsight, we know that these unexplained increases in PP&E were attributable to accounting manipulations. The fact that no legitimate explanation was provided for these accruals by WorldCom's management should have provided an early warning sign that WorldCom's earnings quality was suspect. The lesson to be learned for this example is that large operating accruals lacking legitimate explanations are the calling card of accounting distortions (and, yes, the bad pun is intentional).

6.7   CONCLUSION

Every so often, a writer in the financial press will get upset about accrual accounting and declare that "cash is king," implying that we should use cash-based measures of financial performance over accrual-based measures. We take a more balanced view. Accrual accounting is designed to measure wealth creation in a more accurate and timely manner than simply recording cash receipts and disbursements. For most companies most of the time, these measures add

information. Further, we don't have to choose between cash flows and earnings—
we can have both. By using two different systems to examine a company's activities, we learn much more about what really happened in the past, and we generate
more informed forecasts of the future.

6.8   CASES, LINKS, AND REFERENCES

Case

- Turnaround at Bally Total Fitness? (Questions 2 through 5)

Link

- WorldCom's Form 10-Ks are available at http://www.sec.gov/cgi-bin/
  browse-edgar?type=10-k&dateb=&owner=include&count=40&action=
  getcompany&CIK=0000723527

  The filing dated 2002-03-13 is the last one before the accounting scandal
  broke.

References

- Richardson, S., M. Soliman, R. Sloan, and I. Tuna. (2006). The implications of
  accounting distortions and growth for accruals and profitability. *The Accounting Review* (forthcoming).
- Sloan, R. (1996). Do stock prices fully reflect information in accruals and cash
  flows about future earnings? *The Accounting Review* 71: 289–315.

CHAPTER SEVEN

Structured Forecasting

7.1 INTRODUCTION

Forecasting the future financial statements represents the ultimate goal of all the analyses we have discussed thus far. From a theoretical perspective, equity valuation requires forecasts of the future cash distributions to equity holders. From a practical perspective, however, most analysts focus on forecasting net income. We begin this chapter by reconciling these two perspectives. We lay out a forecasting framework that builds forecasts of the complete set of financial statements in a systematic manner. This framework highlights the joint role of income statement and balance sheet forecasts in generating forecasts of cash distributions to equity holders.

We next discuss broad issues that arise in constructing forecasts for the purpose of valuing equity securities. Should we forecast quarterly financial statements or annual statements? How many years into the future do we need to forecast? What are reasonable assumptions for forecasts that are in the distant future? What balance sheet item should we use as the "plug" that equates assets to liabilities and equity? We close the chapter by showing you how eVal guides you through the forecasting process. With these preliminaries covered, Chapter 8 provides more detailed advice about forecasting each of the line items in the financial statements.

7.2 A SYSTEMATIC FORECASTING FRAMEWORK

The cash distributions a firm pays to its equity holders are the result of a complex and interrelated set of operating, investing, and financing activities. The only sound way to proceed is to first forecast each of these underlying activities and then aggregate their financial implications into a forecast of the ultimate distributions to equity holders. We do this by building forecasts of both the income statement and the balance sheet. By forecasting both financial statements, we can take important interactions into consideration. A good example of the interplay between balance sheet forecasts and income statement forecasts is forecasted interest expense. Your forecast of interest expense on the income statement clearly depends on the amount of debt you forecast on the balance sheet. But the amount of your debt also will depend on your forecasts of the firm's net operating assets and capital structure. And your forecast of the net operating assets clearly depends on

FIGURE 7.1
Systematic
Forecasting
Framework

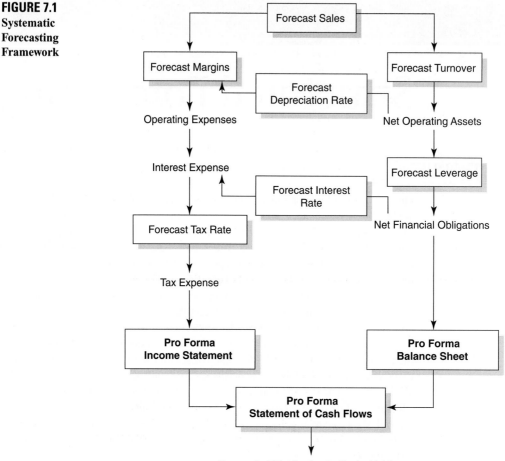

Forecast of Distribution to Equity Holders

your forecast of sales growth. If we are going to keep track of all these interactions, we clearly need to develop a systematic approach to forecasting.

Figure 7.1 illustrates our approach to this forecasting puzzle. The process begins with a forecast of sales. Sales are the primary input to the forecasting process for two reasons. First, recall that the sales transaction is the trigger for the recognition of value creation under GAAP. We forecast operating income by first forecasting sales and then forecasting all of the operating expenses necessary to generate the sales. Second, the sales forecast is our basic statement about how rapidly the firm will grow. This in turn drives our forecasts of the required levels of net operating assets to generate the sales growth and the required amounts of capital to finance the acquisition of the operating assets.

The next two steps in the forecasting process are illustrated in Figure 7.1. On the left side of the figure, we move from the sales forecast to the operating expense forecast by making assumptions about operating margins. On the right side of the figure, we move from the sales forecast to the net operating asset forecast by making assumptions about turnover ratios. You should see that the forecasting process is like applying the Dupont ratio analysis in reverse. Instead of starting with the individual line items in the financial statements and then expressing them as ratios, we forecast the ratios directly and then back into what this implies for the individual line items in the forecast financial statements.

Armed with forecasts of operating expenses and net operating assets (i.e., operating assets less operating liabilities), the next task is to forecast the net financial obligations. Our forecast of net operating assets indicates the total amount of invested capital that is required to support the future business activities. But we still need to forecast the mix of equity and nonequity financing that the firm will use to finance the forecasted level of invested capital. That is, we need to forecast the firm's future leverage. By applying leverage assumptions to the net operating assets, we obtain the required amount of nonequity forms of financing, such as short-term debt, long-term debt, and preferred stock. At this point, you may be tempted to forecast common equity and thus complete the balance sheet. However, we have run out of degrees of freedom. We have forecast every item on the balance sheet except for common equity. Since the balance sheet must balance, we have already made an implicit forecast for common equity. Common equity is the *plug* that is found by subtracting the liabilities from the assets. This is an important point and one to which we return later in the chapter.

We have now forecasted all the line items on the balance sheet. We refer to this forecasted balance sheet as a *pro forma* balance sheet to distinguish it from the actual balance sheets that the firm reported in the past. We still have more work to do on the pro forma income statement. The three items we have omitted are depreciation expense, interest expense, and tax expense. We could not forecast depreciation earlier because it clearly depends on the amount of assets on the balance sheet, so we needed to forecast the asset balance first. Similarly, we couldn't forecast interest or taxes, because interest expense clearly depends on the amount of debt financing and tax expense clearly depends on the magnitude of the interest expense tax shield. We needed the balance sheet forecast of debt before we could construct these income statement forecasts. By applying our forecast of the interest rate to the amount of forecasted debt financing, we generate an interest expense forecast. By deducting our interest expense from our forecast of operating earnings, we generate a forecast of earnings before taxes. Applying a tax rate forecast to earnings before taxes gives our tax expense forecast.

At this point, we are pretty much done forecasting the income statement. You may note that there are still a number of income statement components that we haven't mentioned: items such as gains and losses in other income, extraordinary items, and discontinued operations. Typically, by their very nature, these items are nonrecurring and difficult to forecast. Therefore, ignoring them (i.e., assuming that they are zero) is often the best that we can do. One final item to consider in your income statement forecasts is preferred dividends. If preferred stock is one of the non-common-equity sources of financing represented on the balance sheet, then there typically will be a stated dividend on this stock that should be incorporated in your income statement forecasts. Recall that we are trying to value the common equity, so we must deduct cash distributions to preferred stockholders in order to derive the net cash distributions to common stockholders.

We now have both our pro forma balance sheet and our pro forma income statement. Armed with these two statements, the preparation of our pro forma statement of cash flows is a mechanical task. You should remember from your introductory accounting class that the statement of cash flows can be prepared using the information in the income statement and the beginning and ending balance sheets, so there is nothing left to forecast. And, by referring to the financing section of the statement of cash flows, we can see how our pro forma income statements and balance sheets determine the cash distributions to common equity holders. It is worth emphasizing that we need information from both the pro forma income statement and the pro forma balance sheet to extract our forecasts of distributions to common equity holders. We can see this by recalling the clean surplus relation that we first introduced in Chapter 4:

$$\text{Distributions to Equity} = \text{Net Income} - \text{Increase in Equity}$$

We get the net income forecast from the pro forma income statement, but this alone isn't sufficient for our valuation model. To solve for cash distributions to common equity holders, we also have to deduct the increase in common equity, which is extracted from the beginning and ending balance sheets. This latter adjustment takes account of additional capital that is required to fund the net operating assets of the business. Wall Street analysts often miss this subtlety, focusing almost exclusively on net income. But the clean surplus relation makes it clear that we should be concerned with both how much income is generated *and* how much additional capital has to be invested to generate this income.

7.3 FORECASTING QUARTERLY VERSUS YEARLY FINANCIALS

Exchange-listed firms in the United States are required to prepare financial statements on a quarterly basis. However, for the purpose of building financial forecasts for input into a valuation model, quarterly forecasting is overkill. The value of a firm is determined by its results over the next 10 or 20 years, not the next few quarters. And in addition to providing unnecessary detail, quarterly forecasting requires careful consideration of seasonal effects in financial data. For example, retailers' sales and profits are usually greatest in the fourth quarter, which covers the end-of-year holiday period. A quarterly forecasting interval requires us to build these seasonal patterns into our forecasts. But given that our value estimate will be determined by many years of forecasts, detailed knowledge of the quarterly numbers has little impact on the final answer. As a consequence, most valuation models, including eVal, use an annual interval for building financial statement forecasts. For simplicity, this annual interval typically corresponds with the fiscal year that the company uses for financial reporting purposes.

Despite the use of an annual measurement interval in most valuation models, the quarterly financial statements are still useful. The most recent quarterly financial statements provide the most current information on a firm's performance and financial position. If we are currently in a firm's fourth fiscal quarter and we are attempting to forecast the income statement for the full fiscal year, then we should obviously use the financial statements from the first three quarters as a starting point. But it is very important to be aware of any seasonal effects in the data before extrapolating financial statement data from earlier quarters to later quarters. There are two useful techniques for incorporating seasonal patterns in income statement forecasting. The first is to sum together the most recent four quarters of financial statements. By doing so, you will be sure that any seasonal patterns are present in your annual figure. The cumulative results for the four most recent fiscal quarters are often referred to as the *trailing 12 months* (TTM) or *latest 12 months* (LTM) results. The second technique is to perform *year-over-year* (YOY) comparisons for the most recent quarters. This involves comparing the most recent quarters in the current fiscal year to the corresponding quarters in the previous fiscal year. For example, we compare the third fiscal quarter of the current year to the third fiscal quarter for the previous year. By doing so, we control for any seasonal patterns in the firm's performance. Similar considerations apply to forecasting the balance sheet for the end of the current fiscal year. While the most recent quarterly balance sheet is the timeliest, it also may reflect seasonal patterns in net operating asset balances. For example, most retailers build up inventory during the third fiscal quarter and run it down during the fourth fiscal quarter. If you simply extrapolate the third-quarter inventory balances into the future, you will overstate the inventory necessary to sustain the annual sales. Year-over-year comparisons of quarterly inventory changes are the best technique for controlling for such seasonal patterns.

Another role for quarterly financial statements in valuation is in assessing the ongoing performance of the company relative to your previous forecasts. You may not want to wait until the end of the year to find out whether or not a company is meeting your forecasts. Indeed, quarterly earnings announcements are one of the most important catalysts for a stock price revision, suggesting that most market participants use information in the quarterly financial statements to update their forecasting models. For this reason, it is very useful to prepare explicit quarterly forecasts through the end of the current fiscal year.

7.4 FORECASTING HORIZON

Theoretically speaking, the valuation of an equity security requires us to estimate and discount all the future cash distributions for the infinite future. But, practically speaking, this would require way too many columns on our spreadsheet. Instead, we select a finite horizon over which to prepare explicit forecasts for each year and then we assume that, after this point, the financial statement line items settle down to a constant growth rate. In this way, we describe an infinite series of future cash distributions without having to explicitly derive an infinite number of pro forma financial statements. Oddly enough, the period after the finite forecasting horizon is known as the *terminal period* even though, by definition, it never terminates. In later chapters, we will discuss how the valuation formulas deal with the infinite series of future cash distributions. What we need to concern ourselves with in this chapter is the selection of an appropriate finite forecasting horizon.

The forecasting horizon should begin with the fiscal year that we are currently in and extend out to the point where we can no longer make a better forecast than to simply assume that all the financial statement line items will grow at the same rate as sales. To be more precise, the terminal period should begin when our forecasts meet the following four conditions. First, sales must settle down to a constant growth rate. Second, margins must remain constant. This condition, combined with the constant sales growth rate, ensures that the expenses on the income statement grow at the same constant rate as sales. Third, turnover ratios must remain constant. This condition, combined with the constant sales growth rate, ensures that the net operating assets on the balance sheet grow at the same constant rate as sales. Fourth, financial leverage ratios must remain constant. This condition, combined with the constant sales growth rate, ensures that the financial obligations on the balance sheet grow at the same constant rate as sales. Together, these four conditions ensure that all the items in the income statement and balance sheet will grow at the same constant rate as sales. As a result, cash distributions to equity holders also will grow at this same constant rate.

It is important to note that we do not expect all of these conditions to literally hold beyond the forecasting horizon. In reality, sales growth rates, margins, turnovers, and leverage ratios are all constantly changing and we expect them to continue to change beyond the forecasting horizon. But what is crucial is that we don't expect them to deviate from this constant growth rate in a systematic way. In other words, our forecasts in the terminal period should be unbiased estimates of where we expect these ratios to be in the long run.

How far out do we need to build explicit financial statement forecasts before it is reasonable to assume that things will settle down to this constant long-run equilibrium? It all depends on the nature of the business and the amount of information that is available to build the forecasts. At one extreme, we could be looking at a company in a mature industry with a well-established product, stable demand, a stable production technology, and stable input prices. Moreover, assume that the company offered no forward-looking information about expansion plans, there were no discernible industry trends, and you generally had every reason to believe that "more of the same" is the best description of the future. In such an extreme case, it is reasonable to assume that the sales growth rate, margins, turnovers, and leverage ratios will remain constant at their recent levels. In this simple case, the finite forecasting period is nonexistent and the first year in the forecast period is the terminal period. We generate the forecasted financial statements by naïvely extrapolating the past sales growth rate, margins, turnovers, and leverage ratios into the infinite future. This process is called *straight-lining* because, if sales growth, margins, turnovers, and leverage ratios will all stay constant at their current levels, they would plot against time as a straight line. Straight-lining is the default forecasting assumption that we generally use in eVal. We make this choice because, in the absence of additional information, it is the best that we can do. We'll take a closer look at eVal's default forecasting assumptions at the end of this chapter.

In most circumstances, however, straight-lining is a very naïve forecasting technique. Instead, we should use what we have learned from our analysis of the past to build more sophisticated forecasts of the future. The length of the forecast horizon depends on how far into the future we can reasonably predict variation in the sales growth rate, margins, turnover, and leverage before they settle down to their long-run, steady-state values. Consider each of these variables in turn. Sales growth won't settle to a steady growth rate until industrywide sales stabilize and the firm's market share in the industry stabilizes. Thus, firms in start-up industries or firms that are gaining market share from competitors are likely to require longer forecasting horizons.

Next up are margins. There are two key factors that affect the stability of margins. First, margins are a function of a firm's competitive advantage in the marketplace. Because it is very hard to sustain a competitive advantage for a long period of time, our forecast horizon should be long enough to capture the erosion of any competitive advantage, assuming this is what you believe will happen. Second, margins are subject to systematic accounting distortions. For example, a growing company in an R&D-intensive industry will tend to have its margins temporarily depressed due to the immediate expensing of R&D. Your forecast horizon needs to be long enough to allow any temporary accounting distortions to play out.

Turnover ratios tend to be fairly stable over time, being dictated primarily by the production technology of the firm. However, rapidly growing firms often enjoy economies of scale that lead to increasing turnover ratios as they grow, so you need to anticipate when these economies will be exhausted. Even if the sales growth rate is forecast to hit a steady-state level relatively soon, you might extend the forecast horizon a few years longer if you believe that the firm will continue to reap economies of scale as they grow.

Leverage ratios typically have little influence on the choice of the forecast horizon. A firm's target capital structure generally balances the cost of different types of capital, taking into account the tax benefits of debt and the risk of financial distress. Various factors can cause the actual capital structure to deviate from the target capital structure in the short run, but it is typically quite straightforward for a firm to get back to its target capital structure within a few years. The probability of financial distress is a function of level and variability of firm profitability. As firms mature and profitability settles down to a steady-state growth rate, financial distress becomes less likely, and so firms typically add more debt to their capital structure in order to reap the tax benefits. Thus, if you are preparing forecasts for a young growth firm that is currently primarily equity financed, you will probably want to crank up the amount of debt financing as it reaches maturity.

The above analysis points to two key determinants of the forecast horizon. First, it must be long enough for sales growth to settle down to its steady-state level. Second, it must be long enough for any anticipated erosion of any abnormal profits resulting from competitive advantage in the marketplace. In other words,

TABLE 7.1 Forecast Horizon Guidelines

		Industrywide Growth Prospects		
		Low (mature)	Medium (consolidating)	High (start-up)
Firm-Specific	None	5 years	10 years	20 years
Competitive	Yes, but Only for Short Run	5 years	10 years	20 years
Advantage	Yes, and for Longer Run	10 years	20 years	20 Years

the forecast horizon must be long enough for any abnormal sales growth and abnormal profits to dissipate. For this reason, the forecast horizon is sometimes referred to as the *competitive advantage period*. The selection of the forecast horizon should be based on a thorough analysis of industry growth prospects and the sustainability of any competitive advantage held by the firm in its industry. To get you started, we provide you with some broad-brush guidelines in Table 7.1.

While the table is only intended to provide you with general guidelines, it embodies three important lessons. First, even if you are valuing a firm in a mature industry with no competitive advantage, it is still wise to choose a forecast horizon of at least five years. Doing so will help you resist the temptation to simply straight-line the past. Even firms in mature and competitive industries are sensitive to the business cycle and are subject to demand and supply shocks that can take several years to work their way through the system. A good example here is the airline industry. While mature and competitive, this industry is characterized by large fixed costs and significant demand and supply shocks (business cycle, oil prices, consumer sentiment, terrorist threats, etc.). As a result, growth rates and profit margins can deviate from their long-run competitive equilibrium for several years at a time. (To see this, load the airline industry into eVal using the ticker MG770 and look at how volatile the past financial ratios are.)

The second lesson is that industrywide growth prospects are a very important determinant of the forecast horizon. The reason is that firms in growing industries also tend to be growing, and growth leads to accounting distortions in profit margins. We therefore should try to choose a forecast horizon that is long enough for the industry growth rate to slow down to the economywide growth rate. For a firm in a start-up industry that involves significant research and development and/or marketing expenditures, it can take up to 20 years for the industry to mature. Good examples here are the biotechnology industry today and the computer hardware industry in the 1970s.

The third lesson is that firm-specific competitive advantage is a relatively less-important determinant of the forecast horizon than industrywide growth prospects. Why do we dare make such a sweeping generality? We have found that both students and practicing security analysts are biased toward overestimating how long firms can sustain their competitive advantage. Typically, when a firm has a new product or new service innovation that enables it to generate abnormally high profits, analysts get excited and extrapolate the abnormally high profits far into the future, not realizing that other firms will be quick to imitate the innovation and compete away the abnormal profits. There are some rare exceptions to this rule, such as Microsoft, Coca Cola, and McDonald's, but these are very unusual cases. In these exceptional cases, the firm has usually created a key proprietary asset that gives it some degree of monopoly power. If this is truly the case, then it is reasonable to assume that the firm will sustain its abnormal profits indefinitely, and we can incorporate the abnormal profitability into the terminal value computation. We caution, however, that cases of indefinitely sustainable competitive advantage are rare.

7.5   TERMINAL PERIOD ASSUMPTIONS

Now that we are finished with the forecast horizon, we are ready to talk about the terminal period forecasting assumptions. Recall from the discussion above that the terminal period is the period in which we expect sales growth, margins, turnover ratios, and leverage ratios to settle down to their constant steady-state levels. The assumptions that we make about the levels of these variables will drive the terminal valuation computation and can have a great impact on our overall valuation results. It is therefore important that we choose plausible values for these terminal assumptions. This section provides some guidelines for plausible assumptions or, failing that, describes what assumptions might be considered ridiculous.

The first, most important, terminal value assumption is the terminal sales growth rate. We can offer you some pretty tight guidelines for this one. If a company were to grow at a faster rate than the rest of the economy forever, then it would gradually become a larger and larger proportion of the total economy. Past some point, it would basically take over the whole economy—and then the world and then the universe! It therefore stands to reason that the terminal growth rate cannot be greater than the long-run expected economywide growth rate. Conversely, if a company were to grow more slowly than the economy forever, then it would gradually become a smaller and smaller proportion of the whole economy and eventually disappear. If your company produces a product that you think will eventually become obsolete, then such an assumption is reasonable. However, it is more usual to simply assume that the company will grow at the long-run expected economywide growth rate. This way, the company will maintain its size relative to the overall economy indefinitely. Historically, the annual growth rate in the U.S. economy, as measured by the nominal GDP growth rate, has averaged around 6 percent, composed of roughly 4 percent real growth and 2 percent price inflation. However, in the past decade, it has been closer to 5 percent and the Congressional Budget Office estimates 5 percent nominal GPD growth through 2012 (3 percent real growth and 2 percent price inflation). So, in most cases, a terminal sales growth rate forecast of about 5 percent is reasonable, and it should probably never exceed 7 percent. We use 5 percent as the default terminal value for sales growth in eVal. Finally, for reasons discussed in Chapter 9, your terminal sales growth assumption cannot exceed your cost of equity capital; if it does, you will get error messages.

Next, we must consider the terminal assumptions for margins, turnover ratios, and leverage ratios. Unfortunately, it is not possible to give tight guidelines for each of these assumptions. Recall from Chapter 5 that a company can trade off these performance drivers in an infinite number of ways. For example, more outsourcing will lead to higher turnover and lower margins, while greater product differentiation will lead to lower turnover and higher margins. This makes generalized guidelines impossible. Fortunately, however, we can offer more precise guidelines on the overall combination of assumptions that you choose. Margin, turnover, and leverage combine to give return on equity (ROE). ROE is an accounting measure of the rate of return on investment, and competition tends to force rates of return toward the cost of capital. In fact, if the following two conditions are satisfied, then the terminal ROE should be identical to the cost of equity capital:

1. The firm is operating in a long-run competitive equilibrium.
2. The accounting ROE provides a good measure of the economic rate of return on investment.

Under these conditions, the terminal margin, turnover, and leverage assumptions must combine to give an ROE that is equal to the cost of capital.

What are plausible levels for ROE when we relax these assumptions? Let's relax the first assumption and consider a firm that has a source of competitive advantage that is sustainable indefinitely. In this case, the terminal ROE will be greater than the cost of capital. How much greater depends on how much of a competitive advantage the company is able to sustain. Here again, we caution that it is very difficult to sustain competitive advantage indefinitely. Make sure that you have a very good case for such a scenario before incorporating it into your valuation model. Finally, you should remember that a terminal rate of return that is more than 10 percent above the cost of equity capital is unrealistic. Even if competition fails to drive away the abnormal return, the Federal Trade Commission and Department of Justice will prevent the abnormal return from becoming too large (as Microsoft has recently found out).

Now let's relax the assumption that accounting ROE provides a good measure of the economic rate of return. As discussed in Chapter 4, there are many reasons why accounting rates of return can provide distorted measures of the economic rate of return. Fortunately, most of these distortions disappear when a firm settles down to a steady-state, long-run equilibrium. In particular, most distortions to net income will "wash out" in a steady-state equilibrium. For example, the immediate expensing of R&D tends to downwardly (upwardly) bias income for firms that are spending more (less) on R&D today than they have in the past. But a firm in steady state will be spending a similar amount on R&D today as it did in the past, causing any distortions to wash out. There is, however, one very important class of distortions that don't wash out. These are distortions that are introduced into the denominator of the ROE calculation and arise because GAAP accounting rules do not allow for the capitalization of certain investments. In order to compute an economic rate of return, we need to consider the amount and timing of all past investments that had to be made to generate a cash inflow. Unfortunately, GAAP require many investments that generate cash inflows over multiple future periods to be expensed in the period that they are incurred. The most common examples of such expenditures are R&D, marketing, and administrative expenditures. Note that while the impact of immediate expensing washes out of the income number in steady state, it still causes book value of equity to understate invested capital.

In the face of such accounting distortions, the best way to figure out whether your terminal ROE is reasonable is to do a *pro forma capitalization* of all expenditures that generate future benefits but are immediately expensed under GAAP. This requires you to identify all such expenditures, determine the period over which they are expected to generate future benefits, and then capitalize and amortize them over this period. Once you have done this, you should check that the resulting *pro forma ROE* is within a plausible range of the cost of capital, given any sustainable competitive advantage. An example helps illustrate the importance of making the pro forma adjustments. Pharmaceutical companies have historically generated ROEs that average about 30 percent, whereas the cost of capital in this industry has been in the range of 10 to 15 percent. Is this evidence of monopoly profits? Possibly, but first we need to consider that pharmaceutical companies' annual R&D expenditures have averaged around 25 percent of the book value of equity. Now let's assume that these R&D expenditures generate benefits evenly over the next 12 years, so at any given point there is an average of six years' worth of R&D investment missing from book value. This means we have omitted from book value capitalized R&D equal to about 150 percent of book value (25 percent per year times an average of six years). Hence, if ROE based on as-reported numbers is

$$ROE = \frac{NI}{BKV} = 30\%$$

then pro forma ROE′ is equal to

$$ROE' = \frac{NI}{BKV(1 + 1.5)} = 12\%$$

which is in line with the cost of equity capital. No monopoly profits here!

Forecast Horizon and Terminal Value Assumptions for Kohl's

As we will discuss more in the next chapter, Kohl's is currently in a rapid growth phase. Based on their past growth and on their stated plans for the future, this phase should continue for approximately eight more years. Further, while Kohl's is currently experiencing unusually good performance for the Clothing and Accessories industry, we don't see anything so unique about their strategy that will yield a permanent competitive advantage, and doubt that they can hold onto their current levels of profitability for much longer. Finally, there are no significant accounting distortions in Kohl's financial statements that will cause ROE to be systematically different from the cost of capital. Putting all this together, we set our forecast horizon for Kohl's at 10 years. In addition, we set the terminal period sales growth at 5 percent to match the forecast for the economy. As we fill out our detailed forecasts for Kohl's in the next chapter, we also will be mindful to keep the terminal ROE below 15 percent, which would be a high estimate of the cost of capital in the Clothing and Accessory industry.

7.6 THE BALANCE SHEET "PLUG"

When we build a forecast of the balance sheet that contains 20 line items, we have only 19 degrees of freedom. In other words, since the balance sheet must balance, the forecasts for the first 19 line items determine the forecast for the 20th line item. More generally, regardless of the number of line items on the balance sheet, the forecast of one line item will always have to be set to make sure that the balance sheet balances. We call this line item the balance sheet *plug*. But which line item should we select for the balance sheet plug? The net operating assets are determined by the level and nature of the firm's business activities and should therefore definitely be forecasted, making them unsuitable as a plug. This leaves line items relating to financing activities. These line items are more suitable as a plug, because management can generally adapt them as circumstances require. In other words, management typically decides on their desired level of operating and investing activities and then picks a set of financing activities that provide sufficient capital to fund the operating and investing activities.

While most analysts would agree that the net operating assets should be forecasted directly, there is less agreement on which particular financing line item should be used as a plug. Some analysts use cash as the plug (with a negative cash balance representing a bank overdraft). This has two shortcomings. First, it assumes that management will make no attempt to establish a financing policy that keeps their cash balance at the minimum level necessary to sustain their operating activities. This is a somewhat naïve financing policy (but, then again, it seems to be the one that Microsoft is using). Second, in the case of a bank overdraft, it presupposes that management would be able to secure an overdraft. In the case of a financially distressed firm, this may not be a reasonable supposition.

The other common choice is to plug to common equity. The appeal of this choice is that the common stockholders are the residual claimants of the firm and are thus the natural group to soak up any surpluses or deficits in the firm's financing activities. But this approach also has two shortcomings. First, in the case of a financing surplus, plugging to common equity assumes that management will pay a big dividend or make a big stock repurchase. But many managers instead choose to either keep surplus cash or reinvest it in new projects. Second, in the case of a financing deficit, plugging to common equity assumes that the firm will issue new equity. As with a bank overdraft, this presupposes that management would be able to access capital markets on acceptable terms.

There is no perfect answer to this problem. eVal plugs to common equity, but we warn you not to take the results of this assumption blindly. You should look at the plug amount and ask yourself whether the implied amount of stock issued or repurchased really represents what you think management will do. If not, then you need to iterate back through the other line items in your forecasting model until you get a complete set of forecasts that you are happy with. For instance, if you really believe that management will build a large cash balance rather than repurchase stock (like Microsoft has), then turn up the forecasted cash and the plug to common equity will automatically make the implied stock repurchase to come down.

7.7 FORECASTING WITH eVal

Now let's take a look at how eVal guides you through the forecasting process. Step two of the User's Guide sheet in eVal walks you through the forecasting process. You start by clicking the Input Forecasting Assumptions button. This will bring up the dialog box shown in Figure 7.2 prompting you to select a forecast horizon. The horizon options are 5 years, 10 years, or 20 years. Use the guidelines provided in Section 7.4 to select an appropriate forecast horizon. If you want to select a forecast horizon that is between the options provided, select the next longest forecast horizon and then straight-line your forecasts beyond your desired forecast horizon. For example, if you would like to use a forecast horizon of 14 years, then select a 20-year horizon and straight-line your forecasts for years 15 through 20.

FIGURE 7.2
Forecasting Horizon in eVal

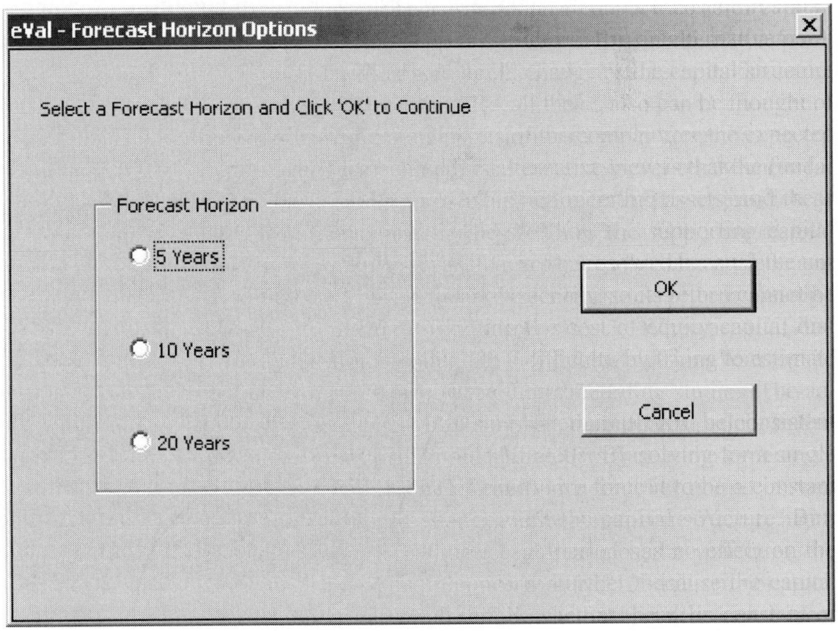

FIGURE 7.3
Forecasting
Assumptions Sheet
in eVal

	A	B	C	D	E	F	G	H	I	Fo
	File Edit View Insert Format Tools Data Window eVal Help									
	A3 ▼ =									
1	**Forecasting Assumptions**									
2	Go To User's Guide		Change Forecast Horizon							
3										
5	Company Name	Kohl's Corporation								
6	Forecast Horizon	10 Years								
7	Estimated Price/Share=$41.77									
8		Actual	Actual	Actual	Actual	Actual	Forecast	Forecast	Forecast	Fo
9	Fiscal Year End Date	1/31/1998	1/30/1999	1/29/2000	2/3/2001	2/2/2002	2/2/2003	2/2/2004	2/2/2005	2/
10										
11	Implied Return on Equity		0.182	0.181	0.191	0.199	0.192	0.191	0.189	
12										
13	Income Statement Assumptions									
14	Sales Growth		20.3%	23.8%	35.0%	21.7%	20.2%	18.7%	17.2%	
15	Cost of Goods Sold/Sales	66.9%	66.5%	66.1%	65.9%	65.7%	65.7%	65.7%	65.7%	
16	R&D/Sales	0.0%	0.0%	0.0%	0.0%	0.0%	0.0%	0.0%	0.0%	
17	SG&A/Sales	22.8%	22.4%	22.1%	21.4%	20.8%	20.8%	20.8%	20.8%	
18	Dep&Amort/Avge PP&E and Intang.		8.1%	7.6%	8.2%	8.0%	8.0%	8.0%	8.0%	
19	Interest Expense/Avge Debt		7.3%	6.5%	7.0%	5.9%	5.9%	5.9%	5.9%	
20	Non-Operating Income/Sales	0.0%	0.0%	0.1%	0.1%	0.1%	0.1%	0.1%	0.1%	
21	Effective Tax Rate	39.9%	39.3%	38.7%	38.5%	38.0%	38.0%	38.0%	38.0%	
22	Minority Interest/After Tax Income	0.0%	0.0%	0.0%	0.0%	0.0%	0.0%	0.0%	0.0%	
23	Other Income/Sales	0.0%	0.0%	0.0%	0.0%	0.0%	0.0%	0.0%	0.0%	
24	Ext. Items & Disc. Ops./Sales	0.0%	0.0%	0.0%	0.0%	0.0%	0.0%	0.0%	0.0%	
25	Pref. Dividends/Avge Pref. Stock		0.0%	0.0%	0.0%	0.0%	0.0%	0.0%	0.0%	
26										
27	Balance Sheet Assumptions:									
28	Working Capital Assumptions									
29	Ending Operating Cash/Sales	1.4%	0.8%	0.9%	2.8%	4.5%	4.5%	4.5%	4.5%	
30	Ending Receivables/Sales	7.8%	7.4%	11.1%	11.1%	11.2%	11.2%	11.2%	11.2%	
31	Ending Inventories/COGS	25.2%	26.2%	26.4%	24.7%	24.3%	24.3%	24.3%	24.3%	
32	Ending Other Current Assets/Sales	0.4%	0.6%	1.0%	1.1%	1.3%	1.3%	1.3%	1.3%	
33	Ending Accounts Payable/COGS	7.4%	8.7%	11.2%	9.9%	9.7%	9.7%	9.7%	9.7%	
34	Ending Taxes Payable/Sales	1.3%	1.3%	1.4%	1.8%	1.7%	1.7%	1.7%	1.7%	
35	Ending Other Current Liabs/Sales	3.1%	3.2%	3.4%	3.1%	3.5%	3.5%	3.5%	3.5%	
36	Other Operating Asset Assumptions									
37	Ending Net PP&E/Sales	24.5%	25.3%	29.7%	28.1%	29.4%	29.4%	29.4%	29.4%	

User's Guide / Financial Statements \ Forecasting Assumptions / User Worksheet / Ratio Analysis / Graphics |◄|

Ready

Selecting a forecast horizon and clicking OK takes you to the Forecasting Assumptions worksheet shown in Figure 7.3. Reading across the columns of this worksheet, you will see 5 years of historical data on each of the forecasting assumptions and 21 years of forecast data. The forecast data pertaining to the forecast horizon that you selected will be shaded yellow, indicating that you are free to edit the values listed in these cells.

We will give you lots of detailed advice on filling in the yellow cells in the next chapter; for now, we just want you to become familiar with the overall way that eVal organizes your forecasting inputs. Reading down the rows of this worksheet, you will see each of the forecasting assumptions laid out following the forecasting framework outlined in Figure 7.1. For instance, we begin with the sales growth rate assumption. If you look at the default forecasting assumptions for sales growth, you will see that it makes a smooth progression over the forecast horizon from its value in the most recent historical year to a terminal year rate of 5 percent. If you change the sales growth forecast for the first year of the forecast period, eVal automatically smoothes between this new growth rate and the terminal growth rate. The default eVal formula for most line items is similar, smoothing between the value in the first forecast period and the value in the terminal forecast period. Therefore, one approach to quickly entering the forecasting assumptions is to forecast the first year and the terminal year and let the formulas smooth out everything in between. Or you can enter the first few years of forecasts and let the formulas smooth from the last year you entered to your terminal year forecast (play with it a bit—you'll soon get the hang of it!). Because eVal starts with the most recent year, you should be particularly wary of unusual changes in this last year—go back and read that MD&A again!

The remaining income statement assumptions forecast the operating margins. The default assumption for most of the income statement items is to simply straight-line their values from the most recent historical year. The exceptions to this rule are Other Income/Sales and Extraordinary Items and Discontinued Operations/Sales. These line items typically contain nonrecurring amounts, so a better default forecasting assumption is that they will be zero in all future periods. Of course, you should always take a close look at the exact nature of the items that have appeared here in the recent past and make your own assessment about the likelihood that they will recur in the future.

The balance sheet assumptions are listed further down the sheet and are presented in four groups. The working capital assumptions are basically forecasts of the turnover ratios, except that we put the balance sheet item in the numerator and divide by the corresponding flow variable (sales or cost of goods sold). This is basically the reciprocal of the turnover ratio. We have found that it is much more intuitive to put the balance sheet item in the numerator when we are trying to forecast the balance sheet item. Note also that we are forecasting the ending balance of the item rather than an average over the period (unlike the turnover ratios in eVal's Ratio Analysis sheet, which are based on average balance sheet amounts). While algebraically possible, forecasting the average balance and then backing into the implied ending balance causes the forecasted ratios to oscillate in very disconcerting ways. Consistent with the way in which we compute turnover ratios, we express inventory and payables as a percentage of cost of goods sold and all of the other working capital accounts as a percentage of sales.

The next two groups of balance sheet forecasting assumptions are the other (noncurrent) operating asset and operating liability assumptions. As with the working capital assumptions, we forecast the ending balance of each of these line items as a percentage of sales. These assumptions fill out the asset side of the balance sheet and the operating portion of the liabilities (i.e., the net operating assets). All that is left on the balance sheet are the financial obligations and equity, which are determined by your financing assumptions. The debt, minority interest, and preferred stock assumptions are statements about the firm's leverage, expressed as a proportion of total assets. Having forecasted the assets, the liabilities, and the preferred stock, the common equity balance is determined—it is the *plug* that we discussed earlier.

Notice that you are allowed to forecast the dividend payout ratio. You may wonder how the ending balance in common equity can be determined if you are free to forecast any dividend you like. Doesn't a dividend reduce the common equity balance? Technically, yes, but since the common equity balance is already determined by your other assumptions, eVal adjusts the implied stock issuances or repurchases to exactly offset any dividend that you forecast. That is, your fore-casted dividends reduce retained earnings, but eVal increases the balance in paid-in capital by exactly the same amount so as to leave common equity unaffected. Play with it a bit and you will see what we mean.

eVal provides you with a few diagnostics to help judge the plausibility of your forecasting assumptions. First, up at the top of the Forecasting Assumptions work-sheet, you will find the Implied Return on Equity. Recall from Section 7.5 that, while it is difficult to provide plausible bounds for each of the individual balance sheet and income statement assumptions, they should all combine to give a return on equity figure that is within a plausible distance from the cost of capital. Second, by returning to the User's Guide and hitting the buttons under step two, you can see a complete ratio and cash flow analysis implied by your assumptions. Do these forecasted ratios jibe with your views about the firm's future? One particularly im-portant item to look at in the cash flow analysis is Net Issuance of Common Stock. As we discussed earlier, this is the amount computed by eVal in order to make your balance sheet balance. A positive amount indicates the amount that will have to be raised through issuance of new stock; a negative amount indicates the amount that will be used to repurchase stock. You should ask yourself if the mar-ket conditions are conducive to raising new stock. Does management intend to use excess cash for stock repurchases? If not, then you need to iterate back through your forecasting assumptions until you have a more plausible scenario.

Suppose management told you they expected the balance in PP&E to be $100 million next year. To hit this amount on your forecasted balance sheet might be a bit tough—you would have to keep changing the PP&E/Sales forecast until you hit exactly $100 million on the financial statements. To make this a bit easier, eVal also let's you enter financial data directly into the financial statements. This is not the way that we recommend you build your forecasts in most cases, but it is some-times helpful. To make this happen, go to the Financial Statements sheet and click the Enter Raw Financial Forecast Data button at the top of the sheet. This will un-protect and shade in yellow all of the financial statement data relating to your cur-rently selected forecast horizon. Upon leaving the Financial Statements work-sheet, all amounts in the Forecasting Assumptions worksheet will be updated to reflect the raw forecast data that you entered. Note that using this option will over-ride and remove all of the smoothing algorithms from the Forecasting Assump-tions worksheet. Please use this feature with care. Once you hit the Enter Raw Fi-nancial Forecast Data button, you have kissed goodbye many of the internal consistency checks in eVal. If your balance sheet no longer balances, take a look in the mirror to see who is to blame.

7.8 FORECASTING EPS

The forecasts discussed so far are all firm-level forecasts. However, investors in public corporations rarely buy the entire firm. Instead, they buy shares represent-ing fractional interests in the firm. For this reason, it is common practice to express certain key forecasts on a *per-share* basis. Expressing forecasts on a per-share basis allows for direct comparisons with stock prices, which are also expressed on a per-share basis. Not surprisingly, the most common component of the financial statements to be expressed on a per-share basis is earnings. Earnings is the key accounting summary measure of firm performance and so it is useful to know just how much earnings a company is generating per share of outstanding common stock. *Earnings per share,* or EPS, is the most commonly published forecast by security analysts. Moreover, the extent to which reported quarterly EPS differs from the consensus analyst forecast of EPS is probably the single most important determinant of short-term movements in stock price.

Given the prevalence of EPS forecasts in practice, it is useful to construct your forecasts of EPS implied by your forecast financial statements. By doing so, you can quickly evaluate whether your forecasts are more optimistic or pessimistic than the forecasts of other analysts following the firm. In theory, the computation of EPS forecasts is quite simple. We simply divide forecast earnings by the forecast weighted-average number of shares outstanding for the period. In practice, however, the forecasting of the weighted-average number of shares outstanding is troublesome. There are two distinct problems. The first is in forecasting the number of shares that will be issued and/or repurchased between now and the end of each future forecasting period. The second is in forecasting the number of common stock equivalents that will be outstanding at the end of future forecasting periods.

The first problem arises because we do not know the future prices at which any stock issuances and repurchases will take place. Our forecast financial statements tell us how many dollars of common equity we expect to issue or repurchase in each future forecasting period. But in order to compute the associated number of shares, we need to know the prices at which these transactions will take place. This introduces a strange circularity into our computations. Remember that one of the main goals of financial statement forecasting is to figure out the value of a share of stock. But in order to forecast EPS, we first need to forecast the future price of a share of stock. If we already knew the latter, we probably wouldn't be bothered about doing the former! Fortunately, there is a pragmatic and internally consistent solution to this circularity problem. We simply assume that our forecasts of the future financial statements at the firmwide level are correct and appropriately incorporated in the firm's stock price. The future stock price is then computed by taking the current intrinsic stock price generated by your forecast financial statements, compounding it at the cost of equity capital, and subtracting any cash dividends paid. The computations are mundane and automated in eVal, so we won't bother with a more detailed description of them here.

The above solution is fine if the current market price of the stock is close to the intrinsic price generated by your forecasting model. But what if the current market price of the stock is very different from the price implied by your model? In this case, either your forecasting model is wrong or the market price is wrong. If you conclude that the former is the case, then you should go back to the drawing board and build a better forecasting model. If you conclude that the latter is the case, then you have identified a mispriced stock. But before computing EPS forecasts, you need to consider the possibility that the firm could issue or repurchase shares of common stock in the future at a market price that differs from intrinsic value. Firms with mispriced stock can influence their own EPS (and intrinsic share price) by engaging in strategic transactions in their own stock. Firms with overpriced stock can increase EPS (and intrinsic share price) by issuing stock, while firms with underpriced stock can increase EPS (and intrinsic share price) by repurchasing stock. This is a complicated topic, and we will defer a more complete discussion to Chapter 12. At this point, you should simply be aware that the procedure used by eVal to compute EPS does not consider such effects.

The second problem in computing EPS concerns the fact that analysts and investors most commonly forecast *diluted* earnings per share. If you are an accounting geek, you will remember that EPS comes in two varieties: basic and diluted. Basic EPS simply involves dividing earnings by shares outstanding. Diluted EPS involves dividing earnings by shares outstanding plus common stock equivalents related to potentially dilutive securities, such as employee stock options and convertible bonds. These potentially dilutive securities represent contingent claims on common equity, and incorporating them helps in figuring out what is likely to be left for the existing common stockholders. Unfortunately, the forecasting of future common stock equivalents is very complicated and difficult to do with much accuracy. We therefore focus on forecasting basic EPS. We can, however, offer you some simple practical advice if you want to forecast diluted EPS. Take a look at the firm's most recent financial statements. The income statement should report both basic and diluted EPS. If these two numbers are very similar, then potentially dilutive securities are probably not that big of a deal, and so ignoring them moving forward is reasonable. If these two numbers differ by, say, 10 percent or more, then common stock equivalents are important and should be considered. A good *base case* forecasting assumption is that the number of common stock equivalents related to potentially dilutive securities will remain constant in the future. But if you are looking at a firm that plans to restructure its employee stock option plan or refinance its convertible debt, you need to pull out your intermediate accounting text and burn some midnight oil.

To make the above discussion more concrete, let's take a look at the EPS forecasts for Kohl's using the default forecasting assumptions in eVal. The EPS forecasts and associated computations are contained in the EPS Forecaster worksheet that can be accessed by clicking the View EPS Forecasts button on the User's Guide worksheet. This worksheet is reproduced in Figure 7.4. The key financial statement inputs to this sheet are the number of common shares outstanding at the most recent balance sheet date, the forecasted price of the company (based on eVal's current forecasting assumptions), the forecast of net income for each future year, and the amount of common equity that is forecast to be issued (repurchased) in each future year. You can follow the formulas in the respective cells to trace each of these inputs back to their source worksheets.

The first computation in the EPS Forecaster worksheet is the forecast of the price at the end of each future year. The price is computed by taking the price at

FIGURE 7.4

EPS Forecaster Sheet in eVal

	A	B	C	D	E	F	G	
1	**EPS Forecaster**	($000, except per share amounts)						
2	Go To User's Guide							
3								
4	Company Name	Kohl's Corporation						
5	Common Shares Outstanding at BS Date	332,167						
6	Equivalent Shares at Valuation Date	332,167						
7	Forecasted Price at Valuation Date	$40.35						
8								
9		Forecast	Forecast	Forecast	Forecast	Forecast	Forecast	Fo
10	Fiscal Year of Forecast	2/2/2003	2/2/2004	2/2/2005	2/2/2006	2/2/2007	2/2/2008	2/2
11	Net Income	590,761	700,011	818,802	945,276	1,076,883	1,210,404	
12	Common Equity Issued (Repurchased)	(26,714)	(73,014)	(135,204)	(215,291)	(314,750)	(434,273)	
13	Forecasted Price at Year End	$42.02	$46.22	$50.84	$55.93	$61.52	$67.67	
14	New Shares Issued (Repurchased)	(636)	(1,580)	(2,659)	(3,849)	(5,116)	(6,417)	
15	Shares Outstanding at End of Year	331,531	329,952	327,292	323,443	318,327	311,909	
16	Forecast EPS	$1.78	$2.12	$2.49	$2.91	$3.36	$3.84	
17	Consensus Analyst Forecast of EPS							
18								
19	Forecast Five Year Growth Rate in EPS	17%		Although not a necessary input for eVal, we recommend that				
20	Consensus Analyst Forecast of Growth			you find the analyst forecasts for your company and store them				
21				in the yellow-shaded cells for comparison purposes.				
22								
23				To obtain analyst forecasts, click here				
24								
25								

the end of the previous year, multiplying by one plus the cost of capital to reflect the expected return for the year, and subtracting the forecast dividend per share for the year. The whole process is initiated using the price forecast computed by eVal. These future price forecasts therefore assume that the eVal forecasting model is the same model that will be reflected in future stock prices. Armed with the forecast price per share, the computation of EPS is straightforward. We first divide common equity issued (repurchased) for the year by forecast price for the year to obtain the number of new shares issued (repurchased) for the year. Next, we compute shares outstanding at the end of each year by adding (subtracting) shares issued (repurchased) for the year to the outstanding balance from the previous year. Finally, we divide net income by the average number of shares outstanding for the year to arrive at our EPS forecast.

One of the most important functions of the EPS Forecaster worksheet is to allow you to compare your EPS forecasts with the consensus analyst forecast. We provide a link at the bottom of the EPS Forecaster worksheet that takes you directly to Thomson Financial's earnings estimates. Where possible, you should compare your forecasts to the consensus analyst EPS forecasts for each of the next two years. You can also compare your revenue forecasts with the analysts' forecasts. You also should compare your forecast of the five-year growth rate in EPS to the corresponding consensus analyst forecast. Deviations between realized EPS and the consensus forecast of EPS are referred to as *earnings surprises* and are an important catalyst for stock price revisions.

7.9   SUMMARY AND CONCLUSION

Forecasting is where the rubber meets the road in equity valuation. A valuation is only as good as the forecasts that support it. And good forecasts only come from a careful synthesis of the findings from your business, accounting, and financial analyses. It is important that you forecast the complete financial statements and that you use a systematic forecasting framework that maintains internal consistency in the resulting statements. It is also important that your forecasting assumptions lead to economically plausible statements about the future.

So far we have talked about forecasting from the 30,000-foot level. The next chapter gets down to the nitty-gritty of forecasting the individual line items on the financial statements.

CHAPTER EIGHT

Forecasting Details

8.1 INTRODUCTION

The last chapter described our general framework for forecasting a firm's future financial performance. In this chapter, we give more specific guidance about how to come up with a reasonable forecast for each specific line item. Obviously, we can't tell you what to forecast in every circumstance; rather, we try to give you a list of things to think about.

As you proceed through the income statement and balance sheet assumptions, you may be plagued by the following two thoughts. The first is that there is always more you could do to develop a better forecast of each item. There is an endless amount of data available—maybe a little more hunting will produce the perfect indicator of the future for the particular variable you are trying to forecast. The second doubt is that, even after all your hard work, you still feel uncertain about the resulting forecast. Both of these feelings are valid, but there is nothing we can do about them; the world is an uncertain place. We offer you a framework to guide you through the forecasting process and we offer you some guidance about what reasonable forecasts might be, but we don't have the crystal ball that perfectly predicts the future.

This chapter will talk you through the individual income statement and balance sheet assumptions that eVal uses to construct the forecasted financial statements. For some of the forecasts, it may help to build a more detailed model and then plug the results from the fancier model into the appropriate income statement or balance sheet assumption. For instance, you may want to forecast sales growth separately for each business segment and then add them up to arrive at the final forecasted sales growth rate. To give you a place to build such detailed models, eVal includes a User Worksheet. This is essentially a blank sheet that you can use for whatever purposes you want. Besides using this sheet to build more detailed models, you can use it to store links to useful news articles, clips from other electronic sources, or pictures of your dog.

After each major category of forecasts, we will develop forecasts for Kohl's in 2001, which is the default data in eVal. The program launches with these data in it; you also can load the 2001 Kohl's data into the program from the Case Data link under the eVal menu. After all the forecasts are developed, we will compare them to what actually happened for a few years after 2001 to see how well we did.

8.2 FORECASTING SALES GROWTH

If God offers to fill in one row of your spreadsheet, this is the one to ask for. Sales growth, or the lack of it, is a huge driver of value. You should bring everything you can to bear on this forecast. eVal shows the firm's past history of sales growth, but this is only a starting point. Extreme levels of sales growth mean-revert very quickly. Nissan and Penman (2001) report that, in a large sample of firms between 1963 and 1999, the top decile of annual sales growth was about 80 percent. However, firms in this decile had sales growth of only about 20 percent in the very next year and only a bit over 10 percent in the year after that. So just because sales growth has been high in the past doesn't mean that sales growth will be high in the future.

Obviously we can't give you a recipe for forecasting sales that will apply to all companies in all situations. What follows is a basic approach along with a list of things that you should consider for most companies. We start by forecasting industry sales growth. With this as a benchmark, you can then ask if the firm is likely to increase or decrease its share of industry sales. This exercise starts with macroeconomic data and works down to a firm-specific forecast. The next step is to consider all the firm-level data in more detail. Regardless of what is going on at the industry level, your firm may behave very differently. What information is there in the firm's own financial statements and other sources that can help you predict their future sales growth?

Forecasting Industry Sales Growth

To build a forecast of industry sales growth, go back to Chapter 2 and look over the list of available macroeconomic data. What are the key drivers of sales in your industry? More importantly, what are the key indicators of *future* sales? For example, the aging of the baby boomers is a very predictable phenomenon that has huge implications for the health care sector. You could study past trends in personal expenditures on health care as a function of the median age of the population. As another example, suppose you are studying a house-building company in the South. The demand for houses is a function of many things, including age demographics, migration patterns across geographic regions, and interest rates. The U.S. government collects detailed statistics on all of these variables. You could estimate the relation between these variables and past housing demand in the South and then extrapolate from this model the demand for future housing.

Building a model of industry sales that predicts the future is no easy task. And, even if you find a set of variables that predicts industry sales very well, your particular firm may buck the trend. Nevertheless, we encourage you to spend some time on this task. Even if your work doesn't result in a great predictor of industry sales, the exercise will help you identify the key drivers of sales and this should help to keep your long-term sales forecasts reasonable. Also, keep in mind that your goal is to predict future sales, not explain past sales. A macroeconomic variable that moves concurrently with industry sales will make for a beautiful graph,

FIGURE 8.1

**Estimating Industry
and Firm Sales from
Macroeconomic Data**

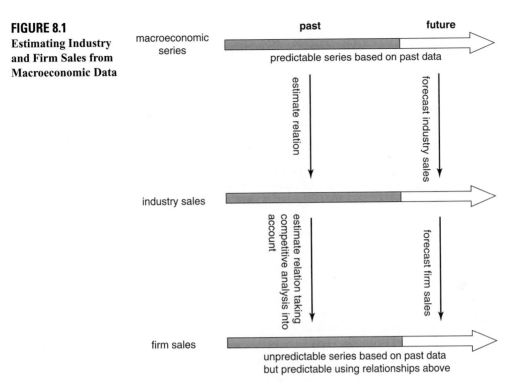

but unless you can generate decent forecasts of the variable, it won't be much help in forecasting future sales. For example, it turns out that the return on the S&P 500 is a great concurrent predictor of demand for cruise vacations; apparently, when the market is up, the "cruising" segment of the population splurges on a great vacation. While this observation makes for a great graph, it is completely useless for predicting future demand for cruise vacations, unless you think you can predict future movements in the S&P 500. And if you can reliably predict future movements in the S&P 500, then you really don't need this book!

Figure 8.1 illustrates how you might think about linking macroeconomic data to industry sales and firm-specific sales. For this to be a useful exercise, you need two key relationships to be very strong. You need the macroeconomic data to be predictable in the future and you need the links between the macroeconomic data, the industry sales, and the firm sales to be strong. If both of these conditions are true, then you can build a sales forecast by first predicting the macroeconomic series, then forecasting industry sales from the macro prediction, and then forecasting firm sales from the industry prediction. Demographic trends, for example, are very predictable macroeconomic phenomena. It would be foolish to ignore these trends if your firm's customers come from a particular slice of the demographic pie. In addition, a number of macroeconomic trends are linked to GDP growth. While GDP growth isn't a simple series to predict, economists put so much effort into forecasting it that you can get decent forecasts from the Web (check out the

Congressional Budget Office or the Conference Board link at the end of the chapter). As an example, personal consumption expenditures on durable goods (e.g., washing machines) tend to grow rapidly as the economy comes out of a recession. If the GDP forecasts indicate a recession is ending, then this is a powerful indicator of a large increase in sales of durable goods in the immediate future. On the other hand, business investment in fixed goods takes much longer to start growing after a recession, so your prediction for an equipment supplier might be much more subdued.

Once you have a forecast of industry sales growth, the next task is to predict how this will relate to your particular firm's sales growth. At this step, you need to consider the intensity of competition from alternative sources for the same products or services. Who are the firm's competitors and how intensely are they competing? The link between industry sales and firm sales is obviously stronger if the firm makes up a significant fraction of the industry. The link is weakest when the firm is small or when the industry is growing rapidly. As an example, the growth in grocery store sales in the United States has been remarkably stable over the past five years, ranging between 2 and 4 percent. No matter how much advertising stores put in the local newspapers, people can only eat so much. However, annual sales growth at Whole Foods has averaged over 20 percent in the past five years as they have expanded from 119 to 175 stores. And Winn-Dixie has averaged –5 percent growth over the past five years, recently filing for bankruptcy, as they lost much of their market share to other store chains. So, while total sales by grocery stores is a very predictable amount, it doesn't provide much guidance for firms such as Whole Foods or Winn-Dixie. Industry sales growth is a better benchmark for a large firm such as Kroger, which makes up about 12 percent of all U.S. grocery store sales ($60 billion out of $510 billion nationwide). In fact, Kroger has grown at only 4 percent annually over the past five years, much closer to the industry average.

The firm-specific facts that we discuss in the next section are typically the main drivers of sales for small and growing firms. In addition, firms with winning strategies may generate unusually large sales growth in the short run by stealing market share from other firms. But in the long run, even these companies can't escape the economic forces of the industry. Whole Foods can't grow at 20 percent forever, even if they take over the entire food industry.

Firm-Specific Influences on Sales Growth

There are many useful predictors of future sales that come from the firm itself. One significant indicator of future sales is the firm's current and future investments, especially in new sales locations, recent promotional campaigns, or new products. Firms make investments to generate future income so, assuming the firm isn't making bad bets, these investments will be harbingers of future sales. As an example, you can divide retail sales growth into growth from opening new stores and growth from increased sales at existing outlets (known as same-store or comparable-store sales growth). California Pizza Kitchen can grow rapidly by opening up new restaurants all over the country, but the very nature of a restaurant puts severe limits on the amount of sales growth that can be generated from the existing locations. Only so many people can squeeze into one booth. Retail companies frequently disclose their plans for new store openings over the next few years; you should use this information to estimate the contribution that new stores will make to total sales growth. You can then combine this with an estimate of the more modest contribution that same-store sales growth will make to arrive at the total sales growth rate (we will do this for Kohl's later in the chapter).

This same logic extends well beyond forecasting in the retail sales business. Most investments are made to generate a sequence of future sales. When the newly invested capital goes online, there is a big burst of new sales, followed by a reasonably steady stream of future sales from that investment. It therefore is useful to distinguish between the large bursts of sales growth that come from newly invested capital and the much lower growth in sales, if any, that comes from the continued operation of the previously invested capital.

You frequently can gain some useful information from the segment disclosure footnote in the financial statements. This footnote describes sales, profits, and investments by major product lines and geographic regions. This information can help focus your attention on the largest sources of sales for the firm and shows you where they are investing for the future. The firm's MD&A (capital resources section) is also a good source of information about the firm's future growth prospects.

Forecasting future sales is very important but very difficult. Take this part of the forecasting task seriously, but also be mindful that some fraction of future sales is inherently unknowable. Floods, pestilence, technological innovation, and the inherent fickleness of the American consumer all combine to make sales a truly random variable. Use all of your collected wisdom to make educated guesses and to put reasonable bounds on your estimates but then move on.

Finally, we would like to repeat the warning from the previous chapter. Do *not* make the terminal year forecast of sales growth very large—7 percent might be a maximum. Think about what it would mean to forecast a large growth rate into perpetuity: as the company grows faster than the world economy, it would slowly but surely take over the entire planet. So unless you mean to forecast this type of world domination, don't let your sales growth forecast get too big in the terminal period.

A Sales Forecast for Kohl's

We will illustrate our approach to forecasting sales using Kohl's. Recall that, in the last chapter, we decided to use a 10-year forecasting horizon for Kohl's. Since Kohl's is a small but rapidly growing firm, the macro approach to forecasting sales might not be very fruitful, at least for the next few years. In the short run, we should forecast their sales based on estimates of their new store growth. However, in the long run, Kohl's will be subject to the undeniable fact that the Clothing and Accessory industry is a relatively stable and slowly growing industry. We will start by looking for the drivers of industry sales growth to guide our terminal period

FIGURE 8.2 **Clothing and Accessories Industry Sales Growth Drivers**

Source: Bureau of Census Retail Sales Survey and Bureau of Economic Analysis NIPA tables.

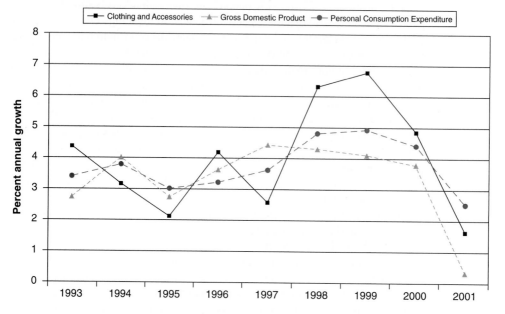

forecast but then develop our more immediate sales forecasts for Kohl's based primarily on company-specific data. We also will develop the forecast as though we are at the end of fiscal 2001 to match the resident data for Kohl's in eVal, and so that we can compare the forecast with what actually happened.

Figure 8.2 illustrates how sales growth in the Clothing and Accessories industry is related to growth in the gross domestic product and particularly to growth in personal consumption expenditures. While growth in Clothing and Accessories sales is more volatile than growth in personal consumption expenditures or GDP, all three series basically move together and average to about the same amounts over time. In addition, consumer expenditure survey data from the Bureau of Labor Statistics shows that the percent of personal consumption expenditures on apparel has remained almost constant over the past few years. Forecasted growth in GDP is therefore likely to be a good predictor of growth in the Clothing and Accessories industry. At the end of 2001, the Congressional Budget Office estimated that nominal GDP growth (real GDP growth plus price inflation) would be 3.4 percent in 2002, increase to 5.2 percent in 2004, and remain relatively constant thereafter. Given the correspondence between GDP growth and growth in the Clothing and Accessories industry, we can use this as our industry forecast. Although Kohl's is likely to grow faster than the industry for some time, eventually it will be governed by these more modest growth forecasts.

Turning to company-specific information, we learn from Kohl's fiscal 2001 10-K that they had 382 stores located primarily in the Midwest and East. They also state that they expect to open 70 new stores in 2002 and 80 new stores in 2003, and plan to continue opening stores at this rate as they grow throughout the country. To estimate how many stores a fully built-out system would contain, we note that in Wisconsin and Michigan, two of Kohl's most developed states, they are averaging 3.5 stores per million people. Extrapolating to the U.S. population of 280 million, this suggests a mature system of about 980 stores (as a point of comparison, Target Stores has 1,400 stores). So we tentatively forecast that they will add 80 stores per year from 2003–2009 in order to meet their growth objectives.

New stores certainly contribute to growth in sales, but, in the retail environment, an equally important statistic is the growth in sales from stores that have been open at least a year, known as comparable-store sales. Kohl's notes with pride in their 2001 MD&A that they enjoyed 6.8 percent comparable-store growth even though the general economy suffered (as a point of comparison, Target Stores had comparable-store sales growth of 4.1 percent in 2001). Looking ahead, Kohl's MD&A notes that, in the future, they expect comparable-store growth rates in the "mid single digits." We interpret this to mean 5 percent.

There are many ways to weave the new-store growth estimate and the comparable-store growth estimate together into a forecast of future sales. We will take only a quick whack at it here. We begin by plotting sales on the number of stores for each year since 1992, as shown in Figure 8.3. Obviously, these two variables are closely related. If we extrapolate the line to 452 stores (382 old plus 70 new), we get a forecast for 2002 of $8,959 million, or 19.6 percent, and the slope of the line indicates that each new store adds about $21 million in sales. The trouble with this estimate is that it doesn't take into account the difference between comparable-store sales growth and sales growth from opening new stores. A slightly more sophisticated approach compounds the growth from adding stores with comparable-store growth. Adding 70 stores to a starting base of 382 is an increase of 18.3 percent. Now suppose that, once a new store is open, it is immediately mature and enjoys the same comparable-store growth as an existing store. In this case, we can compute the growth rate in sales as the

FIGURE 8.3
The Relation between Kohl's Number of Stores and Sales

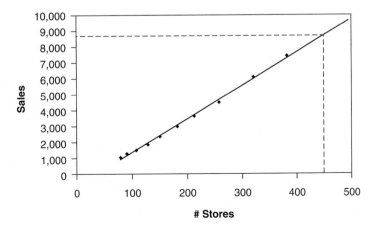

FIGURE 8.4   **Sales History and Sales Forecasts for Kohl's**

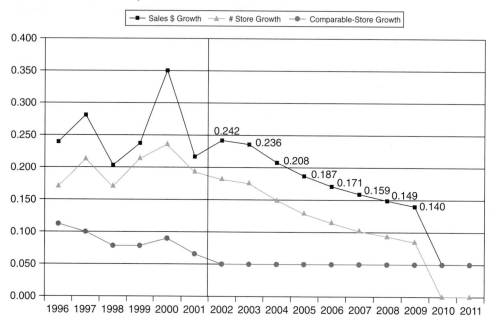

compounded growth in new stores and the comparable-store growth rate. For fiscal 2002, this is (1 + .183)(1 + .05) − 1 = 24.2 percent sales growth. A similar calculation gives 23.6 percent sales growth in 2003, and slowly declining growth rates through 2009, as illustrated in Figure 8.4.

Can Kohl's continue to outperform the industry sales growth forecast of 5 percent for the next 10 years? Based on their past, it certainly seems possible, but remember that every dollar of sales growth Kohl's gets beyond 5 percent is being taken from someone else. As Kohl's continues to enter new markets, it may find increasingly hostile competitors. For this reason, we drop the terminal year sales growth to 5 percent, matching the economywide GDP estimate.

8.3   EXPENSE FORECASTS

As a road map to the expense forecasts, Figure 8.5 shows the income statement assumptions section of eVal's Forecasting Assumptions sheet. Having completed the sales growth forecasts, now it is time to think about how expenses are going to eat away at those revenues.

Many expenses move directly with sales, such as cost of goods sold and selling, general, and administrative expenses, and so we forecast these expenses as a percentage of sales. However, just because the forecast input is a percentage of sales doesn't mean that you should forecast it as a *constant* percent of sales. Firms may enjoy economies of scale as they grow or they may implement cost management

FIGURE 8.5 Income Statement Assumptions for Kohl's

	Actual	Actual	Forecast	Forecast	Forecast	Forecast	Forecast	Forecast	Forecast	Forecast	Forecast	Forecast	TERMINAL YEAR Forecast
Forecasting Assumptions													
Go To User's Guide													
Company Name													
Forecast Horizon													
Estimated Price/Share=$57.91													
Fiscal Year End Date	2/3/2001	2/2/2002	2/2/2003	2/2/2004	2/2/2005	2/2/2006	2/2/2007	2/2/2008	2/2/2009	2/2/2010	2/2/2011	2/2/2012	2/2/2013
Implied Return on Equity	0.191	0.199	0.207	0.223	0.230	0.233	0.233	0.227	0.222	0.216	0.197	0.192	0.197
Interest Expense/Avge Debt	7.0%	5.9%	6.0%	6.0%	6.0%	6.0%	6.0%	6.0%	6.0%	6.0%	6.0%	6.0%	6.0%
Non-Operating Income/Sales	0.1%	0.1%	0.0%	0.0%	0.0%	0.0%	0.0%	0.0%	0.0%	0.0%	0.0%	0.0%	0.0%
Effective Tax Rate	38.5%	38.0%	38.1%	38.2%	38.3%	38.3%	38.3%	38.3%	38.3%	38.3%	38.3%	38.3%	38.3%
Minority Interest/After Tax Income	0.0%	0.0%	0.0%	0.0%	0.0%	0.0%	0.0%	0.0%	0.0%	0.0%	0.0%	0.0%	0.0%
Other Income/Sales	0.0%	0.0%	0.0%	0.0%	0.0%	0.0%	0.0%	0.0%	0.0%	0.0%	0.0%	0.0%	0.0%
Ext. Items & Disc. Ops./Sales	0.0%	0.0%	0.0%	0.0%	0.0%	0.0%	0.0%	0.0%	0.0%	0.0%	0.0%	0.0%	0.0%
Pref. Dividends/Avge Pref. Stock	0.0%	0.0%	0.0%	0.0%	0.0%	0.0%	0.0%	0.0%	0.0%	0.0%	0.0%	0.0%	0.0%

programs; both would lower these expense ratios. In addition, remember that a sales price increase has the same effect as lowering expenses when it comes to forecasting expenses as a percent of sales.

In some cases, the account balances rather than sales levels are the drivers of the income statement items. For example, there is a very strong relation between the debt on the balance sheet and the interest expense on the income statement: the debt balance times the interest rate equals the interest expense. So for interest expense and some other items, the forecast of the income statement item is based on its relation to a balance sheet item.

When forecasting a firm's expense ratios, you should always compare them with their industry peers. As we discussed in Chapter 5, you can load a peer firm or an industry composite into eVal from the Data Center sheet. Alternatively, you can find these statistics at Yahoo!Finance.

Cost of Goods Sold

The ratio of cost of goods sold (COGS) to sales describes how much of every sales dollar is spent directly on providing the product or delivering the service. When forecasting this item, think about how the firm's products or services are viewed in the product market. Can they charge a price premium over their competitors? Is this premium sustainable in the long run? Are there manufacturing efficiencies to be gained that will lower production costs? The effects of competition are first seen in this line item: as a firm is forced to lower its prices in response to competitors' price reductions, this ratio will increase. Much of the ratio analysis of profitability that we discussed in Chapter 5 is designed to help you forecast this item. In addition, you may find some guidance for this forecast by reading the firm's MD&A and earnings announcements. Note that the discussion in the MD&A may be pitched in terms of the gross profit margin, defined as

$$\text{Gross Profit Margin} = 1 - \text{COGS/Sales}$$

So, for example, a pure price increase, with no other changes, will increase the gross profit margin, which reduces the COGS/Sales ratio.

It is possible that a firm's COGS/Sales ratio will exhibit economies of scale if you are forecasting significant sales growth, but this depends on the firm's mix of fixed and variable costs. If the COGS is primarily the cost of purchased inventory, for example, then it will vary directly with sales, so you shouldn't expect economies of scale. On the other hand, if the COGS is due primarily to depreciation (and you are sure that depreciation expense is being included as part of COGS), then as sales increase, the depreciation will not increase proportionally, so this ratio could enjoy some economies of scale. We will discuss how to estimate economies of scale when discussing the forecast for SG&A/Sales, as this is where scale economies typically manifest themselves. If the firm has exhibited some economies of scale that have caused the COGS/Sales ratio to decline in recent years, you should still ask yourself how much longer you expect this trend to continue. Even if the primary component of COGS is depreciation, at some point increasing sales will probably require increasing the asset base, which will engender yet more depreciation.

Along with the firm's own past, the COGS/Sales ratio of a few close competitors is a good place to start when forecasting this ratio. If the firm has a low COGS/Sales ratio relative to its peers, then you need to think about whether or not it can sustain this advantage. If you are analyzing a young firm with no clear cost structure yet exhibited in the data, then using a more mature firm's COGS/Sales ratio in your forecasts is a good idea.

Research and Development Expenses

While there is no necessary relation between research and development (R&D) expenses and sales, many firms budget their R&D expenditures in exactly this way. For instance, Gillette has a stated goal of growing R&D expenditures at the same rate as sales, so the ratio of R&D to sales should remain constant for Gillette. Be particularly cognizant of the stage in a firm's life cycle when forecasting this item. Start-up firms will invest a much larger fraction of their sales in R&D with the intent of bringing this percentage down over time. Also, there may be a relation between the firm's R&D spending and the price premium implied in your COGS forecast. A firm whose strategy is to continually develop new products and sell them at a premium will have a higher R&D to sales ratio and a lower COGS to sales ratio than a firm that copies other firms' products and sells them at a discount. For example, a hallmark of IBM is its research and development activity: it has the largest number of patents granted per year for any firm in the United States for the last six years running. This strategy is reflected in its ratios: IBM's ratio of R&D expense to sales has been fairly constant at about 6 percent, and its gross margin is about 38 percent. In contrast, Dell Computer invests only 1.5 percent of its revenue in R&D, but its gross margin is only 22.5 percent—clearly a different strategy than at IBM.

You should be aware of opportunistic accounting related to R&D on software. Software development costs can be capitalized as an asset once the product is "technologically feasible"—whatever that means—so these expenditures will not show up in R&D expense immediately. Given the vagueness of this definition, companies have considerable flexibility when choosing whether to allocate expenditures to R&D, in which case they are expensed immediately, or to software development, in which case they are classified as an asset and then amortized to expense over a number of years.

Selling, General, and Administrative Expenses

Selling, general, and administrative (SG&A) expenses have some components that move directly with sales, such as commissions paid to the sales force, and other components that are only weakly related to sales, such as clerical staff salaries. The fixed components will give this ratio some economies of scale, so it may decline as a percentage of sales if sales grow. Working against this effect, however, is the fact that many of these expenditures are highly discretionary. For example, when sales are high, the firm may invest in management training programs, but when sales are low, they may cut back on these types of discretionary expenditures. However, there is evidence that SG&A costs are "sticky" in the sense that they increase when times are good, but they fail to decrease when times are bad. You can imagine a firm adding people and assets with careless abandon when sales are growing. But, having gotten use to the assets and people, management might be reluctant to dispose of them quite so quickly when sales start to decline. Examine how this ratio has changed in the past in response to changes in the sales growth rate for evidence of economies of scale. As an example, Figure 8.6 plots the SG&A/Sales and COGS/Sales ratios for Amazon.com over the five years between 2000 and 2004 when sales grew about 150 percent. Note the severe economies of scale for the

FIGURE 8.6   **Economies of Scale in COGS and SG&A for Amazon.com**

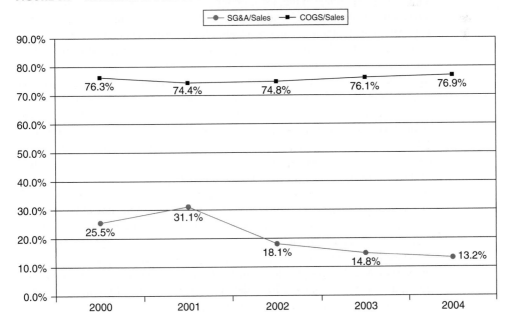

SG&A ratio, which drops from 25.5 percent to 13.2 percent over the five-year period, whereas the COGS ratio hardly changes at all.

To estimate a firm's economies of scale, we need to do a bit more than plot the SG&A ratio on sales for a few years. While such a plot gives some loose guidance, the amount of sales growth is different each year, so the plot doesn't have equal-sized steps across years. To adjust for this, regress the percentage change in SG&A on the percentage change in sales. If the resulting line has a slope of less than one, there are scale economies present. Multiply the slope coefficient times the forecasted percentage growth in sales to get the estimated percentage growth in SG&A (we will give an example using Kohl's in a later section) and then back into what this implies for the SG&A/Sales ratio.

Depreciation and Amortization

The ratio of depreciation and amortization to average (net) property, plant, and equipment (PP&E) and intangibles is forecasted based on the relation between the balance sheet amounts and the income statement amounts. For firms that use straight-line depreciation and replace assets at roughly the same rate as they depreciate them, this ratio is approximately constant and equal to one over *half* the average useful life of the assets (half because, in steady state, the assets are roughly halfway through their useful life, so net PP&E is roughly half gross PP&E). But there are some minor problems with this approach that can't be helped given the typical data that are available as an input to eVal. The general idea is that straight-line depreciation and amortization expenses are charged off uniformly over the asset's life. But, in this case, what we really want to use is *gross* PP&E and intangibles in the denominator of this ratio, not the *net* amount. However, while you can usually find the gross PP&E balance somewhere in the financial statement footnotes, you can rarely find the gross intangibles balance, and neither amount is shown on the face of the balance sheet. The distortion that this introduces is minor for stable firms but large for growing firms because their asset age is changing over time. For a growing firm, this ratio increases as the mix of assets changes from mostly new assets to assets that are, on average, halfway through their useful life. To deal with this, we recommend finding the disclosure in the financial statement footnotes that gives the total gross balance and net balance of PP&E. From this you can compute the proportion of net PP&E to gross PP&E and then multiply the ratio given in eVal by this amount to get an estimate of the ratio of depreciation and amortization expense to *gross* PP&E and intangibles (note that we are assuming that the age mix in intangibles is the same as the age mix in PP&E). One over this amount is an estimate of the useful life of the assets. Enter one over *half* of the useful life estimate as your terminal year forecast. Is this a cool recipe or what?

Another problem that sometimes arises when forecasting depreciation and amortization is that the line item is not shown on the income statement and so is coded as zero by the standardized data providers. If you get the actual financial statements, you can typically find the depreciation and amortization amounts on the statement of cash flows, but this is of only limited value because you don't know what income statement line item the company lumped these expenses into. They could be included as part of COGS, as part of SG&A, or, most likely, divided between these two line items. If you know which line item contains the depreciation and amortization expense, then you can correct the financial statements in eVal by moving the balance to the Depreciation and Amortization line item. Otherwise, all you can do is skip this item and pick it up implicitly in your forecasts of COGS and SG&A.

To forecast the depreciation and amortization expense ratio, you need to think about the type of assets that the firm must deploy to generate sales and how long these assets are expected to last. The footnote that describes the firm's accounting policies typically gives the useful lives of their major types of assets. If the firm primarily uses just one type of asset, then this disclosure is a great guide for your forecast (e.g., if the asset has a 10-year useful life, then forecast 20 percent), but, more commonly, all you learn is that buildings have a 20- to 40-year life, equipment has a 5- to 10-year life, and computers have a 2- to 4-year life. In addition, the intangible asset goodwill is no longer amortized over any period; instead, each year, the accountants ask if it has been "impaired." The consequence of this accounting treatment is that it is virtually impossible to forecast when the consumption of goodwill will show up as an expense in the financial statements. Practically speaking, all you can do is look at how the firm has handled goodwill impairment in the past and hope that this translates into the future.

Interest Expense

The ratio of interest expense to average debt is the firm's average interest rate on all their debt combined. The past rate at which the firm has borrowed is a good indicator of their future borrowing rate, unless you forecast a large change in either the firm's default risk or macro-level interest rates. You also may want to read the debt footnote and see what rate the firm has borrowed at most recently. As a reminder, we warned you in Chapter 5 to beware of interest income that is netted against the company's interest expense. This will make the past interest expense look extremely low when computed as a percent of average debt. If this is the case, then you should find the amount of interest income and move it into the nonoperating income line item on the financial statements. Another complication arises if a firm has convertible debt. Convertible debt carries a lower interest rate because of the value of the conversion option. The easiest method of dealing with this problem is to assume that the firm will issue straight debt in future years at the going market rate of interest (see Chapter 12 for more detail on this issue).

Nonoperating Income

Nonoperating income includes such things as dividends received or interest income on investments, the write-down of assets, and other miscellaneous income. Because this item represents a mix of many things, none of which have obvious drivers, we ask you to forecast it as a percent of sales with the idea that the amounts for these items vary roughly with the firm's size. If the past amounts of nonoperating income are significant, then you should go back to the actual financial statements and figure out what is in this item.

If the nonoperating income is interest or dividends from a financial asset, you need to think about whether that asset will exist in the future. For example, a firm might have an unusually large cash balance if it has recently raised capital but not yet spent it, and this cash balance will beget some interest income. If you believe that the cash will soon be invested in operating assets, then the interest income will soon disappear. Alternatively, the asset might be an investment in another company that was made for strategic reasons and is not expected to change in the near future. In this case, the dividend income or equity method income is likely to continue in the future but will bear no relation to the level of company sales. In this case, you will want to forecast the nonoperating income as a dollar amount and input the result directly on eVal's Financial Statements sheet. The general point is that income rarely falls from the sky, even nonoperating income; rather, it takes assets to produce it. Make sure that you know where these financial assets are on the balance sheet—they may be in cash and marketable securities, they may be in investments, or they may be lumped in with something else—and keep track of the relation between the balance of these assets and your forecast of nonoperating income.

Other items that frequently show up as part of nonoperating income are asset write-downs, impairment charges, and restructuring charges (note that expenses are entered as negative numbers in eVal). While all of these charges sound like one-time events, it is actually quite common for companies to record expenses like these year after year. If you see a string of impairment and restructuring expenses in their past financial statements, then it is very likely that they will continue in the future. In effect, the company is moving normal operating charges into this line item. If this is the case, then your forecasts should treat them as recurring expenses. In addition, if you anticipate a significant asset write-down in the future, possibly because you believe the company's accounting is currently too aggressive, then you should work out more precisely how the write-down will affect this ratio.

Effective Tax Rate

A firm's effective tax rate is the ratio of the tax expense to earnings before income taxes (EBIT). As a ballpark figure, the statutory tax rate for most firms in the United States is 35 percent. To this you add a few percentage points for state and local taxes and possibly deduct a few percentage points for the tax advantages that come from having foreign operations, if your company should be so lucky. The firm's tax footnote contains a great table that explains why the effective tax rate differs from the statutory 35 percent. In accounting language, the items appearing in this table are called *permanent differences* to distinguish them from the *timing differences* that create deferred taxes, as discussed later. You should look through this table with an eye for things that might change in the future. For example, if a company is planning to move its operations from

California, with a flat corporate tax rate of 8.84 percent, to Kansas, with a flat corporate tax rate of 4 percent, it will save 4.84 percent on its effective tax rate (but it will give up the ocean view).

If the firm is losing money (pretax), then its current effective tax rate may be a very poor indicator of its future tax rate. Suppose, for example, that you are examining a young company that has yet to show a profit. The company's losses create net operating loss carryforwards, which can be used to reduce taxes in the future if they become profitable, but can only be booked as assets in the year of the loss under strict conditions. So our young company will probably have an effective tax rate close to zero. But if you forecast that the company will become profitable, then you need to increase the effective tax rate in the future. The company will be able to keep the effective tax rate near zero for a few years beyond the point that it turns profitable by using its net operating loss carryforwards to offset the profit, but eventually profitable companies must pay taxes. We hate to send you there, but the only place you can learn about all this stuff is in the tax footnote. Grab your flashlight and carry a stick.

Minority Interest

Minority interest represents the claim on the income of the consolidated firm of the shareholders in subsidiaries. For most firms, this is zero because they own 100 percent of their subsidiaries, so there are no minority shareholders to make a claim, and you can skip to the next item. However, ignoring this line item for firms that actually have a minority interest can lead to big mistakes, so we include a line for it on eVal's Forecasting Assumptions sheet. These minority shareholders have a claim to some portion of the subsidiary's income, which is being reported as part of the consolidated total. We ask you to forecast this amount as a percent of after-tax income. But since the size of the minority interest claim varies with the subsidiary's income and not the parent company's income, there is no necessary reason that this line item will remain constant. It is generally very difficult to get much information about the subsidiary's income, however, so this scaling variable is the best we can do. If the subsidiary's income moves roughly with the parent's income, then this percentage will be fairly constant.

Other Income

Other income is a bit of a catchall line item. This item differs from the nonoperating income because it is after-tax. You might find the after-tax effects of investment gains/losses or equity method investments here. If this item is nonzero, then you really need to read the actual financial statements to figure out what the company or standardized data providers have put here and whether you believe it will continue in the future. As with nonoperating income, we ask you to forecast this as a percent of sales simply to capture the idea that these items tend to increase with the size of the firm, not because sales is really the driver of these costs. This line item is also a good place to tuck any major adjustments that you might make to the financial statements. For instance, if you want to forecast a large write-off, possibly because you think the company's accounting practices are aggressive, then you can enter the after-tax effect on this line item and keep it nicely separated from the rest of your forecasts.

Preferred Dividends

The ratio of preferred dividends to average preferred stock is quite similar to the ratio of interest expense to debt discussed earlier. This ratio gives the preferred dividend payout percentage, which can usually be found in the financial statement footnotes, or can be inferred from the statement of shareholders' equity. For some firms, you may notice that their balance sheet shows preferred stock outstanding yet shows 0 percent for this ratio in the past data. This occurs because some standardized data providers do not give the preferred stock dividend in their database, so our default entry is zero. If you see a historical balance of preferred stock, then you should get the firm's complete financial statements to look up the historical dividend percentage and input the preferred dividends manually on the Financial Statements sheet in eVal.

Some Final Thoughts about Forecasting the Income Statement

The result of your income statement assumptions is a forecast of the firm's entire sequence of future income statements. For each line item, you should think once again about the transition from the firm's most recent historical performance to its performance in the next few years, through its transition to your terminal year forecasts. As a rough guide, you might think of the near-term performance as being driven by firm-specific activities, such as a rapid expansion plan or a cost-cutting initiative, while the long-term performance as being driven by industrywide and economywide forces, such as changes in consumer spending or technological innovations. Do your forecasts paint a reasonable picture of how the firm might evolve? You will undoubtedly feel more confident about your near-term forecasts than your long-term forecasts; this is simply the reality of forecasting in an uncertain world.

You aren't completely done with your income statement assumptions. These assumptions and the balance sheet assumptions together imply financial ratio and cash flow consequences, and these consequences might be unrealistic. If this is the case, as it usually is after just the first pass, then you need to revisit your income statement assumptions once again.

Expense Forecasts for Kohl's

As an example, we will develop a set of expense forecasts for Kohl's. As input to these forecasts, you may want to refer back to the ratio analysis of Kohl's in Chapter 5. Kohl's has shown a steady improvement in its gross margin over the past few years. In their 2001 MD&A, they attribute the most recent margin improvement to a shift in sales mix to a slightly greater weighting on women's clothes, which carry higher margins than their average product. We also noted in Chapter 5 that Kohl's margins are much better than Target's, their closest competitor. (Recall that you can load Target's 2001 data from the eVal menu.) Since the margin improvement was not attributed to economies of scale and since we don't anticipate a significant shift in the product mix in Kohl's stores, we anticipate no further margin improvements in the near future. Because Kohl's is still relatively young and new, we forecast that they can withstand competitive pressure for the next five years, but then competition will slowly eat away at their margins. As a guide for our long-run forecast, we note that in 2001 Target's COGS/Sales ratio was 68 percent and Saks' was about 64 percent. Placing Kohl's in between these two companies on the cost-leader versus product-differentiator trade-off, we forecast a terminal year ratio of 66 percent. We let eVal smooth years 6 through 10 to this value.

Kohl's has steadily improved its SG&A/Sales ratio each year. In their 2001 MD&A, they state that their goal is to reduce this amount by .2 percent per year. Noting that they have achieved this goal for at least the past five years, we forecast that they will continue to do so for the next five years and then reduce the ratio another .2 percent in the terminal year to reflect long-term efficiency gains. If Kohl's hadn't given us this guidance, we might have estimated the economies of scale in the SG&A. To do so, we regressed the percentage change in SG&A on the percentage change in sales using the past 10 years of data. After forcing the intercept to be zero, the estimated slope of this line is .88. Recalling that sales is forecast to grow 24.2 percent in the next year, this implies that SG&A will grow .88 * 24.2 = 18.9 percent, which implies that the new SG&A/Sales ratio will drop to 20.3 percent. Since this is a bigger savings than management is forecasting, we are going to stick with the .2 percent reduction for our forecast.

Kohl's ratio of depreciation and amortization to the average balance of *net* PP&E and intangibles is 8 percent in the most recent year and has fluctuated between 7.6 and 8.2 percent over the past five years. Because Kohl's is a rapidly growing firm, this ratio will change in a very predictable manner as their growth slows and their asset base is, on average, closer to the 50 percent accumulated depreciation of a stable company (i.e., the assets are halfway through their useful life). From the financial statement footnotes, we learn that the ratio of *gross* PP&E to *net* PP&E is about 1.2. Multiplying the 8 percent ratio by 1.2 gives roughly 10 percent, meaning that the assets have an average useful life of about 10 years. Given the mix of buildings, which have a relatively long life, with store fixtures, which have a relatively short life, this seems like a reasonable estimate. When Kohl's is in steady state and its asset mix is approximately halfway through its useful life at all times, the ratio of depreciation and amortization to *net* PP&E and intangibles will be one over half of the useful life, or 20 percent. We forecast that this ratio will increase smoothly from its current level of 8 percent to a terminal value of 20 percent.

Kohl's most recent interest expense as a percentage of the average debt balance is 5.9 percent. This may seem a bit low, but Kohl's has over a half billion dollars in subordinated convertible debt that, because of its conversion option, has an effective interest rate of only 2.75 percent. Most recently, they issued senior debt at 6.3 percent. We forecast that they will have an effective interest rate of 6 percent in the future, which is the same as Target's most recent rate.

Nonoperating income for Kohl's is due to interest income on their short-term investments. For the past two years, this interest income has been approximately 2.8 percent of the average balance of cash and marketable securities. We do not anticipate that nonoperating income will grow at the same rate as sales because we believe that Kohl's will use these balances to build new stores. Instead, we think nonoperating income will remain approximately 2.8 percent of the cash and marketable securities balance, a reasonable interest rate on this low-risk investment. In the next section, we will forecast that the cash and marketable securities balance will remain at 1.3 percent of sales so, putting this all together, we get

$$\text{Nonoperating Income/Sales} = \text{Nonoperating Income/Cash} \times \text{Cash/Sales}$$

or 2.8% × 1.3% = .0364%. This rounds to zero, which is what we ultimately forecast for nonoperating income.

Finally, Kohl's effective tax rate has declined slightly due to lower state taxes in recently entered markets, as discussed in their MD&A. However, the largest new market that they are just about to enter is California, which has one of the highest state income taxes, so we expect this ratio to increase slightly in the future. Target pays an average of 3.3 percent in state taxes (net of the federal tax benefit, as disclosed in the 2001 annual report), so we will increase Kohl's effective tax rate .1 percent a year for the next three years to bring it in line with Target's rate of 38.3 percent.

We can't do too meaningful ratio analysis on these forecasts yet because many ratios depend on balance sheet items. Moreover, our forecasts of PP&E and debt will affect the depreciation and interest expense lines.

8.4 BALANCE SHEET FORECASTS

The next set of assumptions will construct the balance sheet forecasts. They are organized into assumptions about the net operating assets, consisting of working capital, other operating assets, and other operating liabilities; and assumptions about financing. The net operating assets are forecasted as a percent of sales (or as a percent of COGS) because they are the assets that generate the sales. In contrast, the financial obligations are forecasted as a percent of total assets. As a guide to the balance sheet assumptions, Figure 8.7 shows this portion of the forecasting assumptions sheet in eVal.

8.5 WORKING CAPITAL ASSUMPTIONS

Working capital requirements are driven largely by the operating cycle of the firm. Consequently, all the forecast assumptions in this section are linked to either sales or COGS. A firm's past working capital requirements, and your forecasts of its future requirements, are a statement about the firm's operating efficiency. An improvement in operating efficiency means the firm can generate the same level of gross profit with fewer net assets tied up in working capital.

FIGURE 8.7   Balance Sheet Assumptions for Kohl's

	B	C	D	E	F	G	H	I	J	K	L	M	N
1 Forecasting Assumptions													
2 Go To User's Guide	Change Forecast Horizon												
5 Company Name	Kohl's Corporation												
6 Forecast Horizon	10 Years												
7 Estimated Price/Share=$57.91													
8	Actual	Actual	Actual	Actual	Actual	Forecast	Forecast	Forecast	Forecast	Forecast	Forecast	Forecast	Forecast
9 Fiscal Year End Date	1/31/1998	1/30/1999	1/29/2000	2/3/2001	2/2/2002	2/2/2003	2/2/2004	2/2/2005	2/2/2006	2/2/2007	2/2/2008	2/2/2009	2/2/2010
11 Implied Return on Equity		0.182	0.181	0.191	0.199	0.207	0.223	0.230	0.233	0.233	0.227	0.222	0.216
27 Balance Sheet Assumptions:													
28 Working Capital Assumptions													
29 Ending Operating Cash/Sales	1.4%	0.8%	0.9%	2.8%	4.5%	1.3%	1.3%	1.3%	1.3%	1.3%	1.3%	1.3%	1.3%
30 Ending Receivables/Sales	7.8%	7.4%	11.1%	11.1%	11.2%	11.2%	11.2%	11.2%	11.2%	11.2%	11.2%	11.2%	11.2%
31 Ending Inventories/COGS	25.2%	25.2%	26.4%	24.7%	24.3%	23.3%	22.3%	21.3%	21.3%	21.3%	21.3%	21.3%	21.3%
32 Ending Other Current Assets/Sales	0.4%	0.6%	1.0%	1.1%	1.3%	1.3%	1.3%	1.3%	1.3%	1.3%	1.3%	1.3%	1.3%
33 Ending Accounts Payable/COGS	7.4%	8.7%	11.2%	9.9%	9.7%	10.7%	11.7%	12.7%	12.7%	12.7%	12.7%	12.7%	12.7%
34 Ending Taxes Payable/Sales	1.3%	1.3%	1.4%	1.8%	1.7%	1.7%	1.7%	1.7%	1.7%	1.7%	1.7%	1.7%	1.7%
35 Ending Other Current Liabs/Sales	3.1%	3.2%	3.4%	3.1%	3.5%	3.5%	3.5%	3.5%	3.5%	3.5%	3.5%	3.5%	3.5%
36 Other Operating Asset Assumptions													
37 Ending Net PP&E/Sales	24.5%	25.3%	29.7%	28.1%	29.4%	29.2%	29.2%	29.2%	29.2%	29.2%	29.2%	29.2%	29.2%
38 Ending Investments/Sales	0.0%	0.0%	0.0%	0.0%	0.0%	0.0%	0.0%	0.0%	0.0%	0.0%	0.0%	0.0%	0.0%
39 Ending Intangibles/Sales	1.0%	0.7%	0.4%	0.2%	0.1%	0.1%	0.1%	0.1%	0.1%	0.1%	0.1%	0.1%	0.1%
40 Ending Other Assets/Sales	0.9%	1.1%	3.8%	3.1%	3.4%	3.4%	3.4%	3.4%	3.4%	3.4%	3.4%	3.4%	3.4%
41 Other Operating Liability Assumptions													
42 Other Liabilities/Sales	0.8%	0.8%	0.7%	0.7%	0.6%	0.6%	0.6%	0.6%	0.6%	0.6%	0.6%	0.6%	0.6%
43 Deferred Taxes/Sales	1.5%	1.5%	1.5%	1.4%	1.5%	1.5%	1.5%	1.5%	1.5%	1.5%	1.5%	1.5%	1.5%
44 Financing Assumptions													
45 Current Debt/Total Assets	0.1%	0.1%	3.3%	0.6%	0.3%	0.3%	0.4%	0.4%	0.4%	0.4%	0.4%	0.4%	0.4%
46 Long-Term Debt/Total Assets	19.2%	16.1%	16.9%	20.8%	22.2%	23.2%	24.2%	25.2%	26.2%	27.3%	28.3%	29.3%	30.3%
47 Minority Interest/Total Assets	0.0%	0.0%	0.0%	0.0%	0.0%	0.0%	0.0%	0.0%	0.0%	0.0%	0.0%	0.0%	0.0%
48 Preferred Stock/Total Assets	0.0%	0.0%	0.0%	0.0%	0.0%	0.0%	0.0%	0.0%	0.0%	0.0%	0.0%	0.0%	0.0%
49 Dividend Payout Ratio	0.0%	0.0%	0.0%	0.0%	0.0%	0.0%	0.0%	0.0%	0.0%	0.0%	0.0%	0.0%	0.0%

Financial Statements \ **Forecasting Assumptions** / User Worksheet \ Ratio Analysis \ Graphics \ Cash Flow Analysis \ Valuation Par

Ready

Operating Cash

Every firm requires some amount of operating cash. A typical amount might be 3 percent of sales, but firms vary widely in their holdings of cash and cash equivalents. If your firm has traditionally held a large amount of cash relative to its peers, then it probably doesn't need all this cash for daily operations; rather, part of the balance is really an investment in financial assets. As we discussed in Chapter 5, if the past operating cash balance appears larger than you think necessary for operations, you need to get the as-reported financial statements and make an estimate as to how much of the line item is really operating cash and how much is an investment in financial assets. Once you have an estimate of the amount of true operating cash and the amount of financial assets, you have a few choices about how to proceed. Assuming you think the firm is going to hang onto the financial assets, you can continue to forecast a high ratio of operating cash to sales and then include the interest income from the financial assets in nonoperating income. Alternatively, you can reclassify the financial assets into the Investments line item and forecast its balance separately.

A wilder alternative for dealing with financial assets is to liquidate them in the first forecast period, which you can do in eVal by assuming the Operating Cash/Sales ratio is zero and increasing the dividend payout sufficiently to absorb all the liquidated financial assets. On the surface, this might seem absurd since it is probably unlikely that the firm will make such an extreme change in the next period, but, from a valuation point of view, the present value of a future stream of interest income is equivalent to the liquidation value of the financial assets, so either approach will yield the same valuation (if done carefully). Liquidating the financial assets immediately has the advantage of getting the financial assets out of the picture so we can focus on forecasting the operating variables. For this reason, the liquidation alternative is the most common choice in a traditional discounted cash flow valuation.

Receivables

The ratio of receivables to sales depends directly on the company's collection policy and their customers' ability to pay. A ratio of .25, for instance, means the average receivable was outstanding for .25 of a year, or about 90 days. This is approximate because sales and collections fluctuate through the year, but you get the idea. Insofar as receivable credit is effectively granting the customer an interest-free loan, this is an important strategic decision the firm makes, and one you should think carefully about when forecasting. If the firm's past values of this ratio are constant, then this reflects a consistent collections policy that is unlikely to change in the near future. However, if the ratio is changing significantly or differs drastically from competitors' ratios, then you will need to investigate further. Ask yourself, "What is the firm's relative bargaining power with its customers?" A small firm that supplies a large firm might see a favorable receivables to sales ratio disappear quickly when economic times get tight. A great example of this phenomenon is Salton, maker of the famous George Foreman Grill ("it's a lean, mean grillin' machine!") and other small appliances. They sell the bulk of their goods to a few large retail chains, such Kmart and Wal-Mart, that are not generally known for the generous terms they provide their suppliers. Indeed, between 1998 and 2001, Salton saw the average time it took to collect its receivables go from 41 days to 73 days and its inventory holding period go from 113 days to 143 days as these big customers slowly put on the squeeze.

Inventories

The ratio of inventories to COGS is very similar to the receivables ratio, except that both the numerator and the denominator are computed using historical costs rather than selling prices. The other principal difference is that the company can acquire inventories without selling them, which would increase the numerator without the commensurate increase in the denominator. For that reason, an increasing inventory to COGS ratio is traditionally considered to be a warning sign that the company is having trouble selling its goods. Of course, the common retort is that they are stocking up for a new product release that will send sales skyrocketing. When forecasting this ratio, think about why it might differ from its historical past. Do you anticipate the company implementing a *just-in-time* inventory handling system and thus lowering the required amount of inventory? Alternatively, do you anticipate that the firm's customers or suppliers have so much bargaining power that they will force the firm to hold the inventory for increasingly long periods? Was there some unusual event in the most recent fiscal year that caused the ratio to differ significantly from its normal level?

Other Current Assets

Other current assets include tax refunds, prepaid expenses, and other miscellaneous items. We ask you to forecast this item as a percent of sales because it tends to increase with the size of the firm, so this ratio should be fairly stable. However, if this is a large amount, you really need to look at the published financial statements and see what is included in this line item and decide if it does indeed move with sales.

Accounts Payable

The ratio of accounts payable to COGS is the mirror image of the receivables ratio for the firm's suppliers (with respect to their accounts with the company). It reveals how quickly the firm is paying for the inventory it purchased and sold. Since this is an interest-free loan to the firm, the higher this ratio is the better, assuming, of course, that the firm is capable of paying the loan back. You may forecast that the ratio will increase if you believe that the firm has sufficient power over its suppliers that it can delay paying its bills. When times get tight in the automotive industry, for example, the Big Three automakers don't renegotiate the contract terms with their suppliers—they simply delay paying them for significant periods of time.

Taxes Payable and Other Current Liabilities

Taxes payable frequently show up as a current liability simply because the firm owes taxes as of the end of the fiscal quarter, but they don't have to pay them until a later date.

Other current liabilities include dividends declared but not yet paid, customer deposits, unearned revenue, and other miscellaneous liabilities that will be paid within a year. We ask you to forecast these items as a percent of sales because they tend to increase with the size of the firm, so this ratio should be fairly stable. But, as with other current assets, if the amounts in these categories are significant, you should read the financial statements to see precisely what they are and decide if you think the past ratios are good predictors of the future.

8.6   OTHER OPERATING ASSETS AND LIABILITIES

The key issue for this set of assumptions is determining the size of the firm's future investment in long-lived assets necessary to produce the forecasted sales. Consequently, these items are forecasted as a percent of sales. Your forecasts of these ratios are a statement about the firm's expected production strategy. If the firm outsources much of its production, its investment in assets will be significantly smaller than the investment that is necessary for a more vertically integrated operation. Of course, since outsourcing captures a smaller portion of the value chain, the firm should earn correspondingly smaller margins.

PP&E

To forecast the ratio of PP&E to sales, you should consider the firm's existing capacity relative to your forecast of sales growth. Firms tend to add capacity in large lumps, so as you analyze the firm's past ratio of PP&E to sales, be aware of whether the past ratio amounts were generated by assets operating at full or partial capacity. A good source of information for forecasting this item is the discussion of liquidity and capital resources in the MD&A; in fact, firms often give estimates of future capital expenditures here. And capital-intensive industries, such as steel, automaking, or airlines, often give capacity utilization statistics included in their Selected Data Schedule (Item 6 on Form 10-K). Finally, you can get industry-level statistics on growth rates in investments in different classes of assets from the Bureau of Economic Analysis fixed-asset tables.

It is common for PP&E to rise rapidly during a company's early years and then remain relatively constant thereafter. But note that this pattern does not imply that the *ratio of PP&E to sales* will rise and then flatten out. If the company's sales also are rising rapidly in the early years, this ratio could remain constant throughout the growth and maturity phases of a firm's life cycle. What you really need to think about is whether there are significant economies of scale that the firm will enjoy as it grows. As California Pizza Kitchen expands across the country, its investment in PP&E will necessarily grow at the same rate as sales because there are very few scale economies in a restaurant chain (i.e., having a restaurant in Nebraska has little effect on the cost of opening a restaurant in Oregon). Alternatively, once Iridium puts the necessary satellites in place for its global phone system, sales can grow significantly without additional investment in PP&E.

Another useful fact that can guide your PP&E forecast is the company's disclosures about future capital expenditure plans. These are not required disclosures, but it is not uncommon for a company to discuss these in their MD&A and earnings announcements. Given the beginning balance of PP&E, your forecasted amount of depreciation, and the company's estimate of its capital expenditures, the ending PP&E amount is determined (equivalently, your forecast of ending PP&E determines capital expenditures). The easiest way to get this information into eVal is to play around with your PP&E forecast until the capital expenditures line on the Cash Flow Analysis sheet corresponds with the company's estimate.

Investments

Investments are primarily made up of equity holdings by the firm in other companies. If this amount is significant for your company, then read the financial statements and figure out exactly what this investment represents. We forecast this item as a percent of sales, but there may be no structural reason for the size of the investment to be related to sales. For example, the book retailer Barnes & Noble owns approximately 36 percent of Barnes & Noble.com, which sells books over the Internet. There is no particular reason that Barnes & Noble's investment in this Internet business will increase in lock-step with sales at retail outlets. You have to ask yourself how much additional capital Barnes & Noble will invest in this enterprise.

Intangibles

Intangibles are all those assets that can't be physically touched. To be included in the accounting system, usually the intangible must have been acquired in an arm's-length transaction by the firm. So *purchased* patents, copyrights, licenses, and trademarks would be included, but *internally developed* versions of the same things are not. What you really need to forecast is *purchased* intangibles, but, unfortunately, companies that purchase lots of intangible assets generally develop lots of them internally as well. To make matters worse, the biggest purchased intangible is *goodwill,* defined to be the excess of the purchase price in a corporate acquisition over the fair market value of the identifiable assets (tangible and intangible) received. Because it is only created by an acquisition, goodwill tends to arrive in large and unpredictable lumps. Goodwill, plus the rather arbitrary distinction between purchased and internally developed intangible assets, makes forecasting intangibles very difficult. As with investments, there is no particular reason why this item should remain a constant percent of sales; we use this ratio only because larger firms tend to have more intangibles than smaller firms.

Other Assets and Other Liabilities

Other assets includes many items; some examples are long-term receivables, pre-opening expenses for retail stores, and pension assets. Other liabilities include pension liabilities and other miscellaneous noncurrent liabilities. See the financial statement footnotes for specifics if your firm has a significant amount for these items.

Deferred Taxes

To forecast deferred taxes, you need to think about the firm's tax *timing differences.* You may have noticed that when we forecasted the firm's effective tax rate, we considered "permanent differences" that caused the rate to differ from the statutory 35 percent but did not take into consideration the timing of the tax payments. For example, a firm might have accelerated tax deductions because of an investment in a certain type of asset. In this case, not only does the firm get to deduct the cost of the investment, but it also gets to deduct most of it in the first few years of the asset's useful life. Accountants capture this effect in the balance of deferred taxes, so named because accelerated deductions today mean higher taxes tomorrow when the deductions run out. The firm's specific deferred tax items are described in the footnotes to the financial statements. The principal source for deferred tax liabilities is usually the timing difference between depreciation on PP&E and the tax deductions for these investments. Early in the life of an asset, this will result in deferred tax liabilities (representing the future increase in tax payments when the accelerated tax deductions for the PP&E are exhausted); later this effect will reverse and the liability will shrink back to zero. But as long as the firm is replacing its assets, this liability will remain. If the firm maintains its assets at a fixed level, then the deferred taxes will remain a constant percentage of total assets; the ratio will increase slightly if the asset base is growing. But if you forecast that the firm will shrink its asset base, this ratio will fall dramatically. This is because without new acquisitions of assets, new tax deductions are not generated, causing tax payments to increase and the liability to fall.

Some Final Thoughts about Forecasting the Net Operating Assets

The key statistic coming out of the working capital, other asset, and other liability assumptions is the net operating asset turnover ratio (defined as sales over net operating assets), which is given on the Ratio Analysis sheet in eVal. This statistic summarizes your forecasts of the net operating assets that a firm will need to put in place in order to create the sales that you forecasted. Because a firm's asset turnover is largely determined by its production technology, this ratio typically changes very slowly over time, if it changes at all. Therefore, if your forecasts show this ratio changing dramatically, go back and make sure that you have good reasons for the specific forecasts you have made.

Forecasting Net Operating Assets for Kohl's

Most of Kohl's working capital ratios have remained relatively constant over the five years prior to 2001 (recall from Chapter 5 that the large increase in their receivables collection period that occurred in 1997 was due to a change in accounting, not underlying economics). However, we also noted in Chapter 5 that Target Stores had a much better net operating asset turnover ratio than Kohl's coming into 2001, ranging between 2.6 and 3.2 versus Kohl's most recent value of 2.1. (Recall also that you can see Target Stores' 2001 data in eVal by selecting this for the Case Data link under the eVal menu.)

Starting with the working capital assumptions, we forecast that, in the next year, Kohl's will bring down their balance of operating cash to the level of Target Stores, which is 1.3 percent of sales. This value is also near the industry average. We hold their receivables ratio constant because this has changed very little over the past three years. We forecast that, as Kohl's grows, they will be able to negotiate better deals with their suppliers, including more timely delivery of inventory and longer payment periods. The 2001 inventory-holding period at Target Stores is 58 days; at Kohl's, it is 81 days. We forecast that Kohl's will reduce this ratio by approximately 10 days by 2005, which means that the ratio of inventory to COGS will decrease 1 percent a year for the next three years. (This takes a bit of trial and error in eVal to figure out.) Similarly, Target Stores pays its accounts payable in 52 days; Kohl's pays them in 34 days. We forecast that Kohl's will increase this by 10 days by 2005, which implies that the ratio of accounts payable to COGS will increase by 1 percent per year over the next three years. The other current assets and current liabilities are not described in any greater detail in Kohl's financial statements. We forecast that these items, along with the current taxes payable balance, will remain the same percentage of sales as in the most recent year. None of the items is large enough for this rather naïve assumption to do serious damage.

The biggest remaining net operating asset that we still need to forecast for Kohl's is PP&E. This is a bit tough because Kohl's uses a mix of owned and leased stores, and many of the leased stores are accounted for as operating leases (meaning that they are not part of PP&E; rather, they simply generate rent expense in COGS). Small changes in the mix of owned versus leased stores can have a huge effect on this ratio. Fortunately, we are saved by a disclosure in Kohl's MD&A that they plan to spend $740 million on capital expenditures in 2002. A little guesswork and a lot of toggling between the Forecasting Assumptions sheet and the Cash Flow Analysis sheet in eVal reveals that the forecast of 29.2 percent for PP&E to sales results in approximately $740 million in capital expenditures in fiscal 2002. Since this value is within the range of Kohl's historical past and since the relation between stores and sales is so strong for this type of business, we maintain this ratio until the terminal period. In the terminal period, we reduce it one more percentage point in recognition of the fact that comparable store growth will continue to lower this ratio even after the system of stores is fully developed. We assume that all the remaining forecasting assumptions will stay constant at their levels in the most recent year. This is partly a cost-benefit trade-off; we can't get much information on these items and they aren't a particularly large slice of the pie.

The result of our net operating asset assumptions for Kohl's is that the net operating asset turnover ratio increases from 2.1 in 2001 to 2.3 in the terminal year.

8.7   FINANCING ASSUMPTIONS

The main consideration for this set of assumptions is the firm's long-term capital structure. What is the mix of debt and equity that the firm will employ to support the level of net operating assets you have forecasted? The optimal capital structure for a firm takes into account the risk that debt financing brings with it, as well its tax advantages. Volumes have been written in corporate finance textbooks about optimal capital structure. See, for example, Brealey and Myers (2000). When forecasting this item, you should examine the firm's capital structure in the recent past and the capital structure of other firms in the same industry. In the liquidity section of the MD&A, firms will sometimes discuss their target capital structure; if so, you should use this in your forecasts. Each of the items in this section is forecasted as a percent of total assets.

Current Debt and Long-Term Debt

Current debt is short-term borrowing plus the current portion of long-term debt that is due within a year. Long-term debt, combined with the current debt above, is the firm's total debt financing. These liabilities, unlike the other noncurrent liabilities above, are represented by contractual claims to debt capital providers. As such, they are financing liabilities rather than operating liabilities. Details of a firm's debt contracts are given in the footnotes to the financial statements. Particularly noteworthy is the discussion of short-term borrowing, the allocation of total debt to current and noncurrent portions, and the schedule of future maturities of existing debt.

Minority Interest

Minority interest represents the claim of shareholders in a firm's partially owned subsidiaries. There is no immediate reason why this amount should remain a constant percentage of total assets other than larger firms tend to have larger minority interests, if they have them at all. You could make a more informed estimate of this amount if you knew that the firm intended to acquire a less-than-100-percent interest in another company, or if you knew the firm would not be making any more acquisitions of less than 100 percent, so that this amount might decline as a fraction of total assets. But, in all honestly, it is hard enough to forecast a firm's future acquisition activity without having to also estimate the percentage of ownership they will acquire when they acquire less than 100 percent.

Preferred Stock

Preferred stock is more like long-term debt than equity when it comes to forecasting the value of the firm's common equity. Details of the preferred stock holdings can be found in the financial statement footnotes. You may want to forecast that this item remains a constant dollar value, rather than a constant percentage of total assets, unless the firm specifically says that it intends to continue issuing preferred stock.

Some Final Thoughts on Forecasting the Financing Ratios

The end result of this set of forecasts will be a leverage ratio, defined either as total capital to equity or debt to equity. Like the net operating asset turnover ratio, these ratios tend to be very stable for a firm over time, probably because the optimal capital structure of a firm is driven by fairly stable economic factors. Do not fall into the trap of believing (and forecasting) that a firm will increase its return on equity simply by borrowing to increase its leverage. Remember that more debt begets more interest expense; increasing leverage only increases ROE if the return the firm earns on the new capital exceeds the after-tax cost of debt. Note that the Forecasting Assumptions sheet in eVal automatically takes this into account—you forecast the interest rate in the income statement assumptions and this amount is applied to the forecasted debt balance.

You have now constructed the forecasted balance sheets for your company. The turnover ratio assumptions determine the net operating assets and the financing assumptions determine the financial obligations. The common equity is therefore determined: common equity equals net operating assets less financial obligations.

Dividend Payout Ratio

The dividend payout ratio shown historically is the percent of net income that is paid out as cash dividends. But note that your preceding forecasts completely determine future net income and future total common equity. Hence, your forecasting assumptions already imply the net amount of new common equity that will be issued or discharged (through a dividend or stock repurchase). The dividend payout ratio assumption determines what retained earnings will be, but with a compensating adjustment to paid-in common capital (net) that sets common equity to the level implied by your previous forecasting assumptions. That is, since the future equity balances are already determined, this assumption can only change the composition of the equity. Nonetheless, it is a useful item to forecast, because later, when performing a cash flow analysis, you will be asked to think about the reasonableness of the firm's implied stock issuance activity, and the more they pay out in dividends, the more they need to issue in new equity to finance future growth.

Forecasting Kohl's Financial Obligations

As noted in Chapter 5, Kohl's currently has a relatively low debt to equity ratio at .4 as compared to Target Stores or the industry average, both of which are closer to 1. Kohl's management might be tempted to raise their ROE by increasing their leverage, given that they have a positive spread between RNOA and the net borrowing cost, but a significant increase in leverage would likely cause their future borrowing rate to increase as well. There is no discussion in Kohl's MD&A about changes in leverage, and it has been relatively constant for the past few years. For this reason, we are reluctant to make significant changes in this amount. We forecast that the Current Debt/Total Asset ratio and the Long-Term Debt/Total Asset ratio will steadily increase to 1.5 times their most recent level, ending at terminal values of .45 percent and 33.3 percent, respectively. This will result in a terminal year debt to equity ratio of .85.

8.8   PRO FORMA ANALYSIS OF FORECASTS

Wait! You aren't done yet! Once you get to the bottom of eVal's Forecasting Assumptions sheet, you have completed your *first pass* at forecasting a complete set of financial statements. However, you now need to do some ratio and cash flow analysis on these future financial statements to see how reasonable they really are. Go back to the Ratio Analysis and Cash Flow Analysis sheets in eVal and look at what your forecasts imply for the future ratios and cash flows. Is this what you meant to forecast? Are the implied ROEs and margins consistent with industry norms? If the turnover or leverage ratios are changing significantly, be sure that this is what you really mean because, typically, these ratios are relatively stable over time.

Pro Forma Analysis of Kohl's Forecasts

If you have been busy inputting the Kohl's forecasts that we have made in the previous sections, then you can now examine the implications of those forecasts by returning to the Ratio Analysis and Cash Flow Analysis sheets in eVal. The first thing that jumps out when analyzing the pro forma financial ratios for Kohl's is that the terminal ROE forecast is 20.5 percent, well above any reasonable estimate of their cost of equity capital. Since we don't believe Kohl's has a permanently sustainable competitive advantage, and there are no major accounting distortions that will permanently inflate the ROE, this forecast seems a bit too rosy. Where did we go wrong? After looking over all the financial ratios and pro forma cash flow statements, we see two things that need some adjustment. First, even though we forecast that competitive pressures would increase the COGS/Sales ratio a bit, the net effect of our other forecasts is that the operating margin is 5.5 percent in the terminal period. This is well above the 4 percent operating margin of Target Stores, or Saks, and far above the industry average of about 2.5 percent. If we increase the terminal COGS/Sales ratio to 68 percent, that brings the net operating margin down to 4.3 percent. Second, even though our financing forecasts increased the debt to equity ratio from .4 to .85, we didn't increase the forecasted borrowing rate. If we increase the terminal period Interest Expense/Average Debt to 7 percent, the terminal ROE is 14 percent, a much more reasonable long-term forecast.

We already did some cash flow analysis when we reverse-engineered the PP&E/Sales forecast to hit the capital expenditure amount that Kohl's mentioned in their MD&A. Beyond this, everything else looks reasonable. After the first few years, the pro forma cash from operations is sufficient to fund their capital investment needs. Each year they are forecasted to issue debt and retire equity, which is exactly what we are forecasting that they will do as they increase their leverage ratio.

8.9   WHAT HAPPENED AT KOHL'S?

We developed the forecasts for Kohl's as the end of 2001 so that we could compare the forecasts with what actually happened in 2002–2004. Figure 8.8 compares the estimated and actual results for some key ratios. To see all the results, load the most recent Kohl's data into eVal (ticker = KSS) and look at the historical results.

FIGURE 8.8
Actual and Forecasted Results for Kohl's

Fiscal Year End Date	Forecast 2/2/2003	Forecast 2/2/2004	Forecast 2/2/2005	Actual 2/2/2003	Actual 2/2/2003	Actual 2/2/2005
Annual Growth Rates						
Sales	24.2%	23.6%	20.8%	21.8%	12.7%	13.8%
Advanced Dupont Model						
Net Operating Margin	0.070	0.069	0.068	0.075	0.062	0.066
× Net Operating Asset Turnover	2.237	2.367	2.410	2.066	2.015	2.061
= Return on Net Operating Assets	0.156	0.164	0.165	0.154	0.125	0.136
Net Borrowing Cost (NBC)	0.037	0.038	0.038	0.029	0.037	0.036
Spread (RNOA - NBC)	0.119	0.126	0.127	0.125	0.088	0.099
Financial Leverage (LEV)	0.422	0.465	0.507	0.401	0.325	0.240
ROE = RNOA + LEV*Spread	0.207	0.223	0.229	0.204	0.153	0.160
Turnover Analysis						
Net Operating Asset Turnover	2.237	2.367	2.410	2.066	2.015	2.061
Net Working Capital Turnover	5.872	6.854	7.382	4.888	5.082	5.699
Avge Inventory Holding Period	78.299	75.105	72.565	86.356	85.830	85.499
PP&E Turnover	3.785	3.786	3.747	3.693	3.391	3.200

To begin, we forecast that sales growth in 2002 would be 24.2 percent, based on the belief that Kohl's would open 70 new stores and the comparable-store growth rate would be 5 percent. In 2002, Kohl's actually opened 75 new stores and comparable-store sales growth was 5.3 percent, so why was the actual sales growth only 21.8 percent? Our simple sales growth model compounded growth in the number of stores with growth in sales at existing stores, but this is technically only valid if all stores are equivalent. If the new stores are slightly smaller than average, or if the new stores opened late in the year, or if a new store isn't immediately mature, so it earns less than an existing store, then sales growth will be lower than what the simple model predicts. A combination of all these things caused our sales forecast in 2002 to be a bit too rosy. In 2003 and 2004, the reason the actual growth was lower than the forecasted growth is simple: comparable-store growth fell to –1.6 percent in 2003 and .3 percent in 2004, as compared to our estimate of 5 percent.

In terms of profitability, the 2002 return on equity is very close to our forecast, but the 2003 and 2004 amounts are considerably lower. Turning to the advanced Dupont decomposition shows why. The return on net operating assets was between 3 and 4 percent lower than forecast, mostly due to considerably lower net operating asset turnovers. In terms of specific assets, the inventory holding period was about 86 days, whereas our forecast was that this amount would decrease substantially to about 73 days. And the biggest mistake is that we forecast that the PP&E turnover ratio would remain around 3.75, whereas it fell to 3.4 in 2003 and 3.2 in 2004, as the comparable-store sales growth fell, lowering the efficiency of the PP&E asset. The final contributing factor to the lower-than-forecast ROE is that we estimated a moderate increase in leverage, while Kohl's actually lowered their leverage from .39 in 2001 to .24 in 2004. Since Kohl's has a positive spread, reducing leverage also reduces the actual return on equity.

8.10   CASES, LINKS, AND REFERENCES

Cases

- The Home Depot, Inc.
- Netflix, Inc. (Questions 10 through 12)
- Overstock.com (Questions 10 through 13)
- Forecasting for the Love Boat: Royal Caribbean Cruises in 1998 (Part B)

Links

- Bureau of Economic Analysis: http://www.bea.gov

  In addition to GDP data, this site's fixed asset surveys describe, by industry, quantities of fixed assets, amount spent, net holdings, average age, and so on, of investments in many classes of assets. For example, it gives the amount the electrical machinery industry spent on metalworking machinery (lots) versus farm tractors (very little).

- Bureau of Labor Statistics: http://www.bls.gov

  This is a good source for wages and productivity statistics. It also has fascinating surveys on consumer spending patterns.

- Congressional Budget Office: http://www.cbo.gov

  This is a good source for economic forecasts of GDP and its major components.

- Conference Board: http://www.conference-board.org/

  This site has leading indicators for GDP growth and some interesting consumer confidence data.

- Yahoo!Finance: http://finance.yahoo.com/

- eVal Web site: http://www.mhhe.com/eval2007

References

- Brealey, R., and S. Myers. (2000). *Principles of Corporate Finance*. New York: Irwin/McGraw-Hill.
- Nissim, D., and S. Penman. (2001). Ratio analysis and equity valuation: From research to practice. *Review of Accounting Studies* 6: 109–54.

CHAPTER NINE

The Cost of Capital

9.1 INTRODUCTION

The forecasted financial statements describe an infinite series of future flows of value, either residual income flows or cash flows. In order to combine all these flows into a single estimate of the value today, we need a discount rate, commonly referred to as the firm's *cost of capital*. This chapter explains what it is we are trying to estimate with the cost of capital and it gives some advice about how to make the estimate. But we should be truthful at the outset: there are no good answers to these questions. None of the standard finance models provide estimates that describe the actual data very well. The discount rate that you use in your valuation has a large impact on the result, yet you will rarely feel very confident that the rate you have assumed is the right one. The best we can hope for is a good understanding of what the cost of capital represents and some ballpark range for what a reasonable estimate might be.

This chapter is closely linked to the next chapter on valuation models. You can probably read either one first: your choices are to read about the discount rate used in the valuation models without yet fully understanding the models, or you can read about the models without yet fully understanding the discount rate, one of the most important inputs for the models.

eVal calculates the firm's equity value using residual income models and discounted cash flow models. For both models, it computes the value of the equity directly by discounting the residual income or cash flow each period by the cost of equity capital. eVal also gives you the option to compute the value of the firm to all investors, both equity and nonequity capital providers combined. Computing the value of the equity directly only requires one valuation input: the cost of equity capital. However, computing the value to all investors requires that you also estimate the cost of debt capital and the cost of preferred equity capital, and then weight these pieces correctly to derive a weighted average cost of capital. We begin with the cost of equity capital because it is conceptually the easiest to describe, and it is a necessary input to any equity valuation model.

9.2 COST OF EQUITY CAPITAL

At its most basic level, the cost of equity capital is the expected rate of return that equity investors could earn on their next best alternative investment with an equivalent level of risk (i.e., the opportunity cost of the equity capital). The "equivalent risk" portion of this statement is where the problems lie. What is the correct measure of risk? Risk has something to do with investors' distaste for the uncertainty in future payoffs, but how should we quantify this distaste? Should we quantify risk only by reference to the volatility in the company's underlying cash flows, or should we rely on market prices to infer risk? Should our measure of risk take into consideration the fact that we may or may not hold a diversified portfolio of equity securities? How we estimate the cost of equity capital—the expected return on an investment with "equivalent risk"—depends on the answers to these and other questions.

What Is Risk?

The discount rate that we use in our valuation model serves two purposes. It must account for the time value of money and it must account for the risk of the investment. The time value of money, absent any risk, is a straightforward concept. It is why bank's pay interest on savings accounts and charge interest on risk-free loans. If risk was not an issue, we could use the risk-free interest rate, say the yield on a 10-year U.S. Treasury bond, as our cost of equity capital. Unfortunately, risk is very much an issue.

The forecasted financial statements are your best estimates of how the future will unfold for the company, but it is certainly possible that the actual outcomes could be better or worse. And, even if reality plays out exactly as you forecasted, the market still may not value the firm as you think it should. In short, the payoff to investing in any equity is uncertain. Further, investors generally dislike uncertainty. (What would you rather have: $1 million for sure or a 50/50 gamble between $0 and $2 million?) A fundamental measure of risk would quantify the amount of uncertainty and the investors' distaste for different levels of uncertainty, and then combine these measures in a model of investor decision making. But, while developing a fundamental measure of risk works great on paper, in practice it is very difficult to quantify an investment's level of uncertainty and extremely difficult to quantify investors' distaste for it. Consequently, the standard approach sidesteps the issue by looking at how the market has historically compensated investors for bearing risk. We don't attempt to measure the fundamental risk directly; rather, we measure the compensation that was offered in exchange for bearing it.

Because investors dislike uncertainty, they will only hold a risky security if they are compensated for doing so; higher-risk investments must offer higher expected returns. We measure risk as the additional expected return beyond the risk-free rate that the security offers. The idea is simply that the risk-free rate captures the time value of money, so everything else in the expected return must be compensation for risk. To measure the expected return for different levels of risk, we identify different *risk classes* or *risk factors* and then compute the average past-realized returns for firms in each class. The amount by which the average return in a risk class exceeds the risk-free rate is the *risk premium* for firms in that risk class. The trick, then, is to identify risk classes that group together firms with similar fundamental risk, even though we are punting on actually measuring the fundamental risk itself.

One issue that plays a big part in any discussion of risk is the idea of diversification. A particular equity investment may feel very risky because your estimates of the firm's future cash flows seem quite uncertain, but if the company is only one investment in a large portfolio, then even though its individual payoffs may seem risky, this risk could be diversified away in the portfolio. Consider, for instance, a small hardware store chain in Wisconsin whose cash flows are particularly susceptible to the local Wisconsin economy. But if you hold this investment in a portfolio of stocks that include hardware stores in many other states, then when one state's economy is down, another state's economy may be up, so that the average of all the investments is less volatile than any one investment. Diversification lowers risk. Before you conclude that a particular company has uncertain cash flows and is therefore very risky and warrants a high discount rate, think about the source of the uncertainty. If the source can be diversified away in a portfolio, then the market is probably not willing to compensate investors for bearing the risk.

As a practical answer to the question "what is risk?" we offer two models that identify classes of firms that are considered equally risky. The first model is the capital asset pricing model (CAPM) and the second model is based on the size of the firm.

Capital Asset Pricing Model

Our first pass at quantifying risk is derived from the *capital asset pricing model* (CAPM). Without diving into a semester-long class on the subject, the CAPM says that a firm's expected stock return is given as

$$r_e = r_f + \beta(r_m - r_f)$$

where

r_e = Expected stock return for the firm; equivalently, it is the firm's cost of equity capital

r_f = Risk-free rate of return

r_m = Expected return on the market portfolio

β = The firm's *beta,* which measures the sensitivity of the firm's returns to the market's returns

One assumption underlying the CAPM is that every investor holds a mix of the risk-free bond, which returns r_f, and the entire market portfolio, which is uncertain but returns r_m in expectation. The only source of risk that cannot be diversified away in the market portfolio is variation in the market return and, consequently, the only thing that distinguishes one equity security from another is β, the degree to which the security moves with the market. Firms with high βs are more risky than firms with low βs and firms with the same β are equally risky. Putting it all together, the firm's cost of equity capital is r_e: the risk-free rate r_f captures the time value of money, the market risk premium ($r_m - r_f$) captures the compensation for marketwide risk, and β captures the individual firm's exposure to marketwide risk.

To use this model, you need an estimate of the risk-free rate, an estimate of the market risk premium, and a firm-specific estimate of β. The risk-free rate, measured by the yield on the 10-year U.S. Treasury bond, has ranged between 4 and 7 percent during the last five years. To get the latest value, go to Yahoo! Finance major U.S. indices.

The expected risk premium ($r_m - r_f$) is much more difficult to estimate. This is the amount that investors expect to earn as compensation for bearing the risk of owning the market portfolio. It is the compensation for risk that is currently impounded into the current equity prices, so if you think that equity prices are unusually high, this is equivalent to saying that you think the expected risk premium is unusually low. Historically, the difference between the long-run realized market return and the risk-free return has been somewhere between 2 and 8 percent, but the exact estimate is quite sensitive to the time period of stock return history that is included and how broadly the "market" is defined. For instance, defining the market portfolio as the S&P 500 index, the average risk premium was 7.6 percent over 1926–1998 (Ibbotson and Associates 1998). However, if the market portfolio is defined to include all publicly traded companies and the risk premium is computed over the 1964–1994 period, the average is 5.2 percent (Fama and French 1997). In addition, the standard deviation of this estimate is 2.7 percent, which means that there is a 32 percent chance that the true value lies more than one standard deviation above or below this average. In other words, there is a 68 percent chance that the true value is in a range between 2.5 and 7.9 percent and a 32 percent chance it is even more extreme than these endpoints. None of this should make you feel very confident about your estimate of the expected risk premium.

If the estimate of the expected risk premium is shaky, the estimate of the firm-specific β is even worse. This is typically estimated by regressing the realized r_e on the realized r_m for the past five years of monthly returns. What we are shooting for is a measure of how closely the firm's equity price moves with the broader market. Since the market movement is the only source of risk in the CAPM, a firm with a stronger correlation with the market is a riskier investment. As a benchmark, a firm that perfectly tracked the market would have a β of one; a β of 0.5 would be very low and a β of 1.5 would be very high, by historical standards. The trouble with estimates of firm-specific βs is that they change drastically over time for no apparent reason. For example, IBM's β estimate was 1.5 in 1966 and 0.85 in 1969; it was 0.51 in 1995 and 1.2 in 1998. Surely IBM's fundamental risk didn't change this much during these two three-year periods. Because of this instability, it is not uncommon to use the average β in the firm's industry rather than the firm-specific estimate. But there is also evidence that industry β estimates are themselves unstable, with an average standard deviation of .12 (Fama and French 1997), meaning that there is approximately a 32 percent chance that the true β for an industry with

TABLE 9.1   **Long-Run Industry Beta Estimates**

Source: Fama and French 1997.

Industry	Beta	Industry	Beta
Pharmaceutical Products	0.92	Shipping Containers	1.03
Medical Equipment	1.17	Construction Materials	1.13
Health Care	1.56	Insurance	1.01
Computers	1.04	Precious Metals	0.78
Electronic Equipment	1.38	Miscellaneous	1.26
Business Services	1.34	Transporation	1.21
Measuring and Control Equipment	1.29	Rubber and Plastic Products	1.21
Consumer Goods	0.97	Fabricated Products	1.31
Restaurants, Hotel, Motel	1.32	Apparel	1.24
Alcoholic Beverages	0.92	Chemicals	1.09
Personal Services	1.25	Recreational Products	1.34
Construction	1.28	Shipbuilding, Railroad Equipment	1.19
Retail	1.11	Candy and Soda	1.24
Entertainment	1.35	Petroleum and Natural Gas	085
Food Products	0.87	Nonmetallic Mining	0.98
Agriculture	1.00	Tobacco Products	0.80
Machinery	1.16	Business Supplies	1.11
Printing and Publishing	1.17	Textiles	1.12
Aircraft	1.26	Banking	1.09
Coal	0.96	Telecommunications	0.66
Defense	1.04	Utilities	0.66
Wholesale	1.15	Real Estate	1.17
Trading	1.16	Steel Works, etc.	1.16
Electrical Equipment	1.15	Automobiles and Trucks	1.01

an estimate of one could be lower than 0.88 or higher than 1.12. To compensate for this variation, our best advice is to use an industry β that has been computed over a long time period. Table 9.1 gives industry β estimates computed over the period 1964–1994.

Another source for β estimates, computed for individual stocks over the most recent five-year horizon, is Yahoo! Finance. Enter the company ticker symbol and the select Key Statistics from the resulting screen. If you want to see the industry β computed over the same five-year period, you can go to www.investor.reuters.com (which requires a free registration) and, after entering your company's ticker, hit the Ratio link. Putting this all together, as of February 2006, the firm-specific estimate of β for Kohl's is 0.82. The industry β for the past five years for the Retail—Department and Discount industry is 0.72, and the long-run β estimate for the Retail industry from Table 9.1 is 1.11. If, based on all this, we conclude that our best guess for β is 0.82, and if we combine this with a 4.5 percent risk-free rate (based on 10-year Treasury bonds in February 2006) and a 7.6 percent risk premium (based on the S&P 500 historical average), we get a cost of capital estimate for Kohl's of

$$r_e = 4.5\% + 0.82 * 7.6\% = 10.73\%$$

Recall, however, that the risk premium and the β estimate are noisy. If we allow one standard deviation up or down for each of these estimates, then there is still a 32 percent chance that the true β is below 7.2 percent or above 14.3 percent. So don't feel too smug about your fancy CAPM-derived estimate of the cost of equity capital.

Another reason to question the CAPM estimate is that it fits the actual data very poorly. The CAPM says that the only systematic thing causing different firms to have different stock returns is their beta. So you would think that if you estimated firms' betas at a point in time and then tracked the subsequent stock returns, you should find that firms with higher beta estimates would, on average, have higher subsequent stock returns (as compensation for the extra risk). Unfortunately, many studies have shown that this relation is very weak. Further, you may ask yourself, why are we relying on market prices to tell us about the firm's risk in the first place? The whole premise of this book is that securities can be mispriced, and we can discover the mispricing by our careful analysis. Finally, there is a difference between the realized risk premium over the past 75 years and the expected risk premium going forward. Back in 1926, it would have been difficult to know that the U.S. economy would turn out to be such a huge success story. Part of the difference between the market return and the risk-free rate over this period is simply due to good luck. For this reason, we are inclined to use the lower estimate of 5.2 percent for the risk premium, taken from the Fama and French study. Consistent with this lower estimate, the average cost of equity capital from the 12 countries that have had public exchanges for the longest period of time (approximately 1900–2000) is about 5 percent over the risk-free rate (Dimson, Marsh, and Staunton 2000).

The Size Model

Our second pass at quantifying the risk of an "equivalent investment" is quite simple. Firms of similar size, as measured by their market value, are considered to be in the same risk class. That is, the firm's expected return is

$$r_e = r_f + r_{size}$$

where

r_e = Expected stock return for the firm; equivalently, it is the firm's cost of equity capital

r_f = Risk-free rate of return

r_{size} = Expected return in excess of the risk-free rate for the firm's size decile

This model is motivated by the empirical observation that small firms have historically higher returns than large firms, so the higher return, it is argued, must be compensation for higher risk. The knock on this model is that there is no good explanation for why the size of the firm should drive its nondiversifiable risk. A large firm may have more resources to adapt to changing conditions than a small

TABLE 9.2   **Size-Decile Returns in Excess of Risk-Free Return and CAPM Return**

Source: Ibbotson and Associates 2001.

Decile	Market Value of Largest Company in Decile ($ millions)	Return in Excess of Historical Riskless Rate of 5.2%	Historical Beta	Return in Excess of CAPM Return
1	524,352	6.84%	0.91	−0.20%
2	10,344	8.36	1.04	−0.31
3	4,144	8.93	1.09	0.47
4	2,177	9.38	1.13	1.62
5	1,328	9.95	1.16	0.93
6	840	10.26	1.18	1.08
7	538	10.46	1.24	0.88
8	333	11.38	1.28	1.47
9	193	12.17	1.34	1.74
10	85	15.67	1.42	4.63

firm, but isn't a portfolio of small firms very much like a single large firm with many divisions? Table 9.2 describes 10 size deciles and gives each decile's historical return in excess of the risk-free rate of 5.2 percent, its historical β estimate, and the return in excess of the CAPM-estimated expected return, each estimated from all publicly traded firms from 1926 to 2000.

The first thing to note from Table 9.2 is that the returns increase monotonically as you go from the largest firms (in the 1st decile) to the smallest firms (in the 10th decile). Further, the increase is dramatic: the smallest firms have earned returns in excess of the risk-free rate that are more than double the returns earned by the largest firms. The market has clearly treated these firms as riskier, rewarding investors handsomely, on average, for their willingness to bear this risk. Small firms look riskier from a CAPM perspective as well, with β increasing monotonically from the largest decile of firms to the smallest decile.[1] But, interestingly, even after controlling for the CAPM risk, small firms still had higher returns than large firms, as the final column in Table 9.2 shows. You can combine the CAPM model and the size model using the data in the last column. First, estimate the CAPM expected return for your firm as described in the previous section. Then, add to this the return in excess of the CAPM return, or the *size premium,* as given in the last column of Table 9.2.

Kohl's market capitalization as of February 2006 was approximately $15.6 billion, placing it in the largest decile of firms in Table 9.2. Applying the size model to Kohl's and using 4.5 percent as our current estimate of the risk-free rate, we get

$$r_e = 4.5\% + 6.84\% = 11.34\%$$

[1] While small firms are large in number, they are small in "weight," as measured by their market capitalization. The largest decile of firms is, by definition, only 10 percent of the total count of firms, yet they make up over 70 percent of the total market capitalization in 2000. So even though 9 of the 10 deciles of firms have an average β estimate greater than one, the grand average is still one.

Alternatively, if we add the size premium to the CAPM estimate for Kohl's (computed above), we get

$$r_e = 4.5\% + 0.82 * (7.6\%) - 0.2\% = 10.53\%$$

Does size really measure risk? Should you set your discount rate higher for smaller firms? The empirical evidence in Table 9.2 would certainly say yes. However, the evidence is taken from market prices, so if markets are not completely efficient, maybe we should be more circumspect. Suppose that there was no difference in the fundamental risk of large or small stocks, but market participants consistently undervalued small stocks? Each year, the small stocks would perform better than the large stocks. Their market value would increase and they would move out of the lowest-size decile, and a new crop of small stocks would be born to take their place. If this was the case, then we would see small stocks generating larger returns than large stocks, but it wouldn't be because they were any riskier than large stocks; it would be because the market was inefficiently pricing the small stocks. This story isn't too hard to imagine; small stocks get little analyst coverage, are not held by many institutional investors, and generally fly under the radar of most investors. It seems like a prime place to find market inefficiency.

What Number Do I Put in eVal?

Ultimately there is no good answer to the question "what is the cost of equity capital?" As a practical matter, we want to be able to compare the valuations of different firms on a risk-adjusted basis. If we evaluate 10 firms and then sort them based on the amount we think they are undervalued, we want this sort to reveal relative mispricing, not just differences in the riskiness across the 10 firms. In addition, if we can get the discount rate to adequately control for risk, then we can separate the forecasting exercise from the discounting exercise. We can input our best guesses for the forecasting assumptions without trying to make these estimates compensate for risk as well.

Rather than take the CAPM estimate as truth or the size model estimate as truth, we prefer that you use these models as guides, combining the resulting estimate with your own intuition and some common sense. You might want to ask yourself what rate of return you personally would require on an investment with this firm's level of risk. How much extra return beyond the risk-free rate seems reasonable, given the riskiness of the firm's future payoffs, and evaluated in light of the diversification you have in your portfolio?

The default value for the cost of equity capital in eVal is 10 percent, found on the Valuation Parameters sheet. You can think of it as 5 percent for the risk-free rate and 5 percent for the risk premium; at least it is easy to remember!

There is one constraint on your cost of equity capital input: it must be greater than your assumed terminal growth rate in sales. If this isn't the case, then you are assuming that the firm will grow faster than the discount rate forever. This makes the perpetuity formula in the valuation models invalid; effectively, the value of such a firm is infinite. If you mistakenly violate this condition, eVal will display the error message "Error! cost of equity capital <= growth rate" in red on the relevant valuation sheet. For more discussion, see the section on terminal value forecasts in Chapter 7.

9.3   COST OF NONEQUITY CAPITAL

The only reason you need to consider the cost of nonequity capital is if you are interested in computing the value of all investors' claims on the firm, commonly referred to as the *entity value,* rather than just the equity value. This is also a necessary computation if your approach to valuing the equity is to first value the whole entity and then subtract from this the value of the nonequity claims.

The Valuation Parameters sheet has an optional section for you to enter the cost of capital from debt holders and preferred stockholders. We strongly encourage you to use the same estimates here as you input for the terminal period interest and preferred dividend assumptions on the Forecasting Assumptions sheet. For instance, if your terminal period estimate of the firm's interest rate is 6 percent, we highly recommend inputting 6 percent on the optional Valuation Parameters sheet for the cost of debt. In the short term, a firm may have debt outstanding that has a coupon interest rate different than its market interest rate. However, it would be quite odd to forecast that, forever into the future, the company will somehow manage to issue debt at a rate different than its market rate. Similarly, the cost of preferred stock should probably match your terminal inputs for this item on the Forecasting Assumptions sheet. Note that the value of the equity is already determined by your forecasts and your assumption about the cost of equity capital. Consequently, as you change your assumptions about the cost of debt or the cost of preferred stock, you will change the entity value and the value of the nonequity claims, but the net effect will hold the equity value constant.

Just as with the cost of equity capital, your inputted costs of capital in the optional section should not be smaller than your forecasted terminal period sales growth rate. If they are, then the perpetuity formula we use to compute the present value of the free cash flows to these capital providers is invalid and an error flag will show up on the valuation sheet. Think about what it would mean for the cost of debt to be lower than the growth rate forever. In the terminal period, the growth rate drives the growth in debt, so debt would be growing faster than it was being discounted back and the present value would be infinite (or infinitely negative, depending on whether you are the firm or the debt holder). If your forecasts violate this condition, you will see the message Error! cost of capital <= growth rate on the associated valuation sheet.

9.4   WEIGHTED AVERAGE COST OF CAPITAL

To compute the entity value (as opposed to the equity value), you need a discount rate that reflects the cost of capital from all providers: equity, preferred stock, and debt. Another way to think about this is that we are trying to estimate the cost of equity capital for a hypothetical firm that has the net operating assets of the actual firm but does not have the debt claims or preferred stockholder claims. Consequently, this rate is sometimes referred to as the cost of capital for the unlevered firm, or the expected return on net operating assets (not to be confused with the actual return on net operating assets, as computed in Chapter 5). To see this, examine the basic accounting equation:

$$\text{Net Operating Assets} - \text{Debt} - \text{Preferred Stock} = \text{Common Equity}$$

$$\text{Net Operating Assets} = \text{Common Equity} + \text{Debt} + \text{Preferred Stock}$$

$$\text{Net Operating Assets} = \text{Unlevered Equity}.$$

To compute the cost of capital for this hypothetical firm, a logical approach is to take a weighted average of the cost of equity capital, the cost of preferred stock, and the after-tax cost of debt. The *weighted-average cost of capital* (WACC), labeled r_w, does just this. It is computed as

$$r_w = \frac{r_e P_e + (1 - \text{tax}) r_d P_d + r_{ps} P_{ps}}{P_e + P_d + P_{ps}}$$

where

tax $=$ The firm's estimated effective tax rate

$r_e =$ The firm's estimated cost of equity capital

$r_d =$ The firm's estimated cost of debt capital

$r_{ps} =$ The firm's estimated cost of preferred stock capital

$P_e =$ Resulting value of the firm's common equity

$P_d =$ Resulting value of the firm's debt

$P_{ps} =$ Resulting value of the firm's preferred stock.

The value r_w is the cost of a dollar of additional capital, holding the firm's capital structure constant. Imagine the firm raising the dollar by issuing common equity, preferred stock, and debt in exact proportions to their market values. The weighted-average cost of capital is the natural benchmark for the firm's return on net operating assets, which is the return before any consideration of the firm's financing costs.

Note that the weights used to compute r_w are based on the estimated values of the equity, preferred stock, and debt, not their book values, not their current market values, and not some estimate of their future values in some future capital structure.[2] But this raises a problem. The formula makes reference to P_e, the value of the common equity, yet P_e is exactly what we are trying to find. How can we

[2] The weighted-average cost of capital given here is "after-tax," meaning that the cost of debt has been adjusted down to account for the tax shield of interest (i.e., the $(1 - \text{tax})$ part in the formula). By accounting for the tax deductibility of interest in the discount rate, we do not adjust the free cash flow estimates for the tax benefits of interest. An alternative approach found in some texts is to define WACC on a pre-tax basis (i.e., without the $(1 - \text{tax})$ adjustment in the formula) and then add the tax deduction associated with interest to the free cash flows. This issue is discussed in greater detail in Chapter 10.

weight the different costs of capital based on their estimated values if we don't yet know the estimated value of equity? We sidestep this issue by using the estimate of P_e already found in the model that valued the equity directly. With P_e, P_d, and P_{ps} determined, the value of the entity is simply the sum of these three components. eVal then searches for the value of r_w that discounts the forecasted future free cash flows to all investors back to this predetermined amount. In this way, we find an internally consistent solution for the weighted-average cost of capital and the estimated equity value. This approach is completely valid: given the same series of forecasted financial statements, all valuation models, correctly applied, should yield the same estimate.

What Is Constant and What Is Changing?

In the previous sections, we estimated the cost of equity capital, the cost of preferred stock, and the cost of debt as constants—a single rate that is used to discount flows to each of these capital providers throughout time. We then combined these values using estimates of the value of the equity, preferred stock, and debt to construct the weighted-average cost of capital. However, what if you forecast that the firm's capital structure will change in the future? For instance, suppose you think that the company will drastically increase its ratio of debt to equity in the future. Based on the formula above, if you were to compute the weighted-average cost of capital in the future, it would be different than the r_w based on the current capital structure. Should you base your estimate of r_w on the current capital structure or on the forecasted future capital structure, or should you use a different discount rate each period?

Technically, to be consistent with the assumption of constant costs of capital, the r_w should change with the changing capital structure. But an alternative point of view is that the different costs of capital should change as the capital structure changes in such a way as to hold r_w constant. Recall the r_w also can be thought of as the expected return on the net operating assets of the company, or the expected return on unlevered equity. The idea behind this alternative view is that the fundamental driver of the firm's risks and returns is its net operating assets, and these risks and returns will remain constant regardless of how the supporting capital structure changes. Unfortunately, this issue will never be resolved because the unlevered equity is not a naturally occurring market security, so its return cannot be observed. And, given the difficulty in estimating the cost of equity capital discussed earlier, it seems fruitless to compound this difficulty by trying to estimate how the cost of equity capital will change in the future.

Rather than take a stand on this issue, we simply require that r_w be consistent with the value of the equity when it is computed directly. By solving for a single r_w that reconciles with the estimated value of equity, we force it to be a constant when, technically speaking, it should change with the capital structure. But, practically speaking, changing the r_w estimate each period has no effect on the estimated equity value, which is our main concern. Further, because the capital structure remains constant in the terminal period, whether the r_w is constant or changing also has very little effect on the estimated entity and nonequity values. Think of the single weighted-average cost of capital reported in eVal as an average of the different, theoretically correct, r_w's.

If you see the message "Error! there is no internally-consistent weighted average cost of capital," then eVal is telling you that your assumptions do not allow a feasible solution. For example, if your assumptions imply an equity value of $10 and a debt value of negative $12, then you need an entity value of negative $2 to reconcile these two amounts. But if your forecasts imply positive flows of net operating income, then the entity value cannot be negative, regardless of how high you set the discount r_w. The cases that lead to this error message are rather bizarre, so, if you see the message, there is probably something very wrong with your forecasting assumptions.

9.5   CASES, LINKS, AND REFERENCES

Links

- Yahoo! Finance major U.S. indices: http://finance.yahoo.com/m1?u
- Yahoo! Finance: http://finance.yahoo.com/
- Multex Investor: http://www.multexinvestor.com/

References

- Dimson, E., P. Marsh, and M. Staunton. (2000). *The Millennium Book: A Century of Investment Returns*. London: ABN-AMRO and London Business School.
- Fama, E., and K. French. (1997). Industry costs of capital. *Journal of Financial Economics* 43: 153–93.
- Ibbotson and Associates. (2001). *Stocks, Bonds, Bills, and Inflation*. 2001 Yearbook. Chicago.

Valuation

10.1 INTRODUCTION

The hard work in valuation is already done. The forecasts you developed in Chapters 7 and 8 describe the future evolution of net distributions to equity holders. The cost of equity capital you chose in Chapter 9 determines how valuable future cash flows are today. All that remains is to combine the forecasts with the discount rate to compute the present value of the net distributions to equity holders. Why then are there so many pages in this chapter? It turns out that there are a number of different ways to compute the value of equity. While each of them leads to the same answer, each does so in a way that sheds a different light on the source of value creation. Further, different user groups have historically used different models: accounting types like the residual income models and finance types like the discounted cash flow models. If all you care about is the final answer, any of the models will do. But if you want to see the answer presented in the particular way you learned in some other class or life experience, we have a smorgasbord of models for you to choose from.

There are two features that distinguish the different valuation models. First, the flow variable, the thing that is being discounted, can be either free cash flows or accounting residual income flows (we give precise definitions below). Second, we can compute the value of the flows to equity holders directly, or we can first compute the value of the flows to all investors and then back into the value of the equity claim by subtracting the value of the flows to nonequity capital providers. If we work carefully (and eVal is *very* careful), each model yields exactly the same result. Without boring you with algebraic proof, it should be obvious that each model will get the same answer if you feed each the same inputs. The forecasted financial statements and discount rate assumption *determine* the value; all we have to do is discover it.

All the models we describe allow for the possibility that the firm will live forever, so all models sum over time from the present, labeled time zero, to infinity. It takes a really long time to add up an infinite number of terms one at a time, so at some point in the future, known as the *terminal year,* we need a more succinct way of expressing the present value of the flows in the remaining years. All the models solve this problem the same way, so we defer the discussion of the present value calculations until the end of the chapter and present each model as an infinite sum of terms. But don't worry about this; there is a nifty solution to this problem.

We present all the models in algebraic notation. If you want to work through some numerical examples, the case "Four Valuation Models—One Value" is a good place to start.

10.2 RESIDUAL INCOME VALUATION MODELS

Although actually quite old, the residual income model has recently come back into vogue on Wall Street. Its primary advantage is that it expresses value directly in terms of the financial statements that you worked so hard to estimate, rather than translating these amounts into free cash flows. Define *residual income* RI_t in period t as

$$RI_t = NI_t - r_e CE_{t-1}$$

where

NI_t = Net income available to common equity for the period ending at date t

r_e = Cost of equity capital

CE_{t-1} = Common shareholders' equity at date $t - 1$ (i.e., one year earlier than the NI_t date)

Residual income is the amount by which net income exceeds the capital charge on the book value of common equity invested in the firm. If the firm could deposit its book value in a bank account at the beginning of the year and earn interest at the rate r_e, it would earn $r_e CE_{t-1}$ for the year. Residual income is the amount by which NI_t exceeds or falls short of this benchmark. In this sense, it is *residual*.

The residual income model computes value as the sum of the initial book value plus the present value of future residual income flows. Both the book value and the net income component of residual income are accrual accounting constructs, which may make you incredulous about this model. How can the model work when we know that a firm's accounting book value is an imperfect measure of its market value and that earnings are an imperfect measure of value creation? How can these numbers be used to estimate a firm's market value? The key is to recognize that if book value is understated, then future residual income will be overstated, and by precisely enough to correct for the erroneous book value. For example, if a firm has a missing asset, one that the accounting rules don't recognize, then the asset isn't included in CE_{t-1}, but it produces NI_t, making RI_t positive. In a later section, we will illustrate how all this adds up perfectly.

The easiest version of this model is the one that values the common equity directly.

Residual Income to Common Equity

The algebraic statement of this model is

$$P_e = CE_0 + \sum_{t=1}^{\infty} (1 + r_e)^{-t} RI_t,$$

where

P_e = Estimated market value of common equity as of the last financial statement date

CE_0 = Common shareholders' equity as of the last financial statement date (i.e., time 0)

RI_t = Residual income, equal to $NI_t - r_e CE_{t-1}$, as defined above

r_e = Cost of equity capital

The model starts with the initial stock of accounting value CE_0 and adds to it the discounted sum of expected future residual income flows. The reason a firm's market value P_e will be different than its book value is because it is forecasted to earn residual income in the future. To get a feel for this model, imagine a savings account with $100 in it and a 10 percent interest rate. The book value of this investment, by any reasonable accounting measurement, would be $100. Further, if 10 percent is the market rate of interest on savings accounts, then the return on a similar investment with equivalent risk is probably also 10 percent, so assume r_e = 10 percent. In this case, regardless of deposits or withdrawals (made at the beginning of each year), the earnings each period will be 10 percent of the beginning book value, which is exactly the capital charge $r_e CE_{t-1}$, so residual income in all future periods is zero. Thus, the value of the savings account is $100. If, however, the savings account paid 11 percent interest in some years, yet the discount rate remained 10 percent, then the savings account would earn "residual income" in these years and its market value would exceed $100. Pretty simple.

Figure 10.1 shows the residual income valuation to common equity for Kohl's computed on September 3, 2002, for the fiscal year that ended on February 2, 2002, using the default eVal forecasts. To see this in eVal, first enter 9/3/2002 as the valuation date on the Valuation Parameters sheet and then return to the User's Guide and hit the View Residual Income Valuation button. Each column shows the net income and beginning common equity for the fiscal year, taken directly from the Financial Statements sheet. Residual income is computed from these inputs and then discounted each period, using the default cost of equity capital of 10 percent. The present value of each period's residual income is added up for the first 20 years and then for all the years beyond 20 (this computation is discussed later). The result is added to the book value of common equity as of February 2, 2002, to arrive at $12,057,789 thousand, labeled as the "Forecast Equity Value Before Time Adjustments."

In the previous savings account example, the key comparison was between the discount rate and the rate of interest the account paid. More generally, in a real company, the key comparison is between the forecasted ROE and the cost of equity capital r_e. To see this, multiply and divide RI_t by CE_{t-1} so that

$$RI_t = (NI_t - r_e CE_{t-1}) = (ROE_t - r_e)CE_{t-1},$$

where ROE_t is computed on beginning equity. The expression says that residual income equals the excess of ROE_t over the cost of equity capital times the beginning

FIGURE 10.1 **Residual Income to Common Equity**

Valuation based on eVal defaults as of September 3, 2002, for February 2, 2002, fiscal year end.

	A	B	C	D
1	**Residual Income Valuation**	**($000)**		
2	Go To User's Guide	View Valuation to Common Equity		
3		View Valuation to All Investors		
4	**Company Name**	Kohl's Corporation		
5	Most Recent Fiscal Year End	2/2/2002	NI and CE taken from Financial Statements sheet	
6	Date of Valuation	9/3/2002		
7	Cost of Common Equity	10.00%		
8				
9	Fiscal Year of Forecast	2/2/2003	2/2/2004	2/2/2005
11	**Valuation to Common Equity**			
12	Net Income	590,761	700,011	818,802
13	Common Equity at Beginning of Year	2,791,406	3,355,453	3,982,450
14	Residual Income	311,620	364,466	420,557
15	Present Value of Residual Income	283,291	301,212	315,970
16	Present Value Beyond 20 Years	3,831,760		
17	Present Value of First 20 Years	5,434,623		
18	Common Equity as of			
19	2/2/2002	2,791,406	$= 364{,}466/(1+.10)^2$	
20	Forecast Equity Value Before Time Adj.	12,057,789		
21	Forecasted Value as of Valuation Date	13,402,735		
22	[__] Claims	(1,147,681)	$= 311{,}620/(1+.10)^1$	
23	$= 590{,}761 - .10(2{,}791{,}406)$ quity	12,255,054		
24	Common Shares Outstanding at BS Date	332,167		
25	Equivalent Shares at Valuation Date	332,167		
26	Forecast Price/Share	**$36.89**		
27				
28				

◄ ◄ ► ►│ Graphics / Cash Flow Analysis / Valuation Parameters \ **Residual Income Valuations** / DCF Valuations / EPS Fo ◄│

Ready

common equity book value for the period. If you forecast that the firm's ROE will exceed its cost of equity capital, then residual income will be positive. Stated another way, a firm is worth more than its book value only if it is expected to earn an ROE in excess of its cost of equity capital. Remembering from previous chapters that ROE was our premier measure of profitability, this equation says that profitability creates value.

This expression also demonstrates that size by itself does *not* create value. If $ROE_t = r_e$, then residual income is zero regardless of the value of CE_{t-1}. Similarly, growth in CE_t by itself, does not create value. However, if ROE_t is forecast to exceed r_e in the future, then a firm wants to grow to be as big as possible. Think of it this way: if you forecast that a firm's ROE will always equal its cost of equity capital in the future, then you are really forecasting that the firm will always engage in zero net present value projects. If this is the case, then it doesn't matter how big or small those future projects are; none of them will create value. However, if you forecast that ROE_t will exceed r_e in the future, then you are saying that the firm has positive net present value projects in the future. In this case, you want the projects to be as big as possible; in this case, growth is good. Wall Street analysts frequently confuse the value of growth with the value of profitability when assessing equity securities. Many research reports extol the huge growth potential of a company without explaining how the firm will ever turn the growth into profitability. If the company can't earn a return that is at least as great as its cost of capital, being a big firm just means that it will destroy value faster than a small firm. We suspect that analysts like rapidly growing firms because such firms are likely to require investment-banking services, not because they think they are fundamentally good investment opportunities.

The residual income model has many desirable features. For one thing, it is written in terms of the accounting variables that you worked so hard to forecast. The net income and book value variables come straight from the forecasted financial statements in eVal. More fundamentally, the residual income model describes value in an economically appealing way. Value is driven by profitability and growth. Much of the previous chapters in this book have been aimed at building your intuition for how economic forces and accounting distortions will act on a firm's growth rate and especially on its ROE. By expressing value as a function of these two drivers, the residual income valuation model exploits this intuition.

Finally, because the residual income model is written in terms of accounting numbers, we will use it in the next chapter to describe some popular valuation statistics such as the market-to-book ratio, the price-to-earnings ratio, and the PEG ratio.

Bad Accounting and the Residual Income Valuation Model

Because the residual income model is stated in terms of accounting values, you may worry that distorted accounting measurements will make the model invalid or inaccurate. But, as the next example illustrates, the model is surprisingly resilient to accounting errors. Suppose that the sequence of forecasted common equity and net income, before any consideration of accounting errors, is CE_0, NI_1, CE_1, NI_2, CE_2, NI_3, CE_3 . . . , so that the residual income model yields

$$P_e = CE_0 + \frac{NI_1 - r_eCE_0}{(1+r_e)} + \frac{NI_2 - r_eCE_1}{(1+r_e)^2} + \frac{NI_3 - r_eCE_2}{(1+r_e)^3} + \cdots$$

Now suppose that you are sure that $\$K$ of value is missing from CE_0, possibly due to an R&D investment that cannot be capitalized but is forecasted to payoff in NI_1. You could set out to correct for this error in the accounting model by adding K to CE_0 and subtracting it from your estimate of NI_1; that is, you could recognize the value creation in the current book value rather than waiting for it to materialize in future earnings. In this case the valuation would be

$$P_e = (CE_0 + K) + \frac{NI_1 - K - r_e(CE_0 + K)}{(1+r_e)}$$

$$+ \frac{NI_2 - r_eCE_1}{(1+r_e)^2} + \frac{NI_3 - r_eCE_2}{(1+r_e)^3} + \cdots$$

noting that the addition of K to CE_0 increased book value at date 0 but that the book value at date 1 is back to normal because of the subtraction of K from NI_1. Simple algebra demonstrates that the two valuations are equal. At first blush, this may seem impossible. Shouldn't moving K to the present increase the value estimate, since money has time value? But look carefully at the second term in the second equation; not only has K been deducted from date 1 earnings, but the capital charge is also higher by $r_e K$, thus perfectly correcting for the time value of this manipulation. And you don't even have to forecast *when* the K of additional value will show up in future earnings. Suppose you estimated that the additional value was going to materialize in year two rather than year one, so that your corrected forecasts yielded the following value estimate:

$$P_e = (CE_0 + K) + \frac{NI_1 - r_e(CE_0 + K)}{(1 + r_e)}$$
$$+ \frac{NI_2 - K - r_e(CE_1 + K)}{(1 + r_e)^2} + \frac{NI_3 - r_e CE_2}{(1 + r_e)^3} + \cdots$$

With some hard work, you can show that this again equals the original amount (feeling like this is an algebra test?). By including a capital charge in the definition of residual income, the model perfectly corrects for accounting distortions. Consequently, you really don't need to get involved in correcting the financial statements for accounting distortions; if your forecasts anticipate the unraveling of the accounting distortion, the model will do the rest.

You *should not* conclude from this discussion that it isn't important that you understand accounting distortions. Your forecasts of the future are probably based on observations of the firm's past and, if that past is distorted by poor accounting, then you need to be aware of this. For instance, if the firm has generated unusually high income by capitalizing more expenses than is appropriate, and thus deferred their recognition on the income statement, you need to be aware that future income will suffer when these capitalized expenses start to flow to income (as they surely must in an accrual accounting system).

Residual Income to All Investors

This version of the model is less commonly used but reconciles nicely with the other valuation models. It computes the value of common equity by first computing the value to all capital providers combined, commonly labeled as the *entity value,* and then subtracting from this the value of debt and preferred stock claims. It computes the value of each of these claims as the sum of a beginning balance and the present value of a flow of future residual amounts, just like the previous model.

To express this model algebraically, we need to remind you of some earlier notation. In Chapter 5, we defined NOA_t as the net operating assets of the firm, computed as the total assets less the operating liabilities. Next, define L_t as the accounting value of the debt (current and noncurrent combined) and PS_t as the accounting value of the preferred stock (in Chapter 5, we lumped debt and preferred stock together and labeled them as Net Financial Obligations, but here we will value each separately). By the basic accounting equation, common equity CE_t is given as

$$CE_t = NOA_t - L_t - PS_t$$

In Chapter 5, we also defined NOI_t as the net operating income, computed after tax. It is equal to net income available to common equity holders NI_t plus the after-tax interest that flows to debtholders $(1 - tax)I_t$ and the preferred dividend flows to preferred shareholders PD_t. That is,

$$NOI_t = NI_t + (1 - tax_t)I_t + PD_t$$

where tax_t is the firm's effective tax rate in year t. NOI_t is the amount the firm earned before expenses related to capital providers.

The idea behind the model is that all investors together own NOA_0 and the future stream of after-tax operating income NOI_t. We therefore can compute the value of the entity as the initial balance of NOA_0 plus the present value of the future residual NOI_t stream. Denoting the weighted-average cost of capital as r_w, we define *residual net operating income* as

$$RNOI_t = NOI_t - r_w NOA_{t-1}$$

Note the similarity with residual income defined in the previous section as $RI_t = NI_t - r_e CE_{t-1}$. To compute residual net *operating* income, NI_t is replaced with NOI_t and CE_{t-1} is replaced with NOA_{t-1}.

The *entity value P_f* is then given as

$$P_f = NOA_0 + \sum_{t=1}^{\infty}(1+r_w)^{-t}RNOI_t$$

All investors together own P_f. To find the value of the equity holders' claim, we need to subtract from P_f the value of the debt claim and the value of the preferred stock claim. And, in the spirit of residual income valuation, the value of the debt claim is computed as the initial balance of L_0 plus the present value of the future *residual interest expense* $I_t - r_d L_{t-1}$, where r_d is the cost of debt capital. Similarly, the value of the preferred stock claim is computed as the sum of the initial balance PS_0 and the present value of the future *residual preferred dividends,* using the cost of preferred stock capital r_{ps} as the discount rate. Denoting the debt value as P_d and the preferred stock value as P_{ps}, we get

$$P_d = L_0 + \sum_{t=1}^{\infty}(1+r_d)^{-t}(I_t - r_d L_{t-1})$$

and

$$P_{ps} = PS_0 + \sum_{t=1}^{\infty}(1+r_{ps})^{-t}(PD_t - r_{ps}PS_{t-1}).$$

The entity value is the sum of the value of the common equity, the value of the preferred stock, and the value of the debt:

$$P_f = P_e + P_{ps} + P_d$$

so we can solve for the value of the common equity as

$$P_e = P_f - P_{ps} - P_d$$

This may seem like the long way around to get to a common equity valuation. The advantage of this indirect approach to valuing the equity is that it focuses your attention on the value of the net operating assets and future net operating income of the firm. The idea is that we should first work hard on valuing the entity, since this is the fundamental source of value for the firm, and then worry about how the value gets allocated between the capital providers.

Figure 10.2 illustrates the residual income valuation to all investors for Kohl's as of September 3, 2002, for the fiscal year that ended on February 2, 2002, using the default eVal forecasts. To see this in eVal, hit the View Valuation to All Investors button on the Residual Income Valuations sheet (and be sure you have the valuation date set to September 3, 2002). The figure shows how eVal computes the value of the debt, the value of the preferred stock (which is zero because Kohl's doesn't have any preferred stock), and the entity value. In each case, the value is computed as a beginning balance plus the present value of a residual flow. The figure illustrates a few of the computations. We refer you back to Chapter 5 for the precise definitions of net operating income and net operating assets. Note that the flows to each capital provider are discounted at a different rate: debt is valued using the cost of debt capital (8 percent), preferred stock is valued at the cost of preferred stock (9 percent), and the entity value is computed using the weighted-average cost of capital (shown as 9.6 percent, but in reality it is 9.5978 percent). By subtracting the value of the debt and the value of the preferred stock from the entity value, we arrive at $12,057,789 for the Forecast Equity Value Before Time Adjustment. Note that this is exactly the same amount that we found using the residual income to common equity model in the previous section.

The Tax Shield on Interest

If you have been following all this very carefully, you may have noticed that some money went missing. By definition,

$$NOI_t = NI_t + I_t(1 - tax_t) + PD_t$$

NOI_t is in the income that flows to the entity. Similarly, NI_t is in the income that flows to equity holders, I_t [*without* the $(1 - tax_t)$ adjustment] is in the income that flows to debt holders, and PD_t is the income that flows to preferred stock holders. But what about the $-tax_t I_t$, the *tax shield on interest*? Where did it go? You can think of another agent in our story. For every I_t dollars that the firm sends to debt holders in the way of interest, the government sends $tax_t I_t$ dollars to the firm in the way of tax deductions (because interest is tax deductible). We could value the tax shield on interest separately and then add the result to an estimate of the entity value before any consideration of the tax shield. While this might seem like the most logical approach, the most common approach is to build the value of the tax shield into the entity value by adjusting the weighted-average cost of capital.

FIGURE 10.2   **Residual Income to All Investors**

Valuation based on eVal defaults as of September 3, 2002, for February 2, 2002, fiscal year end.

	A	B	C	D
1	**Residual Income Valuation**	**($000)**		
2	Go To User's Guide	View Valuation to Common Equity		
3		View Valuation to All Investors		
4	**Company Name**	Kohl's Corporation		
5	Most Recent Fiscal Year End	2/2/2002		
6	Date of Valuation	9/3/2002		
7	Cost of Common Equity	10.00%		
8				
9	Fiscal Year of Forecast	2/2/2003	2/2/2004	2/2/2005
53	**Valuation to all Investors**			
54	Cost of Debt	8.00%		
55	Cost of Preferred Stock	9.00%		
56	After Tax Weighted Average Cost of Capital	9.60%		
57				
58	Interest Expense to Debtholders	72,510	86,560	102,020
59	Beginning Book Value of Debt	1,111,838	1,336,502	1,586,240
60	Residual Interest Expense	(16,437)	(20,360)	(24,879)
61	Present Value of Residual Interest Income	(15,219)	(17,456)	(19,750)
62	Value of Debt	(285,758)		
63				
64	Dividends to Preferred Stockholders	0		
65	Beginning Book Value of Preferred Stock	0		
66	Residual Income to Preferred Stock	0		
67	Present Value of Residual Income	0		
68	Value of Preferred Stock	0		
69				
70	Net Operating Income	635,695	753,653	882,024
71	Beginning Net Operating Assets	3,903,244	4,691,956	5,568,690
72	Residual Income to all Investors	261,070	303,328	347,552
73	Present Value of Residual Investor Income	238,207	252,528	264,006
74	Entity Value	11,772,031		
75	Less Value of Debt	285,758		
76	Less Value of Preferred Stock	0		
77	Forecast Equity Value Before Time Adj.	12,057,789		
78		13,402,735		
79		0		

Annotations (callout boxes):

- taken directly from Financial Statements sheet
- $72,510 - .08(1,111,838)$
- $-16,437/(1+.08)^1$
- 1,111,838 + sum of present values of residual interest expense
- $= 261,070/(1+.096)^1$
- = NI + (1−tx)Int. Expense + Pfd. Div. = 590,761 + (1−.38)72,510 + 0
- = CE + Pfd. Stk + LT Debt + ST Debt = 2,791,406 + 0 + 1,095,420 + 16,418
- = 3,903,244 + sum of present values of residual income to all Investors
- = 635,695 − .096(3,903,244)

Recall from Chapter 9 that the weighted-average cost of capital was a mix of the cost of equity capital r_e, the cost of preferred stock capital r_{ps}, and the *after-tax* cost of debt capital $(1 - \text{tax})r_d$. Using the after-tax cost of debt lowers the weighted-average cost of capital that is used to discount the flows to the entity and therefore raises the entity value. Figure 10.3 illustrates the accounting variables and discount rates that each model uses.

FIGURE 10.3 **The Variables in Each Residual Income Valuation Equation**

entity value		common equity value		preferred stock value		debt value		tax shield
P_f		P_e		P_{ps}		P_d		
uses	=	uses	+	uses	+	uses		

	NOA$_t$	=	CE$_t$	+	PS$_t$	+	L_t		
and	NOI$_t$	=	NI$_t$	+	PD$_t$	+	I_t	−	tax$_t I_t$

and discounts using

	r_w	=	r_e	+	r_{ps}	+	r_d

weighted average
of r_e, r_{ps}, and $(1 - \text{tax})r_d$ value of tax$_t I_t$ is incorporated into entity value by using $(1 - \text{tax})r_d$ in r_w computation.

If it strikes you as a bit magical that using the after-tax cost of debt capital is all it takes to get the value of the tax shield on interest built into the entity value, your skepticism is justified. To be theoretically valid, we would need to add some additional assumptions; namely, that the tax rate and leverage ratios remain constant. But, as discussed in Chapter 9, we sidestep this whole issue by allowing eVal to find the internally consistent weighted-average cost of capital for you. You input the cost of equity capital, the pretax cost of debt capital, and the cost of preferred stock capital on the Valuation Parameters sheet, and eVal figures out the weighted-average cost of capital that makes everything balance.

The tax shield on interest is only an issue when valuing the common equity using this indirect approach. When valuing the equity directly, interest payments and the associated tax deductions are just another type of expense that is tax-deductible, no different than utilities or marketing expenses.

10.3 DISCOUNTED CASH FLOW VALUATION

The discounted cash flow (DCF) model focuses on free cash flows rather than earnings flows. eVal computes the DCF model two ways: based on the free cash flows to common equity holders only and based on the free cash flows to all investors—common equity holders, preferred stock holders, and debt holders. With the "all investor" approach, the common equity is valued indirectly as the entity value less the value of the debt and preferred stock claims (just like the residual income to all investors model given in the previous section). The valuation attribute that drives the DCF model, in either form, is free cash flow. Chapter 6 described in detail how this amount could be computed in many different, yet equivalent, ways. These derivations are shown in eVal on the Cash Flow Analysis sheet; you can jump straight to them by hitting the View FCF Computations button. We will give a few formulas for free cash flows here, but we refer you back to Chapter 6 for the details.

DCF to Common Equity

The *free cash flow to common equity* is the primary building block of all our valuation models. It is the net cash distributions to equity holders, labeled D_t. We can compute this amount directly as cash dividends plus stock repurchases less equity issuances. Alternatively, we can use the clean surplus relation and compute D_t based on net income and the change in common equity. That is,

$$CE_t = CE_{t-1} + NI_t - D_t$$

implies that

$$D_t = NI_t - (CE_t - CE_{t-1})$$

This is the cash flow that ultimately determines the value of a common equity claim. Discounting these flows at the cost of equity capital gives us the mother of all valuation models, the *DCF to Common Equity Model,* shown formally as

$$P_e = \sum_{t=1}^{\infty} (1 + r_e)^{-t} D_t$$

where

D_t = Net cash distributions to equity holders, computed as $NI_t - (CE_t - CE_{t-1})$

r_e = Cost of equity capital

Your forecasted financial statements describe net income and common equity forever into the future. From these amounts, we compute D_t and discount these flows at rate r_e. Nothing could be simpler, really. The knock on this model is that it is hard to develop much intuition for future D_t flows. D_t is the distribution of wealth to equity holders, which typically happens much later than the actual creation of wealth. Further, past D_t is a poor predictor of future D_t, so you really need to rely on the financial statements to derive forecasts of future D_t. Your intuition alone won't get you very far.

Since they are all equivalent, it is hard to argue which of the four valuation models is the "original version." Nonetheless, this model is probably the first, most basic, expression of the value of an equity security. The formal derivations of the other models typically start here.[1]

Figure 10.4 illustrates the DCF valuation to common equity for Kohl's as of September 3, 2002, for the fiscal year that ended on February 2, 2002, using the

---

[1] It takes little work to derive the residual income model from the DCF to common equity model. Start with the DCF model and write D_t as $NI_t - (CE_t - CE_{t-1})$. For each future date, substitute for NI_t the value $RI_t + r_e CE_{t-1}$. The first term in the summation (when $t = 1$) is $(1 + r_e)^{-1}[RI_1 + r_e CE_0 - CE_1 + CE_0] = CE_0 + (1 + r_e)^{-1}RI_1 - (1 + r_e)^{-1}CE_1$. The second term in the summation (when $t = 2$) is $(1 + r_e)^{-2}[RI_2 + r_e CE_1 - CE_2 + CE_1] = (1 + r_e)^{-2}RI_2 + (1 + r_e)^{-1}CE_1 - (1 + r_e)^{-2}CE_2$. Adding these two terms together gives $CE_0 + (1 + r_e)^{-1}RI_1 + (1 + r_e)^{-2}RI_2 - (1 + r_e)^{-2}CE_2$. As you can see, we are building the residual income model term by term. Every time we add another term in the summation, we add in the appropriately discounted RI_t term and cancel the last term in the previous sum. Since the summation is infinite, the last term is pushed out infinitely far into the future, and hence has zero present value.

FIGURE 10.4   DCF to Common Equity

Valuation based on eVal defaults as of September 3, 2002, for February 2, 2002, fiscal year end.

	A	B	C	D
1	**DCF Valuations**	**($000)**		
2	Go To User's Guide	View Valuation to Common Equity		
3		View Valuation to All Investors		
4	**Company Name**	Kohl's Corporation		
5	Most Recent Fiscal Year End	2/2/2002		
6	Date of Valuation	9/3/2002		
7	Cost of Common Equity	10.00%		
8				
9	Fiscal Year of Forecast	2/2/2003	2/2/2004	2/2/2005
11	**Valuation to Common Equity**			
12	Free Cash Flow to Common Equity	26,714	73,014	135,204
13	Present Value of FCF	24,285	60,343	101,581
14	Present Value Beyond 20 Years	6,183,403		
15	Present Value of First 20 Years	5,874,386		
16	Forecast Equity Value Before Time Adj.	12,057,789		
17	Forecasted Value as of Valuation Date	13,402,735		
18	Less Value of Contingent Equity Claims	(1,147,681)		
19	Value Attributable to Common Equity	12,255,054		
20	Common Shares Outstanding at BS Date	332,167		
21	Equivalent Shares at Valuation Date	332,167		
22	Forecast Price/Share	**$36.89**		
23				
24				
25				

$$= NI_1 - (CE_1 - CE_0)$$
$$= 590{,}761$$
$$\quad - (3{,}355{,}453 - 2{,}791{,}406)$$

$$= 73{,}014/(1+.10)^2$$

$$= 26{,}714/(1+.10)^1$$

Graphics / Cash Flow Analysis / Valuation Parameters / Residual Income Valuations / DCF Valuations / EPS Fo

Ready

default eVal forecasts. To see this in eVal, hit the View Valuation to Common Equity button on the DCF Valuations sheet (after changing the valuation date to 9/3/2002 on the Valuation Parameters sheet). The figure illustrates the computation of net distributions to common equity holders, labeled as the Free Cash Flow to Common Equity, and a few present value computations for individual years. For details on the computation of free cash flow to common equity, we refer you to Chapter 6, and to the Cash Flow Analysis sheet in eVal. The present value from the first 20 years is added to the present value from beyond 20 years to arrive at the Forecast Equity Value Before Time Adjustments. The details of the present value computations and the time adjustments are discussed in a later section. Note that the final result, before time adjustments, is $12,057,789 thousand, exactly the same result we reached using the residual income models.

DCF to All Investors

When someone in practice says "the DCF model," this is the model they typically have in mind. This model is the warhorse of traditional finance. Unfortunately, because the computation of the *free cash flow to all investors* is rather involved, and because "all investors" models require a weighted-average cost of capital that is consistent with the other costs of capital, it is the rare user who can successfully compute the DCF to all investors model without error. By automating the required computations, eVal makes sure you don't mess up along the way.

Because of the long history this model has enjoyed, a number of different ways to compute the free cash flow to all investors have emerged. We summarize two methods here; we refer you to Chapter 6 for more detailed explanations or to the Cash Flow Analysis sheet in eVal for an example using Kohl's for the year ended February 2, 2002. The free cash flow to all investors, denoted here as C_t, is computed as

$$C_t = NOI_t - (NOA_t - NOA_{t-1})$$

In words, the free cash flow to all investors equals the net operating income less the increase in net operating assets. This should feel right. All investors together claim the cash flows that emanate from the use of the net operating assets. Free cash flow differs from NOI_t because accrual accounting recognizes some NOI_t dollars that are not yet cash dollars, which necessarily means they are still in NOA_t. Subtracting the increase in NOA_t from NOI_t leaves us with the cash that the entity generated from its operations over the period.

You can also compute the free cash flows directly from data given on the statement of cash flows. Just ask yourself, what cash went to each investor group? The company sent equity holders the net distribution D_t (i.e., common dividends plus stock repurchases less equity issuances). The firm sent debt holders interest but received the benefit of the tax deduction on interest $I_t(1 - tax_t)$, and less any increase in principle, denoted ΔL_t. The firm sent preferred stockholders preferred dividends PD_t less any new issuances, denoted ΔPS_t. Putting it all together, we have

$$C_t = D_t + I_t(1 - tax_t) - \Delta L_t + PD_t - \Delta PS_t$$

If you suffer from insomnia and enjoy the finger exercises that only algebra can provide, you can show that this expression for C_t equals the previous one.[2]

Armed with the free cash flow to all investors C_t, we can now compute the *entity value*—the value of the operations to all investors before distinguishing between claimants. Denoting the weighted-average cost of capital as r_w and the entity value as P_f, we have

$$P_f = \sum_{t=1}^{\infty} (1 + r_w)^{-t} C_t$$

and, yes, this version of P_f is exactly equal to the P_f computed using the residual income to all investors model shown in the previous section. To compute the value of the common equity claim, we subtract from P_f the value of the debt P_d and preferred stock P_{ps}. In the spirit of discounting cash flows, each of these non-common-equity claims is itself valued based on the cash flows it receives.

---

[2] Here is the proof. By definition, $NOI_t = NI_t + PD_t + I_t(1 - tax_t)$ and $\Delta NOA_t = \Delta CE_t + \Delta L_t + \Delta PS_t$. Substitute these expressions for NOI_t and $(NOA_t - NOA_{t-1})$ in the first C_t expression. Next, note that by the clean surplus relation, $NI_t = D_t + \Delta CE_t$. Substitute this in for NI_t, cancel the plus and minus ΔCE_t and you have the second expression for C_t.

Denoting the pretax cost of debt as r_d and the cost of preferred stock as r_{ps}, we have

$$P_d = \sum_{t=1}^{\infty} (1 + r_d)^{-t}(I_t - \Delta L_t)$$

and

$$P_{ps} = \sum_{t=1}^{\infty} (1 + r_{ps})^{-t}(\text{PD}_t - \Delta\text{PS}_t)$$

The value of P_d and P_{ps} computed based on cash flows is exactly the same as the value computed in the previous section based on residual flows. Putting it all together, we compute the value of the common equity as

$$P_e = P_f - P_d - P_{ps}$$

Finally, we can mix and match between the residual income model and the discounted cash flow model. For instance, it is not uncommon to compute the value of the debt P_d or the value of the preferred stock using a residual income model, with the added assumption that all future residual flows to these claimants are zero. In other words, the value of the debt and the value of the preferred stock are simply their current book values L_0 and PS_0, respectively. The value of the common equity is then the entity value computed using free cash flows to all investors less the book value of the debt and the book value of preferred stock.

Figure 10.5 illustrates the DCF valuation to all investors for Kohl's as of September 3, 2002, for the fiscal year that ended on February 2, 2002, using the default eVal forecasts. To see this in eVal, hit the View Valuation to All Investors button on the DCF Valuations sheet (after setting the valuation date to 9/3/2002). The figure shows the free cash flows each period to debt and preferred stock (zero in Kohl's case), and then the free cash flows to all investors. Note that the value of debt, the value of preferred stock, and the entity value are each computed using a different discount rate. In particular, the entity value is computed using the weighted-average cost of capital of 9.6 percent (actually, it is 9.5978 percent). This amount was derived by eVal as the rate that equated the equity value when computed directly with the equity value when computed indirectly (i.e. as the entity value less the value of the debt and the value of the preferred stock). Note that the result of $12,057,789, labeled as the Forecast Equity Value Before Time Adjustment, is exactly the same result as in the other three valuation models.

Tax Shield on Interest

Just as in the residual income to all investors model, we need to worry about the tax shield on interest. When the firm pays I_t interest to the debt holders, the government gives the firm a tax deduction worth $\text{tax}_t I_t$. This is why the interest is after-tax in the C_t computation:

$$C_t = D_t + I_t(1 - \text{tax}_t) - \Delta L_t + \text{PD}_t - \Delta\text{PS}_t$$

But notice that the $-\text{tax}_t I_t$ flow, *the tax shield on interest,* isn't getting discounted in the P_e, P_{ps}, or P_d formulas. To see this clearly, Figure 10.6 shows the cash flows

FIGURE 10.5   **DCF to All Investors**

Valuation based on eVal defaults as of September 3, 2002, for February 2, 2002, fiscal year end.

	A	B	C	D
1	**DCF Valuations**	**($000)**		
2	Go To User's Guide	View Valuation to Common Equity		
3		View Valuation to All Investors		
4	**Company Name**	Kohl's Corporation		
5	Most Recent Fiscal Year End	2/2/2002		
6	Date of Valuation	9/3/2002	= Int. Expense – increase in Debt	
7	Cost of Common Equity	10.00%	= 72,510 – 224,664	
8				
9	Fiscal Year of Forecast	2/2/2003	2/2/2004	2/2/2005
53	**Valuation All Investors**			
54	Cost of Debt	8.00%		
55	Cost of Preferred Stock	9.00%		
56	After Tax Weighted Average Cost of Capital	9.60%	= –152,154/(1+.08)²	
57				
58	Free Cash Flow to Debt	(152,154)	(163,178)	(170,262)
59	Present Value of FCF to Debt	(140,884)	(139,899)	(135,160)
60	Value of Debt	(285,758)		
6	= NOI – increase in NOA	0	= –163,178/(1+.08)²	
6	= 635,695 – 788,712 ck			
6	d Stock			
6	taken from Cash Flow Analysis			
6		= –123,082/(1+.096)²		
66	Free Cash Flows to Investors	(153,016)	(123,082)	(73,856)
67	Present Value of FCF to Investors	(139,616)	(102,469)	(56,102)
68	Entity Value	11,772,031		
69	Less Value of Debt	285,758	sum of present values of	
70	Less Value of Preferred Stock	0	FCF to Investors	
71	Forecast Equity Value Before Time Adj.	12,057,789		
72	Forecasted Value as of Valuation Date	13,402,735		

FIGURE 10.6   **The Variables in Each DCF Valuation Equation**

entity value		common equity value		preferred stock value		debt value		tax shield
P_f	=	P_e	+	P_{ps}	+	P_d		
cash flows		cash flows		cash flows		cash flows		cash flows
C_t	=	D_t	+	$PD_t - \Delta PS_t$	+	$I_t - \Delta L_t$	–	$tax_t I_t$

discounted using

r_w	=	r_e	+	r_{ps}	+	r_d

weighted average
of r_e, r_{ps} and $(1-\text{tax})r_d$ value of $tax_t I_t$ is incorporated into entity value by using $(1-\text{tax})r_d$ in r_w computation.

that are being discounted to compute P_e, P_{ps}, and P_d. How, then, can the sum of P_e, P_{ps}, and P_d equal the entity value P_f, which discounts the full C_t flows? The answer is that the value of the tax shield is incorporated into the entity value through the discount rate r_w. Recall from Chapter 9 that the weighted-average cost of capital is a mix of the cost of equity r_e, the cost of preferred stock r_{ps}, and the *after-tax* cost of debt $(1 - \text{tax})r_d$. Using the after-tax cost of debt lowers the weighted-average cost of capital, which raises the present value of the C_t flows in the P_f formula.

While it is relatively easy to see how lowering the weighted-average cost of capital a bit will raise the entity value a bit, it is a bit surprising that the adjustment is exactly the right amount to capture the value of the tax shield. In fact, we are hiding some complications from you. For this to really work out, we would need to assume that the tax rate and the leverage ratio remain constant, yet eVal allows you to forecast whatever tax rates and leverage rates that you like. Rather than constrain your forecasts, we sidestep this whole issue by allowing eVal to find the internally consistent weighted-average cost of capital for you. You input the cost of equity capital, the pretax cost of debt capital, and the cost of preferred stock capital on the Valuation Parameters sheet, and eVal figures out the weighted average cost of capital that makes everything balance. For more information, see the discussion of the weighted-average cost of capital in Chapter 9.

Figuring out how to value the tax shield on interest is only an issue when we want to first value the whole entity and then back into the value of the common equity. If we value the free cash flows to equity directly, then interest and its tax deduction are built into our financial statement forecasts and play out through net income and the book value of equity just like any other expense. What this means is that any debate about valuing the tax shield on interest (and academics love to debate this issue) is really just a debate about how to get the entity value to equal the sum of the debt value, the preferred stock value, and the common equity value.

Figure 10.7 summarizes all four valuation models. The columns describe what is being valued—the equity, the debt, or the preferred stock—and the rows

FIGURE 10.7 Summary of Valuation Equations

Valuation Attribute	Equity Valued Directly as P_e	Equity Valued Indirectly as $P_e = P_f - P_d - P_{ps}$		
	Value of Common Equity P_e	Value of Whole Entity P_f	Value of Debt P_d	Value of Preferred Stock P_{ps}
Cash Flows	$\sum_{t=1}^{T-1} \frac{D_t}{(1+r_e)^t} + \frac{D_T}{(r_e - g)(1+r_e)^{T-1}}$	$\sum_{t=1}^{T-1} \frac{C_t}{(1+r_w)^t} + \frac{C_T}{(r_w - g)(1+r_w)^{T-1}}$	$\sum_{t=1}^{T-1} \frac{I_t - \Delta L_t}{(1+r_d)^t} + \frac{I_T - \Delta L_T}{(r_d - g)(1+r_d)^{T-1}}$	$\sum_{t=1}^{T-1} \frac{\text{PD}_t - \Delta\text{PS}_t}{(1+r_{ps})^t} + \frac{\text{PD}_T - \Delta\text{PS}_T}{(r_{ps} - g)(1+r_{ps})^{T-1}}$
Residual Income	$\text{CE}_0 + \sum_{t=1}^{T-1} \frac{\text{RI}_t}{(1+r_e)^t} + \frac{\text{RI}_T}{(r_e - g)(1+r_e)^{T-1}}$ where $\text{RI}_t = \text{NI}_t - r_e\text{CE}_{t-1}$	$\text{NOA}_0 + \sum_{t=1}^{T-1} \frac{\text{RNOI}_t}{(1+r_w)^t} + \frac{\text{RNOI}_T}{(r_w - g)(1+r_w)^{T-1}}$ where $\text{RNOI}_t = \text{NOI}_t - r_w\text{NOA}_{t-1}$	$L_0 + \sum_{t=1}^{T-1} \frac{\text{RIT}_t}{(1+r_d)^t} + \frac{\text{RIT}_T}{(r_d - g)(1+r_d)^{T-1}}$ where $\text{RIT}_t = I_t - r_d L_{t-1}$	$\text{PS}_0 + \sum_{t=1}^{T-1} \frac{\text{RPD}_t}{(1+r_{ps})^t} + \frac{\text{RPD}_T}{(r_{ps} - g)(1+r_{ps})^{T-1}}$ where $\text{RPD}_t = \text{PD}_t - r_{ps}\text{PS}_{t-1}$

D_t = Cash flow to common equity; $\text{CE}_t = \text{CE}_{t-1} + \text{NI}_t - D_t$
C_t = Cash flow to all investors; $C_t = \text{NOI}_t - \Delta\text{NOA}_t$
L_t = Debt balance at time t
CE_t = Shareholders' equity at time t; $\text{NOA}_t - L_t - \text{PS}_t = \text{CE}_t$
NOI_t = Operating income for the period ending at time t, net of tax
I_t = Interest expense for the period ending at time t,
NI_t = Net income for the period ending at time t; $\text{NI}_t = \text{NOI}_t - (1 - \text{tax})I_t - \text{PD}_t$
NOA_t = Net operating asset balance at time t
PD_t = Preferred dividend at time t

PS_t = Preferred stock balance at time t
r_e = Cost of equity capital
r_d = Cost of debt capital
r_{ps} = Cost of preferred stock capital
r_w = Weighted-average cost of capital:

$$r_w = \frac{r_e P_e + (1 - \text{tax})r_d P_d + r_p P_{ps}}{P_e + P_d + P_{ps}}$$

describe which valuation attribute is being used—free cash flow or residual income. To compute the infinite sum of flows, each expression makes use of the perpetuity formula discussed in the next section.

10.4 PRESENT VALUE COMPUTATIONS

All four valuation models given above compute value as the present value of an infinite series of flows of the valuation attribute, either residual income or free cash flow. Since it is impossibly time consuming to compute the present value of an infinite series term by term, all valuation models compute the present value term by term up to the *terminal year* and then compute the present value beyond the terminal year using the formula for a growing perpetuity. In case you have forgotten, the present value of a growing perpetuity of payments, starting with K one year from now and growing at rate g forever after, discounted at rate r, is given by the following formula

$$\frac{K}{(1+r)} + \frac{(1+g)K}{(1+r)^2} + \frac{(1+g)^2K}{(1+r)^3} + \frac{(1+g)^3K}{(1+r)^4} + \cdots = \frac{K}{(r-g)}$$

The left-hand side of the formula shows the sequence of terms that continue in perpetuity in the present value computation and the right-hand side of the formula shows the simplified result.

Before the terminal year, your forecasts can be as wild as you like. Each year's forecasts will imply a flow of valuation attributes, however unusual, and the model will compute the present value of each year's flow. However, starting with the terminal year, your forecasts are constrained to behave in a more predictable manner. Sales growth is fixed at the rate you input into eVal in the terminal year and this becomes the g in the perpetuity formula. Profit margins, asset turnovers, and leverage ratios also are assumed to remain constant after the terminal year. These forecasts imply well-defined financial statements forever into the future, and they are financial statements that will generate residual income flows and free cash flows that will grow forever at rate g. Once everything is safely growing at this known rate, we can compute the present value of the subsequent flows using the formula given above.

In previous chapters, we noted that your terminal growth forecast should not exceed the discount rate; otherwise, the present value is infinite. In terms of the formula given above, if g is greater than r, then the result is negative, but you shouldn't try to attach any meaning to this. The formula is simply undefined when g exceeds r.

Let's use the growing perpetuity formula to rewrite the residual income to common equity model. The model given earlier is

$$P_e = CE_0 + \sum_{t=1}^{\infty} (1+r_e)^{-t} RI_t.$$

Now suppose that, starting in year T, the financial statement forecasts imply that residual income will be RI_T and then grow at rate g forever after. We can now compute the present value as

$$P_e = \text{CE}_0 + \sum_{t=1}^{T-1}(1+r_e)^{-t}\text{RI}_t + \frac{\text{RI}_T}{(r_e - g)(1+r_e)^{T-1}}$$

The first two terms are the present value for years 1 through $T-1$ and the last term is the present value for years T and forever after. To apply the formula for a growing perpetuity in this setting, you need to think carefully about when the different residual income flows take place. The residual income in year T is RI_T; it is $\text{RI}_T(1 + g)$ in year $T + 1$, and so on, growing forever at rate g. If we were standing in year $T-1$ and wanted to compute the present value of this growing perpetuity, we would apply the formula and get

$$\frac{\text{RI}_T}{r_e - g}$$

But we want the present value at time 0, not time $T-1$, so we need to discount back $T-1$ more years. To do this, we divide by $(1 + r_e)^{T-1}$, as shown in the denominator of the last term.

All of the other valuation models handle the present value computations exactly the same way. After the financial statement forecasts become sufficiently stable, insofar as they imply a smooth sequence of future free cash flows or residual income flows, the perpetuity formula kicks in to compute the remaining present value. As a summary, Figure 10.7 gives the precise definition of each model.

So what is the value of T, the terminal year? In eVal, it is always 23 years. This may not seem like the most obvious choice, so let us explain. On the Forecasting Assumptions sheet, the longest horizon you can pick for making detailed forecasts is 20 years. After 20 years, it is assumed that all relationships stabilize and grow at the terminal sales growth rate. However, many of the forecasting assumptions in eVal are based on relationships between income statement amounts and *average* balance sheet amounts, so it takes two more years for all the relationships among the financial statements to stabilize and yield steady sequences of cash flows and residual income flows. If you pick the 5-year or 10-year forecasting horizon, the cash flows and residual income flows stabilize sooner, but we still get the same present value if we discount each year individually until we get out to year 23. In general, you should be very cautious about using the perpetuity formula too soon. Many of the financial statement relationships change around the transition from the finite horizon to the steady state that follows after the terminal year. Because year T is the starting value for an infinite stream of future values, even a small error in the year T cash flow or residual income flow gets greatly amplified, resulting in a big mistake in the valuation. Because the terminal value calculation is important, yet tedious, we let eVal handle the calculation.

Adjusting the Present Value to the Present

Figure 10.8 illustrates eVal's present value computations for the DCF to common equity and the residual income to common equity models. The amounts are from Kohl's, valued as of September 3, 2002, for the fiscal year ended February 2, 2002,

FIGURE 10.8

Kohl's Present Value Computations

Valuation based on eVal defaults as of September 3, 2002, for February 2, 2002, fiscal year end.

DCF Valuation to Common Equity

11	Valuation to Common Equity	
12	Free Cash Flow to Common Equity	26,714
13	Present Value of FCF	24,285
14	Present Value Beyond 20 Years	6,183,403
15	Present Value of First 20 Years	5,874,386
16	Forecast Equity Value Before Time Adj.	12,057,789
17	Forecasted Value as of Valuation Date	13,402,735
18	Less Value of Contingent Equity Claims	(1,147,681)
19	Value Attributable to Common Equity	12,255,054
20	Common Shares Outstanding at BS Date	332,167
21	Equivalent Shares at Valuation Date	332,167
22	Forecast Price/Share	**$36.89**

Residual Income Valuation to Common Equity

11	Valuation to Common Equity	
12	Net Income	590,761
13	Common Equity at Beginning of Year	2,791,406
14	Residual Income	311,620
15	Present Value of Residual Income	283,291
16	Present Value Beyond 20 Years	3,831,760
17	Present Value of First 20 Years	5,434,623
18	Common Equity as of	
19	2/2/2002	2,791,406
20	Forecast Equity Value Before Time Adj.	12,057,789
21	Forecasted Value as of Valuation Date	13,402,735
22	Less Value of Contingent Equity Claims	(1,147,681)
23	Value Attributable to Common Equity	12,255,054
24	Common Shares Outstanding at BS Date	332,167
25	Equivalent Shares at Valuation Date	332,167
26	Forecast Price/Share	**$36.89**

using the default forecasting settings. Consider the DCF to common equity, shown in the top panel. eVal adds Present Value of First 20 Years and Present Value Beyond 20 Years to arrive at the Forecast Equity Value Before Time Adjustment. Comparing the two amounts shows that a little less than half of the total value of the cash flows arrives in the first 20 years. But now compare this to the residual income model in the bottom half of Figure 10.8.

The residual income model also shows values for the first 20 years and beyond 20 years, but they aren't the same as for the DCF model. In particular, the value beyond 20 years is much smaller and, if we consider the value of Common Equity as of 2/2/2002 as part of the value during the first 20 years, then the residual income model shows a significantly greater portion of value arriving much earlier than the DCF model. Both models arrive at the same Forecast Equity Value Before Time Adjustment, but why do they allocate the value differently across time? The answer reveals a fundamental difference in the way the two models characterize value creation. The residual income model counts the balance of common equity as value already earned and counts net income as value created, regardless of the actual cash flow. The DCF model, in contrast, waits for the actual cash to arrive. Another way to say this is that the DCF treats investment as a consumption of value (cash is leaving the firm) while the residual income model treats investment as a store of value (assets are put on the books). The two models ultimately get to the same total value because they are based on the same underlying financial statement forecasts, but they differ drastically on when they say the value is created.

Regardless of which model you are working with, it is useful to think about when the model says that value is being created. In most cases, you are probably more confident about your forecasts during the first 20 years than you are about your forecasts beyond 20 years, so if most of the value is concentrated more than 20 years away, then you might be less confident in your valuation. Are we more confident in the residual income model than in the DCF model because it records valuation creation sooner? The answer is absolutely not. One model can be derived algebraically from the other and so it would be silly to be more confident of the left-hand side of an equation than the right-hand side. Whatever uncertainty you have in your forecasts about book value and net income translate into exactly the same amount of uncertainty in future net distributions to common equity holders.[3]

So far we have discussed the present value calculations as of the end of the fiscal year for the most recent financial statements, which is February 2, 2002, in the Kohl's example, and have worked our way down Figure 10.8 to the line labeled Forecast Equity Value Before Time Adjustment. There are two more present value adjustments that take us to the next line, labeled Forecasted Value as of Valuation Date. First, the present value computation treats the cash flows and residual income flows as though they are realized on the last day of the fiscal year. In reality, wealth is distributed somewhat more evenly throughout the year. To correct for this, we multiply the value estimate by $(1 + r_e/2)$. This effectively moves the flows forward six months in time. Second, you will typically want to compute the value as of the day you are thinking of trading the stock, not the last day of the last fiscal year. You can enter whatever valuation date you like on eVal's Valuation Parameters sheet; the default is the current date. eVal then computes the fraction of the year (ρ) between the inputted date and the fiscal year end, and multiplies the value estimate by $(1 + r_e\rho)$ to get the present value as of the inputted date. This adjusts your valuation estimate for the passage of time between the last set of financial statements and the date entered. As time passes, you get closer to the estimated future values, so their present value increases. In the Kohl's example in Figure 10.8,

---

[3] Lundholm and O'Keefe (2001) provide careful discussion of this issue, along with a list of common errors in the implementation of each model that generate apparent, but not real, differences between the residual income model and DCF models.

the valuation date is September 3, 2002, which is 58.6 percent of the way through the next fiscal year. Putting these two time value adjustments together, and using the default cost of equity capital in eVal of 10 percent, the adjustment to go from the Forecast Equity Value Before Time Adjustment to the Forecasted Value as of Valuation Date is

$$12,057,789(1 + .10/2)(1 + .10(.5861)) = 13,402,735$$

There are two other adjustments we need to make before we get to the final estimate of price per share. These are discussed in the next section.

Solving for the Implied Cost of Equity Capital

So far we have input our estimate of the cost of equity capital and then solved for the value of the equity by discounting the cash flows or residual income flows using this estimate. But we can change the order of things. At the bottom of the Valuation Parameters sheet, there is a calculator that takes as input a price per share and then finds the cost of equity capital that would yield this price. For example, we found earlier that the estimated value of Kohl's stock as of September 3, 2002, is $36.89 per share, based on eVal's default forecasts, discounted at the default cost of equity capital rate of 10 percent, and after subtracting $1,147,681 thousand for contingent claims (see the next section). However, on September 3, 2002, Kohl's stock was trading at about $70 per share. If we input $70 into the calculator, we get an implied cost of equity capital of 7.98 percent (try it yourself!). To find this amount, eVal keeps guessing discount rates until the value of the firm is the price you input in the calculator. This means that if investors' expectations at September 3, 2002, are the same as the default eVal forecasts, and the market is efficient (meaning that the price of $70 per share is "correct"), then investors should expect to earn a 7.98 percent return on their Kohl's investment. They may not earn this return every year—in fact, even if the future cash flows materialize exactly as the eVal forecasts predict, all the model says for sure is that the annualized return over the life of the firm will be 7.98 percent. If 7.98 percent strikes you as an unreasonably low return for an investment as risky as Kohl's, then effectively you are saying that investors' beliefs are more optimistic than the eVal defaults (but recall that our detailed forecasts were less optimistic) or the market price for Kohl's stock is too high. For instance, if you believe that the true cost of equity capital for Kohl's is 10 percent, but the calculator says the implied rate is 7.98 percent, then the annualized *alpha* on Kohl's stock is 7.98 percent −10 percent = −2.02 percent. This means that if the market corrects this mispricing and you hold a short position in Kohl's, you would expect to earn 2.02 percent in excess of the risk-adjusted return.

There is one cautionary note we need to offer before turning you loose with the implied cost of capital calculator. If your forecasts imply that some future cash flows will be positive and others will be negative, then it is possible for there to be more than one discount rate that equates the value of the future cash flows with the price you input, but only one of these values will be correct. eVal will pick the most reasonable amount (and by that we mean the amount closest to 10 percent), but if your cash flow forecasts are both positive and negative and the calculator yields a value that is negative or is extremely high, then you should disregard it.

10.5   VALUING CONTINGENT CLAIMS AND OTHER ADJUSTMENTS

The value of *contingent claims* represents your estimate of the value of other potential claims on the firm that are not currently recognized in the financial statements or in your estimates. These might be stock warrants, the convertible component of a debt issue, or existing employee stock options. They all have the feature that value is transferred from existing shareholders to future shareholders if the claim is exercised and equity is issued at a price below its intrinsic value. Forming a precise estimate of this loss in value can be quite complicated. We will describe how to compute a lower bound for this value, how to approximate it more accurately using the *contingent claims calculator* in eVal, and then discuss some limitations to both of these approaches.

At this point, we are trying to estimate the value of existing contingent claims; Chapter 12 confronts the even more thorny issue of estimating the value of contingent claims to be issued in the future. We will focus on estimating the value of employee stock options; the other types of contingent claims can be estimated in similar fashion. Start by reading the firm's financial statement footnote on employee stock options. Here they tell you the number of options outstanding in different ranges of option exercise prices. If the option can be exercised at a low price and the stock is currently trading at a high price, then each option is worth *at least* the difference between these two amounts. That is, the option is *in the money* by the difference between these two amounts. But this only represents a lower bound on the value of the option because it doesn't account for the fact that the stock price might increase even more before the option must be exercised. How likely this is to occur depends on the life of the option and the volatility in the stock price. There are a number of ways to put all these puzzle pieces together and form an option pricing model. eVal offers you a calculator that uses the most popular solution: the Black-Scholes Option Pricing Model. Let

S = Current stock price

K = Exercise or "strike" price

y = Long-term forecasted annual dividend yield

r = Annual risk-free interest rate

t = Number of years before the option expires

σ = Standard deviation of the log of the value of the stock price

$N(\bullet)$ = Cumulative standard normal distribution function

The Black-Scholes formula is then

$$optionvalue = Se^{-yt}N(d_1) - Ke^{-rt}N(d_2)$$

where

$$d_1 = \frac{\ln\left(\dfrac{S}{K}\right) + \left(r - y + \dfrac{\sigma^2}{2}\right) t}{\sigma \sqrt{t}}$$

$$d_2 = d_1 - \sigma \sqrt{t}$$

Without attempting to derive the specific form of this model, we offer some observations about it. First, note that the option's value increases with the gap between the current stock price S and the option's exercise price K. The deeper the option is in the money, the more valuable it is. Second, the option's value increases with t, the number of years remaining before the option expires, and with σ, the stock price volatility. Third, the option value decreases with the dividend yield y because future dividends decrease the future stock price, all else equal. Actually evaluating this formula by hand would be quite difficult because the function $N(\bullet)$ is itself quite complicated. Instead, the contingent claims calculator on the Valuation Parameters sheet in eVal takes your inputted parameters and does the calculation for you.

Most of the inputs to the contingent claims calculator are obvious, but the one that you may not have a good feel for is the annual standard deviation of the log of the stock price. A good source for this data item is the employee stock option footnote. Companies provide an estimate of this amount because they are required to estimate the value of options issued to employees during the current fiscal year. Prior to 2006 firms would report this amount only in the footnote; now they must expense it. A ballpark figure is 30 percent, which is the default amount given in the contingent claims calculator.

A problem with the Black-Scholes estimate given by the contingent claims calculator is that real live employees frequently do not behave exactly like the model says they should. In particular, it has been shown that employees overwhelmingly exercise their options well before the option's expiration date. This doesn't make sense, from the model's point of view, because the option still has additional value right up to the expiration date. From the common equity holder's point of view, however, this is good news because less value is being given away to the employees. It also means that the Black-Scholes estimate might be too high. Your final estimate might be something higher than the simple difference between the current stock price and the exercise price and something less than the full Black-Scholes amount given in the contingent claims calculator.

Generally, the company reports a range of exercise prices and gives the weighted average of the exercise price, years to expiration, and other details for each set of options in the range. You need to estimate the value of the options separately for each exercise price and corresponding number of shares under option at that exercise price. In Figure 10.9, we illustrate the inputs to the contingent claims calculator using the stock option footnote from Kohl's 10-K for the year ended February 2, 2002.

To use the data from Kohl's footnote in the contingent claims calculator, we need to assume that all the options in an exercise price range have the weighted-average exercise price and years remaining on the contractual life. We also take the

FIGURE 10.9
Estimated Value of Kohl's Options Outstanding as of February 2, 2002

Excerpt from Kohl's 10-K for the year ended 2/2/2002	Exercise Price Range		
	$1.75 to $9.49	$9.50 to $35.49	$35.50 to $71.82
Options outstanding..................................	7,253,245	5,940,700	8,059,851
Weighted average exercise price of options outstanding $	6.57 $	24.63 $	54.72
Weighted average remaining contractual life of options outstanding...	3.4	11.3	13.9

Estimated Value of Options Outstanding (in thousands)*

Options with Exercise Price Range of $1.75–$9.49	$432,610
Options with Exercise Price Range of $9.50–$35.49	$322,270
Options with Exercise Price Range of $35.50–71.82	$392,801
Total Value ($000)	**$1,147,681**

*Other inputs to the Contingent Claims Calculator are a risk-free rate of 6%, a dividend yield of 0% and stock return volatility of 40%, as given in Kohl's 10-K, and a $65 current stock price, which was the price just after the fiscal year end.

risk-free interest rate, the dividend yield, and the volatility estimates from the Kohl's footnote. The net result is that the outstanding options have a Black-Scholes value of $1,14,7681 thousand, or over a billion dollars, as shown in Figure 10.8 for the line labeled Less Value of Contingent Equity Claims. A billion dollars is a little over 5 percent of Kohl's market capitalization at the end of fiscal 2001.

This adjustment for contingent claims only captures the effect of existing contingent claims. What if you expect that the firm will continue to issue options or other contingent securities in the future? As we discuss in Chapter 12, the best way to handle this is to estimate the dollar value of the to-be-issued contingent claims and record them as an expense in your forecasted financial statements.

Adjusting for Stock Splits and Stock Dividends

If the firm has undertaken a stock split or stock dividend, as opposed to a cash dividend, between the date of the financial statements you are using and the valuation date, then you need to adjust for this by inputting a *dilution factor* on the eVal Valuation Parameters sheet. For example, if your firm does a two-for-one stock split after the date of the financial statements, then the number of shares outstanding doubles, resulting in a dilution factor of two. If we failed to account for the split, then our per-share valuation estimate and all of our EPS forecasts would be twice what they should be. To see a list of recent splits for a company, go to Yahoo! Finance, type the company's ticker, and select the Chart option under More Info. You only have to adjust for splits since the most recent balance sheet date loaded in eVal. Don't include any splits made before that date.

What if the firm issues new shares for cash or as part of the acquisition of another company? Interestingly, you do not need to adjust for this *if* you believe the shares were issued at their true intrinsic value. In a stock split or stock dividend, the number of shares increases but nothing of economic value is added to the firm, so adjusting the number of shares completely captures the effect of this event.

However, if the firm receives something of economic value in exchange for the shares, then value of the firm increases along with the number of shares. If the new shares are issued at a price equal to their intrinsic value, then the increase in firm value exactly offsets the dilution caused by the increase in the number of shares. To make this perfectly clear, imagine a firm that consists of $100 in a bank account and has one share outstanding, so its intrinsic value is $100 per share. If the firm issues another share for $100 and deposits it in the bank, the firm is now worth $200 and has two shares, so it is still worth $100 per share. Complications arise, however, if the firm issues the stock at $90 or $110. In this case, there is a wealth transfer between the original owners and the new investors. Situations such as this raise thorny issues in valuation. Fundamentally, what is the value of an overvalued stock that can issue equity at its inflated price? We will ignore such complications in this chapter and take them up in a serious way in Chapter 12.

The last stock split for Kohl's was in April 2000, well before the February 2, 2002, fiscal year end, so we don't need to adjust the number of shares in our computations for a valuation on September 3, 2002. Consequently, the Common Shares Outstanding at Balance Sheet Date and the Equivalent Shares at Valuation Date are the same amount in Figure 10.8.

Putting It All Together

The valuation formulas given in the first part of the chapter compute the present value as of the most recent fiscal year end, assuming that all cash flows and residual income flows happen on the last day of each year. We then adjusted this value up by a half-year's worth of time value because the flows typically happen evenly throughout the year, not on the last day. We also adjusted the value up to the date that we are actually doing the valuation (or whatever date we want), rather than the end of the most recent fiscal year. We then subtract the value of any contingent claims and adjust the number of shares for any stock splits or stock dividends that occurred between the fiscal year end and the valuation date. The final result is our forecast of the intrinsic price per share. This is what you think the stock is really worth. For Kohl's, the final result is $36.89 per share, as illustrated on the last line of Figure 10.8. Recall that the valuation date is set to September 3, 2002, and we simply used the default eVal forecasts. If we input all the more detailed forecasts developed in Chapter 8, the value drops to about $30 per share. This is less than half of the market price of Kohl's at September 3, 2002, so the market is expecting much better performance from Kohl's than is implied by the eVal defaults and by our more carefully developed estimates. With hindsight, who was right? Recall that in the last section of Chapter 8, we showed that Kohl's profitability in 2002–2004 was actually lower than our detailed forecasts. Correspondingly, the price dropped to the $40-per-share range over the same period.

The Model Summary sheet in eVal gives a quick snapshot of the firm's historical performance, the profitability and growth implications of your detailed forecasts, and the resulting price-per-share estimate. It also shows the market-to-book and price-to-earnings ratios that are implied by your estimated price; these ratios are discussed in the next chapter.

If the value estimate is ridiculously far from the current market price and you feel reasonably confident in your forecasts, here are a few things to check. First, are you sure you have the correct number of shares outstanding? If there was a stock split after the fiscal year end, then you may be off by 100 percent in your estimate. Second, what if the estimated price is negative? Literally, a negative price means that you would pay this amount to *not* have to own the stock. We allow eVal to arrive at this conclusion if it is the logical implication of your forecasts and cost of capital inputs, but we don't really expect you to get out your checkbook. If the estimated price is negative, it means that the present value of the cash flows that the equity holders are forecasted to send *to* the firm is greater than the present value of the cash flows that the equity holders are forecasted to receive *from* the firm. If this was literally true, then an equity holder might indeed be willing to pay to not have to own the stock. But since the firm can't force the equity holders to keep sending it money, and since equity holders are not liable to third parties for the firm's losses, the real lower bound on price is zero. If the price is negative, you would simply refuse to own the stock, and you can do this for free. We let eVal report a negative price because it shows you the logical implications of your forecasts. If you really think the firm has positive value, you need to revise your forecasts accordingly. To identify the economic source of a price estimate that is negative, or far too low, look at the series of ROE forecasts. Value is destroyed each period that the ROE is below the firm's cost of equity capital. If this situation continues on for too long, or for periods with very high growth, the net result will be a negative stock price. Negative stock prices are discussed in more detail in Chapter 12.

eVal's Model Summary sheet also has a handy tool for conducting a sensitivity analysis of your valuation. You feed the model a horizon, a beginning ROE, a terminal ROE, a beginning sales growth rate, a terminal sales growth rate, and a cost of equity capital. The model then estimates the value of the firm by extrapolating a linear progression between the beginning and ending ROEs and the sales growth rates. You can use this to see how small changes in your estimates affect your valuation. You also can use this tool to do a "quick and dirty" valuation of a company that you might be interested in studying further.

10.6 CASES, LINKS, AND REFERENCES

Cases

- The Valuation of Amazon.com in June 2001
- Encom Corporation (Stage 3)
- Four Valuation Models—One Value
- Evaluating Intel's Earnings Torpedo
- Overstock.com (Questions 14 through 17)
- Can Salton Swing? (Questions 5 and 6)

Links

- eVal Web site: http://www.mhhe.com/eval2007
- Yahoo! Finance: http://yahoo.finance.com

Reference

- Lundholm, R., and T. O'Keefe. (2001). Reconciling value estimates from the discounted cash flow model and the residual income model. *Contemporary Accounting Research* 18: 311–35.

CHAPTER ELEVEN

Valuation Ratios

11.1 INTRODUCTION

In Chapter 5, we converted the financial statement data into ratios in order to reveal underlying economic properties and to make the data comparable across companies and over time. For the same reason, we can more easily compare the valuation of different companies by scaling our estimated value by some accounting data. In this section, we derive the market-to-book ratio, the price-to-earnings ratio, and a new innovation known as the PEG ratio, and we discuss what each ratio reveals about the market's expectations about the company's future. These ratios are commonly used summary statistics for a firm's valuation and each can be found on financial information portals, such as Multex Investor or Yahoo! Finance. After we discuss each ratio, we will give some historical and current benchmarks to get you grounded.

We offer a word of caution before proceeding. As we found in the last chapter, a valuation depends on an infinite series of forecasted financial data. Only in very special cases is it possible to value a firm based on just its current book value or its current earnings. Consequently, it is unlikely that you will be able to take a quick look at the price-to-earnings ratio or market-to-book ratio and know if a firm is mispriced. Rather, these ratios can help you to make a quick assessment of the expectations built into a firm's current market price.

11.2 THE MARKET-TO-BOOK RATIO

This ratio divides the current market value of equity (P_e) by the book value of equity from the most recent financial statements (CE_0). If we start with the residual income to common equity model and divide everything by CE_0, we get

$$\frac{P_e}{CE_0} = 1 + \sum_{t=1}^{\infty} \frac{(ROE_t - r_e)\frac{CE_{t-1}}{CE_0}}{(1+r_e)^t}$$

where ROE_t is defined relative to beginning equity: $ROE_t = NI_t/CE_{t-1}$.

The first thing to note from this formula is that if you forecast that $ROE_t = r_e$ every period in the future, then the firm is worth exactly its book value (i.e., CE_0). This is like a savings account: every period it pays interest at exactly its discount rate and so every period it is worth exactly the balance in the account. When firms have a market-to-book ratio greater than one, the market expects that, on average, they will earn an ROE_t higher than r_e in the future.

Note that the CE_{t-1}/CE_0 term in the numerator is the *cumulative* growth in beginning common equity each period. In other words, in year one it equals one, in year two it equals CE_1/CE_0, in year three it equals CE_2/CE_0, and so on. The numerator in our expression for the market-to-book ratio is therefore the firm's abnormal profitability ($ROE_t - r_e$) times its cumulative growth in beginning book value (CE_t/CE_0). This simple observation speaks volumes. A firm is worth more than its book value only if it is expected to have an ROE_t greater than r_e (as we keep repeating). Assuming the firm is expected to meet this profitability threshold, growth and profitability are multiplicative. This means that really high valuations come about when firms have both high profitability *and* high growth.

To give you a few reference points, suppose that ROE is forecasted to be constant forever, and equity is forecasted to grow at rate *g* forever. In this case, the market-to-book ratio can be simplified to

$$\frac{P_e}{CE_0} = 1 + \frac{ROE - r_e}{r_e - g}$$

Suppose the firm has a 10 percent cost of equity capital, a forecasted constant ROE of 20 percent, and a perpetual growth rate of 5 percent. By historical standards, these would be very rosy forecasts. Using the preceding formula gives a P_e/CE_0 ratio of three. As a contrast, the market-to-book ratio for Kohl's was greater than eight in 2002—it has since come down to about three as of 2006. Kohl's ROE was close to 20 percent in 2002, so why such a high valuation ratio? One reason is that their growth had been about 25 percent per year for the past few years, and the market might have similar growth far into the future. Clearly, Kohl's can't sustain that rate of growth forever, so our simplified formula isn't going to work in this case. But, loosely speaking, Kohl's was expected to be more than twice as valuable as the hypothetical firm with 20 percent ROE and 5 percent perpetual growth. We will give lots of historical statistics later in the chapter, but as a final benchmark, the median market-to-book ratio between 1974 and 2004 for all publicly traded companies was 1.5; the bottom 25 percent were below 0.93 and the top 25 percent were above 2.5.

The market-to-book ratio is a very useful summary measure. It gives you a quick sense of what the market must think about the future growth and profitability of the firm. Of course, like everything else in valuation, our intuition can be thwarted by distortions in accounting. A good example of this is Kellogg, the maker of breakfast cereals ("they're great!"). You may not think of Kellogg as a high-flying, fast-growing stock. And it isn't; annualized growth over the past five years is only about 5 percent. Nonetheless, it has a market-to-book ratio greater than 10! The story behind this is relatively simple. The great value of Kellogg is in its brands, yet none of this value is on Kellogg's balance sheet. Most of their brands have been developed internally over many years, and GAAP accounting doesn't capitalize internally developed intangible assets. Consequently, Kellogg's book value vastly understates its economic value, causing its current ROE to exceed 50 percent. If we plug a constant 50 percent ROE and a perpetual 5 percent growth rate into our simplified P_e/CE_0 model, assuming a 10 percent cost of equity capital, we get a market-to-book ratio of 9.

11.3 THE PRICE-TO-EARNINGS RATIO

This ratio divides the current market price per share by the past annual earnings per share, computed either as the most recent annual figure or as the sum of the past four quarters of earnings. It takes a fair bit of algebra, but you can derive the following expression from the residual income model:

$$\frac{P_e}{NI_0} = \frac{1+r_e}{r_e}\left(1 + \sum_{t=1}^{\infty} \frac{\Delta RI_t}{(1+r_e)^t \, NI_0}\right) - \frac{D_0}{NI_0}$$

where ΔRI_t is the *change in* residual income between date t and date $t-1$, D_0 is the net distribution to common equity holders, and NI_0 is the net income for period *zero* (i.e., so that $CE_0 = CE_{-1} + NI_0 - D_0$).

To understand what this ratio measures, ignore the D_0/NI_0 term for the time being; this is the dividend payout ratio for the current year, and it is typically less than one. If $\Delta RI_t = 0$ forever (e.g., residual income is a constant) and $r_e = 10$ percent, then the price-to-earnings expression is $(1 + r_e)/r_e = 11$. The reason the price-to-earnings ratio typically differs from 11 is because of the summation term inside the brackets. Now look carefully at the summation term. It is the sum of the *changes* in residual income, scaled by the current period's net income, as opposed to the sum of the levels of residual income that you saw in the residual income model. So the price-to-earnings ratio will be greater than 11 if the market expects residual income to grow and it will be less than 11 if the market expects residual income to shrink. It doesn't matter whether the *level* of residual income is positive or negative, only the direction and size of the expected change. This is very different from the market-to-book ratio, which was large only if the expected *level* of residual income was large and positive.

What will cause residual income to grow? Obviously, growth in net income will contribute to growth in residual income, but the relation is subtler than this. For *residual* income to grow, net income must grow *faster than* book value grows. This is much tougher than simply growing net income. We can illustrate this better by stating the change in residual income in relative terms. Divide ΔRI_t by common equity at time $t-1$ to get

$$\frac{\Delta RI_t}{CE_{t-1}} = (ROE_t - ROE_{t-1}) + g_{t-1}(ROE_t - r_e)$$

where ROE_t is defined as NI_t/CE_{t-1} and g_{t-1} is the percentage growth in common equity from date $t-2$ to $t-1$. Suppose that $g_{t-1} = 0$, so that book value has not grown and the second term is zero. In this case, if the firm can deploy the existing book value more profitably, $(ROE_t - ROE_{t-1})$ will be positive and ΔRI_t will increase. Alternatively, suppose that ROE_t is greater than r_e by a constant amount each period. In this case, the first term in brackets is zero but, since the firm has positive net present value investments, growing book value increases income faster than the increase in book value, so again ΔRI_t will increase.

One logical benchmark for the price-to-earnings ratio that we have already discussed is to assume that residual income is a constant in perpetuity, and that the current dividend payout (D_0/NI_0) is zero, so that

$$\frac{P_e}{NI_0} = \frac{1 + r_e}{r_e}$$

If r_e = 10 percent, then this gives a price-to-earnings ratio of 11, as discussed above. A related benchmark is the *forward price-to-earnings ratio,* defined as P_e divided by the forecasted net income for next year, NI_1. In this case, assuming residual income is a constant perpetuity, we get

$$P_e = CE_0 + \frac{RI_1}{r_e} = CE_0 + \frac{NI_1 - rCE_0}{r_e} = \frac{NI_1}{r_e}$$

or

$$\frac{P_e}{NI_1} = \frac{1}{r_e}$$

If r_e = 10 percent, then we get a price-to-forward-earnings ratio of 10. For all companies with positive earnings between 1974 and 2004, the median price-to-earnings ratio was 13.5; the bottom 25 percent were below 8.6 and the top 25 percent were above 21.9. If NI_0 is negative, the price-to-earnings ratio isn't really meaningful, so we have excluded these firms. But you can think of firms with negative earnings as having very high price-earnings ratios—in the sense that they have a positive price even though they have negative earnings. Clearly, these companies must return to profitability if they are to create value for their shareholders. We will give values for the distribution of price-to-earnings ratios in different industries in the next section.

11.4   THE PEG RATIO

We have one more valuation ratio to discuss, the PEG ratio, which stands for price-earnings-growth. It is defined as follows:

$$\text{PEG Ratio} = \frac{\text{Price-to-Earnings Ratio}}{\text{Earnings Growth} \times 100} = \frac{P_e/NI_1}{\left(\dfrac{NI_2 - NI_1}{NI_1}\right) \times 100}$$

Note that the price-to-earnings ratio in the numerator is the forward ratio (i.e., the denominator is the forecast of next year's net income) and the earnings growth rate defined here is growth from one year ahead to two years ahead. The earnings growth rate is frequently defined over a longer period, say three to five years, but it still must be an annualized percentage. By defining it as given above, we can reconcile this ratio with a legitimate valuation model. As we will explain shortly, the benchmark for the PEG ratio is one. Stocks with a PEG under one are considered undervalued and those with a PEG greater than one are considered overvalued (per the Yahoo! Education Web site).

This ratio is a rough heuristic. The idea is that the price-to-earnings ratio measures the amount of earnings growth that is reflected in the market price so, if we compare this ratio with forecasted earnings growth, we can see whether the market price correctly reflects the forecasted growth and thus determine whether a stock is underpriced or overpriced. This seems reasonable, but why is one the magic benchmark? Academics have searched for special cases of a more general valuation model that will make this formula true, but with only limited success. Here is one such case.

Define the forecasted *abnormal earnings* at time $t + 1$ as

$$ae_{t+1} = NI_{t+1} - [NI_t + r_e(NI_t - D_t)]$$

This amount is *abnormal* in the following sense. At time $t + 1$, you expect to earn the same net income as you did at time t, plus interest on any amount that you didn't distribute to equity holders ($NI_t - D_t$). This is the amount in square brackets. The amount by which NI_{t+1} exceeds or falls short of this amount is therefore "abnormal."

The PEG ratio follows from a valid valuation model when two conditions hold. First, net distributions to equity holders are forecasted to be zero one year ahead (i.e., $D_1 = 0$). This implies that forecasted abnormal earnings in year two are

$$ae_2 = NI_2 - (1 + r_e)NI_1$$

Second, forecasted net income and net dividends from year three forward are such that abnormal earnings are constant and equal to the abnormal earnings in year two, computed assuming $D_1 = 0$. That is,

$$ae_t = ae_2 \text{ for } t \geq 2$$

If these assumptions are met, then one can show that

$$P_e = \frac{NI_2 - NI_1}{r_e^2}$$

Constructing the PEG ratio from this simple valuation model gives

$$\frac{P_e/NI_1}{\left(\dfrac{NI_2 - NI_1}{NI_1}\right) \times 100} = \frac{1}{r_e^2 \times 100}$$

If r_e is 10 percent, then this gives a PEG ratio of one. And if all these assumptions hold, then stocks with a PEG ratio less than one are undervalued and stocks with a PEG ratio greater than one are overvalued.

As you can see, with some work, we can beat the PEG ratio back into our world of theoretically valid valuation models. But the real question is, how reasonable are the assumptions that were necessary to get the job done? We had to assume that *abnormal earnings* are constant forever in the future, and equal to the abnormal earnings computed based on the forecasted earnings for the next two years. We also had to assume that net distributions to equity holders are forecasted to be zero next year. Finally, for the ratio to be benchmarked at one, we needed to assume the cost of equity capital is 10 percent.

To put the underlying model that supports the PEG ratio into perspective, we can rewrite price in this special case as

$$P_e = \frac{\text{NI}_1}{r_e} + \frac{\text{NI}_2 - (1 + r_e)\text{NI}_1}{r_e^2}$$

Note that the first term is the price we would get if we assumed that the forward price-to-earnings ratio is a constant (i.e., $P_e = \text{NI}_1/r_e$). In the previous section, we showed that a constant forward price-to-earnings ratio occurs when residual income is a constant perpetuity (i.e., $\text{NI}_t - r_e\text{CE}_{t-1}$ is constant for all t). The model supporting the PEG ratio adds to this a bonus for abnormal earnings between year two and year one. In this sense, the model behind the PEG ratio is more sensitive to future growth than the forward price-to-earnings ratio, which is exactly what the PEG ratio was intended to do. If you were an analyst trying to "sell" investors on a stock with high forecasted growth in the near term, the PEG ratio is a good tool because it makes such stocks look more reasonably valued. However, there is no evidence that such stocks are actually undervalued; they just look this way when evaluated using the PEG ratio.

11.5   PUTTING SOME VALUATION RATIOS TOGETHER

The market-to-book ratio is simply a scaled version of the residual income model and is therefore clearly focused on measuring value. Because the price-to-earnings ratio scales by earnings in the most recent year, it is much more focused on expected growth. It is driven by how much residual income will increase in the future relative to earnings today. And, to wrap all of this up into a neat package, note that

$$\frac{P_e}{\text{CE}_0} = \frac{\text{NI}_0}{\text{CE}_0} \times \frac{P_e}{\text{NI}_0}$$

or

$$\text{Market-to-Book Ratio} = \text{ROE}_0 \times \text{Price-to-Earnings Ratio}$$

defining ROE_0 now as the return on *ending* equity.

Remember how we hammered away on the idea that value is created by a combination of profitability and growth? Here we see this once again. The market-to-book ratio is the product of profitability, measured as ROE_0, and growth, measured loosely by the price-to-earnings ratio.

The market-to-book and price-to-earnings ratios together give you a great snapshot of the market's expectations about the firm. To help you develop a feel for what a big or small ratio is, we have plotted the median market-to-book and price-to-earnings ratios each year from 1974 to 2004 in Figure 11.1.

FIGURE 11.1
Valuation Ratios through Time

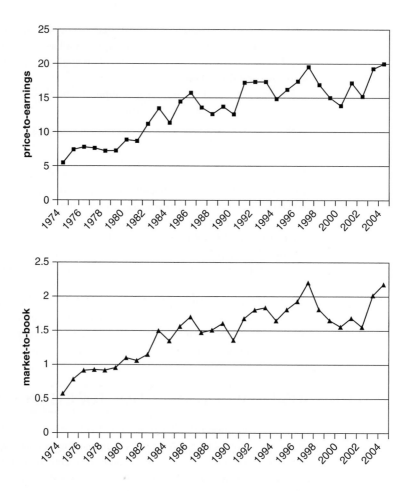

Two observations are immediately clear from the figure. First, valuations relative to fundamentals (i.e., net income and common equity) have been drifting steadily up over the past 20 years. This may be due to steadily declining interest rates over the same period, increasingly optimistic estimates about future growth and profitability, or a steady decline in the ability of accounting measures to capture true value. Which interpretation is correct is unclear; scholars and practitioners have championed each. The second observation is that the "dot.com" bubble reached its peak in fiscal 1999, partially deflated, and may be present again. At the end of 2004, the economywide market-to-book ratio was about 2.3 and the economywide price-to-earnings ratio was about 20. Both amounts are roughly twice as high as the values during the 1980s.

The valuation ratios not only change over time but also vary greatly across different sectors of the economy. Figure 11.2 plots the market-to-book and price-to-earnings ratios as of March 1, 2006, for 10 economic sectors, as defined by the S&P 1500 Supercomposite.

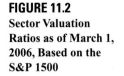

FIGURE 11.2
Sector Valuation Ratios as of March 1, 2006, Based on the S&P 1500

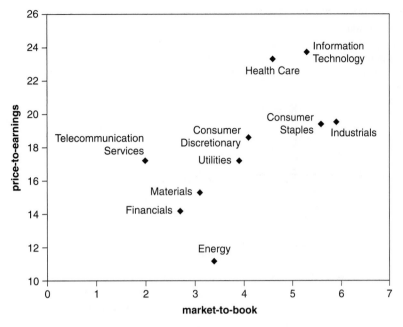

Note the huge difference between the energy sector and the information technology or health care sectors. Not surprisingly, the market sees more growth potential and more future profitability in technology and health care than it sees in energy. This doesn't mean that energy stocks are a bad investment and technology and health care are good investments. In fact, if it means anything, it is more likely that the market is overpricing technology and health care stocks and underpricing energy. We will return to the issue of picking stocks based on these simple valuation ratios in the next section.

We can use the market-to-book ratio and the price-to-earnings ratio together to see how the market views different firms in an industry. Figure 11.3 plots the valuation ratio for some representative firms in the Retail—Department Store industry.

The figure is divided loosely into four regions. Firms that are low on both dimensions are labeled as *value* and firms that are high on both dimensions are labeled *glamour*. The off-diagonal categories identify more unusual firms. Firms that have very high price-to-earnings ratios but relatively low market-to-book ratios are labeled *turnarounds*. They currently have very little earnings but, based on a big restructuring, a new CEO, or blind faith, the market expects that they will have lots more earnings in the future. The future earnings growth may not coincide with a high ROE so, while the price-to-earnings ratio is very high, the market-to-book ratio is still low. At the other extreme we have *harvesters*. Imagine a firm that has lots of profitability but only moderate growth. Without much anticipated growth, the price-to-earnings ratio would be relatively low while the high ROE would generate a high market-to-book ratio.

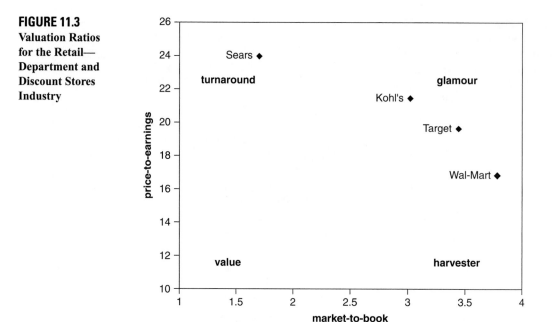

*Ratios computed on September 3, 2002.

You can see from Figure 11.3 that Kohl's, Target, and Wal-Mart sort neatly in terms of growth and profitability. Wal-Mart is the most profitable of the three but has the lowest future growth prospects (probably because it is already so large). Kohl's has higher growth prospects, so its price-to-earnings ratio is higher, but it is not expected to be as profitable as the almighty Wal-Mart. Target lies somewhere between Kohl's and Wal-Mart on both dimensions. The other dot on the figure, Sears, has a considerably lower market-to-book ratio but a much higher price-to-earnings ratio. Does Sears really have such strong growth prospects? Probably not, but remember that the denominator of the price-to-earnings ratio is a single year's earnings, so if the most recent year is a very small profit, as was the case for Sears, then the small denominator can cause the entire ratio to be very large. What the ratio is saying is that, relative to a particularly poor year, the market believes Sears does indeed have good growth prospects. In prior years, Sears was in the *value* quadrant of the graph, with both low growth and low profitability.

Can You Make Money with This?

The market-to-book and price-to-earnings ratios both compare the current market price to an accounting measure of fundamental value. It is natural to ask whether or not firms that are extreme on either of these measures tend to move back to an average value. Do these statistics mean-revert? And further, if they do mean-revert, is it because the price corrects itself or is it because price predicts a

TABLE 11.1   **Portfolio Returns to Different Price-to-Fundamental Investment Strategies**

Next Year's Return	Market-to-Book Ratio	Price-to-Earnings Ratio	Book Value + 0.62 × Residual Income
Return on bottom 10% of ratio	19.1%	20.7%	21.0%
Return on top 10% of ratio	11.8%	11.8%	11.1%
Hedge return	7.3%	8.9%	9.9%

Returns are for investments in the top or bottom 10 percent of the indicated ratio for all publicly traded firms between 1976 and 1995. The portfolio position is taken three months after the fiscal year end and held for 12 months. See Dechow, Hutton, and Sloan (1999) for details.

future movement in the accounting fundamentals? If the correction is due to future price changes, then it may be possible to form a trading strategy based on these ratios.

Before giving you the answers to these titillating questions, we want to stress that the whole point of this book is to teach you how to develop a detailed forecast of the firm's future financial statements and then translate these forecasts into a value estimate. We expect you to arrive at a value estimate that is far superior to what you could get simply by looking at the company's earnings and book value and then comparing each to price. But with that thought in mind, the short answer is yes; historically you would have made a bit of money by trading solely on the market-to-book and price-to-earnings ratios.

Table 11.1 gives the details of three different investment strategies based only on the accounting book value and earnings.

Each strategy sorts the firms on their price-to-fundamental ratio, where the fundamental is either value, earnings, or a combination of the two, and then buys firms with the lowest ratios and sells firms with the highest ratios. The portfolios are formed three months after the fiscal year end (to be sure that the book value and earnings data are publicly available) and are held for one year. The tests are conducted over a large sample of firms from 1976 to 1995. The first column of the table shows that the decile of firms with the lowest market-to-book ratio earned an average return of 19.1 percent while the decile of firms with the highest market-to-book earned an average return of only 11.8 percent. Our hedge portfolio has no exposure to marketwide risk because it is equally long and short in the same dollar value of stocks, yet it would have returned 7.3 percent (i.e., it made 19.1 percent on the long position and lost 11.8 percent on the short position). The second column of the table shows a similar result for portfolios based on the price-to-earnings ratio. The hedge return to this strategy is 8.9 percent. The third column computes a crude *value* measure based on the current book value and residual income. It is defined as

$$V_e = CE_0 + 0.62RI_0$$

where the value 0.62 is based on an estimate of the rate at which residual income mean-reverts in the entire economy. The strategy then computes the P_e/V_e ratio and forms portfolios. As shown in the table, the hedge return to this portfolio is 9.9 percent, with no exposure to marketwide movements in price.

These hedge returns are quite large by Wall Street standards. A hedge return is equally long and short in the same dollar amounts, so it is a zero net investment, at least in principle. Of course, you can't walk into a brokerage house and open an account with zero dollars. But imagine that you invested your wealth in a fund that tracked the entire market and, in addition, you took the zero net position in the hedge portfolio described above. This combined strategy would beat the market return by almost 10 percent. A money manager who consistently beat the market by 10 percent would be a god on Wall Street, so is it really this easy? Not really. First, the actual transaction costs of taking a long position in 10 percent of the market and a short position in a different 10 percent of the market would be prohibitively costly. A truly implementable strategy would have to limit itself to a much smaller set of firms, and this smaller set of firms may not have the same returns as those documented in Table 11.1. Further, while the hedge portfolio has no exposure to marketwide price movements, it still may have a significant exposure to other types of risk. What if all the long positions are in technology stocks and all the short positions are in utilities? It is certainly possible that tech stocks will go down and utility stocks will go up and you would lose a lot of money. The hedge portfolio is market-neutral, but it certainly isn't without risk. In fact, the return to the market-to-book strategy is so thoroughly documented that many finance professors refer to it as a *risk factor*, although it isn't clear exactly what fundamental risk such a strategy exposes one to. This is always the debate: is it an exploitable return or is it compensation for bearing risk? Finally, even if this profitable strategy was available in the past, there is no guarantee that it will be available in the future. If enough investors notice this pattern in the data and invest to profit on it, they will push the price of low price-to-fundamental stocks up and push the price of high price-to-fundamental stocks down, eliminating the hedge return in the process.

11.6   CASES, LINKS, AND REFERENCES

Case

- Determinants of Valuation Ratios: The Restaurant Industry in 2003

Links

- eVal Web site: http://www.mhhe.com/eval2007
- Multex Investor: http://www.multexinvestor.com/home.asp
- Yahoo! Finance: http://yahoo.finance.com
- Yahoo! Education: http://biz.yahoo.com/edu/

Reference

- Dechow, P., A. Hutton, and R. Sloan. (1999). An empirical assessment of the residual income valuation model. *Journal of Accounting and Economics* 26.

Some Complications

12.1   INTRODUCTION

Up until this point, the valuation step has been quite straightforward. Given a series of forecast financial statements and the key valuation parameters, we just let eVal crank out the valuation. Unfortunately, life is not always this simple. In this chapter, we discuss some of the most common complications that arise in the valuation step. We stress that eVal does not provide any "quick fix" solutions to these complications. Instead, it is up to you, now as an educated valuation specialist, to make sure that you anticipate these complications. Remember, as we have stated many times before, the maxim "garbage-in, garbage out" is the order of the day.

There are two primary categories of complications. The first category relates to negative values and the abandonment option. If you load a company that is losing money into eVal, you will typically find that the default valuation is negative. What does this mean? Stocks never have negative values in real life. This category of complications is the subject of Section 12.2.

The second category of complications relates to value creation and destruction through financing transactions. eVal simply computes the intrinsic value of the company to the existing stockholders, assuming that they will be the only participants in all future net cash distributions. But what if the existing stockholders let some new stockholders invest in the company at a price that is different from intrinsic value? Whenever a company issues or repurchases common stock at a price other than intrinsic value, it creates or destroys value for the existing stockholders. This category of complications is the subject of Section 12.3.

12.2   NEGATIVE VALUES AND THE ABANDONMENT OPTION

Negative Values

In Chapter 10, we discussed what it means for eVal to return a negative stock price. In this section, we revisit this issue and offer some advice about how to deal with this unusual situation. A negative stock valuation is actually not an uncommon occurrence in eVal if you simply use eVal's default forecasting assumptions on a company with losses in its most recent year. Yet in the real world we never see negative stock prices. To understand why eVal generates negative stock prices,

FIGURE 12.1
eVal Model Summary
for Sepracor

Model Summary		Sensitivity Analysis	
Go To User's Guide		Reset to Current	
Historical Data For:		**Forecast Horizon** 5 10 20	10 Years
SEPRACOR INC			
Most Recent Fiscal Year End:	12/31/2001	**This Year's ROE (%)**	89.18%
Average ROE (last five years)	-174.12%		
Sales Growth (last five years)	133.42%	**Terminal Year's ROE (%)**	75.72%
Forecast Data:		**This Year's Sales Growth (%)**	71.75%
Forecast Horizon	10 Years		
This Year's ROE	89.18%	**Terminal Year's Sales Growth (%)**	5.00%
Terminal Year's ROE	75.72%		
This Year's Sales Growth	71.75%	**Cost of Equity Capital (%)**	10.00%
Terminal Year's Sales Growth	5.00%		
This Year's Forecast EPS	-$4.87	**Estimated Price/Share**	-$928.89
Forecast 5 Year EPS Growth	53.16%		
Valuation Data:		Sensitivity analysis allows you to assess the impact of changing key assumptions on the estimated price per share. Note that the sensitivity analysis uses a linear smoothing algorithm to compute ROE and Sales Growth between the current year and the terminal year, so it may provide a different price estimate from your detailed analysis even with the same key forecasting assumptions.	
Cost of Equity Capital	10.00%		
Valuation Date	1/6/2003		
Estimated Price/Share	-$930.86		
Estimated Price/Earnings Ratio	190.96		
Estimated Market/Book Ratio	231.63		

let's look at a specific example. Figure 12.1 provides the Valuation Summary sheet for a company called Sepracor as of the end of fiscal 2001.

Sepracor is a biotechnology company that has many drugs under development but only a small number that are currently generating revenue. Consequently, sales revenues are smaller than the combined amount of R&D and SG&A expense, and Sepracor has reported substantial losses for the last several years. The valuation in Figure 12.1 was obtained using the default forecasting assumptions in eVal. Note that the estimated price per share is –$930.86. The summary of the forecast data indicates a current ROE of 89 percent and a terminal ROE of 75 percent. How can ROE be positive if the company is making losses? Well, it turns out that the company has made such large cumulative losses that its common equity is negative. When we divide the negative earnings by the negative common equity, we get a positive ROE. But the positive ROE is clearly not meaningful when the equity base is negative.[1] You should always check that the book value of common equity is positive before trying to interpret the ROE. If we were to look into the details of the forecasted financials, we would see that Sepracor is forecast to have negative earnings, residual income, and cash flows for every future period—clearly a bleak future. We also see that sales are forecast to grow at 72 percent in the current year, trending down to 5 percent in the terminal year. When we combine the negative earnings, cash flows, and residual income with the aggressive sales growth, we get a huge negative valuation. According to our forecasts, Sepracor has a money-losing business model and plans to continue to grow the business, thereby losing even more money in the future.

---

[1] Note that we can still use the residual income valuation model when the book value of common equity is negative. We just can't divide earnings or residual income by a negative book value number and meaningfully interpret the resulting ratio.

FIGURE 12.2
eVal DCF Valuations
for Sepracor

	A	B	C	D	E	F
	AIU ▾ ▪ =B1b+bbU+bb4-bbd					
1	**DCF Valuations**	**($000)**				
2	Go To User's Guide	View Valuation to Common Equity				
3		View Valuation to All Investors				
4	**Company Name**	SEPRACOR INC				
5	Most Recent Fiscal Year End	12/31/2001				
6	Date of Valuation	1/6/2003				
7	Cost of Common Equity	10.00%				
8						
9	Fiscal Year of Forecast	12/31/2002	12/31/2003	12/31/2004	12/31/2005	12/31/2006
11	**Valuation to Common Equity**					
12	Free Cash Flow to Common Equity	(155,042)	(278,772)	(480,795)	(794,230)	(1,254,584)
13	Present Value of FCF	(140,948)	(230,390)	(361,229)	(542,470)	(778,998)
14	Present Value Beyond 20 Years	(32,824,658)				
15	Present Value of First 20 Years	(29,991,172)				
16	Forecast Equity Value Before Time Adj	(62,815,831)				
17	Forecasted Value as of Valuation Date	(72,662,212)				
18	Less Value of Contingent Equity Claims	0				
19	Value Attributable to Common Equity	(72,662,212)				
20	Common Shares Outstanding at BS Date	78,059				
21	Equivalent Shares at Valuation Date	78,059				
22	Forecast Price/Share	-$930.86				
23						

Now look at Sepracor's forecasted future free cash flows on eVal's DCF Valuation sheet, which is reproduced in Figure 12.2. In 2002, Sepracor is forecast to have negative free cash flow to common equity of over $155 million. By 2006, the amount of negative free cash flow is forecast to grow to over $1.2 billion. This means that, in order to keep operating the business consistent with our forecasts, enormous amounts of new common equity will have to be issued. If the existing stockholders act as forecast in our eVal model, then they will have to provide huge amounts of new equity injections into Sepracor, even though they will never get a positive cash dividend payment in return. Under this scenario, the value of the company to the existing stockholders is clearly negative because of the negative present value of the additional cash infusions that they plan to make.

Why then do we never observe negative stock prices? The reason is that stockholders have limited liability. Management and creditors can never force the existing stockholders to pay more cash into the company, so the least that a stock can ever be worth is zero. This is where the eVal model doesn't jibe with reality. We have forecast that stockholders will be willing to pay in additional cash indefinitely, and eVal took the present value of those negative cash flows to common equity holders, but, in reality, stockholders are likely to abandon the company and it will cease operations. The most obvious limitation of our forecasting model is that we have extrapolated Sepracor's past losses into the indefinite future. But in reality, the stockholders of Sepracor hope that profitability will improve as drugs that are currently under development start generating revenues.

Given that we never observe negative stock prices in the real world, why do we allow them to arise in eVal? The reason is that we want you to see just how bad an investment in such a company would really be. How much value are you forecasting that the company can destroy as investors send good money chasing after bad? We know that the price will never actually be negative. Interpret the negative value estimate as the amount that investors would pay to *not have to own the stock*. This gives you a feel for just how bad the forecasted future of the company really is.

The present value computations in eVal assume that existing stockholders will finance any additional cash infusions implied by your forecasts. While we know that this is unrealistic, what if the existing management and stockholders are able to "hoodwink" new investors into providing the additional capital? While this would be a negative net present value proposition for the new investors, it is possible that the existing stockholders could make themselves better off at the expense of the new investors. This is one of the reasons why investment bankers who can "sell any deal" are able to charge such high fees. Figuring out the amount of wealth transfers between existing stockholders and new capital providers is complicated, and we will address this issue in more detail in Section 12.3.

The Abandonment Option

We have now established that equity cannot have a negative value in practice because stockholders have limited liability. They are free to walk away from the company and cannot be forced to provide additional capital to fund money-losing operations or pay creditors. This stockholder right is sometimes referred to as the *abandonment option*. As with most options, the abandonment option has value. In this section, we will examine the abandonment option in more detail.

The forecasting assumptions we discussed in Chapter 8 are our "best guesses" for what we think the values will be in the future. They are each a point estimate of the most likely outcome rather than ranges of many possible outcomes. But, in reality, any number of possible outcomes could arise for most of our assumptions. To see how sensitive your forecasts are to some key assumptions, play with the Sensitivity Analysis tool on the Model Summary sheet in eVal (shown in Figure 12.1 above). As long as the range of reasonable valuations is symmetric around our most likely estimate, and all the valuations are positive, then the most likely valuation estimate is also the expected value of the investment. Unfortunately, the abandonment option can introduce significant asymmetries into the range of possible valuation outcomes. In particular, since equity values can never be negative, the left tail of the possible range of valuation outcomes is truncated at zero. The result is that the most likely point estimate valuation can seriously underestimate the true valuation when we take the abandonment option into consideration. We illustrate the effect of the abandonment option in Figure 12.3.

Figure 12.3 charts the probability distribution of possible valuation outcomes for three different scenarios. In each of the three scenarios, the most likely point estimate of value, represented by the peak of the valuation distribution, is $100. Sensitivity analysis reveals the range of other possible valuation outcomes. The first chart represents a low-variance scenario, where the range in possible valuation outcomes is quite closely clustered around the most likely estimate of $100. Note also that the range of possible outcomes is symmetric and all values are positive. This first scenario represents the typical case, where the range of possible valuation outcomes is symmetric around the most likely point estimate valuation, all reasonable valuations are positive, and so the most likely point estimate valuation is our best estimate of the true valuation.

FIGURE 12.3
Probability
Distributions of
Valuation Outcomes
for Three Different
Scenarios

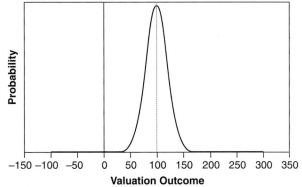

Probability Distribution of Valuation Outcomes for Low-Variance Firm

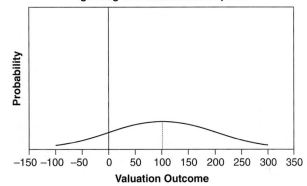

**Probability Distribution of Valuation Outcomes for High-Variance Firm
Ignoring the Abandonment Option**

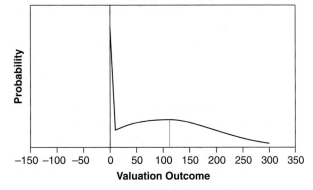

**Probability Distribution of Valuation Outcomes for High-Variance Firm
Incorporating the Abandonment Option**

The second chart represents a high-variance scenario, where the range of possible valuation outcomes varies widely around the most likely point estimate of $100. As with the first chart, the range of possible outcomes continues to be symmetric around the most likely valuation estimate of $100, so the expected value is still $100, but a significant range of the possible valuation outcomes in the second chart falls below zero. As discussed above, all the negative valuations are unreasonable because the existing stockholders will not indefinitely continue to invest good money after bad; rather they will exercise their abandonment option and refuse to contribute additional capital.

The range of possible valuation outcomes, assuming that stockholders optimally exercise their abandonment option, is shown in the third chart of Figure 12.3. In this chart, the distribution of possible valuation outcomes is truncated at zero. All of the possible negative valuation outcomes in the second chart are now concentrated at zero. Note that stockholders still keep all of the upside in the case of very positive valuation outcomes, but they avoid the downside in the case of negative valuation outcomes. As a result, the expected valuation of the investment is now greater than the most likely point estimate of $100. In the particular case shown in the third chart, the expected value works out to be about $110. Thus, by using the most likely point estimate valuation, we would have undervalued the stock by about 10 percent.

What determines the value of the abandonment option? The third chart in Figure 12.3 should make it clear that the greater the probability of a negative valuation outcome, the greater the value of the abandonment option. The lower the most likely point estimate valuation and the greater the variance of possible valuation outcomes, the greater the probability of a negative outcome, and the greater the value of the abandonment option. Thus, the abandonment option tends to be the greatest in money-losing companies with great uncertainty in future outcomes. A company such as Sepracor is a very good example. Owning a share in this company is like owning an option on the small chance that they will strike it big on some new drug.

To determine whether there is an abandonment option in play, you should always conduct sensitivity analysis for a *worst-case* scenario. If this scenario yields a negative valuation, then the abandonment option has positive value. To make the analysis tractable, this worst-case valuation scenario should represent a plausible outcome—assumptions that you feel have maybe a 25 percent chance of occurring. You also should think about a representative *best-case* valuation scenario. By assigning probabilities to each of these scenarios and assigning a value of zero to the negative valuation outcomes, you can compute the expected value of the stock *after* incorporating the abandonment option. Table 12.1 provides some representative computations assuming that the most likely outcome has a probability of 50 percent and the best- and worst-case scenarios each has a probability of 25 percent.

The table provides four representative cases. The first two cases represent a "healthy" firm, with a most likely valuation outcome of $100. The second two cases represent a "distressed" firm, with a most likely valuation outcome of $0. The first and third cases represent a "low-variance" firm, with the best and worst

TABLE 12.1   Value of Abandonment Option

	Worst Case (25% prob.)	Most Likely Case (50% prob.)	Best Case (25% prob.)	Value without Abandonment Option	Value with Abandonment Option
Healthy low-variance firm	$50	$100	$150	$100	$100
Healthy high-variance firm	−$50	$100	$250	$100	$112.5
Distressed low-variance firm	−$50	$0	$50	$0	$12.5
Distressed high-variance firm	−$150	$0	$150	$0	$37.5

case scenarios deviating from the most likely case by $50. The second and fourth cases represent a "high-variance" firm, with the best and worst case scenarios deviating from the most likely case by $150. We compute the value without the abandonment option by summing the products of each of the valuation outcomes with their respective probabilities. We compute the value with the abandonment option using the same procedure, but after assigning a value of $0 to all negative valuation outcomes.

For the first case, of the healthy, low-variance firm, even the worst-case valuation outcome is positive, so the abandonment option has no value. In the second case, of the healthy, high-variance firm, the worst-case outcome has a negative value, giving value to the abandonment option. The value without the abandonment option is $100 and with the abandonment option is $112.5, so the value of the abandonment option is $12.5. Higher variance results in a greater value for the abandonment option. In the third case, of the distressed, low-variance firm, the worst-case valuation outcome is again negative, giving a value of $12.5 to the abandonment option. In the fourth case, of the distressed, high-variance firm, the worst-case valuation outcome is very negative, resulting in an abandonment value of $37.5. Financial distress combines with high variance to give great value to the abandonment option. Note that in this fourth case, the value of the company with the abandonment option is $37.5, even though the most likely valuation outcome is zero. Ignoring the abandonment option can result in serious undervaluation.

12.3   CREATING AND DESTROYING VALUE THROUGH FINANCING TRANSACTIONS

Common Equity Transactions

The valuation computations in eVal assume that all future net cash distributions to common stockholders will accrue to the current common stockholders or, if the current shareholders sell their shares to someone else, they do so at the share's intrinsic value. In reality, this is often not the case. Companies frequently issue new shares of stock to new stockholders and repurchase shares of stock from existing stockholders, and do so at values that are wildly different from the stock's intrinsic value. An obvious question is whether these transactions can create or destroy value. The answer is a resounding yes, and there have been numerous spectacular cases where companies have created or destroyed value for stockholders through transactions in their own common stock.

To keep things simple, we will start by assuming that we have created a valuation model in eVal that correctly forecasts the future net cash distributions to common stockholders; that is, it captures the share's intrinsic value. By discounting these future cash distributions, eVal arrives at the value of common equity to the existing stockholders as a group. eVal then divides by the number of common shares outstanding to arrive at the estimate of intrinsic value per share. As long as all of the current stockholders continue to hold their stock and no new stock is sold, then the current stockholders will all realize this intrinsic value.

But what if some existing stockholders sell their stock to new stockholders? Well, as long as these transactions take place at intrinsic value, no wealth is transferred between the selling stockholders and the buying stockholders. However, if these transactions take place at a price that differs from the intrinsic value, there is a wealth transfer between the old selling stockholders and the new buying stockholders. If trades take place above intrinsic value, the selling stockholders gain at the expense of the buying stockholders. Conversely, if trades take place below intrinsic value, the selling stockholders gain at the expense of the buying stockholders. These results should come as no surprise. After all, one of the key goals of eVal is to help you profit from buying underpriced securities and selling overpriced securities. The important point to emphasize at this juncture is that the value of the stock to ongoing stockholders continues to be the intrinsic value computed by eVal, regardless of the price at which trades take place between old and new stockholders.

But what if the company itself trades in its own stock? Well, as long as these trades take place at intrinsic value, again there are no wealth transfers. But if these trades take place at a price different from intrinsic value, then there are wealth transfers between the existing stockholders and the stockholders transacting with the company. Table 12.2 summarizes the direction of the wealth transfers.

The important issue here is that the ultimate value of a stock to an ongoing stockholder is determined not only by the intrinsic value of the stock, but also by

TABLE 12.2
Wealth Transfers in Stock Transactions

	Company Repurchases Stock from Existing Stockholders	Company Sells Stock to New Stockholders
Transaction takes place at a price above intrinsic value	Wealth is transferred from ongoing stockholders to selling stockholders	Wealth is transferred from buying stockholders to ongoing stockholders
Transaction takes place at a price below intrinsic value	Wealth is transferred from selling stockholders to ongoing stockholders	Wealth is transferred from ongoing stockholders to buying stockholders

the extent to which the company transacts in its own stock at a price differing from intrinsic value. This means that the market value of a stock is a potentially important determinant of the value of the stock even to a stockholder with no plans to trade the stock. A couple of examples help to clarify this fact. First, consider the case of a company with an intrinsic value of common equity of $1,000 and 10 shares outstanding. The intrinsic value per share is $100. Next assume that this company is able to issue an additional 10 shares at $300 per share. The company has a revised intrinsic value of $4,000 and 20 shares outstanding, giving an intrinsic value of $200 per share. By issuing new shares at a price that exceeds intrinsic value, the company has created additional intrinsic value for ongoing stockholders.

As a second example, begin again with a company that has intrinsic value of common equity of $1,000 and 10 shares outstanding. But now assume that this company's stock is only trading at $50 per share. If this company repurchases six shares of its own stock, it will have a revised intrinsic value of $700 and four shares outstanding, giving an intrinsic value per share of $175. By repurchasing shares at a price below intrinsic value, the company has created additional intrinsic value for ongoing stockholders.

The above analysis has important implications for the valuation of an equity security. If the market value of the security differs from its intrinsic value, then we must consider the potential for the company to engage in transactions in its own stock to take advantage of this misvaluation. You can probably see that this argument has an element of circularity to it. If a company's market price is an important determinant of its intrinsic value, then how should we determine the appropriate market price? For this reason, stock prices can get caught up in speculative bubbles. But, at the end of the day, these speculative bubbles simply transfer wealth from one set of stockholders to another. The intrinsic value of a firm's total common equity is still determined only by the present value of its future net cash distributions.

It is difficult to identify airtight examples of firms issuing or repurchasing equity at prices different from the intrinsic value because we never really know for sure what a firm's intrinsic value is. Nonetheless, we offer AOL's acquisition of Time Warner as a likely illustration. In January 2000, AOL was trading at total market value of $164 billion, a value that was difficult to justify based on forecasts of their future cash flows. AOL cashed in on their high stock price by issuing shares of AOL stock in exchange for Time Warner's stock. Whereas AOL had mostly Internet assets and a customer base with fading loyalty, Time Warner had hard assets, including magazines, cable networks, and recording studios. The acquisition converted AOL's overvalued stock into assets that had real value. In this way, they created value for the original AOL shareholders, but at the expense of the Time Warner shareholders. It didn't take long for the market to find its way back to intrinsic value. Prior to the merger announcement, Time Warner had a market value of about $84 billion. By the time the deal closed a year later, the value of the combined entity had fallen to approximately $109 billion, not much more than the original value of Time Warner all by itself. Absent the acquisition, the original AOL shareholders may have had nothing in terms of future cash flows. As it stood, they owned 54 percent of the new entity—and the original Time Warner shareholders, who used to own 100 percent of the valuable part of the new entity, now owned only 46 percent. On February 3, 2003, the merged AOL Time Warner had a market value of only $52 billion, much to the chagrin of the original Time Warner owners.

From a practical perspective, how can we address the issue of potential wealth distributions resulting from a company trading in its own stock? Well, we should always be aware of significant deviations between the current market value of a stock and our estimate of its intrinsic value. If a company's market price exceeds its intrinsic value, we should consider whether the company is likely to issue new shares of stock. These issuances can take the form of seasoned equity offerings or stock-for-stock acquisitions of other companies. If such issuances are likely, then we should try to quantify their impact on stock values for ongoing stockholders. If a company's market price is below its intrinsic value, we should consider whether management is likely to undertake stock repurchases. If repurchases are likely, then we should try to quantify their impact on stock values for ongoing stockholders. You may have noticed that our guidance is somewhat vague on this issue. This is no coincidence. A company's ability to create and destroy value for ongoing stockholders by transacting in its own stock is one of the most difficult valuation issues to grapple with. Trying to forecast how much value will be created or destroyed is like trying to forecast when a Ponzi scheme will collapse.

The creation and destruction of value through financing activities is not restricted to transactions in a company's common stock. If companies are able to issue debt or preferred stock at inflated values, then they will likewise create value for existing stockholders. But there is one key difference for these noncommon-equity forms of financing. We explicitly forecast these events in our eVal model. Hence, as long as we correctly forecast the favorable or unfavorable terms of this nonequity capital, their impact on the value of common equity will be incorporated by eVal.

Contingent Equity Claims

Issuing contingent equity claims is another way to create or destroy value through financing transactions. Contingent equity claims take many forms, including company warrants, employee stock options, and the conversion options on bonds. These contingent equity claims give their holders the right to purchase shares of common stock at prices that may differ from intrinsic value, and are in many cases well below intrinsic value. If such rights are exercised, then wealth is transferred between the ongoing stockholders and the new stockholders exercising their contingent equity claims. The accounting for contingent equity claims varies depending on the form the claim takes, but none of the existing accounting rules correctly reflect the impact of contingent equity claims on the intrinsic value of a share of common stock.

We can give you a simple (but admittedly crude) procedure for dealing with contingent equity claims. To the extent that a company has *existing* outstanding contingent equity claims, you should simply value those claims and incorporate them into your eVal computation using the contingent claims calculator described in Chapter 10. To the extent that you forecast a company will issue contingent equity claims in the *future*, capture the economic effect of this by forecasting that the company will instead engage in a "plain vanilla" transaction that has a similar effect to actually issuing contingent claims. For instance, with warrants, you should simply assume that the company will issue common stock of equivalent value. For employee stock options, simply assume that the company will pay cash compensation of equivalent value. The accounting rules for stock compensation changed beginning in 2006, so financial statements now have an estimate of the value of options issued to employees, which should help you forecast the future compensation value. For the issuance of convertible bonds, simply assume that the company will issue plain bonds at the market interest rate. Note that these alternative transactions are not exactly economically equivalent to issuing contingent equity claims. But the key differences hinge on changes in the future stock price of the company. And if we knew how the future stock price was going to change, we wouldn't need to do a valuation in the first place. By replacing the contingent claim transactions with their plain-vanilla equivalents, we obtain an estimate of intrinsic value that abstracts from the circularity of trying to determine a firm's current value while assuming that you can forecast changes in its expected future value.

12.4   CASES, LINKS, AND REFERENCES

Cases

- The AOL Time Warner Merger
- The Valuation of Amazon.com in June 2001

Link

- eVal Web site: www.mhhe.com/eval2007

PART TWO

Cases

The AOL Time Warner Merger*

On January 10, 2000, AOL and Time Warner announced their intention to merge to create the world's first Internet-age media and communications company. The proposed deal represented the biggest corporate merger of all time, with the merged entity valued at approximately $350 billion. The deal was also unique in that it combined one of the leading names from the booming "new economy" with one of the largest "old economy" media companies. While the deal was billed by AOL and Time Warner as a "merger of equals," AOL was generally recognized as the "acquiror" and Time Warner as the "target." The objective of this case is to understand the structure and financial implications of the merger. Further details concerning the proposed merger are provided in the online exhibits included with the case, which can be found at www.mhhe.com/eval2007.

Finally, you can load the case data for AOL into eVal (the AOL data are already adjusted for the November 1999 stock split) and examine the valuation. (*Note:* The case data are imported from the eVal Users' Guide by selecting Input Historical Data → Import Case Data → then picking AOL.) Please use the number of shares on pages 13 and 16 of the proxy statement (2,255 for AOL and 1,301.5 for TW).

QUESTIONS

1. Describe the major synergies and other sources of value creation associated with the merger.
2. The terms of the merger represent a significant premium to Time Warner shareholders. Quantify this premium.
3. Do you think that the additional value created by the deal is sufficient to justify the premium being offered to Time Warner shareholders?
4. Estimate AOL's premerger intrinsic value by importing AOL's historical financial statements into eVal, setting the forecast horizon to 10 years and the valuation date to January 10, 2000, and leaving all other assumptions at their default values. What is the intrinsic stock price for AOL? Do you think that this is a reasonable premerger valuation?

* This case was prepared by Richard Sloan as the basis for class discussion. Copyright © 2001 by Richard Sloan.

5. Assume that the default assumptions in question 4 are appropriate for a pre-merger AOL and that the addition of Time Warner to AOL increases the value of AOL by exactly the $142 billion purchase price given in the online Exhibit 2 (i.e., the acquisition is a zero NPV investment). Compute AOL's post-merger intrinsic stock price. You do not need to use eVal for this question.

6. Reconcile the pre- and post-merger intrinsic valuations in questions 4 and 5. Why did a zero NPV investment change the value of AOL's intrinsic stock price?

7. Estimate whether the merger will be accretive (i.e., increase AOL's near-term EPS relative to what EPS would have been if the merger hadn't taken place) or dilutive (i.e., decrease AOL's near-term EPS relative to what EPS would have been if the merger hadn't taken place).

The Valuation of Amazon.com in June 2001*

BACKGROUND

Amazon.com was one of the darlings of the Internet stock boom of the late 1990s. Opening its virtual doors in 1995, Amazon's original mission was to use the Internet to transform book buying into the fastest, easiest, and most enjoyable shopping experience possible. Amazon went public in May of 1997, with an offer price of $18 per share, and opened at $29.25 per share. Over the next five years, Amazon's stock price went on a wild ride, peaking at over $100 per share in December 1999. During this period, Amazon split its shares by a factor of 12, implying a split-adjusted price of over $1,200 per share relative to its $18 offer price—a gain of over 6,000 percent in less than three years. Since December of 1999, however, Amazon's stock price, like many of its dot.com counterparts, has seen a steady decline. In June of 2001, Amazon's stock price had declined to $12 per share.

By June 2001, Amazon had grown into the leading inventory-carrying shopping destination on the Internet. Its new mission was "to be the place customers can go to find/discover anything they might want to buy online." The company had indeed expanded its product line to include items such as music and consumer electronics and had opened operations in the United Kingdom, Germany, France, and Japan. Sales had grown from just $16 million in 1996 to almost $3 billion in 2001. Despite this rapid growth, there were some problems. Perhaps most importantly, Amazon had yet to report a profit. Moreover, sales growth was declining and was forecast by management to drop to 20–30 percent for fiscal 2001.

Wall Street analysts expressed widely divergent opinions concerning Amazon's future. At one extreme, some analysts argued that it was time to value Amazon like a "real-world" retailer. Pointing to its lack of a profitable business model combined with its high leverage and declining levels of working capital, these analysts

---

* This case was prepared by Professor Richard Sloan as the basis for class discussion, rather than to illustrate either effective or ineffective handling of a business situation. Copyright © 2001 by Richard Sloan.

forecast that Amazon could face a serious credit problem and possibly even bankruptcy before the end of fiscal 2001. For example, Ravi Suria, a convertible bond analyst with Lehman Brothers, argued that

> We believe that the low levels of working capital could trigger a creditor squeeze in the second half of the year, creating considerable downside risk to revenue and cash estimates for the second half.[1]

At the opposite extreme, some analysts saw Amazon as the dominant player in an important new industry. Armed with its valuable customer list and e-commerce brand name, these analysts saw Amazon as the future Wal-Mart of "e-tailing." These analysts believed that margin improvement and scale economies would soon enable Amazon to turn profitable. For example, Mary Meeker and Mark Mahoney, equity analysts with Morgan Stanley Dean Witter, argued that

> Total worldwide online retail sales are expected to grow nicely over the next 3–5 years, and Amazon.com, with 32MM+ cumulative customers and one of the strongest e-commerce brands, should be well positioned to benefit from this growth.[2]

Accordingly, these analysts reiterated their "Long-Term Outperform" rating on Amazon.com. Amazon's management shared this optimistic view of their company's future with Chairman and CEO Jeff Bezos, promising pro forma operating profitability by the fourth quarter of 2001.

ASSIGNMENT

Your assignment is to use eVal to provide a comprehensive valuation analysis of Amazon as of June 30, 2001. To assist you with this task, three online exhibits are provided at www.mhhe.com/eval2007.

The exhibits are (a) Amazon.com's fiscal 2000 annual report, (b) financial results for the first fiscal quarter of 2001, and (c) a valuation model for Amazon.com that is based on a leading sell-side research report on Amazon dated June 21, 2001. The valuation model includes both short-term income statement forecasts and a formal DCF valuation model (a rare event indeed for sell-side research!). Note that no balance sheet forecasts were provided in the report.

TASKS

1. Load the Amazon.com data into eVal (note that the case data are imported from the eVal Users' Guide by selecting Input Historical Data → Import Case Data → and picking Amazon). Select a 10-year forecast horizon, set the valuation date to June 30, 2001, and examine the default valuation provided by eVal.

[1] Ravi Suria, Research Report on Amazon.com, *Lehman Brothers Convertible Bond Research,* February 6, 2001.

[2] Mary Meeker and Mark Mahoney, Research Report on Amazon.com, *Morgan Stanley Dean Witter Equity Research,* June 21, 2001.

You will note that the default estimate is a negative number. This seems odd, because limited liability prevents real-world stock prices from being negative. Explain why eVal provides a negative value.

2. Use eVal to *approximately* reconstruct the sell-side valuation model provided at the third online exhibit to this case. Your approximation should be close enough that the resulting eVal valuation is between $10 and $20 per share. You will have to make some additional assumptions in your eVal model because the valuation model provided is very terse. Provide a critical evaluation of this valuation model, paying special attention to the forecasted financial ratios implied by the model. [*Hints*: (a) As you change the forecasting assumptions, refer to the "Computation of Free Cash Flow to Investors" portion of the Cash Flow Analysis sheet to see the resulting free cash flows, and (b) to cleanly isolate depreciation in your forecasts, move 84460 out of SG&A and into Depreciation on the fiscal 2000 historical income statement.]

3. Use eVal to conduct a sensitivity analysis on the valuation model you constructed above with respect to the future EBITDA assumptions. First, construct a model in which EBITDA as a percent of revenue is higher by 0.20 than in the above model for every future forecast period. Second, construct a model in which EBITDA as a percent of revenue is lower by 0.20 than in the above model for every future forecast period. [To be clear, EBITDA is forecasted to be 5 percent of revenue in 2003; in your first model this will be 25 percent and in your second model it will be −15 percent, and you will make similar adjustments to all other years in the forecast horizon.]

4. Assume that there is a one-third probability of each of the three valuation scenarios you have computed above. What would this imply about the value of Amazon.com? How does this compare to the original valuation provided in the sell-side valuation model? Explain the sources of any differences. Based on the sum of all your analysis, what do you think Amazon.com was worth at June 30, 2001?

Turnaround at Bally Total Fitness?*

By 1999, the 1996 spin-off of Bally Total Fitness (ticker=BFT) from Bally Entertainment had all the elements of a classic turnaround story. Under the leadership of President and CEO Lee Hillman, stagnant sales and losses had been converted to rapidly growing sales and profits. With over 4 million members and 350 facilities, BFT had firmly established itself as the dominant player in the growing health club business. However, despite its apparent success, BFT was experiencing mixed reactions from Wall Street. After reaching an all-time high of close to $40 in early 1998, BFT's stock price had dropped back into the $20s. The initial drop in its stock price was prompted by concerns about BFT's accounting procedures that appeared in the *Wall Street Journal*:

> The nation's largest health-club chain is getting worked over by skeptical investors, who quarrel with its accounting methods. The questions started at the end of July, when Bally Total Fitness Holdings reported an unexpectedly encouraging second-quarter profit of eight cents a share. The bulls credit new health programs and more than $100 million of revenue from a successful installment-membership plan devised by the two former accountants who run Bally, Chief Executive Officer Lee Hillman and John Dwyer, chief financial officer. But bears don't believe in the turnaround of the previously none-too-healthy fitness centers. They cite puzzling changes in depreciation and gaps between cash collection and anticipated revenue. And they don't think Chicago-based Bally is keeping enough reserves for membership fees that may not be paid. If Bally's accounting was more conservative, "it would have lost significant amounts of money, instead of making eight cents" in the quarter, says money manager Blair Baker of Precept Capital Management in Dallas.[1]

Related concerns continued to plague BFT's stock price into 1999. Short sellers continually targeted the stock, with 4 million shares shorted by the middle of 1999, representing over one-third of BFT's float and 20 times BFT's average daily

---

volume. As a result, BFT's stock price looked cheap compared to its expected future earnings performance, as indicated below:

BFT: Earnings Growth and Related Pricing Ratios, 1999

	Last Five Years	This Year (Dec. 1999)	Next Year (Dec. 2000)	Next Five Years	Price/Earn (Dec. 1999)	PEG Ratio (Next Five Years)
Bally Total Fitness Holding Corp	n/a	202.0%	49.6%	35.0%	14.2	0.4
Leisure and recreation services	2.1%	3.7	21.7	18.8	46.9	2.5
S&P 500	10.3	11.3	10.1	7.5	28.0	3.7

Source: Yahoo! Finance Website (1999).

Wall Street's sentiments about BFT also were reflected in its dwindling sell-side analyst coverage. From the beginning of 1998 through the middle of 1999, First Call indicated that sell-side analyst coverage declined from 6 to 3, while the consensus sell-side recommendation slid from 1.3 to 2.0. Merrill Lynch, who also happens to be BFT's primary investment banker, continued to be BFT's strongest sell-side supporter. Merrill analyst Seth Weber issued the following comments in response to continued criticism of BFT's accounting policies:

> Shares of Bally Total Fitness have been under pressure on another negative report. In our view, the report had no new information and basically rehashed the same issues we addressed last year. We recommend investors particularly use any weaknesses in the stock as a buying opportunity . . . With respect to the report, it discusses BFT's membership growth, deferral accounting and cash flow—all issues we feel comfortable with.[2]

Details concerning BFT's business strategy and financial performance are provided in BFT's Form 10-K for the year ended December 31, 1998. This document is available as an online exhibit at www.mhhe.com/eval2007.

QUESTIONS

1. Evaluate BFT's business strategy, identifying the key success factors and risks.
2. Evaluate the appropriateness of BFT's revenue recognition policy with respect to financed memberships. Your evaluation should address
   - Whether the policy is consistent with GAAP.
   - Whether the policy is consistent with the underlying economics of the business.
3. Recast BFT's 1998 income statement assuming that BFT recognized (and had always recognized) membership revenues when cash was received from

[2] Research comment on Bally Total Fitness Holding Corp., *Merrill Lynch*, September 29, 1999.

members. List any assumptions or approximations that you make. (Financials are available in Excel format at www.mhhe.com/eval2007.)

4. Explain the major reasons for any differences between the original and recast financial statements. Do you think that the recast financial statements represent BFT's economic performance better or worse than the numbers reported by the company?

5. What actions would you advise BFT's management take in order to increase investor confidence in BFT's financial condition? What are the pros and cons of these actions?

Boston Chicken, Inc.*

At the end of 1996, Boston Chicken was one of the hottest names on Wall Street. Operating in the highly competitive restaurant industry, the chain had grown from 18 stores in 1991 to over 1,000 stores in 1996 and in its short history had raised over $1 billion in public offerings. EPS had grown from just $0.06 in 1993 to $1.01 in 1996, representing an annual growth rate of well over 100 percent. At the end of 1996, Boston Chicken traded around $40, representing a price-earnings multiple of 40 and a market-book ratio of 3. The company's spectacular success was attributed to the leadership of a group of investors headed by Scott Beck, former vice chairman of Blockbuster Entertainment, who took control in 1992. Enthusiasm for the company in 1994 was summarized in *The Washington Post* as follows:

> Perhaps no company better captures the spirit of the new economy than Boston Chicken Inc., the hottest of last year's hot stock offerings, which aims to do for the rotisserie what Col. Sanders did for the deep fryer . . . But Boston Chicken is not really about poultry—it is about developing a market-winning formula for picking real estate, designing stores, organizing a franchise operation and analyzing data.[1]

However, enthusiasm for the company was not universal. Doug Kass, research chief of brokerage J. W. Charles of Boca Raton, Florida, commented:

> I wouldn't touch Boston Chicken with a 10-foot rotisserie spit. I'm concerned with some major accounting issues, excessive stock valuation, surging competition and heavy dependence on a single product.[2]

Boston Chicken's management staunchly defended the company against such criticism. CFO Mark Stephens responded:

> We've got great chicken, great side items, our accounting is fine, and we're growing like a weed. When you get a big profile, it's natural for people to shoot at you.

Boston Chicken also took two steps to reduce its reliance on rotisserie chicken in 1995. First, Boston Chicken extended its food offerings to include turkey, ham, and meatloaf, and concurrently changed the name of its stores to Boston Market.

---

* This case was prepared by Professor Richard Sloan as the basis for class discussion, rather than to illustrate either effective or ineffective handling of a business situation. Copyright © 1998 by Richard Sloan.

[1] From Steven Pearlstein, "Boston Chicken: Hot Stuff," *The Washington Post*, July 4, 1994. © 1994, The Washington Post. Reprinted with permission.

[2] Dan Dorfman, "Pros Roast Chicken Stock," *USA Today*, August 12, 1994.

Second, Boston Chicken diversified its food offerings further by investing in ENBC, which was created through the combination of a number of leading bagel retailers.

Against this backdrop, Boston Chicken entered 1997 with plans to open over 300 additional restaurants over the next 12 months. The continued expansion was to be financed through the issuance of over $400 million of convertible debt in the first half of 1997. Enthusiasm for Boston Chicken remained high on Wall Street, with many Wall Street analysts recommending the stock as a "strong buy."

Details concerning Boston Chicken's business strategy and financial performance and expansion plans are provided in the company's Form 10-K for the year ended December 29, 1996. This document is available as an online exhibit at www.mhhe.com/eval2007.

QUESTIONS

1. Evaluate the structure of the restaurant industry and its ability to generate profits over the long run. As a starting point, consider the five forces of competition:
   - Competition from substitutes.
   - Rivalry between established competitors.
   - Threat of entry.
   - Bargaining power of customers.
   - Bargaining power of suppliers.

2. Some analysts argue that Boston Chicken (BOST) is primarily in the business of operating restaurants. Other analysts argue that BOST is primarily a franchiser, as opposed to an operator of restaurants. Still others argue that BOST is primarily a financial institution that lends money to operators of restaurants. Based on the information provided in the case, what do you view as BOST's primary business and why?

3. Evaluate BOST's strategy for creating competitive advantage. What are the key success factors and risks associated with this strategy?

4. Evaluate the quality of BOST's earnings.

5. Restate BOST's earnings using a method that better reflects the underlying economics of the business. (Financials are available in Excel format at www.mhhe.com/eval2007.)

6. Assuming that BOST continues to use its current accounting methods, what future event(s) are likely to cause its quality of earnings problems to surface (i.e., what future event(s) will cause BOST's future earnings to be lower because current earnings are potentially overstated)?

Four Valuation Models—One Value*

This case is designed to give you some practice computing the inputs to and final value estimate from some of the most standard valuation models. After you do the computations by hand, or if you give up in frustration, you can verify them using eVal (the details for using eVal are given in part B of the case). Part C of the case illustrates how accounting distortions flow through the different valuation models. We refer you to Chapter 10, "Valuation," for the precise definitions of the valuation models and their inputs.

The forecasted financial statements that extend into the infinite horizon are given in Figure 1. In addition, you should assume that the cost of equity capital is 10 percent, the pretax cost of debt is also 10 percent, and the effective tax rate is 40 percent. Also assume there are 1,000 shares outstanding and divide your valuation by 1,000 to get the price per share.

FINANCIAL STATEMENT FORECASTS

Given in Figure 1 is one historical year and four forecasted years of financial statements for our example company. Note that the sales growth is 20 percent in year one and 5 percent in years two and beyond. However, because depreciation expense and interest expense are based on average balances, net income doesn't start growing at 5 percent each year until year three (i.e., $NI_{2002}(1 + .05) = NI_{2003}$). Common shareholders' equity also starts growing at 5 percent in year three (i.e., $CE_{2002}(1 + .05) = CE_{2003}$).

QUESTIONS

Part A. The Four Valuation Models

Free Cash Flow to Common Equity Valuation Model

1. Find the forecasted free cash flow to common equity for 2001 and beyond.
2. Compute the value of common equity as of December 31, 2000, using the free cash flow to common equity model.

---

* This case was prepared by Russell Lundholm as the basis for class discussion. Copyright © 2002 by Russell Lundholm.

FIGURE 1

Financial Statement Forecasts

7		Actual	Forecast	Forecast	Forecast	Forecast
8	Fiscal Year End (MM/DD/YYYY)	12/31/2000	12/31/2001	12/31/2002	12/31/2003	12/31/2004
10	**Income Statement**					
11						
12	Sales (Net)	20,000	24,000	25,200	26,460	27,783
13	Cost of Goods Sold	(12,000)	(14,400)	(15,120)	(15,876)	(16,670)
14	Gross Profit	8,000	9,600	10,080	10,584	11,113
17	EBITDA	8,000	9,600	10,080	10,584	11,113
18	Depreciation & Amortization	(2,000)	(2,200)	(2,460)	(2,583)	(2,712)
19	EBIT	6,000	7,400	7,620	8,001	8,401
20	Interest Expense	(1,000)	(1,100)	(1,230)	(1,292)	(1,356)
22	EBT	5,000	6,300	6,390	6,710	7,045
23	Income Taxes	(2,000)	(2,520)	(2,556)	(2,684)	(2,818)
25	Other Income (Loss)	0	0	0	0	0
26	Net Income Before Ext. Items	3,000	3,780	3,834	4,026	4,227
29	Net Income (available to common	3,000	3,780	3,834	4,026	4,227
30						
31	**Balance Sheet**					
32						
33	Operating Cash and Market. Sec.	1,000	1,000	0	0	0
37	Total Current Assets	1,000	1,000	0	0	0
38	PP&E (Net)	20,000	24,000	25,200	26,460	27,783
41	Other Assets	0	0	0	0	0
42	Total Assets	21,000	25,000	25,200	26,460	27,783
43						
49	Long-Term Debt	10,000	12,000	12,600	13,230	13,892
53	Total Liabilities	10,000	12,000	12,600	13,230	13,892
55	Paid in Common Capital (Net)	10,000	8,220	3,986	590	(2,975)
56	Retained Earnings	1,000	4,780	8,614	12,640	16,867
57	Total Common Equity	11,000	13,000	12,600	13,230	13,892
58	Total Liabilities and Equity	21,000	25,000	25,200	26,460	27,783

Residual Income to Common Equity Valuation Model

3. Find the forecasted residual income for 2001 and beyond.

4. Compute the value of common equity as of December 31, 2000, using the residual income to common equity model.

Free Cash Flow to All Investors Valuation Model

5. Find the forecasted free cash flow to all investors for 2001 and beyond.

6. Compute the after-tax weighted-average cost of capital.

7. Compute the value of common equity by first computing the value of the free cash flows to all investors (i.e., the entity value) and then subtracting the value of the cash flows to debt holders. *Note*: At this point, the estimated value will only be approximately the same as in the other models.

8. Recompute the entity value using a discount rate of 9.3646 percent and then find the value of the equity. Why is there a discrepancy between the answers to questions 7 and 8?

9. Without doing any computations, contrast the residual income to all investors model with the free cash flow to all investors model.

Residual Income to All Investors Valuation Model

We will skip the computations for this model. You can see them in eVal under the Residual Income Valuations tab.

Practice on Haggar Inc. (the makers of the #2 brand in pants!)

In the appendix, you will find the income statement, balance sheets, and cash flow statement for Haggar Inc. for the fiscal year ending September 30, 2002.

10. Compute the free cash flow to common equity using only the income statement and balance sheet for Haggar in fiscal 2002 and then reconcile this amount with the free cash flow to common equity computed directly from the statement of cash flows.

11. Compute the free cash flow to all investors using only the income statement and balance sheet for Haggar in fiscal 2002 and then reconcile this amount with the free cash flow to all investors computed directly from the statement of cash flows. *Note*: Book overdrafts are included in accounts payable.

Part B. Verifying Your Computations with eVal

Load the data for the case into eVal by hitting the Input Historical Data button on the main User's Guide sheet, choosing the Import Case Data option, and then choosing Four Valuation Models Case. To generate the financial statements shown in Figure 1, go to the Forecasting Assumptions sheet and set

- The forecast horizon to five years.
- The first year sales growth to 20 percent and the sales growth for years 2002 and beyond to 5 percent.
- The operating cash/sales ratio forecast to 4.167 percent in year 2001 and 0 percent in years 2002 and beyond.
- The long-term debt/total asset ratio forecast to 48 percent in year 2001 and 50 percent in years 2002 and beyond.

These changes will yield the financial statements shown in Figure 1. Finally, go to the Valuation Parameters sheet and set

- The cost of equity capital to 10 percent.
- The cost of debt capital to 10 percent.
- The valuation date to July 9, 2000.

By setting the valuation date halfway into the fiscal year, we remove the half-year time value adjustment in eVal and make the computations much easier to see. If you have followed all these instructions carefully, the price shown on the financial statements sheet (or anywhere else) should be $61.25. If this isn't the case, look carefully at the Financial Statements sheet in eVal and be sure that the forecasted net income and common shareholders' equity is exactly as shown in Figure 1. If these are okay and the price still isn't $61.25, then double-check your settings on the Valuation Parameters sheet. More importantly, if your answers to Part A of the case are not all $6,125,000/1,000 shares = $61.25 per share, then go to the Residual Income Valuations sheet or DCF Valuations sheet and see where your computations differ from eVal's.

Part C. Accounting Distortions

This part of the case answers the question "how do accounting distortions, intentional or unintentional, affect the valuation models?" As an example, suppose that our company shifts $2,000 of noncash income from fiscal 2002 to fiscal 2001. There are many ways they could do this: accelerating the recognition of revenue or deferring the recognition of an expense. Because the shifted income is not a real cash flow, it must necessarily increase an asset account in 2001 by $2,000, and this account will reverse in 2002. To make the computations transparent, suppose the shifted income was in the line item Other Income and the associated asset account was Other Assets. Further, suppose that all other income statement items, assets, and liabilities remain the same (common shareholders' equity will obviously change).

1. Alter the financial statements in Figure 1 to show the income shifting just described. Based on these new financial statements (*not* eVal), compute the value of common equity as of December 31, 2000, using the residual income to common equity model.

2. The income shifting clearly moves the recognition of net income forward in time and money has time value, so why has this accounting distortion not changed the value of the equity? (*Hint*: Your answer to question 1 should match the value you computed in Part A: $61.25 per share.)

3. To completely clarify the answer to question 2, compute the free cash flows to common equity from the revised financial statements. Compare your answer to the cash flows you computed in Part A.

4. To illustrate the irrelevance of accounting distortions in eVal, make the following changes to the financial statement forecasts that you entered in Part B:

    • Hit the Enter Raw Forecast Data button on the financial statements sheet and enter $2,000 of Other Income in year 2001 and −$2,000 in year 2002.

    • Enter $2,000 for Other Assets in year 2001. It is already entered as zero in 2002.

    • Reenter $12,000 for Long-Term Debt in 2001; otherwise the default forecasting algorithms in eVal will change debt slightly. eVal will automatically change Retained Earnings so that the balance sheet balances.

    If you made all these changes correctly, you should once again have a $61.25 per share value. Now, to see how general this result really is, alter your forecasts so that the distortion doesn't reverse until 2004 (i.e., that Other Asset maintains its balance of $2,000 until 2004, when the −$2,000 of Other Income is recorded). Note once again that the value is unchanged.

5. What about distortions in the existing financial statements? Suppose that you feel that there are $1,000 of unrecorded assets, such as an internally developed intangible asset. Suppose that you restate the year 2000 financial statements in Figure 1 by adding $1,000 to Other Assets and Retained Earnings. Further,

suppose that your forecasted financial statements remain exactly as in Figure 1, with the exception that Retained Earnings is $1,000 larger and Paid in Common Capital is $1,000 smaller. In eVal be sure to set Other Assets back to zero in 2001 and beyond. What is your valuation now? Explain why the valuation changed in the amount that it did. (*Hint*: Follow the net dividends each period.)

APPENDIX   Haggar Inc. Financial Statements

Consolidated Statements of Operations and Comprehensive Income (In thousands, except per share amounts)

Year Ended September 30

	2002	2001	2000
Net sales	$ 481,831	$ 444,570	$ 432,855
Cost of goods sold	351,704	307,796	287,392
Reorganization costs	(3,812)	20,150	—
Gross profit	133,939	116,624	145,463
Selling, general and administrative expenses	(118,442)	(123,972)	(128,849)
Royalty income	1,326	1,856	2,436
Other income (expense), net	613	(107)	1,370
Interest expense	(3,600)	(5,140)	(4,084)
Income (loss) before provision (benefit) for income taxes and cumulative effect of accounting change	13,836	(10,739)	16,336
Provision (benefit) for income taxes	5,823	(2,069)	7,054
Income (loss) before cumulative effect of accounting change	$ 8,013	$ (8,670)	$ 9,282
Cumulative effect of accounting change	(15,578)	—	—
Net income (loss)	$ (7,565)	$ (8,670)	$ 9,282
Other comprehensive income (loss):			
Cumulative translation adjustment	16	15	(565)
Comprehensive income (loss)	$ (7,549)	$ (8,655)	$ 8,717
Net Income (Loss) Per Common Share			
Basic			
Income (loss) before cumulative effect of accounting change	$ 1.25	$ (1.34)	$ 1.38
Cumulative effect of accounting change	(2.44)	—	—
Net income (loss)	$ (1.19)	$ (1.34)	$ 1.38

Net Income (Loss) Per Common Share

	2002	2001	2000
Diluted			
Income (loss) before cumulative effect of accounting change	$ 1.25	$ (1.34)	$ 1.37
Cumulative effect of accounting change	(2.42)	—	—
Net income (loss)	$ (1.17)	$ (1.34)	$ 1.37
Weighted average number of common shares outstanding—Basic	6,385	6,485	6,733
Weighted average number of common shares and common share-equivalents outstanding—Diluted	6,429	6,485	6,786

Haggar Corp. and Subsidiaries
Consolidated Balance Sheets (In thousands)

September 30

	2002	2001
Assets		
Current assets:		
Cash and cash equivalents	$ 4,124	$ 7,800
Accounts receivable, net	64,284	71,299
Inventories	100,996	97,726
Property held for sale	2,157	—
Deferred tax benefit	12,087	11,290
Other current assets	2,766	2,215
Total current assets	186,414	190,330
Property, plant and equipment, net	46,195	51,975
Goodwill, net	9,472	25,050
Other assets	7,896	7,870
Total assets	$ 249,977	$ 275,225
Liabilities and Stockholders' Equity		
Current liabilities:		
Accounts payable	$ 30,542	$ 35,645
Accrued liabilities	39,448	25,374
Accrued wages and other employee compensation	6,713	5,103
Accrued workers' compensation	4,468	3,645
Current portion of long-term debt	3,742	4,021
Total current liabilities	84,913	73,788
Long-term debt	21,343	49,338
Total liabilities	106,256	123,126

(*continued*)

Haggar Corp. and Subsidiaries

September 30

	2002	2001
Stockholders' equity:		
Common stock—par value $0.10 per share; 25,000,000 shares authorized and 8,660,609 and 8,591,000 shares issued at September 30, 2002 and 2001, respectively	866	859
Additional paid-in capital	42,911	42,014
Cumulative translation adjustment	(534)	(550)
Retained earnings	125,439	134,310
	168,682	176,633
Less: Treasury stock, 2,242,205 and 2,203,705 shares at cost at September 30, 2002 and 2001, respectively	(24,961)	(24,534)
Total stockholders' equity	143,721	152,099
Total liabilities and stockholders' equity	$ 249,977	$ 275,225

Haggar Corp. and Subsidiaries
Consolidated Statements of Cash Flows (In thousands)

Year Ended September 30

	2002	2001	2000
Cash Flows from Operating Activities			
Net income (loss)	$ (7,565)	$ (8,670)	$ 9,282
Adjustments to reconcile net income (loss) to net cash provided by (used in) operating activities:			
Cumulative effect of accounting change	15,578	—	—
Depreciation and amortization	8,561	11,813	13,824
(Gain) loss on disposal of property, plant and equipment	(272)	2,458	(867)
Reversal of net realizable value on property held for sale	(2,157)	—	—
Deferred tax expense (benefit)	(129)	(666)	1,476
Changes in assets and liabilities:			
Accounts receivable, net	7,015	(2,986)	(4,791)
Inventories	(3,270)	(5,145)	(6,596)
Other current assets	(551)	(478)	(98)
Accounts payable	(11,103)	10,469	(7,854)
Accrued liabilities	14,074	2,404	(4,984)
Accrued wages and other employee compensation	1,610	(1,003)	(908)
Accrued workers' compensation	823	(296)	(834)
Deferred long-term income tax liability	—	—	(867)
Net cash provided by (used in) operating activities	22,614	7,900	(3,217)

Year Ended September 30

	2002	2001	2000
Cash Flows from Investing Activities			
Purchases of property, plant, and equipment	(3,334)	(5,266)	(10,626)
Proceeds from sale of property, plant, and equipment	135	38	1,563
Increase in other assets	(4)	(1,075)	(2,852)
Net cash used in investing activities	(3,203)	(6,303)	(11,915)
Cash Flows from Financing Activities			
Purchases of treasury stock at cost	(427)	(1,807)	(8,191)
Proceeds from issuance of long-term debt	494,000	105,000	156,000
Proceeds from issuance of common stock	904	84	72
Payments on long-term debt	(522,274)	(102,020)	(131,064)
Increase in book overdrafts	6,000	—	—
Payments of cash dividends	(1,306)	(1,307)	(1,262)
Net cash (used in) provided by financing activities	(23,103)	(50)	15,555
Effects of exchange rates on cash and cash equivalents	16	15	(565)
Increase (decrease) in cash and cash equivalents	(3,676)	1,562	(142)
Cash and cash equivalents, beginning of period	7,800	6,238	6,380
Cash and cash equivalents, end of period	$ 4,124	$ 7,800	$ 6,238

EnCom Corporation*

INTRODUCTION

EnCom is a fictitious corporation that is designed to illustrate (i) the impact of aggressive and conservative accounting on the quality of earnings and (ii) the correspondence between the discounted free cash flow model (DCF) and residual income model (RIM) approaches to equity valuation.

EnCom is a very simple corporation that operates a business for just five years. At the end of each year, all free cash flow generated by the business is paid out to the owners as a dividend. The case proceeds in three stages:

1. We value EnCom using the traditional DCF approach and we also compute EnCom's internal rate of return (IRR) and prepare accrual-based financial statements for EnCom. This first-stage analysis serves as a benchmark for the second two stages.

2. We introduce a marketing project representing an incremental investment opportunity for EnCom. By considering different methods of accounting for the marketing project, we illustrate the impact of aggressive and conservative accounting on the quality of earnings.

3. We use the RIM approach to valuing EnCom. This stage illustrates the correspondence between the DCF and RIM approaches to valuation and also illustrates the robustness of RIM valuations to accounting distortions.

INITIAL CASE FACTS

EnCom commences business and engages in operating activities for five periods, with data as follow:

- The initial required investment in property plant at the beginning of the first period is $1,000. The equipment has a five-year useful life and zero salvage value. For accounting purposes, the equipment is depreciated using the straight-line method and all depreciation is treated as a period expense (i.e., it is not part of cost of goods sold).

---

* This case was prepared by Professor Richard Sloan as the basis for class discussion, rather than to illustrate either effective or ineffective handling of a business situation. Copyright © 2003 by Richard Sloan.

- Sales per period are $1,200, with half of the sales revenue received in cash at the end of the period in which the sale is made and the other half received in cash at the end of the following period.
- The cost of goods sold is $720, with all inventory acquired for cash at the end of the period prior to the period in which the sale is made.
- There are no other expenses or sources of income and no other required working capital or investment requirements.
- At end of each period, all free cash flow is paid out as a dividend.
- The discount rate is 10 percent.

STAGE ONE QUESTIONS

1. What is the total initial investment that is required at the beginning of the first period in order to start EnCom?
2. Compute the value of EnCom immediately after the initial investment at the beginning of period one using the discounted free cash flow method.
3. Compute EnCom's internal rate of return.
4. Prepare financial statements (income statements and balance sheets) for EnCom for each of the five periods that it is in business.
5. Compare EnCom's free cash flows and earnings for each of the five periods. Overall, which of the two measures do you think provides the best measure of EnCom's periodic performance? Why?
6. Compute EnCom's return on equity (ROE, computed as earnings for the period divided by book value of equity at the beginning of the period) for each of the five periods. Compare EnCom's ROE for each period to EnCom's IRR and provide a qualitative explanation for any major differences.

ADDITIONAL CASE FACTS FOR STAGE TWO

An incremental investment project is available to EnCom, with data as follow:

- EnCom can engage in a marketing campaign during period one, with total marketing costs of $300, payable in cash at the end of period one.
- The marketing project increases cash inflows at the end of periods one, two, and three by $150 per period.
- All other facts remain the same.

STAGE TWO QUESTIONS

1. Compute the value of EnCom with the incremental project immediately after the initial investment at the beginning of period one using the discounted free cash flow method. Should EnCom invest in the incremental project?
2. Compute EnCom's IRR with the incremental investment project.

3. Assume that EnCom accounts for the incremental marketing project by expensing all marketing costs in the period they are incurred. Prepare financial statements for each of the five periods under this accounting assumption. Do you think this accounting assumption is aggressive, conservative, or neutral?

4. Assume that EnCom accounts for the incremental marketing project by capitalizing marketing costs and then amortizing them in proportion to the benefits received. Prepare financial statements for each of the five periods under this accounting assumption. Do you think this accounting assumption is aggressive, conservative, or neutral?

5. Assume that EnCom accounts for the incremental marketing project by capitalizing marketing costs and then expensing all of these costs in the first period in which no benefits are received from the project. Prepare financial statements for each of the five periods under this accounting assumption. Do you think this accounting assumption is aggressive, conservative, or neutral?

6. Which of the above three accounting methods do you think provides the best measure of EnCom's periodic performance? Why?

7. Compute EnCom's ROE for each of the five periods using each of the above three accounting methods. Explain how each of the different accounting methods impacts EnCom's ROE.

8. Using the insights from the EnCom example, provide a qualitative explanation of the impact of aggressive and conservative accounting on a firm's ROE relative to its IRR.

STAGE THREE QUESTIONS

1. Provide a separate residual income valuation for EnCom immediately after the start of business using each of the three accounting methods from stage two.

2. In question 1 above, you should have arrived at the same valuation regardless of the accounting method employed. Provide a qualitative explanation as to why the different accounting methods have no impact on the valuation.

GAAP versus the Street: Three Cases of Conflicting Quarterly Earnings Announcements*

1. THE GREAT ATLANTIC AND PACIFIC TEA COMPANY, INC. (NYSE: GAP)

On March 16, 1999, GAP announced results for the fourth fiscal quarter of 1998, ended February 27, 1999. A copy of the press release containing the announcement and other pertinent extracts from GAP's 1998 Form 10-K is available as an online exhibit at www.mhhe.com/eval2007.

Following the announcement, the analyst tracking services First Call, Zacks, and I/B/E/S reported the following earnings surprise information for the quarter:

Tracking Service	Consensus Forecast of EPS	Actual EPS
First Call	$0.18	$0.19
Zacks	$0.18	$0.19
I/B/E/S	$0.22	$0.19

While each of the tracking services reported actual EPS at 0.19, GAP's fiscal 1999 Form 10-K indicates that EPS for the quarter, computed according to GAAP, was a loss of −$2.31.

* This case was prepared by Professor Richard Sloan as the basis for class discussion, rather than to illustrate either effective or ineffective handling of a business situation. Copyright © 2000 by Richard Sloan.

Questions

1. Identify the reason(s) for the difference between the actual EPS numbers reported by the analyst tracking services and the EPS number computed according to GAAP and reported in the Form 10-K.

2. Which of the alternative EPS numbers do you think best represents the performance of the company for the quarter? Explain your answer.

II. INTEL CORPORATION (NASDAQ: INTC)

On October 12, 1999, INTC announced results for the third fiscal quarter of 1999. A copy of the press release containing the announcement is available as an online exhibit at www.mhhe.com/eval2007.

The analyst tracking services First Call, Zacks, and I/B/E/S reported the following earnings surprise information for the quarter:

Tracking Service	Consensus Forecast of EPS	Actual EPS
First Call	$0.57	$0.55
Zacks	$0.57	$0.55
I/B/E/S	$0.57	$0.55

While each of the tracking services reported actual EPS at $0.55, INTC's fiscal 1999 third-quarter Form 10-Q indicates that EPS for the quarter, computed according to GAAP, was $0.42.

Questions

1. Identify the reason(s) for the difference between the actual EPS numbers reported by the analyst tracking services and the EPS number computed according to GAAP.

2. Which of the alternative EPS numbers do you think best represents the performance of the company for the quarter? Explain your answer.

III. AMAZON.COM, INC. (NASDAQ: AMZN)

Go to http://www.amazon.com and find the investor relations link (it might be under About Amazon.Com, but it changes location periodically). Find the most recent quarterly press release announcing their quarterly financial results. You also may see a 10-Q or 10-K filing, but look for the press release that generally precedes this filing.

Questions

1. Read the press release and see if you can determine AMZN's GAAP EPS for the quarter.

2. See if you can determine "The Street's" EPS number for the same quarter, as reported by First Call (access through http://finance.yahoo.com) and Zacks (access through http://moneycentral.msn.com/investor).

3. Identify the reason(s) for the difference between the actual EPS numbers reported by the analyst tracking services and the EPS number computed according to GAAP.

4. Which of the alternative EPS numbers do you think best represents the performance of the company for the quarter? Explain your answer.

The Home Depot, Inc.*

This is a real-time forecasting case. Your objective is to forecast The Home Depot's (NYSE: HD) income statement, balance sheet, and statement of cash flows for the current fiscal quarter. You will be evaluated on both the methodology underlying your forecasting model and the extent to which you accurately forecast The Home Depot's financial statements. You should place particular emphasis on trying to generate an accurate forecast of The Home Depot's EPS for the quarter.

The Home Depot makes a good pedagogical real-time forecasting case for several reasons:

- It is a large and important company (component of both the S&P 500 and the DJIA).
- A wealth of information about the company is readily available on the Web.
- Its basic business operation/strategy is well known and easy to understand.
- Its rapid growth illustrates forecasting techniques specific to growth companies.
- The seasonal nature of its business illustrates forecasting techniques specific to companies with seasonals.
- It is followed by a large number of sell-side analysts, who each publishes its own forecasting models.

We recommend that you use the following framework and links in constructing your forecasting model:

1. Familiarize yourself with The Home Depot's business strategy and financial performance. You will find most of the information available from the Financial Info link on http://www.homedepot.com. Make sure that you study The Home Depot's recent Form 10-Ks and Form 10-Qs. You also may find it useful to compare The Home Depot's performance with industry benchmarks and major competitors. Try http://moneycentral.msn.com/investor/, enter HD for the ticker, and then go to Financial Results/Ratios. Also check out http://www.lowes.com/.

* This case was prepared by Richard Sloan as the basis for classroom discussion. Copyright © 2000 by Richard Sloan.

2. Familiarize yourself with The Home Depot's expansion plans. Company press releases and the MD&A sections of the Form 10-Ks and Form 10-Qs are your best sources of information. This information is again available from the Financial Info link on http://www.homedepot.com.

3. Familiarize yourself with any information made available during the quarter that may have a bearing on The Home Depot's results. For example, did Home Depot's management issue any earnings forecasts or pre-announcements? Was consumer spending relatively high during the quarter? Have any competitors already reported quarter's results? What was the weather like around the United States and how might this impact The Home Depot's sales?

4. Use the forecasting framework developed in the course, along with the insights generated by your analysis in steps one though four above, to prepare The Home Depot's pro forma financials for the current quarter. Your forecast should be based on more detailed analysis than simply repeating management's guidance.

5. Do a "reality check" on your forecasting model by comparing your model to the models published by leading Wall Street sell-side analysts and by comparing your EPS forecasts to the consensus sell-side forecast. You can often obtain full-text sell-side analyst reports from research libraries.

Evaluating Intel's Earnings Torpedo*

On September 21, 2000, Intel Corporation, the world's largest manufacturer of computer chips, issued an earnings warning indicating that third-quarter revenue was anticipated to be below previous expectations. This announcement prompted a huge sell-off in Intel's stock, which drove the price down from $61.48 to $47.94 over the course of the next 24 hours. This 22 percent stock price drop took place on daily volume of 300 million shares, a new record for the NASDAQ. In this case, you will build pro forma financial statements for Intel based on both Wall Street's expectations prior to Intel's earnings warning and Wall Street's revised expectations after the warning. You will then evaluate whether Intel's stock price decline was justified by the information in the earnings warning.

Intel's revenue growth was 11.9 percent in 1999 and had grown at an average annual rate of just over 12.5 percent for the five years ending in 1999. A surge in the worldwide demand for computer chips resulted in strong revenue growth in the first two quarters of 2000, with year-over-year revenue growth for the first and second quarter of 12.5 percent and 23.0 percent, respectively. In the press release accompanying the announcement of the financial results for the second quarter, Craig Barrett, president and CEO of Intel, stated that "looking forward, we expect to see strong demand continue into the second half." Based on this guidance, most Wall Street analysts were expecting Intel's third-quarter revenue to be between $8.8 million and $9.3 million, representing year-over-year quarterly growth of between 20 and 27 percent, and sequential quarterly growth of between 6 and 12 percent.

Intel released its earnings warning after the close of regular trading hours on September 21, 2000. The full text of the press release is attached as Exhibit 1. In this press release, Intel indicated that it "now expects revenue growth for the third quarter to be approximately 3 to 5 percent higher than second quarter revenue of $8.3 billion."

* This case was prepared by Richard G. Sloan, Professor of Accounting at the University of Michigan Business School, for the purpose of class discussion, rather than to indicate the effective or ineffective handling of a business situation. Copyright © 2001 by Richard G. Sloan.

EXHIBIT 1
**Intel Third-Quarter
Revenue to Be Below
Expectations**
Demand in Europe
weaker than expected.

SANTA CLARA, Calif., Sept. 21, 2000—Intel's third quarter revenue is anticipated to be below the company's previous expectations, primarily due to weaker demand in Europe, the company said today. The company now expects revenue for the third quarter to be approximately 3 to 5 percent higher than second quarter revenue of $8.3 billion.

The company expects gross margin percentage for the third quarter to be 62 percent, plus or minus a point, lower than the company's previous expectations of approximately 63 to 64 percent. Interest and other income is expected to be approximately $900 million for the third quarter, up from the company's previous expectations of $800 million.

Business Outlook

The following statements are based on current expectations. These statements are forward-looking, and actual results may differ materially. These statements do not reflect the potential impact of any mergers or acquisitions that may be completed after the date of this release.

- The company expects revenue for the third quarter of 2000 to be approximately 3 to 5 percent higher than second quarter revenue of $8.3 billion.

- The company expects gross margin percentage for the third quarter to be 62 percent, plus or minus a point. Gross margin percentage for 2000 is expected to be 63 percent, plus or minus a few points. In the short term, Intel's gross margin percentage varies primarily with revenue levels and product mix as well as changes in unit costs.

- Expenses (R&D, excluding in-process R&D, plus MG&A) in the third quarter of 2000 are expected to be up 7 to 9 percent from second quarter expenses of $2.2 billion, primarily due to higher spending on marketing programs and R&D initiatives in new business areas. Expenses are dependent in part on the level of revenue.

- R&D spending, excluding in-process R&D, is expected to be approximately $4.0 billion for 2000.

- The company expects interest and other income for the third quarter of 2000 to be approximately $900 million. Interest and other is dependent in part on interest rates, cash balances, equity market levels and volatility, the realization of expected gains on investments, including gains on investments acquired by third parties, and assuming no unanticipated items.

- The tax rate for 2000 is expected to be approximately 31.8 percent, excluding the impact of the previously announced agreement with the Internal Revenue Service and acquisition-related costs.

- Capital spending for 2000 is expected to be approximately $6.0 billion.

- Depreciation is expected to be approximately $790 million in the third quarter and $3.4 billion for the full year 2000.

- Amortization of goodwill and other acquisition-related intangibles is expected to be approximately $400 million in the third quarter and $1.5 billion for the full year 2000.

(continued)

EXHIBIT 1
Intel Third-Quarter
Revenue to Be Below
Expectations
(continued)

Copies of this earnings release and Intel's annual report can be obtained via the Internet at http://www.intc.com/ or by calling Intel's transfer agent, Computershare Investor Services, L.L.C. (formerly named Harris Trust and Savings Bank), at (800) 298-0146.

Intel, the world's largest chip maker, is also a leading manufacturer of computer, networking and communications products.

The above statements contained in this outlook are forward-looking statements that involve a number of risks and uncertainties. In addition to factors discussed above, among other factors that could cause actual results to differ materially are the following: business and economic conditions and growth in the computing industry in various geographic regions; changes in customer order patterns; changes in the mixes of microprocessor types and speeds, purchased components and other products; competitive factors, such as rival chip architectures and manufacturing technologies, competing software-compatible microprocessors and acceptance of new products in specific market segments; pricing pressures; development and timing of introduction of compelling software applications; insufficient, excess or obsolete inventory and variations in inventory valuation; continued success in technological advances, including development and implementation of new processes and strategic products for specific market segments; execution of the manufacturing ramp, including the transition to the 0.18-micron process technology; shortage of manufacturing capacity; the ability to grow new networking, communications, wireless and other Internet-related businesses and successfully integrate and operate any acquired businesses; unanticipated costs or other adverse effects associated with processors and other products containing errata (deviations from published specifications); litigation involving antitrust, intellectual property, consumer and other issues; and other risk factors listed from time to time in the company's SEC reports, including but not limited to the report on Form 10-Q for the quarter ended July 1, 2000 (Part I, Item 2, Outlook section).

Based on the information provided above and using the eVal software to facilitate your analysis, perform the following tasks:

1. Import the data for this case into eVal. (*Note*: The Intel case data are imported from the eVal Users' Guide by selecting the sequence of buttons Input Historical Data → Import eVal Case Data → Intel.) For the purpose of this case, you should set the valuation date to September 22, 2000, and the cost of equity capital to 12 percent on the Valuation Parameters worksheet.

2. Based on Wall Street's expectations immediately *before* Intel's earnings warning, provide a set of forecasting assumptions that (approximately) justify Intel's $61.48 prewarning stock price.

3. Based on Wall Street's expectations immediately *after* Intel's earnings warning, provide a set of forecasting assumptions that (approximately) justify Intel's $47.94 post-warning stock price.

4. Based on your analysis in questions one through three, evaluate whether the 22 percent stock price drop was a reasonable response to the news about valuation fundamentals in Intel's earnings warning. To the extent that you do not think the stock price drop was justified, speculate as to why it occurred.

Interpreting Margin and Turnover Ratios*

INTRODUCTION

Return on investment is the product of profit margin and turnover, as illustrated by the Dupont model:

$$\frac{\text{Income}}{\text{Investment}} = \frac{\text{Income}}{\text{Sales}} \times \frac{\text{Sales}}{\text{Investment}}$$

In this exercise, you will use eVal to get a better understanding of the determinants of profit margins and turnover ratios and the trade-offs that are made between them. The Ratio Analysis worksheet in eVal computes profit margins and turnover ratios for you. In particular, lines 30 and 31 of this worksheet compute profit margins and turnover ratios using net operating assets as the measure of investment. We will use these two lines for our analysis.

DETERMINANT 1: INDUSTRY PRODUCTION TECHNOLOGY

One key determinant of margins and turnover ratios is the production technology of the industry in which a firm operates. Some industries require large investments in capital in order to produce relatively small amounts of sales, resulting in low turnover ratios. In order for investments in such industries to provide a competitive rate of return, profit margins must be high enough to compensate for the low turnover. A good example of such an industry is Telecom Services.

To load the Telecom Services industry into eVal, go to the Data Center worksheet, enter the Telecom Services industry code MG844 in the ticker input box, and click the Go button. To view margin and turnover ratios for this industry, go to the Ratio Analysis worksheet and study lines 30 and 31. Net operating assets turns are less than one per year. The considerable investment in the wireline infrastructure that is required to operate a telecom services business results in very low turnover. To provide a competitive rate of return, net operating margin must be relatively high. Net operating profit margins have historically averaged over 10 percent in this industry.

A good example of an industry at the other end of the spectrum is Discount Variety Stores. To load this industry into eVal, go to the Data Center worksheet, enter the Discount Variety Stores industry code MG732 in the ticker input box, and click the Go button. To view margin and turnover ratios for this industry, go to the Ratio Analysis worksheet and study lines 30 and 31. Net operating asset turns are greater than three times per year. This industry uses very basic stores that are designed to accommodate high volumes of sales. But competition is fierce, and profit margins are extremely low, resulting in competitive rates of return.

Question

1. Using eVal, identify another example of an industry that operates with low turnover ratios and high margins and another example of an industry that operates with high turnover ratios and low margins. In each case, explain the features of the industry's production technology that lead to these ratios.

DETERMINANT 2: BUSINESS STRATEGY–PRODUCT DIFFERENTIATION VERSUS COST LEADERSHIP

Another key determinant of margins and turnover ratios is the extent to which a firm follows a product differentiation versus a cost leadership strategy. A product differentiation strategy requires higher investment to generate a differentiated product, resulting in lower turnover. A successful strategy also should generate higher margins. A cost leadership strategy, in contrast, generates the basic product more efficiently, resulting in higher turnover and lower margins.

Question

2. Using eVal, identify an example of a product differentiator and an example of a cost leader within a particular industry. In each case, try to select an example where the strategy is appropriately reflected in the turnover ratios and explain the source of the different ratios.

DETERMINANT 3: CORPORATE STRATEGY–VERTICAL INTEGRATION VERSUS OUTSOURCING

Another key determinant of margins and turnover ratios is the extent to which a firm follows a strategy of vertical integration versus outsourcing. Outsourcing requires less investment in operating capacity, but also necessitates the sharing of margins with the outsourcing partner. Relative to vertical integration, outsourcing therefore results in higher turnover and lower margins. The franchising of retail outlets, the leasing of productive capacity, and the securitization and sale of customer receivables can all be considered as forms of outsourcing.

Question

3. Using eVal, identify an example of a vertical integrator and an example of an outsourcer within a particular industry. In each case, try to select an example where the strategy is appropriately reflected in the turnover ratios and explain the source of the different ratios.

Netflix, Inc.*

By early 2005, Netflix had revolutionized the movie rental industry, growing to 3 million subscribers in its eight short years of existence. Netflix's tremendous success was primarily attributable to its innovative business model, built on two disarmingly retro technologies: the DVD and the U.S. Postal Service. For a monthly subscription fee averaging $18, consumers gain access to an unlimited number of rentable DVDs, most delivered within a couple of days of being ordered online.

This was not the first business success for Netflix founder and CEO, 44-year-old Reed Hastings. Hastings had already sold his first company, Pure-Software, in the mid-1990s for $750 million. He then went back to school, getting a master's in education from Stanford, and subsequently became president of the California Board of Education. His career in education ended around the time he rented *Apollo 13* from a Blockbuster store. After getting socked for $40 in late fees, Hastings began wondering why video rentals don't work like health clubs, which give members unlimited access for a flat monthly fee. His original business plan relied on mailing VHS cassettes to customers, but in 1997 he realized that DVDs, still new at that time, would be a much easier and more durable format for mailing.

Hastings started Netflix in 1998 from a warehouse in the heart of Silicon Valley. By early 2005, Netflix had 35 warehouses around the country, mailing out over 1 million DVDs per day to customers. Netflix had increased its subscriber base to 9 percent of households in its local San Francisco Bay area market and just 2.3 percent of households in the rest of the country, leaving plenty of room for future growth. Netflix's success had caught the attention of industry giants, who struggled to imitate Netflix's business model. Both Blockbuster and Wal-Mart introduced services similar to Netflix but couldn't match Netflix's combination of excellent customer servicing and shrewd marketing. Wal-Mart subsequently exited this business in May 2005, outsourcing it to Netflix.

Yet competition and rapid expansion were taking their toll on Netflix's profitability. Quarterly EPS peeked at $0.29 in the third quarter of 2004 and had dropped to $0.08 by the fourth quarter of 2004, with a loss projected for the first quarter of 2005. The lower profitability stemmed primarily from squeezed margins due to greater competition and more aggressive use of the unlimited rental option by subscribers. Netflix's stock price followed its earnings, plunging from almost $40 in early 2004 to just $12 by early 2005. But even this seemed like a rich valuation given that losses were being projected for the first quarter of 2005.

* This case was prepared by Professor Richard Sloan as the basis for class discussion, rather than to illustrate either effective or ineffective handling of a business situation. Copyright © 2005 by Richard Sloan.

Critics argued that Netflix was simply pricing its service too cheaply. The video rental market had long depended on hefty late fees to drive profitability. By eliminating late fees and allowing unlimited rentals, it seemed that Netflix was simply selling its service at too low a price to earn a respectable profit. Netflix countered that its low profitability was attributable to ongoing investments in growing its subscriber base. Once this subscriber base matured, economies of scale, strong subscriber retention, and reduced subscriber usage of the unlimited rental option were expected to deliver healthy profits.

While having appeal in the current marketplace, Netflix's argument had one fundamental flaw. Its business model was likely to become obsolete in a few short years. A similar fate had met America Online almost a decade earlier. America Online invested heavily in building the largest subscriber base in the online content provider business, only to see this business rendered largely obsolete by the ISP (Internet service provider) business a few years later. Few industry observers expected mail delivery of DVDs to be the long-run delivery format for movie rentals. Video on demand through cable and satellite TV companies and Internet downloading were widely expected to become the standard delivery channels within the next decade.

Despite these concerns, Netflix marched full steam ahead with its aggressive growth strategy. Numerous Wall Street analysts applauded this strategy and recommended the stock as a "buy" to their brokerage clients. For example, a representative analyst argued that.[1]

> **We are raising our EPS estimates and increasing our 12-month price target to $34.** We expect record levels of subscriber acquisitions during 2005 to bode well for future profitability and we are increasing our 2005 EPS estimate to $0.34 and our 2006 EPS estimate to $1.13. We are reiterating our Buy rating and increasing our price target to $34 (30 × 2006 EPS) based on increased 2006 estimates.

Detailed information on Netflix's business strategy, financial situation, and expansion plans are provided in its Form 10-K for the year ended December 31, 2004. For comparative purposes, similar information also is provided for Blockbuster in its Form 10-K for the corresponding period. These documents are available as online exhibits at www.mhhe.com/eval2007.

QUESTIONS

Business Strategy Analysis

1. Identify Netflix's source(s) of competitive advantage in the movie rental business relative to (i) traditional bricks-and-mortar video rental outlets, such as Hollywood Entertainment, and (ii) Web-based services offering the downloading of movies over the Internet, such as Movielink.

2. Evaluate the sustainability of Netflix's current sources of competitive advantage in the movie rental business.

[1] This analyst quote represents the case-writer's personal synthesis of the published views of the numerous analysts that were bullish on the stock in 2005.

Accounting Analysis

3. Contrast and evaluate how Netflix and Blockbuster account for their movie rental libraries. Do you think that any differences are justified?

4. Assume that instead of using its current accounting practices for its DVD library, Netflix instead expensed all costs associated with its DVD library as they were incurred. Estimate the *operating income* Netflix would have reported for the year ended December 31, 2004.

5. Briefly explain why Netflix's provision for income taxes (i.e., tax expense) for its 2004 fiscal year is so small.

Ratio Analysis

6. Compute rental library turnover ratios for Netflix and Blockbuster for fiscal year 2004. Carefully justify your choice of numerator in each of these ratios.

7. Identify the major reason(s) for the difference between the two turnover ratios that you computed above. Be as specific as possible.

8. Compute the gross margin earned on *movie rentals* for Netflix and Blockbuster for fiscal year 2004.

9. Identify the major reason(s) for the difference between the two margins that you computed above. Be as specific as possible.

Forecasting Analysis

10. Load the Netflix case data into eVal and provide a set of forecasting assumptions that yield a $0.34 EPS estimate for FY2005 and a $1.13 EPS forecast for FY2006. (*Note*: The Netflix case data are imported from the eVal Users' Guide by selecting the sequence of buttons Input Historical Data → Import Case Data → Netflix.)

11. Evaluate the plausibility of the forecasting scenario you provided in answer to the preceding question.

12. Define and evaluate the "churn" metric computed by Netflix and explain why low churn is crucial to Netflix's long-run profitability.

Valuation Analysis

13. Load the Netflix case data into eVal, set the valuation date to March 1, 2005, and critically evaluate the default valuation provided by eVal. (*Note*: The Netflix case data are imported from the eVal Users' Guide by selecting the sequence of buttons Input Historical Data → Import eVal Case Data → Netflix.)

14. In early 2005, Netflix was trading at around $12 per share. Using eVal, provide a set of forecasting assumptions that approximates this price. Use a cost of equity capital of 10 percent and a valuation date of March 1, 2005. Do you think that these forecasting assumptions are plausible?

15. Evaluate the method used to establish the price target of $34 quoted in the introduction to the case.

Overstock.com*

At the beginning of 2004, Overstock.com, Inc., was one of the hottest growth stocks on Wall Street. Operating in the highly competitive "e-tail" industry, the company had grown revenue from less than $2 million in 1999 to over $200 million in 2003. By March of 2004, Overstock.com's stock price had risen to around $30, representing a price-sales multiple of 2 and a market-book multiple of 10. The company's spectacular rise was attributed in large part to its high-achieving chief executive, Dr. Patrick Byrne. Byrne, who holds a master's from Cambridge University and a doctorate from Stanford University, had previously run a subsidiary of Warren Buffett's Berkshire Hathaway. Enthusiasm for the company in early 2004 was summarized in *The Washington Post* as follows:

> Fifty-five venture capitalists turned down Patrick Byrne's discount-shopping Web site for funding at the peak of dot-com investing mania. So the graduate of Walt Whitman High, Stanford University and Warren Buffett's real-world school of business funded it himself. Five years later, Overstock Inc. is a publicly traded company, pulling in nearly 7 million shoppers a month to its Internet bargain bazaar and ranking right up there with Target.com and BestBuy.com as one of the Web's top 20 e-commerce sites. But Byrne, its maverick chief executive, won't be satisfied until Overstock.com becomes a household name on par with eBay and Amazon.com, the Internet's top shopping hangouts, each of which draws more than 30 million people a month.[1]

The news, however, was not all good. Overstock.com had yet to report a positive annual profit and had only logged one quarterly profit, with that being back in the fourth quarter of 2002. The last 12 months had seen the departure of the company's chief financial officer, chief operating officer, and president. Moreover, competition was heating up from the likes of industry giants Amazon.com and eBay as well as smaller start-ups, such as privately held SmartBargains.com.

Against this backdrop, Overstock.com entered 2004 with plans to raise an additional $50 million, primarily to fund the inventory acquisitions necessary to maintain the company's aggressive growth plans. Its capital-raising plans called for the issuance of 1.5 million additional shares through an offering underwritten by W. R. Hambrecht and Co. and JMP Securities. Enthusiasm for Overstock.com

---

* This case was prepared by Professor Richard Sloan as the basis for class discussion, rather than to illustrate either effective or ineffective handling of a business situation. Copyright © 2005 by Richard Sloan.

[1] Leslie Walker, "Underestimated Overstock.com Aims Higher," *The Washington Post,* December 4, 2003. © 2003, The Washington Post. Reprinted with permission.

remained high on Wall Street, with analysts at both W. R. Hambrecht and JMP Securities issuing "buy" recommendations on the stock. Analysts at W. R. Hambrecht summarized their investment opinion as follows:

> **Reiterating Buy rating and increasing price target to $40.** Our price target implies an enterprise value to CY04 revenue of 1.4x, vs. a 1.1x multiple for OSTK's discount retailing peers and vs. 8.7x for internet bellwethers AMZN and eBay (EBAY: Buy Rated). We think OSTK shares deserve a premium to its discount retailing peers because of the company's superior top-line growth prospects.[2]

Detailed information on Overstock.com's business strategy, financial situation, and expansion plans are provided in its Form 10-K for the year ended December 31, 2003. This document is available as an online exhibit at www.mhhe.com/eval2007.

QUESTIONS

Business Strategy Analysis

1. Evaluate the structure of the Internet retailing (e-tailing) industry and its ability to generate profits over the long run. As a starting point, consider the five forces of competition:
   - Competition from substitutes.
   - Rivalry between established competitors.
   - Threat of entry.
   - Bargaining power of customers.
   - Bargaining power of suppliers.

2. Evaluate Overstock.com's strategy for creating competitive advantage, identifying the key success factors and risks associated with this strategy. Make sure to evaluate Overstock.com's business strategy relative to established e-tailers such as Amazon.com, traditional liquidation retailers such as TJX Companies, and other liquidation e-tailers such as SmartBargains.com.

Accounting Analysis

3. Identify Overstock.com's critical accounting policies. Briefly comment on whether you think that these accounting policies fairly present Overstock's financial performance.

4. The growth rate in Overstock's total revenue from 2002 to 2003 exceeded 150 percent. Do you think that this growth rate is sustainable? Explain your answer.

---

[2] William J. Lennan and Andrew Mackay, "OSTK: Beating Amazon.com on NYT Bestsellers, but What Does It Mean for Margins?" *W. R. Hambrecht and Co. Research Report,* March 10, 2004.

5. The growth rate in Overstock's gross profit from 2002 to 2003 was less than 50 percent, despite the fact that total revenue grew by over 150 percent. Explain why the growth rate in gross profit was so much lower.

6. Overstock.com has reported substantial losses in each of the last three years. Do you think these accounting losses provide a good reflection of Overstock.com's underlying economic performance? If you answered no to the first part of this question, how might you go about restating Overstock.com's accounting results in order to better reflect Overstock.com's underlying economic performance?

Ratio Analysis

7. Maximizing return on equity involves a trade-off between operating profitability (margin on sales) and turnover (efficiency of asset utilization). Consider the different business models of

   - A closeout e-tailer, such as Overstock.com (OSTK).
   - A regular e-tailer, such as Amazon.com (AMZN).
   - A traditional closeout retailer, such as Ross Stores (ROST).
   - A department store retailer, such as May Department Stores (MAY).

8. Discuss how the different business models involved in each of these categories will influence the trade-off between profitability and turnover.

9. Figures 1, 2, and 3 are eVal Ratio Analysis outputs for AMZN, ROST, and MAY through the end of fiscal 2003. Using eVal, load the Overstock.com case data and conduct a ratio analysis for OSTK. (*Note*: The Overstock.com case data are imported from the eVal Users' Guide by selecting the sequence of buttons Input Historical Data → Import Case Data → Overstock.com.) Provide both a time-series analysis of OSTK from 2001 through 2003 and a cross-sectional analysis using AMZN, ROST, and MAY as comparison companies. Summarize what you learn about the key strengths and weaknesses of OSTK's financial performance.

Forecasting

This is a real-time forecasting case. Your objective is to forecast Overstock.com's income statement, balance sheet, and statement of cash flows for its current fiscal quarter. You should place particular emphasis on trying to generate an accurate forecast of Overstock.com's current quarter EPS (both basic EPS and diluted EPS). Use the following framework and data sources in constructing your forecasting model:

10. Familiarize yourself with Overstock.com's business strategy and financial performance. You will find most of the information available from the Investor Relations link at the bottom of Overstock.com's homepage (http://www.overstock.com). Make sure that you review Overstock.com's recent SEC filings and press releases.

FIGURE 1   Ratio Analysis for Amazon.com

	Actual 12/31/1999	Actual 12/31/2000	Actual 12/31/2001	Actual 12/31/2002	Actual 12/31/2003
Annual Growth Rates					
Sales		68.4%	13.1%	26.0%	33.8%
Assets		−13.6%	−23.3%	21.6%	8.6%
Common Equity		−463.2%	#N/A	#N/A	#N/A
Earnings		#N/A	#N/A	#N/A	#N/A
Free Cash Flow to Investors			#N/A	−1,308.2%	#N/A
Sustainable Growth Rate			47.1%	10.7%	−3.0%
Profitability					
Return on Equity		4.027	0.471	0.107	(0.030)
Return on Equity (b4 nonrecurring)		2.267	0.307	0.027	(0.118)
Return on Net Operating Assets		(0.876)	(0.449)	(0.007)	0.179
Basic Dupont Model					
Net Profit Margin	(0.439)	(0.511)	(0.182)	(0.038)	0.007
× Total Asset Turnover		1.199	1.655	2.168	2.535
× Total Leverage		(6.572)	(1.567)	(1.299)	(1.738)
= Return on Equity		4.027	0.471	0.107	(0.030)
Advanced Dupont Model					
Net Operating Margin	(0.387)	(0.464)	(0.137)	(0.002)	0.031
× Net Operating Asset Turnover		1.889	3.273	4.713	5.686
= Return on Net Operating Assets		(0.876)	(0.449)	(0.007)	0.179
Net Borrowing Cost (NBC)		0.072	0.065	0.064	0.061
Spread (RNOA − NBC)		(0.948)	(0.513)	(0.072)	0.117
Financial Leverage (LEV)		(5.171)	(1.793)	(1.598)	(1.775)
ROE = RNOA + LEV * Spread		4.027	0.471	0.107	(0.030)
Margin Analysis					
Gross Margin	0.218	0.238	0.239	0.273	0.253
EBITDA Margin	(0.192)	(0.123)	(0.032)	0.049	0.066
EBIT Margin	(0.364)	(0.240)	(0.074)	0.027	0.051
Net Operating Margin (b4 nonrec.)	(0.364)	(0.240)	(0.074)	0.027	0.051
Net Operating Margin	(0.387)	(0.464)	(0.137)	(0.002)	0.031
Turnover Analysis					
Net Operating Asset Turnover		1.889	3.273	4.713	5.686
Net Working Capital Turnover		8.002	8.867	9.098	9.272
Avge Days to Collect Receivables		0.000	0.000	5.210	8.472
Avge Inventory Holding Period		34.261	24.458	22.103	23.043
Avge Days to Pay Payables		80.458	70.558	69.293	68.349
PP&E Turnover		8.076	9.786	15.389	22.704

FIGURE 2 Ratio Analysis for Ross Stores

	Fiscal Year End Date				
	Actual 12/31/1999	Actual 12/31/2000	Actual 12/31/2001	Actual 12/31/2002	Actual 12/31/2003
Annual Growth Rates					
Sales		9.7%	10.2%	18.2%	11.0%
Assets		2.9%	11.0%	25.7%	21.7%
Common Equity		−1.2%	16.4%	18.1%	17.4%
Earnings		1.1%	2.2%	29.8%	13.4%
Free Cash Flow to Investors			#N/A	−336.3%	#N/A
Sustainable Growth Rate			28.0%	31.4%	30.1%
Profitability					
Return on Equity		0.323	0.306	0.339	0.326
Return on Equity (b4 nonrecurring)		0.323	0.306	0.339	0.326
Return on Net Operating Assets		0.306	0.292	0.332	0.310
Basic Dupont Model					
Net Profit Margin	0.061	0.056	0.052	0.057	0.058
× Total Asset Turnover		2.818	2.903	2.890	2.598
× Total Leverage		2.043	2.033	2.058	2.158
= Return on Equity		0.323	0.306	0.339	0.326
Advanced Dupont Model					
Net Operating Margin	0.061	0.057	0.053	0.057	0.058
× Net Operating Asset Turnover		5.391	5.551	5.824	5.321
= Return on Net Operating Assets		0.036	0.292	0.332	0.310
Net Borrowing Cost (NBC)		0.066	0.060	0.014	0.000
Spread (RNOA − NBC)		0.240	0.231	0.318	0.310
Financial Leverage (LEV)		0.068	0.063	0.021	0.054
ROE = RNOA + LEV * Spread		0.323	0.306	0.339	0.326
Margin Analysis					
Gross Margin	0.314	0.312	0.311	0.274	0.275
EBITDA Margin	0.123	0.114	0.107	0.112	0.115
EBIT Margin	0.103	0.093	0.086	0.094	0.095
Net Operating Margin (b4 nonrec.)	0.063	0.057	0.053	0.057	0.058
Net Operating Margin	0.061	0.057	0.053	0.057	0.058
Turnover Analysis					
Net Operating Asset Turnover		5.391	5.551	5.824	5.321
Net Working Capital Turnover		12.847	13.087	13.552	11.131
Avge Days to Collect Receivables		2.028	2.136	2.010	2.031
Avge Inventory Holding Period		103.866	104.916	95.437	100.076
Avge Days to Pay Payables		52.056	52.599	52.606	56.791
PP&E Turnover		9.426	9.433	9.619	8.841

FIGURE 3   Ratio Analysis for May Department Stores

	Fiscal Year End Date				
	Actual 12/31/1999	Actual 12/31/2000	Actual 12/31/2001	Actual 12/31/2002	Actual 12/31/2003
Annual Growth Rates					
Sales		4.7%	−2.3%	−4.8%	−1.1%
Assets		5.8%	3.0%	0.1%	1.3%
Common Equity		−5.4%	−0.4%	5.1%	3.9%
Earnings		−7.5%	−18.6%	−23.4%	−20.6%
Free Cash Flow to Investors			#N/A	162.5%	−26.3%
Sustainable Growth Rate			9.6%	5.5.%	2.6%
Profitability					
Return on Equity		0.212	0.178	0.133	0.11
Return on Equity (b4 nonrecurring)		0.210	0.177	0.147	0.154
Return on Net Operating Assets		0.131	0.107	0.091	0.078
Basic Dupont Model					
Net Profit Margin	0.065	0.058	0.048	0.039	0.031
× Total Asset Turnover		1.289	1.207	1.131	1.110
× Total Leverage		2.838	3.053	3.029	2.922
= Return on Equity		0.212	0.178	0.133	0.101
Advanced Dupont Model					
Net Operating Margin	0.080	0.074	0.065	0.058	0.049
× Net Operating Asset Turnover		1.764	1.650	1.585	1.609
= Return on Net Operating Assets		0.131	0.107	0.091	0.078
Net Borrowing Cost (NBC)		0.055	0.050	0.055	0.056
Spread (RNOA − NBC)		0.075	0.057	0.036	0.022
Financial Leverage (LEV)		1.074	1.233	1.161	1.016
ROE = RNOA + LEV * Spread		0.212	0.178	0.133	0.101
Margin Analysis					
Gross Margin	0.358	0.351	0.350	0.340	0.339
EBITDA Margin	0.164	0.156	0.145	0.134	0.138
EBIT Margin	0.131	0.120	0.105	0.093	0.096
Net Operating Margin (b4 nonrec.)	0.079	0.074	0.065	0.062	0.065
Net Operating Margin	0.080	0.074	0.065	0.058	0.049
Turnover Analysis					
Net Operating Asset Turnover		1.764	1.650	1.585	1.609
Net Working Capital Turnover		4.758	4.837	5.327	5.293
Avge Days to Collect Receivables		53.501	51.744	49.768	47.817
Avge Inventory Holding Period		111.519	115.175	117.459	115.828
Avge Days to Pay Payables		39.162	39.121	43.396	46.779
PP&E Turnover		3.002	2.790	2.515	2.514

11. Familiarize yourself with Overstock.com's expansion plans. Company press releases and the MD&A sections of the Form 10-Ks and Form 10-Qs are your best sources of information. This information is again available from the Investor Relations link at the bottom of Overstock.com's homepage.

12. Use the forecasting framework developed in the course, along with the insights generated by your analyses in questions 1 and 2 above to prepare forecasts of Overstock.com's income statement, balance sheet, and statement of cash flows for the current quarter.

13. Do a "reality check" on your forecasting model by comparing your EPS forecasts to sell-side analysts' forecasts (available at the following link: http://finance.yahoo.com/q/ae?s=OSTK).

Valuation Analysis

14. The case introduction summarizes an investment opinion issued by analysts at W. R. Hambrecht on March 10, 2004. Critically evaluate the valuation method(s) used to justify the $40 price target contained in this opinion.

15. Load the Overstock.com case data into eVal and critically evaluate the default valuation provided by eVal. (*Note*: The Overstock.com case data are imported from the eVal Users' Guide by selecting the sequence of buttons Input Historical Data → Import eVal Case Data → Overstock.com.)

16. In early 2004, Overstock.com was trading at around $30 per share. Using eVal, provide a set of forecasting assumptions that approximate this price. Use a cost of equity capital of 10 percent and a valuation date of March 10, 2004. Do you think that these forecasting assumptions are plausible?

17. Using eVal, provide your own valuation of Overstock.com on March 10, 2004. Select what you consider to be the most plausible set of forecasting assumptions and justify these selections. Use a cost of equity capital of 10 percent and a valuation date of March 10, 2004.

Pre-Paid Legal Services*

The third week of October 1999 was a truly bizarre week in the history of Pre-Paid Legal Services (NYSE: PPD). It was marked by the following significant events.

Monday, October 18:	PPD's stock price opens at $36 on the NYSE, slightly above its Friday close of $35.50.
	Forbes magazine names PPD as number 13 on its annual list of the best 200 small companies in America.
Tuesday, October 19:	PPD announces record results for the third quarter of 1999. EPS increased 50 percent, meeting Wall Street's expectations and marking PPD's 25th consecutive quarter of increased revenues and earnings. The full text of PPD's earnings announcement is attached as Exhibit 1.
	Following the announcement, PPD's stock price plummets by over 20 percent in frenzied trading on the NYSE.
Wednesday, October 20:	After taking the night to digest PPD's earnings announcement, investors again pummel PPD's stock price, forcing it down another 10 percent. PPD steps into the market in an effort to shore up its stock price, repurchasing 140,000 shares over the remainder of the week.
Friday, October 22:	PPD's stock price closes at $25, a loss for the week of over 30 percent.

* This case was prepared by Professor Richard Sloan as the basis for class discussion, rather than to illustrate either effective or ineffective handling of a business situation. Copyright © 1999 by Richard Sloan.

EXHIBIT 1
Pre-Paid Announces
Record Third
Quarter Results

Earnings per share up 50 percent and recruiting up 42 percent
ADA, OK, October 19, 1999—Pre-Paid Legal Services, Inc. (NYSE:PPD), today reported record results for the third quarter and for the nine months ended September 30, 1999. As a result of the 1998 fourth quarter acquisition of TPN, Inc. ("TPN") that was accounted for as a pooling of interests, the 1998 periods have been restated to include the operating results of TPN.

Net income for the third quarter of 1999 rose 49 percent to $9,870,000 from $6,611,000 for the prior year's period, while total revenues rose 23 percent to $49,025,000 from $39,809,000 for the prior year's period despite planned decreases of $4.8 million in TPN product sales. The Company's membership revenues increased 41 percent to $39,748,000 from $28,105,000 for the same period last year. Earnings per share, diluted, increased 50 percent to 42 cents per share from 28 cents per diluted share for last year's comparable quarter.

Nine-month net income during 1999 increased 56 percent to $28,524,000 from $18,296,000 for the first three quarters of 1998. Earnings per share, diluted, for the 1999 nine-month period increased 59 percent to $1.21 per share from 76 cents per diluted share for last year's comparable period. Revenues for the nine months were up 20 percent to $141,567,000 from $117,500,000 for the initial nine months of the prior year despite planned decreases of $19 million in TPN product sales.

Even though commission advances increased $9.2 million as a result of increasing membership sales during the third quarter of 1999, cash flow from operations was $5,119,000, a decrease of $379,000, or 7 percent, from the cash flow of $5,498,000 for the comparable quarter of 1998. Cash flow from operations for the first nine months of 1999 was $12.9 million compared to $8.8 million for the comparable period of 1998, an increase of $4.1 million, or 46 percent. At September 30, 1999, the Company had cash and investment balances exceeding $42,500,000.

For the third quarter of 1999, the Company added 134,725 new members, 41 percent above the 95,619 new members added during the same period of 1998. New sales associates recruited during the third quarter of 1999 were 22,493 compared to 15,820 for the comparable period of 1998, an increase of 42 percent.

"We are obviously very pleased with our third quarter operating results, but more than ever, firmly believe the best is yet to come. As we celebrate our 28th year in business, we are in the best financial condition in our history with cash and investment balances of more than $42.5 million, no long term debt and significant positive cash flow while still continuing to grow our membership revenues at better than 40 percent. Our continued revenue growth, financial condition, enhanced Internet presence and increases in recruiting all contribute to our belief that the best is still ahead of us," Harland Stonecipher, Chairman, said.

Pre-Paid Legal Services, Inc., develops, underwrites and markets legal service plans nationally. The plans provide for legal service benefits, including unlimited attorney consultation, will preparation, traffic violation defense, automobile-related criminal charges, letter writing, document preparation and review and a general trial defense benefit. More information can be located at the Company's homepage on the worldwide web at prepaidlegal.com.

FIGURE 1
Pre-Paid Legal
Services, Inc.,
Financial Highlights
(Unaudited)
(Dollars and shares in
000s, except per share
amounts)

	Three Months Ended		Nine Months Ended	
	9/30/99	9/30/98	9/30/99	9/30/98
Revenues:				
Membership premiums	$39.748	$28,105	$112,017	$78.443
Product sales	1,256	6,102	4,426	23,437
Associate services	5,832	4,093	16,201	23,437
Interest income	897	819	2,665	1,881
Other	1,292	690	6,204	1,929
	49,025	39,809	141,567	117,500
Costs and expenses:				
Membership benefits	13,764	9,297	37,388	25,893
Product costs	790	3,711	2,899	14,321
Commissions	9,819	6,422	26,200	17,299
General and administrative	4,428	5,074	13,938	17,971
Associate services and direct marketing expenses	3,767	3,306	10,637	10,518
Depreciation and amortization	688	823	2,372	2,025
Premium taxes	389	277	1,090	908
Other	285	—	3,160	—
	33,839	28,910	97,684	88,935
Income before income taxes	15,186	10,899	43,883	28,565
Provision for income taxes	5,316	4,288	15,359	10,269
Net income	9,870	6,611	28,524	18,296
Less dividends on preferred shares	2	2	7	7
Net income applicable to common shares	$9,868	$6,609	$28,517	$18,289
Basic earnings per common share	$.43	$.28	$1.23	$.78
Diluted earnings per common share	$.42	$.28	$1.21	$.76
Weighted average number of common shares:				
Basic	22,927	23,496	23,246	23,446
Diluted	23,313	23,887	23,587	23,926
Net cash provided by operating activities	$5,119	$5,498	$12,852	$8,790
New membership sales	134,725	95,619	376,424	273,048
New sales associates recruited	22,493	15,820	68,035	46,530
Number of active memberships at end of period	759,341	546,358		

Statements in this press release other than purely historical information, including statements relating to the Company's future plans and objectives and expected operating results, constitute forward-looking statements within the meaning of Section 21E of the Securities Exchange Act of 1934. Forward-looking statements are based on certain assumptions which may not be correct and are subject to all of the risks and uncertainties incident to the Company's business which are described in the reports and statements filed by the Company with the Securities and Exchange Commission. As a result, actual results may vary materially from those described in the forward-looking statements.

Fred Russell, a Tulsa money manager who rates PPD as one of his favorite companies, explains the stock price drop as follows:

The stock price drop is typical of Wall Street's reaction to significant news. Included in Tuesday's earnings statement was a somewhat complex accounting of increased commission payments. This caused short-term pain during the period for Pre-Paid, but the upswing in sales should benefit the company in the long run.[1]

PPD investor relations spokesperson Melanie Danielson notes that

Another factor was the impact of comments made by a short-seller on CNBC on Tuesday. The seller pointed out that the company's cash flow for the third quarter, reported Tuesday, was $5.1 million, down $379,000 from the same period in 1998.[2]

Information concerning PPD's business strategy, accounting policies, and financial condition is provided in PPD's Form 10-K for 1998. Relevant portions of this document are available as an online exhibit at www.mhhe.com/eval2007.

QUESTIONS

1. Identify and evaluate the key elements of PPD's business strategy. Make sure you understand the product they are selling and how they go about selling it.
2. Identify the problem revealed by the third-quarter earnings announcement that resulted in PPD's stock price drop. What was the cause of this problem?
3. Suggest an alternative method of accounting for the transactions that led to the problem identified in Question 2 above and recompute PPD's earnings using this method.
4. Do you think that earnings computed using the method you identified in Question 3 above provide a better or a worse indication of PPD's actual performance?
5. What actions would you advise PPD's management take in response to investors' reaction to the third-quarter earnings announcement?
6. What information would you seek from PPD's subsequent press releases and SEC filings in order to determine whether the price reaction to the third quarter announcement was warranted?

[1] "Oklahoma-Based Legal Services Firm's Stock Price Plummets 22 Percent," *Tribune Business News,* October 20, 1999.
[2] Ibid.

Determinants of Valuation Ratios: The Restaurant Industry in 2003*

The restaurant industry has always represented a prime example of a competitive industry. New innovations are easily observed and imitated, start-up costs are generally quite low, and the entry and exit of new players is frequent. Despite the intense competition, a wide range of valuation ratios are typically observed in the industry. The year 2003 was no exception. It was characterized by the following industry medians:

Industry Median ROE = 14.1 percent

Industry Median Consensus Analyst Forecast of Five-Year EPS
   Growth = 17.5 percent

Industry Median Price-to-Earnings Ratio = 18.6

Industry Median Market-to-Book Ratio = 2.5

The brief sketches of four restaurant companies on the following pages illustrate the variety of experiences within the industry.

REQUIRED

Based on the information provided for each of the following four companies, rank the companies as to whether you expect them to have a higher or lower market-to-book ratio and a higher or lower price-to-earnings ratio relative to the median firm in the industry.

Dave & Busters, Inc.

Dave & Buster's, Inc., is an operator of large-format, high-volume regional entertainment complexes. Each entertainment complex offers an extensive array of entertainment attractions such as pocket billiards, shuffleboard, interactive simulators, and virtual reality systems, plus traditional carnival-style games of skill. In addition, the complexes offer a full menu of food and beverages. As of February 2, 2003, it operated 32 entertainment complexes across the United States, with an average age of 5.1 years per location.

Summary financial data are presented below:

Book Value of Equity/Share = $13.38

2002 EPS = $0.41

Consensus Analyst Forecast of 2003 EPS = $0.80

Consensus Analyst Forecast of Five-Year EPS Growth = 20 percent

Darden Restaurants, Inc.

Darden Restaurants, Inc., is a casual-dining restaurant company in the United States. The company operates 1,131 restaurants in 49 states, including 629 Red Lobster, 472 Olive Garden, 21 Bahama Breeze, and 9 Smokey Bones BBQ Sports Bar restaurants. Darden has no restaurants in Alaska. In addition, the Company operates 37 restaurants in Canada, including 32 Red Lobster and 5 Olive Garden restaurants. Darden also operates one Olive Garden Cafe in the United States. The company operates all of its North American restaurants. In Japan, Red Lobster Japan Partners, a Japanese retailer unaffiliated with Darden, operates 34 Red Lobster restaurants pursuant to an area development and franchise agreement.

Summary financial data are presented below:

Book Value of Equity/Share = $7.12

2002 EPS = $1.31

Consensus Analyst Forecast of 2003 EPS = $1.42

Consensus Analyst Forecast of Five-Year EPS Growth = 14 percent

Panera Bread Company

Panera Bread Company operates a retail bakery-cafe business and franchising business under the concept names Panera Bread Company and Saint Louis Bread Company. As of December 28, 2002, the company's retail operations consisted of 132 company-owned and 346 franchise-operated bakery-cafes (including one specialty bakery-cafe). Panera Bread specializes in meeting consumer dining needs by providing food, including fresh baked goods, made-to-order sandwiches on baked breads, soups, salads, custom-roasted coffees, and other cafe beverages, and targets suburban dwellers and workers by offering a specialty bakery and cafe experience with a neighborhood emphasis. The company's bakery-cafes are principally located in suburban, strip-mall and regional-mall locations. Its business operates in 32 states.

Summary financial data are presented below:

Book Value of Equity/Share = $5.57

2002 EPS = $0.81

Consensus Analyst Forecast of 2003 EPS = $1.00

Consensus Analyst Forecast of Five-Year EPS Growth = 35 percent

Lone Star Steakhouse

Lone Star Steakhouse & Saloon, Inc., owns and operates a chain of midpriced, full-service, casual-dining restaurants in the United States, as well as in Australia. As of March 10, 2003, the company owned and operated 249 midpriced, full-service, casual-dining restaurants located in the United States operating under the trade name Lone Star Steakhouse & Saloon or Lone Star Cafe. The company has 20 upscale steakhouse restaurants, with 5 operating as Del Frisco's Double Eagle Steak House restaurants and 15 operating as Sullivan's Steakhouse restaurants. It also operates a midpriced restaurant operating as Frankie's Italian Grille. In addition, a licensee operates three Lone Star restaurants in California and another licensee operates a Del Frisco's restaurant in Orlando, Florida. The company operates 20 Lone Star Steakhouse & Saloon restaurants in Australia and a licensee operates a Lone Star Steakhouse & Saloon restaurant in Guam.

Summary financial data are presented below:

Book Value of Equity/Share = $20.54

2002 EPS = $1.30

Consensus Analyst Forecast of 2003 EPS = $1.37

Consensus Analyst Forecast of Five-Year EPS Growth = 9 percent

Forecasting for the Love Boat: Royal Caribbean Cruises in 1998*

Much like Kate Winslet leaning over the bow of the *Titanic,* the North American cruise industry seems poised to either take flight or suffer a precipitous fall. The number of cruise passengers has grown from 500,000 in 1970 to 5,400,000 in 1998, a compounded average of 8.9 percent per year. Further, as the baby boomers mature, an increasing proportion of the population will fit the profile of a typical cruise customer—someone between 40 and 59 years old earning about $60,000. But all the news isn't bright. Based on the number of new ships that have already been ordered by major operators, the number of available berths in the North American market is expected to increase by over 40 percent in the next five years. Will the increase in demand for cruise vacations be sufficient to fill all the cabins on these new ships? Given the large fixed costs of operating a cruise vessel and the debt necessary to fund this capacity expansion, the cruise industry risks an encounter with an iceberg as it steams into the new millennium.

This case focuses on Royal Caribbean Cruises in 1998. The first part of the case asks you to conduct a detailed analysis of Royal Caribbean's past financial statements and to compare them with their rival, Carnival Cruises. The second part of the case asks you to forecast the financial performance of Royal Caribbean for the next three years. Note that the chilling effect of September 11, 2001, on the travel and vacation business occurs mostly after the three years that you will be forecasting, so you don't have to pretend that you don't know about this major event.

The case material that follows will provide you with a comprehensive picture of the North American cruise industry as it stood in 1998 along with specific

* Professor Russell Lundholm prepared this case at the University of Michigan Business School in 2002 as the basis for class discussion. Sources for this case include the Cruise Line International Association Market Overview, Cruise Industry News, the Tourism Industry Association of America, Royal Caribbean Cruises' 1998 10-K filing, and Carnival Cruises' 1998 10-K filing. I thank Cheryl Fenske at the Cruise Line International Association for her help in obtaining 1998 data.

financial and operating details of Royal Caribbean Cruises and Carnival Cruises. There is a wealth of information available and no single correct way to put it all together in your financial analysis and forecasts. Please limit your analysis to the information available in the case. The data supporting the graphs in this case are given in the appendix and are included with the case's Excel files, along with files containing input data for eVal. (Please note that Global Access did not code Royal Caribbean's preferred dividend. You will need to modify the financial statements in eVal to correct for this.)

THE NORTH AMERICAN CRUISE INDUSTRY IN 1998

Cruise ships travel the world. Royal Caribbean Cruises, for instance, offers 175 destinations on six different continents. What defines the North American market is not the destination but the point of sale. Hence, North Americans purchase their trips in North America but may fly to any part of the world to embark on a "North American" cruise. While all major cruise lines offer "air and sea" options, this is really just a convenience for their customers. The air portion is priced at cost, and this portion of the trip is handled completely by the airline. Virtually all cruise purchases take place through a local travel agent.

Demand for cruise vacations has grown rapidly over the past two decades as Figure 1 illustrates, with the only decrease in demand occurring in 1994–1995. Further, the average length of a cruise trip has grown to approximately 6.6 days, reaching levels not experienced since the early 1980s. Because of the fixed/ variable cost structure in the cruise industry, longer trips are typically more profitable than short trips, so the industry has welcomed this trend.

The North American cruise industry is composed of two very large companies and many small ones. Carnival Cruise Lines is the largest firm with 33 ships carrying 2,045,000 passengers in 1998, 38 percent of the North American cruise market. Royal Caribbean Cruises is the second largest company with 16 ships

FIGURE 1
Growth in Demand for Cruise Vacations

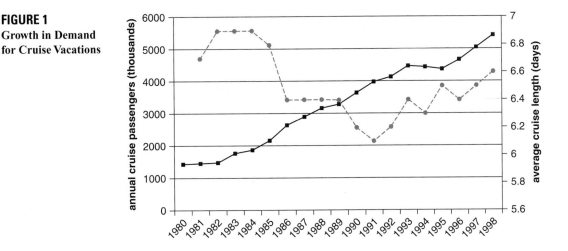

FIGURE 2
Relative Market
Shares of Cruise
Lines

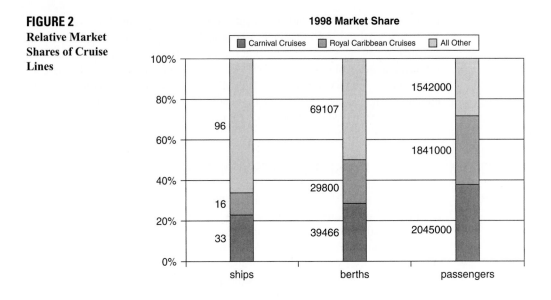

carrying 1,841,000 passengers in 1998, a total of 34 percent of the North American market. A host of smaller cruise lines make up the rest of the industry, dividing 1,542,000 passengers between 96 vessels. The relative market shares are illustrated in Figure 2.

THE CRUISE EXPERIENCE

The cruise industry offers a wide variety of ship sizes, luxury levels, and itineraries. From small, quasi-research vessels that probe Artic passages to massive "mega-ships" that resemble floating Malls of America, the cruise industry offers something for everyone. The Caribbean is the most common destination for cruises sold in North America, as seen in the table below, with approximately 39 percent of all passenger-days devoted to this destination. However, the table also shows that there has been a significant increase in demand for trips to locations such as the Mediterranean, Alaska, and Europe. The latest trend is for huge ships that carry as many as 3,000 guests and offer a wide variety of entertainment alternatives. Such vessels feature rock climbing, ice skating, miniature golf, cinemas, discos, spa facilities, libraries, casinos, extensive live entertainment, and entire shopping malls, all onboard the ship. The focus of these cruise alternatives is on the vessel, rather than the destination. Bob Dickinson, the president of Carnival Cruises, remarked, "Now, the cruise itself is the destination—magnificent floating resorts. To me, the itinerary is a little Green Stamp, a little extra thing."

Destination	1987		1995		1998	
	Total Bed-Days	Percent of Total	Total Bed-Days	Percent of Total	Total Bed-Days	Percent of Total
Caribbean	8,828,791	43.3	15,254,551	42.8	17,117,659	38.7
Mediterranean	841,051	4.1	3,477,729	9.8	5,092,530	11.25
Alaska	1,715,197	8.4	3,008,146	8.4	3,790,816	8.6
Bahamas	1,922,386	9.4	2,761,224	7.7	2,891,352	6.5
Transcanal	970,191	4.8	2,277,201	6.4	2,612,788	5.9
Mexico West	1,131,462	5.6	1,754,312	4.9	2,421,126	5.5
Europe	357,516	1.8	1,582,589	4.4	3,714,437	8.4
Bermuda	1,141,121	5.6	1,094,707	3.1	1,094,982	2.5
South America	620,396	3.0	255,830	0.7	943,392	2.1
Transatlantic	339,388	1.7	658,928	1.8	725,040	1.6
Hawaii	602,728	3.0	601,542	1.7	745,216	1.7
All other (15 other locations)	1,906,767	9.4	2,935,123	14.4	3,091,374	15.2
Total	20,376,994	100.0	35,661,882	100.0	44,240,712	100.0

WHO'S ONBOARD

Obviously, different types of cruises attract different types of customers. Nonetheless, certain demographic profiles are most likely to take a cruise. The table below compares the demographic profile of those who have taken a cruise with the entire U.S. population over the age of 24. Generally, the population of past cruisers is older, wealthier, and better educated than the entire population.

Demographic Profile		Ever Cruised	Past Five-Year Cruisers	Population over Age 24
Gender:	Male	49%	51%	50%
	Female	51%	48%	49%
Age:	25–under 40 years	27%	28%	43%
	40–59 years	42%	42%	44%
	60 years or older	32%	30%	13%
	Average	51 years	50 years	43 years
	Median	51 years	51 years	42 years
Marital status:	Married	76%	78%	69%
	Not married	24%	22%	31%
Household composition:	Have children under 18	37%	35%	54%
	Adults only	63%	65%	46%
	Occupants	3	3	3

(*continued*)

(*continued*)

Demographic Profile		Ever Cruised	Past Five-Year Cruisers	Population over Age 24
Education:	Some college or less	42%	36%	54%
	College graduate or more	58%	64%	46%
Household income:	$20,000–$29,999	8%	5%	13%
	$30,000–$39,999	12%	10%	17%
	$40,000–$59,999	32%	31%	31%
	$60,000–$99,999	28%	30%	29%
	$100,000 or more	20%	25%	9%
	Average	$72,600	$79,100	$60,400
	Median	$58,500	$64,500	$51,800

FIGURE 3
Types of Cruise Line Customers

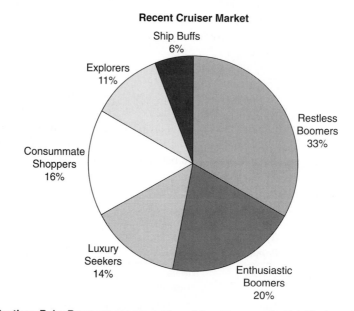

Recent Cruiser Market

Restless Baby Boomers are newest to cruising. They are at a Point in time when they may be trying different vacation experiences.
Enthusiastic Baby Boomers are already convinced about cruising and its many activities. They live intense, stressful lives and look to vacations generally, and cruises in particular, for the escape and relaxation they offer.
Luxury Seekers can afford, and are willing to spend money for, deluxe accommodations and pampering.
Consummate Shoppers are looking for the best value in a vacation and in a cruise.
Explorers are well-educated, well-traveled individuals with an intellectual interest and curiosity about different destinations.
Ship Buffs are the most senior segment: they have cruised extensively and expect to continue because they find the on-board experience of cruising so pleasurable and comfortable.

Examining those who have cruised most recently reveals a few different types of customers, as Figure 3 illustrates, but most seek the relaxation and pampering that a cruise can provide. Indeed, when the recent cruiser population was asked what cruising offered that was superior to other types of vacations, the top three responses were "being pampered," "fine dining," and "hassle free."

SUPPLY OF AVAILABLE BERTHS

The supply of available berths as of 1998 was shown earlier in Figure 2. Further, because the lead time necessary to design and build a cruise ship is approximately three years, a reasonably accurate forecast of future supply is available for the next three years, as seen in the table below (more detailed information about Royal Caribbean's new ships is available later in the case). It is more difficult to estimate the amount of capacity that will be retired in the future. Over the past five years, 48 ships with a total of 28,900 berths have been retired or moved out of the North American market. However, many of these retirements occurred because of a 1997 deadline to meet the heightened safety requirements imposed by the International Maritime Organization. From 1994 through 1996, retirements exceeded 7,000 berths per year but have slowed considerably since then.

| | New Capacity | | | | | | | |
| | 1999 | | 2000 | | 2001 | | Total New | |
	Ships	Berths	Ships	Berths	Ships	Berths	Ships	Berths
Carnival Cruises (includes Holland brand)	3	5,480	2	6,180	2	3,900	7	15,560
Royal Caribbean Cruises (includes Celebrity brand)	1	3,100	2	5,100	3	6,100	6	14,300
All other cruise lines	7	7,794	2	2,800	4	6,296	13	16,890
Total new ships/berths	11	16,374	6	14,080	9	16,296	26	46,750

DEMAND FOR A CRUISE VACATION

To date, only 11 percent of the U.S. population has ever taken a cruise. However, a recent cruise industry survey of people over the age of 24 found that 56 percent are interested in cruising sometime in the future and 31 percent responded that they will definitely take a cruise in the next five years. Demographic trends also favor the cruise industry. As the demographic profile showed, 42 percent of recent cruise passengers are between the ages of 40 and 59. As the baby boomers age, this segment of the U.S. population is estimated to grow at more than three times the national population growth rate over the next three years, as seen in Figure 4.

Along with growth in the U.S. population, it is possible that the amount of vacation time per individual will increase over time. Numerous studies have shown that the baby boomer generation values recreation more highly than previous

FIGURE 4
Annual Population Growth Rates by Age

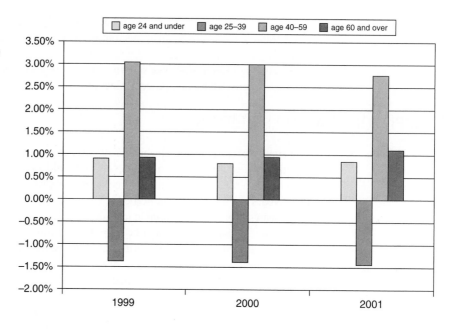

FIGURE 5
Growth Rates in the U.S. Gross Domestic Product (GDP), Personal Consumption, and Recreation Expenditures

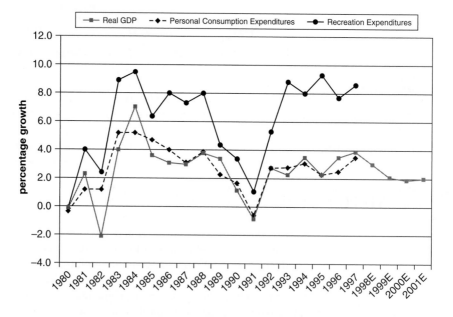

generations. This is illustrated in Figure 5, which plots growth rates in the U.S. gross domestic product (GDP), personal consumption, and recreation expenditures. As the figure shows, growth in personal consumption maps closely to growth in the gross domestic product (GDP). By comparison, recreation spending has grown faster than personal consumption in every year since 1980, with the gap

FIGURE 6
Average Number of Vacation Days

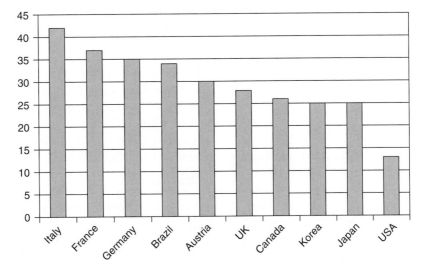

between the two increasing dramatically after the 1991 recession. This increase is widely attributed to the consumption tastes of the baby boomer generation. The figure also shows the 1998 Congressional Budget Office's forecasts for future GDP growth.

Finally, U.S. residents vacation far less than the citizens of all other developed countries, averaging just 13 days per year. As Figure 6 illustrates, even the hardworking Japanese and Koreans vacation almost twice as much as Americans. Italians, living the good life, vacation more than three times as much. It is certainly possible that Americans will increase their vacation expenditures even more in the future.

PART A. COMPREHENSIVE FINANCIAL ANALYSIS

Your task for this part of the case is to conduct a comprehensive financial analysis of Royal Caribbean Cruises and to compare their performance with Carnival Cruises. Excerpts from Royal Caribbean's 20-F filing and Carnival's 10-K filing are included as online exhibits at www.mhhe.com/eval2007.

You will need to import the case data into eVal. (*Note*: The Royal Caribbean case data are imported from the eVal Users' Guide by selecting the sequence of buttons Input Historical Data → Import Case Data → Royal Caribbean. Similar steps load the Carnival data.) You should compare the financial statements in eVal with the ones in the 20-F and 10-K filings so that you can see exactly what data are used to compute each ratio and make any necessary adjustments. The definitions of each ratio are given in Part One of this textbook. Note that Royal Caribbean paid a preferred stock dividend of $12.5 million in 1998 but that this amount is not in the eVal data. You will have to correct the financial statements once they are loaded into eVal.

1. Compare the growth rates of Royal Caribbean and Carnival Cruises. What are the advantages to being large in this industry?
2. Compute the 1998 net operating income, net financing expense, average net operating assets, and average net financial obligations from the financial statements in Royal Caribbean's 20-F filing.
3. Using your answers to the previous question, compute return on equity (ROE) and then decompose ROE using the advanced Dupont decomposition:

$$ROE = RNOA + Leverage \times Spread$$

How does your decomposition compare to the one provided by eVal?

4. Using the financial ratios provided by eVal, evaluate any trends in Royal Caribbean's return on equity, compare it with Carnival Cruise's return on equity, and discuss the main causes of any differences.
5. Now consider each of the main drivers of return on equity: margins, turnovers, and leverage. Using eVal's output as a starting point, evaluate any trends and compare Royal Caribbean with Carnival Cruises in each of these areas. Only note what is exceptional—do not discuss every possible ratio.
6. Does a dollar of revenue increase bring about a constant increase in expenses for Royal Caribbean, or do they enjoy economies of scale? Estimate any economies of scale that might be present.
7. Approximately 35 percent of Carnival Cruise's passengers also book their air travel through the cruise company (as an "air and sea" package) while only 25 percent of Royal Caribbean's passengers include the air portion in their booking. Conceptually, how will this affect your ratio comparison of the two companies and discuss how you might adjust the data to remove this distortion?

PART B. FINANCIAL FORECASTS

This part of the case asks you to forecast the financial performance of Royal Caribbean for the next three years. This is where you should bring together the industry facts given in the beginning of the case, the results of your financial analysis, and your understanding of Royal Caribbean's unique attributes gleaned from a careful reading of their SEC filings. Note that, while the events of September 11, 2001, had a dramatic effect on subsequent travel and tourism, this is largely after the periods you are forecasting. In their 2001 annual report, Royal Caribbean estimates a net cost of $47.7 million due to passenger's inability to fly to their departure locations, subsequent cancellations, and other costs incurred as a direct result of this event. Make your forecasts without regard to this event, but then subtract an extraordinary loss of $47.7 million from your final income estimate to control for this effect.

Your answers will not be graded on their accuracy but, rather, on the logic you give to support them. Use eVal to derive the forecasted financial data. Although your answers should be in the format given in eVal, your analysis should be *far more detailed* than a simple extrapolation from Royal Caribbean's past performance (as the eVal defaults will do). Note that Royal Caribbean paid a preferred stock dividend of $12.5 million in 1998 but that this amount is not in the Global Access data. You will have to correct the financial statements once they are loaded into eVal. (*Note*: The Royal Caribbean case data are imported from the eVal Users' Guide by selecting the sequence of buttons Input Historical Data → Import Case Data → Royal Caribbean. Similar steps load the Carnival data.) Excerpts from Royal Caribbean's 20-F filing and Carnival's 10-K filing are included as online exhibits at www.mhhe.com/eval2007

1. Based on all the information provided in the case, forecast Royal Caribbean's gross revenue for 1999, 2000, and 2001. Please explain your reasoning.

2. Forecast the remaining portions of the income statement for 1999, 2000, and 2001. Comment only on the forecast components that differ significantly from past trends or ratios—do not discuss each line item if you don't have anything substantive to say.

3. Forecast complete balance sheets for the end of 1999, 2000, and 2001. Comment only on the forecast components that differ significantly from past trends or ratios—do not discuss each line item if you don't have anything substantive to say.

4. Can Royal Caribbean afford to purchase the ships that it has on order in the next three years? How do you anticipate that these acquisitions will be financed?

5. For this question, do not use eVal (because it is easier not to). Suppose your analysis indicated that Royal Caribbean will spend $810,261 thousand on additions to property and equipment in 1999. Given this, estimate the ending balance of property and equipment for 1999.

6. For this question, do not use eVal (because it is easier not to). Suppose your analysis indicated that Royal Caribbean's 1999 ending balance of customer deposits was $515,308 thousand. Estimate the amount of cash collected from customers in 1999.

Can Salton Swing?*

Sales growth and profitability are the two pillars of a high valuation. And, based on these two measures, Salton Inc.—the maker of the BreadMan bread machine, the Juiceman juice extractor, and the George Foreman electric grill—looks fabulous. As of fiscal 2000 (ending July 1, 2000), the average ROE for the past four years has been 50.5 percent, and the average annual sales growth has been 70.6 percent. Allowing eVal to extrapolate this past performance over the next ten years yields a valuation as of September 30, 2000 (approximately when the 10-K was filed), of over $1,400 per share. At the time, Salton's stock was trading at an all-time high, but this was still only $40 per share, and in the subsequent year it drifted back down to a $20 range. The purpose of this case is to figure out why the market expects so little out of Salton compared to its historical fundamentals, and to decide if this is an appropriate valuation or a severely undervalued stock.

To aid you in your analysis, there are online exhibits at www.mhhe.com/eval2007. These exhibits include excerpts from the fiscal 2000 10-K filing and an Excel file with ratio analysis for the four competitor firms and Salton. Finally, to input the case data into eVal, go to Input Historical Data; then select Input eVal Case Data and find the Salton case.

BACKGROUND

In their 10-K, Salton states that they have the leading domestic market share in toasters, juice extractors, indoor grills, bread makers, griddles, waffle makers, and buffet hotplates, and a strong presence in a number of other related products. They either own or license a number of major brand names, including Toastmaster, Maxim, Breadman, Juiceman, George Foreman Grills, White-Westinghouse, Farberware, Melitta, Timex, and Kenmore. Three principal product lines—George Foreman Grills, Juiceman, and Breadman—accounted for 55.2 percent of sales in fiscal 2000 and 55.4 percent of sales in fiscal 1999. All small appliances combined account for 89 percent of total sales in fiscal 2000.

Salton predominately sells its products to mass merchandisers and department stores, with only a small Internet business selling directly to consumers through

* Professor Russell Lundholm prepared this case as the basis for class discussion. Copyright © 2001 by Russell Lundholm.

infomercials and the company Web site. Its largest two customers in fiscal 2000 were Wal-Mart and Kmart, representing 13 and 12 percent of its sales, respectively. The top five customers in fiscal 2000 represented 46 percent of total sales. With only minor exceptions, it has no long-term contracts with any of its customers.[1]

Salton manufactures its products in the Far East using over 45 unaffiliated suppliers, although the largest producer accounted for 38 percent of purchases in fiscal 2000. Its purchases are typically denominated in U.S. dollars, limiting exposure to foreign currency risk. Finally, Salton must place a firm purchase commitment with its suppliers approximately 6 to 12 months prior to receiving a firm commitment from its customer.

THE DEAL WITH GEORGE

Salton's hottest product line is the George Foreman Grill, an electric grill that comes in various sizes and colors, and in both indoor and outdoor versions. The original agreement with George Foreman (former heavy-weight boxing champion of the world) was that Mr. Foreman received in royalty fees 60 percent of the gross profit from this product line.[2] But midway through fiscal 2000, and effective as of the beginning of fiscal 2000, Salton negotiated a significant change in this agreement. Instead of annual royalty payments, Salton purchased the rights to the George Foreman trademark in perpetuity, paying with shares of Salton stock valued at $23.75 million and a note payable for $113.75 million, payable in five annual payments (one of which occurred in fiscal 2000). All together, the present value of consideration given for the trademark was $122 million, which is being amortized over 15 years.

QUESTIONS

1. Consider the competitive forces at work in the small-appliance industry. Do you think Salton can sustain its unusually high profits and return on equity in this industry?

2. For comparison purposes, the online exhibits for the case give a ratio analysis from eVal for four of Salton's competitors: Applica, Maytag, Sunbeam, and Whirlpool. Based on the Dupont analysis, how has Salton generated such a large return on equity relative to these other firms? Do you see any significant trends or changes in Salton's ratios over time?

3. For the past two years, Salton has stated in their Management Discussion and Analysis that a significant source of their sales growth has been from the George Foreman product line. Estimate what fraction of total sales is due to these products?

---

[1] Salton has a contract with Kmart that technically runs though June 30, 2004, but Kmart can terminate the agreement without cause after June 30, 2002. Consequently, this contract by itself does not represent a sustainable competitive advantage.

[2] December 9, 1999, company press release.

4. The deal with George Foreman has both real economic effects and cosmetic accounting effects that will bear upon your forecasts of Salton's future income. Discuss each. How will the deal with George Foreman change the relationship between sales and other income statement items?

5. Suppose you believe that the George Foreman trademark is grossly overvalued in Salton's books; in fact, rather than its book value of approximately $113.9 million ($122 million less $8.1 million in amortization), you believe it is worthless. Discuss the different ways you could express this belief in your forecast inputs to eVal.

6. Load the case data for Salton into eVal. Change the valuation date to be September 30, 2000, roughly the release date of the fiscal 2000 10-K. If you leave everything else at the default eVal levels, the resulting value estimate is approximately $1,400 per share. Modify the forecasting assumptions to represent a more realistic scenario. If you believe the Foreman trademark is overvalued, you may also want to modify the financial statements to correct for this distortion. Putting it all together, is Salton still an undervalued stock?

A Tale of Two Movie Theaters*

This case compares the financial statistics of two movie theater companies: one that defaulted on its debt and filed for bankruptcy in 2000 and the one that did not. Your task is to predict which company will ultimately be the one that declares bankruptcy. Until the solution of the case is presented, we will refer to the two companies as *Country Cinema* and *City Screens*.

THE MOVIE THEATER INDUSTRY

Attending a theatrical movie remains a thriving entertainment activity in North America, with ticket sales topping $7.6 billion in 2000. While the number of movie attendees has declined slightly in recent years, the decline has been more than offset by increases in ticket prices, resulting in healthy year-to-year ticket revenue growth (see Figure 1). But despite the overall increase in sales, the movie theater industry has struggled in recent years. The number of screens has increased 34 percent since 1995, somewhat less than the total box office sales growth, but the cost of operating so many new screens has outstripped the increase in revenue. Multiplexes, theaters with eight or more screens, have become the industry standard, and megaplexes, theaters with at least 10 screens and stadium-style seating, have grown rapidly in popularity. While the multiscreen theater format offers many advantageous operating features—the ability to optimally match the theater size with the audience and a more evenly spaced demand for concession services—it also has required significant capital expenditures on stadium seating and state-of-the-art sound and projection equipment. The popularity of the new theater options has caused many older theaters to suffer, necessitating asset write-downs. Finally, the increased competition between screens has caused marketing costs to rise 54 percent since 1995 and shorter runs have raised the rental fees to distributors (which average about 50 percent of the total box office).[1]

---

* Professor Russell Lundholm prepared this case as the basis of class discussion.

[1] First-run motion picture rental fees are generally the greater of (i) 70 percent of box office admissions, gradually declining to as low as 30 percent over a period of four to seven weeks, and (ii) a specified percentage (i.e., 90 percent) of the excess of box office receipts over a negotiated allowance for theater expenses (commonly known as a "90/10" clause). Second-run motion picture rental fees typically begin at 35 percent of box office admissions and often decline to 30 percent after the first week. (Source: 10-K of City Screens.)

FIGURE 1

North American
Movie Theater
Statistics

Source: Motion Picture
Association of America.

	Box Office Gross Sales	Average Ticket Price	Attendance	Number of Screens	Number of Theaters	Average Screens per Theater
1995	$5494 M	$4.35	1263 M	27805	7744	3.6
1996	$5912 M	$4.42	1339 M	29690	7798	3.8
1997	$6366 M	$4.59	1388 M	31640	7480	4.2
1998	$6949 M	$4.69	1481 M	34186	7418	4.6
1999	$7448 M	$5.08	1465 M	37185	7551	4.9
2000	$7661 M	$5.39	1421 M	37396	7421	5.0

TWO MOVIE THEATER COMPANIES

The two companies in this case are approximately the same size, each with approximately 2,800 screens as of fiscal 2000. For each company, ticket sales constitute approximately 65 percent of revenues, followed by concessions, which make up roughly 30 percent of revenues, with the remainder coming from video games and on-screen advertising. The two companies differ significantly in the size of town they operate in. *Country Cinema*, as we will call it, targets small to mid-sized communities. As of 2000, the management of Country Cinema believes it was the sole exhibitor in approximately 65 percent of its areas. In contrast, *City Screens* operates 69 percent of its domestic screens in the 20 largest "designated market areas" (as defined by Nielsen Media), as well as operating in certain large international cities.

WHO WILL DEFAULT: COUNTRY CINEMA OR CITY SCREENS?

From 1995 to 2000, both companies were expanding rapidly and changing over to multiplex and megaplex theater formats. And both were borrowing heavily to fund their growth and remodeling costs. But one company stumbles in the summer of 2000 and defaults on its loans. The summer season is traditionally the highest-volume period for movie theater attendance, but the summer of 2000 failed to deliver any blockbuster movies and attendance suffered. Consequently, one of the companies did not generate sufficient cash flow to stay within its loan covenants.

The detailed requirements of each company's loan covenants fill hundreds of pages, but the basic idea behind them is very simple. The covenants place limits on additional borrowing and on payments to equity holders. They also describe a number of financial health measures so that, if the company starts to get too sick, the bank can declare the loan in technical default. This makes the loan immediately due and payable in full, allowing the bank the opportunity to claim assets before they are all gone.

Two measures of financial health for Country Cinema and City Screens are the total leverage ratio, roughly defined as total debt/EBITDA before nonrecurring items, and the fixed charges coverage ratio, roughly defined as EBITDA plus rent/interest plus rent, where rent is the rent expense on operating leases and debt includes capital leases. At the time of the case, both companies were required to maintain the total leverage ratio below 6 and the fixed charges coverage ratio above 1.25. However, the precise definition of EBITDA differed between the two companies. The definition of EBITDA in the Country Cinema covenants was basically the traditional earnings before interest, taxes, depreciation, and amortization, and before any nonrecurring items such as gains/losses on asset sales or restructuring charges. For City Screens, the definition was more forward-looking, excluding the performance of theaters scheduled to close and extrapolating into the near future the performance of theaters that were recently opened.

REQUIREMENTS

Your task is simply to forecast which company you believe will default in the summer of 2000 and justify your prediction. It will aid your analysis greatly if you forecast the next year's financial statements for both firms. There are much data available to you. The case materials are as follows:

1. You can load the case data into eVal and examine the credit risk statistics at the bottom of the Ratio Analysis sheet. (*Note:* The case data are imported from the eVal User's Guide by selecting Input Historical Data → Import Case Data → then picking either Country Cinema of City Screens.)

2. Note that the 1998 fiscal year end for City Screens is actually April 1, 1999.

The fiscal 1998 financial statements and excerpts from the MD&A for both companies are available as online exhibits at www.mhhe.com/eval2007.

Please note: The exact definitions of the financial health measures given in the loan covenants for each company are extremely detailed, and you do not have sufficient information to reconstruct them. The details about the covenants given above and a general investigation into the financial health, risk exposure, and, most importantly, a forecast of the future for each company will be sufficient to guide your analysis.

COUNTRY CINEMA FINANCIAL RATIOS

	Fiscal Year-End Date			
	12/31/1995	12/31/1996	12/31/1997	12/31/1998
Analysis of Credit Risk				
Net Income to Total Assets	0.027	−0.015	0.033	−0.044
Implied default probability	3.0%	5.5%	3.0%	5.5%
Total Liabilities to Total Assets	0.613	0.636	0.673	0.676
Implied default probability	4.5%	5.5%	5.5%	5.5%
Quick Ratio	0.553	0.337	0.323	0.226
limplied default probability	5.0%	9.0%	9.0%	9.0%
EBIT to Interest Expense	2.36	2.66	2.41	1.89
Implied default probability	3.0%	3.0%	3.0%	5.0%
Inventory Holding Period	7.12	5.51	5.98	7.11
Implied default probability	3.9%	3.9%	3.9%	3.9%
Annual Sales Growth	11.3%	17.0%	7.5%	5.0%
Implied default probability	3.0%	3.2%	3.0%	3.0%
Average implied default probability	3.7%	5.0%	4.6%	5.3%
Other Ratios				
Rent expense (from footnotes)	45,600	54,800	57,600	66,800
Fixed Charge Coverage	1.79	1.83	1.82	1.66
Total Debt/EBITDA	3.5	3.21	4.05	3.96
(before nonrecurring charges)				

CITY SCREENS FINANCIAL RATIOS

	Fiscal Year-End Date			
	3/28/1996	4/3/1997	4/2/1998	4/1/1999
Analysis of Credit Risk				
Net Income to Total Assets	0.057	0.026	−0.031	−0.016
Implied default probability	2.0%	3.0%	5.5%	5.5%
Total Liabilities to Total Assets	0.671	0.764	0.825	0.882
Implied default probability	5.5%	7.0%	9.0%	9.0%
Quick Ratio	0.296	0.256	0.132	0.167
Implied default probability	9.0%	9.0%	9.0%	9.0%
EBIT to Interest Expense	2.38	2.74	1.03	0.34
Implied default probability	3.0%	3.0%	7.0%	7.0%
Inventory Holding Period	0.00	0.00	0.00	0.00
Implied default probability	3.0%	3.0%	3.0%	3.0%
Annual Sales Growth	16.5%	14.4%	13.3%	20.4%
Implied default probability	3.2%	3.0%	3.0%	3.2%
Average implied default probability	4.3%	4.7%	6.1%	6.1%
Other Ratios				
Rent expense (from footnotes)	64,813	80,061	106,383	165,370
Fixed Charge Coverage	1.89	1.89	1.5	1.31
Total Debt/EBITDA	1.67	3.31	3.78	5.95
(before nonrecurring charges)				

Getting Started with eVal

The eVal software is an integral part of this book. While you can definitely read each chapter without sitting next to your computer, we assume that you will be using eVal to construct your valuation models and therefore will need a bit of instruction on how to interact with the software. Unlike many other valuation software programs, eVal is *not* a black box. This book and the software are woven together to teach you exactly why your valuation model produces the answer that it does. Of course, we think eVal is much more than an instructional tool—we think it is a great general-purpose valuation program that will vastly improve the quality of your life (or, at least, the quality of your valuations). But, even if you ultimately use some other valuation software, it will be much easier to learn another program after having first learned eVal.

INSTALLING AND RUNNING eVal

Insert the eVal CD into your computer. If the installation program doesn't launch immediately, then navigate to the CD drive for your computer and double-click the setup.exe file. Because there is a ton of financial data included with eVal, the installation can take up to 10 minutes to run and require up to 20 MB of space on your hard drive. If you need to uninstall eVal for some reason, then go to your Control Panel (usually found under the Settings submenu on your Start menu) and select Add/Remove Programs.

Once eVal is installed on your computer, it can be started by double-clicking the eVal icon on your desktop or by navigating to the eVal program icon using the Start menu. If you have the security level for Microsoft Office set to Medium, a warning message will appear notifying you that the program file contains macros authored by Russell Lundholm and Richard Sloan but that these macros have not been authenticated. *You must enable macros* for eVal to function! If your security level is set to High or Very High, then you will not even be able to enable macros, and eVal will not funtion. You must therefore lower you security settings to Medium or Low. To change your security settings in Excel, open Excel, go to the Tools menu, then to the Macros submenu and select Security.

USING eVal

The first chapter gives you an overview of eVal and the rest of the book shows you all the beauty and nuance that it contains. But if you want to start clicking buttons right now, that's fine—you can't break anything. The program is really just a customized Excel file, so if you are familiar with Excel, then everything should look pretty familiar. You can only change the yellow cells; everything else is copy-protected so that you don't accidentally mess up the program. The main eVal file is "Read Only," so to save your work you must pick another file name.

APPENDIX B

Hemscott Data Industry and Sector Group Codes

1		**BASIC MATERIALS**
11		CHEMICALS
	110	Chemicals—Major Diversified
	111	Synthetics
	112	Agricultural Chemicals
	113	Specialty Chemicals
12		ENERGY
	120	Major Integrated Oil & Gas
	121	Independent Oil & Gas
	122	Oil & Gas Refining & Marketing
	123	Oil & Gas Drilling & Exploration
	124	Oil & Gas Equipment & Services
	125	Oil & Gas Pipelines
13		METALS & MINING
	130	Steel & Iron
	131	Copper
	132	Aluminum
	133	Industrial Metals & Minerals
	134	Gold
	135	Silver
	136	Nonmetallic Mineral Mining
2		**CONGLOMERATES**
21		CONGLOMERATES
	210	Conglomerates
3		**CONSUMER GOODS**
31		CONSUMER DURABLES
	310	Appliances
	311	Home Furnishings & Fixtures

	312	Housewares & Accessories
	313	Business Equipment
	314	Electronic Equipment
	315	Toys & Games
	316	Sporting Goods
	317	Recreational Goods, Other
	318	Photographic Equipment & Supplies
32		CONSUMER NONDURABLES
	320	Textile—Apparel Clothing
	321	Textile—Apparel Footwear & Accessories
	322	Rubber & Plastics
	323	Personal Products
	324	Paper & Paper Products
	325	Packaging & Containers
	326	Cleaning Products
	327	Office Supplies
33		AUTOMOTIVE
	330	Auto Manufacturers—Major
	331	Trucks & Other Vehicles
	332	Recreational Vehicles
	333	Auto Parts
34		FOOD & BEVERAGE
	340	Food—Major Diversified
	341	Farm Products
	342	Processed & Packaged Goods
	343	Meat Products
	344	Dairy Products
	345	Confectioners
	346	Beverages—Brewers
	347	Beverages—Wineries & Distillers
	348	Beverages—Soft Drinks

35		TOBACCO
	350	Cigarettes
	351	Tobacco Products, Other

4   FINANCIAL

41		BANKING
	410	Money Center Banks
	411	Regional—Northeast Banks
	412	Regional—Mid-Atlantic Banks
	413	Regional—Southeast Banks
	414	Regional—Midwest Banks
	415	Regional—Southwest Banks
	416	Regional—Pacific Banks
	417	Foreign Money Center Banks
	418	Foreign Regional Banks
	419	Savings & Loans
42		FINANCIAL SERVICES
	420	Investment Brokerage—National
	421	Investment Brokerage—Regional
	422	Asset Management
	423	Diversified Investments
	424	Credit Services
	425	Closed-End Fund—Debt
	426	Closed-End Fund—Equity
	427	Closed-End Fund—Foreign
43		INSURANCE
	430	Life Insurance
	431	Accident & Health Insurance
	432	Property & Casualty Insurance
	433	Surety & Title Insurance
	434	Insurance Brokers
44		REAL ESTATE
	440	REIT—Diversified
	441	REIT—Office
	442	REIT—Healthcare Facilities
	443	REIT—Hotel/Motel
	444	REIT—Industrial
	445	REIT—Residential
	446	REIT—Retail
	447	Mortgage Investment
	448	Property Management
	449	Real Estate Development

5   HEALTH CARE

51		DRUGS
	510	Drug Manufacturers—Major
	511	Drug Manufacturers—Other
	512	Drugs—Generic
	513	Drug Delivery
	514	Drug-Related Products
	515	Biotechnology
	516	Diagnostic Substances
52		HEALTH SERVICES
	520	Medical Instruments & Supplies
	521	Medical Appliances & Equipment
	522	Health Care Plans
	523	Long-Term Care Facilities
	524	Hospitals
	525	Medical Laboratories & Research
	526	Home Health Care
	527	Medical Practitioners
	528	Specialized Health Services

6   INDUSTRIAL GOODS

61		AEROSPACE/DEFENSE
	610	Aerospace/Defense—Major Diversified
	611	Aerospace/Defense Products & Services
62		MANUFACTURING
	620	Farm & Construction Machinery
	621	Industrial Equipment & Components
	622	Diversified Machinery
	623	Pollution & Treatment Controls
	624	Machine Tools & Accessories
	625	Small Tools & Accessories
	626	Metal Fabrication
	627	Industrial Electrical Equipment
	628	Textile Manufacturing
63		MATERIALS & CONSTRUCTION
	630	Residential Construction
	631	Manufactured Housing
	632	Lumber, Wood Production
	633	Cement
	634	General Building Materials
	635	Heavy Construction
	636	General Contractors
	637	Waste Management

7   SERVICES

71		LEISURE
	710	Lodging
	711	Resorts & Casinos
	712	Restaurants
	713	Specialty Eateries

714	Gaming Activities	
715	Sporting Activities	
716	General Entertainment	

72 **MEDIA**

720	Advertising Agencies
721	Marketing Services
722	Entertainment—Diversified
723	Broadcasting—TV
724	Broadcasting—Radio
725	CATV Systems
726	Movie Production, Theaters
727	Publishing—Newspapers
728	Publishing—Periodicals
729	Publishing—Books

73 **RETAIL**

730	Apparel Stores
731	Department Stores
732	Discount, Variety Stores
733	Drug Stores
734	Grocery Stores
735	Electronics Stores
736	Home Improvement Stores
737	Home Furnishing Stores
738	Auto Parts Stores
739	Catalog & Mail Order Houses

74 **SPECIALTY RETAIL**

740	Sporting Goods Stores
741	Toy & Hobby Stores
742	Jewelry Stores
743	Music & Video Stores
744	Auto Dealerships
745	Specialty Retail, Other

75 **WHOLESALE**

750	Auto Parts Wholesale
751	Building Materials Wholesale
752	Industrial Equipment Wholesale
753	Electronics Wholesale
754	Medical Equipment Wholesale
755	Computers Wholesale
756	Drugs Wholesale
757	Food Wholesale
758	Basic Materials Wholesale
759	Wholesale, Other

76 **DIVERSIFIED SERVICES**

760	Business Services
761	Rental & Leasing Services
762	Personal Services
763	Consumer Services
764	Staffing & Outsourcing Services
765	Security & Protection Services
766	Education & Training Services
767	Technical Services
768	Research Services
769	Management Services

77 **TRANSPORTATION**

770	Major Airlines
771	Regional Airlines
772	Air Services, Other
773	Air Delivery & Freight Services
774	Trucking
775	Shipping
776	Railroads

8 **TECHNOLOGY**

81 **COMPUTER HARDWARE**

810	Diversified Computer Systems
811	Personal Computers
812	Computer-Based Systems
813	Data Storage Devices
814	Networking & Communication Devices
815	Computer Peripherals

82 **COMPUTER SOFTWARE & SERVICES**

820	Multimedia & Graphics Software
821	Application Software
822	Technical & System Software
823	Security Software & Services
824	Information Technology Services
825	Healthcare Information Services
826	Business Software & Services
827	Information & Delivery Services

83 **ELECTRONICS**

830	Semiconductor—Broad Line
831	Semiconductor—Memory Chips
832	Semiconductor—Specialized
833	Semiconductor—Integrated Circuits
834	Semiconductor Equipment & Materials
835	Printed Circuit Boards
836	Diversified Electronics
837	Scientific & Technical Instruments

84 **TELECOMMUNICATIONS**

840	Wireless Communications
841	Communication Equipment
842	Processing Systems & Products
843	Long-Distance Carriers

	844	Telecom Services—Domestic	**9**	**UTILITIES**
	845	Telecom Services—Foreign		
	846	Diversified Communication Services	91	UTILITIES
85		INTERNET	910	Foreign Utilities
			911	Electric Utilities
	850	Internet Service Providers	912	Gas Utilities
	851	Internet Information Providers	913	Diversified Utilities
	852	Internet Software & Services	914	Water Utilities

Standardized Financial Statement Data Definitions

This appendix provides general definitions of the standardized financial statement data items used by eVal. These definitions should be interpreted as broad guidelines rather than precise rules. For more precise definitions of the standardized financial statement data items provided by Hemscott Data, COMPUSTAT, and Thomson Research, you should refer to the user documentation supplied with these products. There are many subtle differences and ambiguities in the way these three services construct their standardized databases. However, from a user's perspective, it is sufficient that you have a good understanding of how the standardized data for the company you are analyzing in eVal has been mapped from the as-reported data.

In applying these definitions, recall that eVal follows two important conventions in coding all financial statement data. First, all dollar and share amounts are recorded in thousands. Second, all line items that reduce their respective net income, asset, liability, or equity totals are recorded as negative amounts. For example, cost of goods sold, dividends, and an accumulated deficit in retained earnings all represent amounts that would be recorded as negatives in eVal.

Below, we provide definitions for eVal's standardized financial statement data items in the order that they appear in eVal's Financial Statements worksheet.

The cell "Company Name" at the top of the Financial Statements sheet is simply the name of the company, abbreviated to a reasonable length where appropriate.

The cell "Common Shares Outstanding" at the top of the Financial Statements sheet is defined as the total number of common shares issued net of the number of common treasury shares at the most recent fiscal year end (in thousands).

The cells labeled "Fiscal Year End (MM/DD/YY)" contain the date of the end of the fiscal year for the financial statement data entered in that column, in MM/DD/YY format (for example, December 31, 1999, would be entered as 12/31/99).

INCOME STATEMENT

The line item "Sales (Net)" represents gross sales reduced by cash discounts, trade discounts, and returned sales and allowances for which credit is given to customers.

The line item "Cost of Goods Sold" represents all costs directly allocated by the company to production, such as material, labor, and overhead.

The line item "Gross Profit" is computed as as Sales (Net) plus Cost of Goods Sold.

The line item "R&D Expense" (Research and Development Expense) represents all costs that relate to the development of new products or services.

The line item "SG&A Expense" (Selling, General, and Administrative Expense) represents expenses incurred in the normal operating activities of the company that are not allocated to Cost of Goods Sold or classified as R&D Expense.

The line item "EBITDA" (Earnings before Interest, Tax, Depreciation, and Amortization) is computed as Gross Profit plus R&D Expense plus SG&A Expense.

The line item "Depreciation and Amortization" represents noncash charges for the periodic allocation of the cost of property, plant, equipment, intangible assets, and wasting assets.

The line item "EBIT" (Earnings before Interest and Taxes) is computed as EBITDA plus Depreciation and Amortization.

The line item "Interest Expense" represents the periodic cost of securing short- and long-term debt. Ideally, this item should be presented gross of interest income. However, in cases where a firm reports interest expense net of interest income without disclosing the gross amounts, this line item will represent interest expense net of interest income.

The line item "Non-Operating Income (Loss)" represents the net amount of any income or expense items that are not directly related to the normal operating activities of the company. This item commonly includes interest and other investment income, earnings from equity affiliates, and charges related to asset impairments.

The line item "EBT" (Earnings before Taxes) is computed as EBIT plus Interest Expense plus Non-Operating Income (Loss).

The line item "Income Taxes" represents all expenses recognized in relation to taxes imposed by federal, state, and foreign taxing authorities.

The line item "Minority Interest in Earnings" represents the fraction of the income of consolidated subsidiaries that is attributable to minority stockholders in the subsidiary.

The line item "Other Income (Loss)" represents any miscellaneous nonoperating income or expense items that are reported on an after-tax basis.

The line item "Net Income Before Ext. Items" (Net Income before Extraordinary Items and Discontinued Operations) is computed as EBT plus Income Taxes plus Minority Interest in Earnings plus Other Income (Loss).

The line item "Ext. Items & Disc. Ops" (Extraordinary Items and Discontinued Operations) represents the income statement effects of extraordinary items, discontinued operations, and accounting changes.

The line item "Preferred Dividends" represents the total amount of the preferred dividend requirements on cumulative preferred stock and the dividends paid on noncumulative preferred stock. If using Global Access data, see the discussion of its treatment of preferred dividends in Appendix D.

The line item "Net Income (available to common)" is computed as Net Income Before Ext. Items plus Ext. Items & Disc. Ops plus Preferred Dividends.

BALANCE SHEET

The line item "Cash and Marketable Securities" represents cash and all securities that are readily convertible into cash.

The line item "Receivables" represents amounts of cash due from others, generally within the next year, net of any applicable allowances.

The line item "Inventories" represents merchandise bought for resale and material and supplies purchased for use in operating activities.

The line item "Other Current Assets" represents current assets other than Cash and Marketable Securities, Receivables, and Inventories.

The line item "Total Current Assets" is computed as Cash and Marketable Securities plus Receivables plus Inventories plus Other Current Assets.

The line item "PP&E (Net)" (Net Property, Plant, and Equipment) represents the cost of tangible fixed property, plant, and equipment used in the production of revenues, less accumulated depreciation.

The line item "Investments" represents long-term investments, including equity investments in unconsolidated affiliated companies.

The line item "Intangibles" represents the cost of all intangible assets including goodwill, less accumulated amortization.

The line item "Other Assets" represents long-term assets other than PP&E, Investments, and Intangibles.

The line item "Total Assets" is computed as Total Current Assets plus PP&E plus Investments plus Intangibles plus Other Assets.

The line item "Current Debt" represents the total carrying value of short-term borrowings with an original maturity of one year or less plus the current portion of long-term debt (long-term debt coming due within one year), including the current portion of capital lease obligations.

The line item "Accounts Payable" represents trade obligations due within the next year or the normal operating cycle of the company.

The line item "Income Taxes Payable" represents income taxes that are due and owing to the taxing authorities within the next year.

The line item "Other Current Liabilities" represents current liabilities other than Current Debt, Accounts Payable, and Income Taxes Payable and includes accrued expenses and dividends payable.

The line item "Total Current Liabilities" is computed as Current Debt plus Accounts Payable plus Income Taxes Payable plus Other Current Liabilities.

The line item "Long-Term Debt" represents the total carrying value of debt obligations due in more than one year, including the long-term portion of bonds, mortgages, and capital lease obligations.

The line item "Other Liabilities" represents long-term liabilities other than Long-Term Debt, Deferred Taxes, and Minority Interest and includes pension and other post-retirement liabilities.

The line item "Deferred Taxes" represents the accumulated tax deferrals attributable to timing differences in income recognition for financial reporting and tax purposes. Where applicable, this item also includes the carrying value of any deferred tax credits.

The line item "Minority Interest" represents the fraction of the carrying value of the common equity of consolidated subsidiaries that is attributable to minority stockholders in the subsidiary.

The line item "Total Liabilities" is computed as Total Current Liabilities plus Long-Term Debt plus Other Liabilities plus Deferred Taxes plus Minority Interest.

The line item "Preferred Stock" represents the total net carrying value of preferred stock. If using Global Access data, see the discussion on its treatment of preferred stock in Appendix D.

The line item "Paid in Common Capital (Net)" represents the total net carrying value of all common equity accounts other than retained earnings. This item regularly includes the net effects of common stock at par, additional paid-in capital, treasury stock, unrealized gains and losses, and unearned stock compensation.

The line item "Retained Earnings" represents the cumulative earnings of the company, net of cumulative dividend distributions. In cases where this item is negative, it is typically referred to as the accumulated deficit.

The line item "Total Common Equity" is computed as Paid in Common Capital (Net) plus Retained Earnings.

The line item "Total Liabilities and Equity" is computed as Total Liabilities plus Preferred Stock plus Total Common Equity.

STATEMENT OF RETAINED EARNINGS

The line item "Beg. Retained Earnings" (Beginning Value of Retained Earnings) represents the ending value of Retained Earnings for the previous fiscal year, as defined for the Balance Sheet above.

The line item "Net Income" represents Net Income, as defined for the Income Statement above.

The line item "Common Dividends" represents the total amount of cash dividends declared on common stock for the year.

The line item "Clean Surplus Plug (Ignore)" represents the total net effect of all items other than Net Income and Common Dividends that affected Retained Earnings during the fiscal year. Items that regularly enter this category are treasury stock transactions accounted for using the par value method, stock dividends, prior period adjustments, and retroactive accounting changes. Since future treasury stock transactions are assumed to flow through paid-in capital (i.e., the cost method) and since the rest of these adjustments refer to the past, this item is zero in the future forecasted financial statements. That's why we keep telling you to *ignore* it.

The line item "End. Retained Earnings" (Ending Value of Retained Earnings) represents the value of Retained Earnings for the current fiscal year, as defined for the Balance Sheet above.

Importing Data from a Saved File

eVal provides four options for importing data from a saved file:

- Import data from Thomson Research.
- Import data from WRDS.
- Import data from COMPUSTAT template.
- Import data from MarketGuide template.

Importing the historical data is a two-step process. First, you access the data from the third-party data provider and then save it in the form specified below. This step does not involve eVal. Second, you import the data into eVal by selecting the option that matches your data source. This is accomplished by opening the eVal User's Guide sheet, clicking the Input Historical Data button, clicking the Import Data from a Saved File button, choosing the appropriate data input option, and clicking the OK button.

Note: The following instructions for accessing data from third-party data providers are correct as of this writing, but these providers may change their data formats, URLs, and so forth, at any time. If you encounter problems following the instructions below, please check the eVal Web site for updated instructions.

IMPORTING DATA FROM THOMSON RESEARCH

Thomson Research (also known as Global Access) provides access to spreadsheet financials for historical data coded from SEC filings. This service is accessible through the electronic libraries of many leading business schools, and also offers individual subscriptions. A key advantage of using Thomson Research is that the data are provided in preformatted Excel spreadsheets. Thus, all you have to do is download the appropriate spreadsheet to your computer. Thomson Research provides a number of preformatted "Spreadsheet Financials" and the "SEC 10-K History (10-Year) spreadsheet" provides the data required by eVal. If you have a subscription to Thomson Research, you can save the appropriate spreadsheet for the company of your choice as follows:

1. Log on to the Thomson Research service at http://research.thomsonib.com/. (*Note*: This is a subscription database that is password protected. If your institution has a subscription to Thomson Research, then you will probably have to enter the Web site through the appropriate proxy server at your institution in order to gain access.)
2. Select your company by entering the company name or ticker in the box at the top left of the screen and clicking the Go button.
3. Under the Spreadsheet Financials heading, click on the link to SEC 10-K History (10-Year).
4. You should now have the option to open or save this spreadsheet file. The easiest approach is to save the file on your computer, remembering the name and location under which it is stored. If the file opens in your browser without giving you the option of saving it, open up a blank Excel spreadsheet and then cut and paste the contents of the Thomson Research spreadsheet to your new spreadsheet, being very careful to paste the data to the exact same cells as in the original Thomson Research spreadsheet.
5. Before you try to load the saved data into eVal, we recommend closing your browser. If you don't do this, then Excel may be running in the browser window, which may interfere with eVal's import routine.

You can now read these data into eVal by selecting the Data from Thomson Research data input option and following the prompts to tell eVal where the saved spreadsheet file is located. Once this is done, eVal will automatically import all available historical data, and you will be ready to start analyzing your company.

IMPORTING DATA FROM WRDS

WRDS (Wharton Research and Data Services) is a division of the Wharton School of Business. Most leading business schools subscribe to WRDS, and access is often given to students through class accounts. Like Thomson Research, WRDS offers preformatted financial statements for download. WRDS obtains the financial statement data from the COMPUSTAT database and downloads them in HTML format. If you have a subscription to WRDS, you can save the appropriate spreadsheet for the company of your choice as follows:

1. Access the WRDS server at http://wrds.wharton.upenn.edu/ and log in. (*Note*: This is a subscription service that is password protected.)
2. Click on the Tools link on the left-hand side of the screen and then click on Financial Statements (Annually Updated) in the Compustat Tools list.
3. In the Step 1 drop-down box, select Complete Financial Statements.
4. In the Step 2 drop-down box, select the most recent five years of annual data. For example, if data are available through 2005, select a beginning date of 2001 and an ending date of 2005. *User's note*: It is important that you select exactly

five years' worth of data; otherwise eVal will not import the data into the correct columns.

5. In the Step 3 drop-down box, enter an appropriate identifier for your company.

6. Click the Submit Request button, wait for link to the resulting HTML file to load in a separate window, and then save the resulting HTML file on your computer, remembering the name and location under which it is stored. You can save the data file by right-clicking the link to the file and selecting the Save Target As command.

You can now read the data in this HTML file directly into eVal by selecting the Data from WRDS data input option and following the prompts to tell eVal where the file is located. Excel takes care of converting the HTML file to Excel format. Once this is done, eVal will automatically import all available historical data, and you will be ready to start analyzing these data.

IMPORTING DATA FROM A COMPUSTAT TEMPLATE

This data import option is not supported in the current version of eVal. We include it for the benefit of users of prior versions of eVal who still have files stored in this format.

IMPORTING DATA FROM A MARKETGUIDE TEMPLATE

This data import option is not supported in the current version of eVal. We include it for the benefit of users of prior versions of eVal who still have files stored in this format.

Index